P9-CAY-017

CHAUCER AND RELIGION

Chaucer's writings (the *Canterbury Tales*, *Troilus and Criseyde*, lyrics and dream poems) are here freshly examined in relation to the religions, the religious traditions and the religious controversies of his era. Using a variety of theoretical, critical and historical approaches, the essays deal with topics that include Chaucer and Wycliffism; Chaucer's dream poetry and religion; Chaucer and secularity; gender, sex and marriage; the cult of the saints, pilgrimage, and the Virgin Mary; Chaucer's handling of morality; representations of Judaism and Islam; fabliaux and religion; Chaucer's use of the Bible; death and mutability in the *Canterbury Tales*; and, additionally, a range of issues related to teaching Chaucer in Britain and America today.

CHRISTIANITY AND CULTURE

ISSUES IN TEACHING AND RESEARCH

ISSN 1740–9896

Series Editors

Dee Dyas
Helen Phillips

The volumes in this series focus on key topics in the cultures of the past and the role of religion in these cultures. Each offers a collection of new essays by leading scholars, which aim to cover the major subjects in a particular area or period, and to provide teachers, researchers and students with the best of the current thinking on the subject. They also discuss the issues involved in teaching, in an objective way, the often distant and sometimes alien concepts of the religious cultures of past centuries in a modern, secular, multi-cultural society.

Already published

1. The Christian Tradition in Anglo-Saxon England: Approaches to Current Scholarship and Teaching
edited by Paul Cavill

2. Approaching Medieval English Anchoritic and Mystical Texts
edited by Dee Dyas, Valerie Edden and Roger Ellis

3. Christianity and Romance in Medieval England
edited by Rosalind Field, Phillipa Hardman and Michelle Sweeney

CHAUCER AND RELIGION

Edited by

HELEN PHILLIPS

D. S. BREWER

© Editors and Contributors 2010

All Rights Reserved. Except as permitted under current legislation
no part of this work may be photocopied, stored in a retrieval system,
published, performed in public, adapted, broadcast,
transmitted, recorded or reproduced in any form or by any means,
without the prior permission of the copyright owner

First published 2010
D. S. Brewer, Cambridge

Transferred to digital printing

ISBN 978 1 84384 229 3

D. S. Brewer is an imprint of Boydell & Brewer Ltd
PO Box 9, Woodbridge, Suffolk IP12 3DF, UK
and of Boydell & Brewer Inc.
668 Mt Hope Avenue, Rochester, NY 14620, USA
website: www.boydellandbrewer.com

A CiP catalogue record for this title is available
from the British Library

The publisher has no responsibility for the continued existence or accuracy
of URLs for external or third-party internet websites referred to in this book,
and does not guarantee that any content on such websites is,
or will remain, accurate or appropriate.

This publication is printed on acid-free paper

Typeset by Word and Page, Chester

Contents

General Editors' Foreword

This series addresses the challenge that the study of literature, history and material culture of the past often poses for modern researchers, students and teachers, because the religious assumptions of previous centuries are remote from the world-views of contemporary people. The volumes in the series aim to provide research, discussion and critical perspectives on the role of religion and the historical inter-relationships of religion, society and culture, each focusing on a particular period or topic. They are designed primarily for those in university research, teaching and study, but their subjects and approaches are also likely to be of interest to readers and teachers more widely. Each volume offers a collection of essays by leading scholars and critics, providing an authoritative and balanced overview of the subject in the light of current research.

Central to the aims of the series is a conviction of the importance of the inter-relationship of research and teaching and the belief that the best teaching is that which is informed by the best contemporary research and thinking. The series is produced in association with the Christianity and Culture project, which seeks to explore how past religious culture can be studied and taught in modern multi-cultural, multi-faith, and in many respects secular, societies, in an objective and academic way. While the major part of each volume will be a sequence of specially commissioned essays, designed to provide a comprehensive survey of a topic, and addressing the issues, information and research relevant for an informed and up-to-date study of the religious culture of a past society and culture, volumes will also discuss how they can most effectively be presented, and made accessible, to students. Each book will therefore both give space specifically to consideration of methods of teaching historical religious culture, and contain essays in which teachers in higher education from a range of countries and contexts discuss issues and materials, and suggest approaches and answers.

Acknowledgements

Many people have helped with the conception and completion of this volume. Special thanks are due to Caroline Palmer at Boydell and Brewer, the most wise and helpful of editors. Also to Graham Caie, Dee Dyas, Rosalind Field, Rob Gossedge, Rachel Jones, Stephen Knight and Clive Tolley. And to Derek Brewer, who died before the book was published but who gave enormous advice, inimitably experienced and encouraging, early on in its planning.

Helen Phillips

Contributors

Anthony Bale, Birkbeck, University of London
Alcuin Blamires, Goldsmiths, University of London
Laurel Broughton, University of Vermont
Graham D. Caie, Glasgow University
Helen Cooper, University of Cambridge
Roger Dalrymple, Buckinghamshire University College
Dee Dyas, University of York
D. Thomas Hanks, Baylor University
Stephen Knight, Cardiff University
Frances M. McCormack, National University of Ireland, Galway
Carl Phelpstead, Cardiff University
Helen Phillips, Cardiff University
David Raybin, Eastern Illinois University
Sherry L. Reames, University of Wisconsin – Madison
Gillian Rudd, Liverpool University

Abbreviations

EETS ES	Early English Text Society, Extra Series
EETS OS	Early English Text Society, Original Series
Riverside Chaucer	*The Riverside Chaucer*, ed. Larry D. Benson, 3rd edn (Boston, MA, 1987)

Unless otherwise indicated, references to Chaucer's works are to the *Riverside Chaucer* edition and the abbreviations for his individual works given there (p. 779) are used.

Introduction

HELEN COOPER

Writing about Chaucer and religion is a very different matter from writing about, for instance, T. S. Eliot and religion. For Eliot, Christianity, in the form of high Anglicanism, was an option that he embraced as a living faith, and that increasingly shaped and coloured his poetry. His task, in an unashamedly materialist and increasingly agnostic or atheist world, was to find a poetic language that would convey the thoughts and feelings that informed that faith even to those who did not share it: to make space for religion in a world that saw no need for it. For Chaucer, Christianity was a given, and faith was effectively the only option available. It presented itself to him primarily as the medium in which he and his society lived and worked. For a few of his contemporaries, it was as an all-absorbing spiritual devotion; for everybody, it was the basis of their work and their play, of economics and politics and medicine and science and the arts. Most people would never have seen a picture or a sculpture that was not religious in subject, or had a holiday that was not marked out as a holy day.

That very saturation of the culture in religion, however, can make it seem as if religion were merely a pre-scientific way of talking about the same things that drive the modern world: as if medieval expressions of devotion were merely the surface gloss on phenomena that were in fact economic, sociological or political, or even pathological. For all the new visibility given to religion and religious practices in the modern study of the past, it remains almost part of our scholarly credentials not to treat religious conviction seriously. The assumption seems to be that whatever the medieval ego may pretend to itself about pious motivation, the medieval id always had its fist deep in the till, grubbing for money or for power. No doubt that was often true, and Chaucer generously confirms our suspicions; but he also reminds us, if we read him whole, that it is too easy just to transfer back into the past our own secular assumptions about what 'really' drove individuals. Devotion was not always driven by financial self-interest; mystical experience was something more, or other, than neurosis. There is more going on in Chaucer's works, and in his society, than is encompassed by his satire alone, and we need to learn to pay attention. Satire itself requires a common belief system, a set of values shared between author and reader, if it is to work at all; and for Chaucer, that system is a Christian one. These are the issues this book addresses.

For all practical purposes, Christianity for Chaucer took the form of the

Catholicism that was common to all of Western Europe, with the pope at its head (though in his lifetime there were two rival popes, one based at Rome and one at Avignon) and its hierarchy of cardinals and archbishops, bishops and archdeacons and priests. It had its most visible form in the churches. The village church was normally the largest and most substantial building in every parish, and the vast cathedrals and abbeys dwarfed their surrounding towns or dominated the more isolated landscapes. Christian rituals shaped everyone's life: birth and baptism and the churching of the mother, confession and penitence and the last rites administered to the dying – but not necessarily marriage, which required only that vows should be willingly exchanged by the parties: a situation that created an abundance of business for the ecclesiastical courts that attempted to control sexual activity. Taxes too were most consistently a religious matter: while the king and the local lord of the manor had the right to levy a tax on particular occasions or under particular circumstances, it was the tithe of all one's income or produce paid to the local priest that was the most evident and consistent form of taxation. And even more than taxes, death was the business of the Church, for after death the soul left the material world altogether and passed into God's hands. His judgement would assign it to heaven, hell or, most likely, the in-between condition of Purgatory, passage through which could be speeded by Masses sung on its behalf through the benefaction of the living; only at the Last Judgement, when soul and body were reunited, would an eternity of salvation or damnation ultimately supersede any more partial condition, and the economic investment of the earthly Church in the state of the soul come to an end.

Time within this world was measured as God's. Early in the eighth century, Bede had developed for practical use the idea of counting the years as before and after Christ (AD is *anno domini*, in the year of our Lord), in the system still used now even if the terminology has been secularised into the 'common era'. Calendar dates were rarely specified as days of the month (though Chaucer does this much more than his contemporaries): the calendar itself was primarily religious, with a date being marked not as 9/11, but as St Omer's Day. The calendar lived out in daily practices recorded in an endlessly repeating annual cycle the great events of Christ's life, the Nativity, the Passion and the Resurrection; the witness borne to the faith by the saints; and, in Advent, a reminder of the Judgement to come. Other holy days too were marked by their own particular rituals and processions: Candlemas and Corpus Christi, the feast day of the patron saint of the parish church or of one of the numerous religious guilds that absorbed a good proportion of the population. Lent and comparable periods of fasting prescribed what one could eat and when one could make love to one's spouse. The basic calendar and the core texts of the liturgy, including the Little Hours of the Virgin, the Office of the Dead and the Penitential Psalms, were increasingly available to the laity (though still in Latin) in the form of primers, more often known now as Books of Hours: these were often highly decorated, but by the time of Chaucer's death they were becoming widely available in less elaborate forms to gentry and townsmen, and, especially, women.[1] Mechanical clocks were still rare, and the time of day was

1 There is an excellent account of them and their use in the interior spiritual life of the laity in Eamon Duffy, *Marking the Hours: English People and their Prayers 1240–1570* (New Haven and London, 2006), pp. 3–64.

most often measured in terms of the seven liturgical offices – lauds, prime, nones and so on – or by the movements of the created cosmos, dawn and noon and nightfall. Church bells, almost universal in parish churches by the early Middle Ages, rang for every Mass and some other services, and for particular ecclesiastical celebrations: 'clock' is itself derived from words meaning 'bell'. It was only the arrival of the mechanical clock that commodified time (the first recorded strike over working hours happened in the vineyards of France late in the fourteenth century). Before that, it was part of God's creation, and no more than a temporary island bounded by eternity.

Space and place and travel likewise transmuted easily into a journey to God. Pilgrimage always had something allegorical about it, of the pilgrimage of the soul; literal pilgrimage to shrines and holy places replicated that in physical form. A few pilgrims made their way to the Holy Land (including, famously, Chaucer's Wife of Bath); most contented themselves with the shrines where relics of Christ's Passion or the Virgin were preserved (fragments of the Cross, a vial of milk), or, most often, of individual saints. Saints served as the intercessors between humankind and God, and were regularly invoked in prayer. Each had his or her own speciality. St Margaret, who had emerged unscathed from the belly of a diabolic dragon, was the patron saint of childbirth, and a safe delivery could be assisted through the mother's contact with her girdle (or a replica of it, though there were a good number of 'originals' across Europe) or even a copy of her Life. Every church contained chapels to and images of individual saints, often including a local one, in addition to its own patronal dedicatee, with candles lit before them to mark the parish's veneration or the prayers of particular individuals. Pilgrimage constituted a special event beyond those everyday processes of veneration. Not all pilgrims, of course, had their minds always on higher things; but in an age when curiosity was officially classified as a distraction from concentration on the things of God, the desire for new sights and for travel could be legitimated through the practice of pilgrimage. Motives are rarely pure, and for many pilgrims, no doubt, such a desire mingled with genuine penitence for sin, or the hope of a cure for illness or disability, or, as Chaucer specifies for his own pilgrims, with thanks for a cure received.

The great majority of the population of Chaucer's England worked on the land. At the top of the hierarchy were the king and the nobility, those who held territory directly from the king in return for political and military support. All of these would have had private chapels within their castles and manors, and a staff of chaplains. Below them were the gentry, hereditary landholders who normally held their land from one of the great lords; they too might well employ a chaplain of their own. Rapidly enlarging in numbers and importance were the craftsmen and townsmen and merchants, the forebears of the middle classes. This group and the gentry between them provided most of those who had positions within the Church, as priests or chaplains or administrators, or who took vows as friars or monks or nuns. It was only those who were sufficiently well off, or were supported by the piety of a wealthy patron, who had the option of entering the Church as a career, and there was a wide range of motivations for doing so. A genuine vocation for a life of withdrawal and prayer could lead a man, or, less frequently, a woman, to a monastery or nunnery or to the solitary life of the anchorhold. Parents might also urge such a life on a younger son or daughter, as a kind of gift to God that would be repaid at Judgement Day; and life as a professed religious in most monastic orders offered security and a reasonably comfortable lifestyle. Ordination as a priest might likewise be led by a desire to serve God and society, or as the first step in upward mobility in the Church hierarchy or secular administration. Most people who wanted an education normally had to do so through ecclesiastical institutions, as the double meaning of 'clerical' still indicates: relating either to clerics, or to clerks and secretaries and anyone who is concerned with writing. Household chaplains were often used to teach younger children in basic literacy, and the sons of the great would often have a tutor who might be a literate knight rather than a cleric. We know nothing about Chaucer's education, and indeed in many respects he appears anomalous (just as he is anomalous in appearing in court service as a squire when he came from a mercantile rather than gentry background); by whatever means he acquired it, he had a good knowledge of Latin. He read widely in Latin works, even though he used a crib when one was available and picked up some of his knowledge of biblical, classical and patristic works at second hand. As the son of a vintner in the great trading centre of London, he may have grown up bilingual in Anglo-Norman and English, and he acquired Italian later as part of his professional kit as a diplomat as well as a poet. French was still, in his childhood, a prerequisite for learning Latin, but modern languages did not officially figure on the educational curriculum. In his later life his closest associates included men who had spent time at the religious institutions of Oxford or Cambridge, but he was never a student there himself. The royal administration in which he worked was substantially staffed by clerics, and it was nothing unusual for bishops to hold high secular office. On occasion they would even join military expeditions.

The belief system encompassed everyone from the peasant labouring in the fields, who replicated the punishment inflicted on Adam that he should earn his bread in the sweat of his brow (Genesis 3: 19), to the king who was crowned in a religious ceremony that included anointing with holy oil in an act that rendered his person and his office uniquely sacred within his own realm. The principles by which monarch and serf lived were all based on religion. Arguments about prices and incomes and political actions invariably started from religious premises, about just price, due reward, God-instituted hierarchies, rightful rulers, and so on. Just what those premises might be was not, however, clear-cut: religious principles were as likely to intensify as to prevent argument, and conclusions were likely to depend on other considerations altogether. The gentry and aristocracy, who regarded social hierarchy as God-given, at least since the Fall, may have been appalled by the slogan of the English Rising of 1381 –

> When Adam delved, and Eve span,
> Who was then the gentleman?

– but that too was a direct appeal to God's creation of humankind, an assertion that social stratification was not part of the divine ordination. It is a small step from there to Chaucer's repeated assertions that true gentility, *gentilesse*, is a matter of virtue, not birth, though the proponents of that view never took it as a basis for rebellion. At the top of the hierarchy, the fact of coronation made the deposition of a crowned king all the more problematic, as was made all too clear in 1399; but if a king could no longer govern, or if the opposition to him was too powerful, his anointing never saved him. Of course kings, and usurpers, did not always do the virtuous thing, any more than all workers laboured for the love of God and their neighbour (Langland has plenty to say about that, and Chaucer never claims that his Plowman is a typical peasant), but that ideal was always held up before them. All behaviour, public and private, took shape against a consciousness of damnation; for whether you attended to the fact or not, you would be faced with the balance sheet of your deeds at Judgement Day, and would not escape punishment.

This very all-pervasiveness of religion, and the difficulty of separating it off from the institutions of the Church, can make it difficult now to get any full sense of medieval spirituality, the inward movement of the soul towards God that gave many men and women a deeply committed vocation and inspired the mystics who lived alongside the workers and bureaucrats and lovers and warriors of Chaucer's England. Scholarship is wary of belief systems, especially those it does not share (to parody only a little: minority rights and democracy good; orthodox religion, patriarchy and monarchy bad), and criticism rightly takes as its premise that professed motives may not be enough.[2] It is both impossible and undesirable to study the Middle Ages merely on its own premises; it is equally undesirable to study it solely on ours, though that is all too possible. It is much too easy to treat devotion in every case as a veneer rather than as a substance; the very saturation of the culture with religion can appear to drain the piety out of it. Even at the time, the distance between the individual soul and God that had become entrenched within the ecclesiastical structures and hierarchies was perceived as a difficulty that needed to be addressed. Some of Chaucer's contemporaries devoted their lives to God; many more sought a more direct access to the spiritual life without going so far as to abandon the secular world for a life of withdrawal or contemplation. One such way was through affective piety, the invitation to seek spiritual insight through compassionate meditation on the sufferings of Christ or the Virgin.[3] Another way, which emerged when Chaucer was at the height of his poetic career, bypassed the institutions of the Church altogether, in the movement known as Wycliffism or Lollardy: a religious movement that urged a return to a simpler, more biblical form of Christianity, that abandoned belief in transubstantiation and wanted to see the dismantling of ecclesiastical power and wealth, and that believed that the Bible should be available to everyone, Latin-literate or not, in full English translation. It amounted to a frontal attack on the privileges of the Church, and the Church responded by declaring it heretical. In the fifteenth century, Lollardy became not only a way of worship or a way of life, but a faith to die for; and a number of men and women were prepared to be martyred for their belief in a fresh and more direct form of Christian faith.

Chaucer's own relationship to all such matters is hard to evaluate. He was

[2] For a particularly full and sympathetic account, see Eamon Duffy, *The Stripping of the Altars: Traditional Religion in England 1400–1580* (New Haven and London, 1992); despite notionally starting in the year of Chaucer's death, much of the first part holds good for the late fourteenth century too. The book has been criticized on the grounds that it is too sympathetic: that if its account of the late-medieval Church were all simply true, the Reformation could never have happened.

[3] See *Mysticism and Spirituality in Medieval England*, ed. William F. Pollard and Robert Boenig (Cambridge, 1997).

certainly ready to show characters within his works, especially suffering women such as Custance and Griselda, appealing to the sufferings of the Virgin; and he wrote – or, to be more precise, produced a creative translation of – a fine hymn to the Virgin, the *ABC*, a poem that in its alphabetical shaping insists on God as alpha and omega, His Word as the basis of the universe. Apart from the *ABC*, only one of Chaucer's short poems spoken without any intermediary, the 'Ballad of Good Counsel' usually known as *Truth*, addresses devotional issues directly, and that urges a friend, and through him mankind in general, to embark on the 'heye wey' of the pilgrimage of life; but even that works primarily through good prudential advice on how to avoid trouble in this world. His most powerful religious poetry, the shorter hymns to the Virgin embedded within the prologues to the *Prioress's Tale* and the *Second Nun's Tale* and the closing stanza of *Troilus*, is drawn from the greatest religious poet of the Middle Ages, Dante, who died some twenty years before Chaucer was born; and it is interesting, though it is not at all obvious what conclusions one should draw from it, that he looks to Dante for such material more extensively than to the liturgy. Italian was still little known internationally, and Chaucer is the first non-native speaker of Italian we know of to show a knowledge of his work. We are extraordinarily lucky that he should have been a comparably great poet, and that he wrote in English. Chaucer resisted Dante's larger theological ideas, however, in particular his readiness to declare the judgement of God on all the representatives of humankind he portrays in the *Divine Comedy*. It was a principle of faith, shared by Chaucer, that one could not predict the final divine judgement on one's fellow men; he indeed repeatedly points out that all human judgement is fallible, and especially in matters that touch on God's preserve.

The degree of Chaucer's involvement with Lollardy has been a matter of intense debate, with the weight of the argument falling towards his being in sympathy with many of its aims rather than being a committed member of the movement. The Wife of Bath has traces of Lollardy about her; so in many ways does the Parson, in his outspokenness at many of the abuses of the Church and his belief in the letter of the text, though his tale also affirms an orthodox belief in confession and the Mass.[4] One could oppose the corruption that beset the Church, its concern with power and politics and the accretion of wealth, without being heretical, and it is never decisively clear whether, or how far, Chaucer went beyond an acute consciousness of the pervasiveness of such corruption into theological dissidence. His satire varies in intensity to match the different targets he has in sight. Love of money, as many of the secular pilgrims make evident, is a near-universal human attribute; what distinguishes the ecclesiastics is their greater distance from the ideal of life that their careers ought to show. Chaucer was not alone in casting friars as symbolic of the worst of religious corruption, since St Francis had founded the first fraternal order with such high ideals, of absolute poverty and service, and the gap between those original principles and current practice was devastatingly clear. Even so, Chaucer's own Friar Huberd is a tabloid example of scandal rather than a norm: it is worth bearing in mind too that friars seem to have suffered an

[4] The major study of Lollardy is Anne M. Hudson, *The Premature Reformation: Wycliffite Texts and Lollard History* (Oxford, 1988). Studies on Chaucer include Alcuin Blamires, 'The Wife of Bath and Lollardy', *Medium Ævum* 58 (1989), 224–42, and Frances McCormack, *Chaucer and the Culture of Dissent: The Lollard Context and Subtext of the Parson's Tale* (Dublin, 2007).

unusually high mortality rate in the Black Death of 1348, presumably because so many of them placed their duties to the sick and dying above preserving their own lives. Chaucer's harshest criticism is reserved for those whose love of money is allowed to divert lay people from the path to heaven, as the Pardoner is happy to let souls go blackberrying so long as their owners are gullible enough to believe in his own offer of salvation guaranteed in return for cash. What the Pardoner does was illegal by any standards, but the doctrine of indulgences and the cult of relics opened too easy a way to abuse. Lollardy was fuelled by the perception of all such matters, but its core was theological, to do with the nature of God and the right ways to live and to worship Him, and Chaucer's own theological beliefs remain hidden from us. All we know is that in his late fifties, he took lodgings within the precincts of Westminster Abbey, and after his death was buried inside the church itself, close to one of the most important shrines in England.

Chaucer was above all a poet of this world, not of the next. Religious structures of one kind or another are pervasive in his work, above all because they were pervasive in his society. An assortment of ecclesiastical office-holders famously throngs his world; but he also makes an abundance of allusions to the liturgy, the Bible and the Christian Fathers such as show an extensive knowledge of belief and doctrine. He very rarely, however, writes the kind of religious poetry that preoccupied most of his contemporaries: William Langland, who in *Piers Plowman* tried to bring the individual's pilgrimage to truth into a single focus with economic, political and social life; John Gower, whose *Miroir de l'Omme* (the 'mirror of mankind'), a huge penitential work written in Anglo-French that constituted almost a third of his entire poetic output, is a kind of verse equivalent of the *Parson's Tale*; *Pearl* and *Patience* and *Cleanness*, homiletic poems on submission to God probably written by the same man who wrote the secular *Sir Gawain and the Green Knight*. Chaucer writes just one saint's life, the life of St Cecilia that in the *Canterbury Tales* is assigned to the Second Nun, though it seems likely that it was written originally as a free-standing work. The Miracle of the Virgin that constitutes the *Prioress's Tale*, by contrast, has its genesis, so far as is known, entirely within the Canterbury sequence, as do the secular tales with a hagiographic edge, the Man of Law's tale of Custance and the Clerk's of Griselda. They function, in other words, primarily as part of the larger story-collection, which, for all its pilgrimage opening and penitential ending, is overwhelmingly secular in focus.

Even secular genres, such as romance, could be shaped to endorse familiar patterns of piety, but that is a move that Chaucer largely resists, and it is clear that he does so intentionally. His two greatest works that have some claim to be romances, *Troilus* and the *Knight's Tale*, are set in a pre-Christian pagan world where Catholic sexual morality does not apply, but also where the metaphysical seekings of the central characters can never receive a Christian answer: where there are no comforting reassurances available about the overriding providence of a loving God or the hope of salvation. *Troilus* defines itself as a tragedy rather than a romance, and both works acknowledge a grounding in classical epic. What Chaucer does offer his pagans is a philosophy drawn from Boethius that offers something comparable from within the reach of reason, without the further exercise of a Christian faith. It is important that he does so; but for the characters themselves, the Boethian answers never really take root, and their most urgent metaphysical questionings – about whether human agency is in fact driven by arbitrary forces beyond its control, or why the innocent should suffer – remain unresolved.

Does that amount to an account of Chaucer as a religious sceptic? 'Scepticism' is a term often applied to him, though as a quality – 'Chaucerian scepticism' – more than as a matter of personal belief.[5] It is a quality so evident in his work that it is tempting to take it as dominant. It is, however, most pervasive in those more secular works that are most widely read now, so it risks existing as a consequence of our own preferences rather than his own full practice. A reading of his work that privileged the *ABC* and *Truth*, the *Man of Law's Tale* and *Second Nun's Tale*, the *Parson's Tale* and the *Retractions*, would produce a very different sense of his beliefs from one that concentrated on *Troilus*, the *Miller's Tale*, and the Wife of Bath. This does not mean that to create a Chaucer of religious commitment we would have to choose the worse poetry, or the prose, over the work that has made him recognized as arguably the greatest non-dramatic poet Britain has ever known. *Troilus* may have to turn its back on its own story to achieve its Christian ending, but Chaucer is the first author to make its central character a man who so restlessly seeks the principles by which humankind lives. Pilgrims such as the Miller and the Pardoner may most attract modern readers, but they would not mean what they do without the frank admiration for Christian virtue in the Plowman and Parson. His interest in the world and the people who inhabit it, not least their fallibility, and his refusal always and only to measure things in the terms prescribed by the Church, enable his poetry to make the transition easily into the modern world; but to write out his deep grounding in human ethics, and the ultimate grounding of those ethics in Christianity, is to misunderstand him profoundly.

The essays in this collection approach these questions not only from a variety of standpoints, but with a variety of purposes in mind: to illuminate devotional practice, or the contexts of religion in fourteenth-century England, or the traditions underlying Chaucer's own religious writing, or the detail of his texts, or how we might best communicate all of that to our students. Graham Caie considers how the members of that common wele might have accessed the Bible, in an age when full clerical Latin literacy was confined to a few and lay vernacular literacy was still unusual, and measures his answers against Chaucer's pilgrims and the use and misuse they make of the Scriptures. Frances McCormack explores the difficult question of Wycliffite influence both in terms of Chaucer's possible allusions and sympathies and also of the complex engagement of readers in a period of instability and disorder. Carl Phelpstead focuses on the importance given to the training for a good death in the *artes moriendi*, handbooks on how to die well, and on the doctrines associated with death and Purgatory and the single Christian community of the living and the dead. Alcuin Blamires writes his way tightly into the quotidian world of sex and marriage and the Church's attempts to regulate them through canon law, as well as describing the higher spiritual reaches represented by virginity. Helen Phillips writes on Chaucer's romances – 'the matter of Chaucer', as she terms it, to emphasize their distinctiveness in comparison with the

[5] The idea was sensitively promoted by Sheila Delany, *Chaucer's House of Fame: The Poetics of Skeptical Fideism* (Chicago and London, 1972).

standard 'matters' of Troy, Charlemagne and Arthur – to try to establish their own placing in relation to the great sexual debates of the age, and to draw out Chaucer's attempts to negotiate between the values accorded to human emotion by romance and by Boethius's *Consolation of Philosophy* or the teachings of the Church. A very different genre, and one that looks less susceptible to religious readings, is addressed by Stephen Knight's exploration of the relationship between clerics and churls which seems a recurrent feature of fabliaux. His close study examines who swears by whom and when in the fabliaux, the churls' tales; he suggests that the detail of the stories should be read as the verbal equivalent of the pictorial parodies found in the margins of the great Psalters. Laurel Broughton offers a study of Chaucer's saints, in particular Becket and the Blessed Virgin, and the imagery that accompanies them. Sherry Reames places his religious poetry, and most particularly the various hymns to the Virgin contained in his work, in the context of late-medieval piety. Anthony Bale reminds us that, however great was the influence of the Church within Chaucer's England, Christianity was not the only religion known: the Jews might have been expelled from England a century earlier, but they still had some physical presence in London and a much greater presence in the Italian cities that Chaucer visited, as well as being a constant in religious teaching and in popular stories; and the Saracens were not only all-purpose villains (like Nazis or Russians) but regular trading partners, the originating purveyors of spices and silks to the wealthy of England. Dee Dyas examines Chaucer's frame-story motif, of a company of pilgrims, in relation not only to the practice of contemporary pilgrimage but also in relation to the multiple communities to which medieval Christians belonged. Writing on Chaucer's shorter poems, Helen Phillips and Stephen Knight both examine how relationships between secular and spiritual discourses interact in not only the wording but the structures of the dream poems and lyrics.

The final group of essays addresses the issues raised by teaching Chaucer, and the religious issues within Chaucer, through case studies as to what has been found to work well. David Raybin approaches Chaucer's texts in comparison with each other, with the emphasis less on religion as such than on the more familiar and accessible field of ethics; Roger Dalrymple gives examples of enquiry-based learning that link Chaucer's text with comparable contemporary writing, and so place him within the larger Middle English context such as his earliest readers would have taken for granted. The essays by Gillian Rudd and Thomas Hanks consider the state of play for teaching the religious elements of Chaucer and methods for introducing modern students to these, and they find good grounds for optimism for the future even while recognizing the challenges. The hope is that this book will assist with those challenges, and help to justify the optimism.

Contexts and Critical Approaches

1

Love, Marriage, Sex, Gender

ALCUIN BLAMIRES

THERE ARE MOMENTS when Chaucer's writings can sound peculiarly modern. One such moment comes when a knight's extravagantly lyrical description of a woman he has loved provokes a sceptical reaction from the narrator of the *Book of the Duchess*. The narrator observes that he can well believe that the woman seemed the very loveliest to behold, to anyone who looked at her *with the knight's eyes* ('Whoso had loked hir with your eyen', *BD* 1051). That detachment and relativism in thinking about personal attraction has a twenty-first-century flavour.

On the other hand, there is much in Chaucer that will seem alien, at least to many in the modern Western world. Sexual intercourse between unattached consenting adults is by no means now widely taken to be a 'sin' of fornication, but the Wife of Bath recalls that amorous escapades are reckoned sinful ('Allas, allas! That evere love was synne!', III 614). Stranger still to modern sensibilities, medieval Christian doctrine pronounced sexual intercourse even between *married* partners to be sinful under various circumstances, as we shall see in detail later. A hint of this is found in the *Miller's Tale*, when the student Nicholas is developing his crafty plan to bed a carpenter's wife under cover of the hypothetical approach of a new Noah's Flood. Nicholas coolly warns the carpenter that on the auspicious night of the projected flood he must sleep well away from his wife so that 'bitwixe yow shal be no synne, / Namoore in lookyng than ther shal in deede' (I 3590–1). 'No synne' evidently means no sex – not even sexual thoughts prompted by 'looking'.

There are both general and specific resonances from Christian doctrine here. The general presumption was that marital (let alone extra-marital) intercourse was always, as it were, on the verge of sinfulness by reason of its satisfaction of clamorous physical urges, even when a man and wife engaged in it for reasons approved by the Church. Sex was held to be incongruous with prayerfulness, because 'the presence of the Holy Spirit is not given at the time when conjugal acts are undertaken'.[1] The specific presumption is that abstinence from sex would be strongly advisable in a context where danger is looming. If Noah's family abstained from sex as a precaution before the Deluge, a married Oxford artisan faced with a flood should copy their example.[2]

1 Pierre Payer, *The Bridling of Desire: Views of Sex in the Later Middle Ages* (Toronto, 1993), p. 101, quoting Gratian, the compiler of an important book of Church law. Payer's chapter 4 (pp. 84–110) on 'Legitimate Reasons for Marital Relations' is particularly valuable.

2 The idea Chaucer invokes is not from the Bible (Genesis 6–9) but medieval elaboration of it, e.g. as seen in a discussion of lechery in a contemporary commentary on the Ten Commandments: married people

Matters of sexual conduct, these and others, were not options reserved for private conscience. The Church possessed elaborate judicial machinery, separate from the civil courts, to police sexual behaviour and marriage. Single individuals engaging in consensual sex – 'fornicating' – could be had up before the Church courts. We shall see that the *Friar's Tale* and the *Clerk's Tale* are examples of texts which demonstrate the active power of the Church's legal machinery. As Chaucer writes, he interacts with the regulations and expectations of fourteenth-century Christianity in the spheres of gender, sexuality, love and marriage.[3] We have already touched on abstinence from sex, and will make virginity our starting point.

Virginity

The physical virginity of a girl prior to marriage was a general matter of concern in medieval society since it corroborated her uncontaminated contribution to her husband's bloodline through childbirth once she married. However, from early times (thanks in large part to views expressed in the Epistles of St Paul) the Church had developed an extravagant valuation of virginity that went far beyond merely physical definition. Virginity was seen as a possible life-choice, in which one could devote oneself more comprehensively to spirituality than in marriage. In fact virginity, in this thinking, altogether transcended the normal marital state: 'freedom from sexual intercourse, the life of contemplation fit for angels in this world, extends into eternity'.[4] However, it was for women in particular that virginity was seen as the crowning condition. There was a triad of categories to which the Church habitually assigned women. Uppermost was the category of virginity, warranting the top spiritual reward: below it, in descending order of merit, were chaste widowhood, and marriage.

Celibacy – the state of dedicated singleness – was an important criterion of priesthood and the extensive male religious orders in the Middle Ages. Why, therefore, did the concept of virginity tend to be most emotively associated with women? Two reasons may be suggested. One arose from the physiology of intercourse: a persistent element of Christian thought imagined a woman's initially intact body, once penetrated and inseminated, to be 'stained' or 'defiled', as though deprived of a kind of ritual purity – a notion still available to us in the word 'deflowered'. The other reason lay in what had become a cardinal point of Christian doctrine – the belief that Mary mother of Jesus, universal intercessor and female role model, had remained virgin despite conceiving.

should avoid sex in 'holy time' and 'times of prayer', just as 'in the time of the approach of Noah's Flood, because of the harsh tribulation and fear that they were in, Noah and his three sons refrained from sex for a whole year, and slept apart from their wives so that by abstinence and prayer they might the more readily be saved from peril'; *Dives and Pauper*, ed. Priscilla H. Barnum, 2 vols, EETS os 275, 288 (Oxford, 1976, 1980), I, pt. 2, p. 59 (my modernization). The underlying principle derives from 1 Corinthians 7: 29–34, esp. 'He who is without a wife gives thought to the things of the Lord, how to please the Lord. But he who is joined in marriage gives thought to worldly things, how to please his wife.'

3 The doctrines are elaborately surveyed in James A. Brundage, *Law, Sex, and Christian Society in Medieval Europe* (Chicago, 1987), and summarized in *Handbook of Medieval Sexuality*, ed. Vern L. Bullough and James A. Brundage (New York, 1996).

4 Augustine, *The Good of Marriage*; in *De bono coniugali*, ed. and trans. P. G. Walsh (Oxford, 2001), p. 19.

Virginity had consequently assumed a metaphorical breadth of meaning. As the historian of sexuality Karras observes, in medieval Christian thinking virginity was a *psychological* as much as *physiological* concept – a state of mind, a behavioural attitude, an aspiration to transcend bodily matters.[5] The fourteen-year-old Virginia in the *Physician's Tale* manifests both facets of virginity. With maidenly modesty she is resolute never to sin with her body, and therefore avoids social occasions conducive to flirtation (VI 61–5). She also puts us in mind of the more abstract notion of virginity, for we are told that her disposition led her to be as chaste 'in spirit' as in body, and so she *flowered* in virginity (43–4). A virginity that both presupposes and transcends routine medieval virtues of maidenliness (such as suppression of appetite, diligence, and obedience to one's father) is likewise briefly and powerfully ascribed to Griselda, the Marquis's choice of bride in the *Clerk's Tale*: 'in the brest of hire virginitee / Ther was enclosed rype and sad corage [mature and steadfast spirit]' (IV 219–20). Although Griselda's marriage ends her physical virginity early in the tale, her subsequent role in the narrative remains a demonstration of the metaphorical, elevated notion of a virginity of spirit, a 'rype and sad corage'.

Going back once more to Virginia's case, her self-suppressing virginal personality is pointedly distinguished from the 'boldness' which, the tale suggests, many women develop as wives (VI 68, 71). Yet paradoxically, traditional Christian stories of early saints' lives supplied stirring role models of militant, 'bold' virgins, such as St Katharine of Alexandria, who held out against authoritative males who tried to coerce them into marriage or into the 'wrong' religion. In the *Second Nun's Tale* the virgin heroine Cecilia is empowered by her faith and by her virginity to convert her bridegroom into agreeing a non-sexual marital relationship. She shows herself charismatically able to debate matters of faith confidently ('boldely', VIII 319). But from the point of view of a pagan Roman official whom she resists, her confidence seems aggressive and arrogant. He demands that she drop her 'booldnesse' (487) towards him and sacrifice to Rome's gods. According to circumstances, then, Christian virginity may be alternatively self-effacing like Virginia's or 'bold' like Cecilia's; alternately humble in spirit or spirited (131, 319).

The *Second Nun's Tale* is Chaucer's only major shot at representing militant Christian virginity,[6] though as we shall see he is also interested in assertive Amazonian virginity. Nevertheless in general – with the ambivalent exception of the Wife of Bath's *Prologue* – his writing remains respectful of the Christian valuation of virginity. He is particularly responsive to the subject of threats to female virginity, which offer narrative possibilities of pathos surrounding the victim; and particularly responsive to the destruction of *consent* in the act of actual or threatened violation. Consent was a key concept in Christian understanding of marriage, so we will come back to it later in the chapter. Consent to intercourse was also a matter in which the Church courts took a strong interest, and it is to the control of sexual matters by these courts that we will now briefly turn.

5 Ruth Mazo Karras, *Sexuality in Medieval Europe: Doing unto Others* (Abingdon, 2005), p. 53.

6 Custance in the *Man of Law's Tale* is a model of the allied but less exalted phenomenon of spiritually protected marital *chastity*.

Sexuality, Marriage and the Church Courts

The *Friar's Tale* focuses on a vicious summoner, and generates a sense of outrage against ecclesiastical corruption. A summoner was a minor official operating on behalf of a regional ecclesiastical judiciary presided over by an archdeacon. Among the matters over which the archdeacon's court had jurisdiction, accurately listed by Chaucer, cases concerning fornication – whether by laypersons or by priests – duly figure prominently in historical records. Court proceedings for fornication might result in a penance, typically a flogging, but the penance could increasingly be bought off with a fine.[7] Graft and bribery were in fact endemic in the system. Whether or not summoners used prostitutes as 'snouts' to lead them to male sexual offenders, and then fleeced these as the Friar claims, there is no doubt that the courts had a reputation for homing in on sexual matters as a soft target. In the *Friar's Tale*, the summoner flings a claim at the widow of the tale, his intended victim, that he has previously paid on her behalf a fine levied on her by the court for her 'correccioun' (punishment) on a charge of adultery (III 1613–17). The adultery allegation is palpably plucked out of thin air as the summoner manoeuvres to extort cash from her. It is a sharp reminder of the abuses arising from the Church's sweeping institutional authority in matters of sexual and marital behaviour.

Like several other writers in late-fourteenth-century England (a melting pot of reformist thinking) Chaucer engages candidly with those abuses. Readers of the *Reeve's Tale* encounter a Cambridgeshire parson who – far from being celibate as the Church required of its priests – has illicitly fathered the wife of a local miller. The parson cherishes dynastic ambitions. He intends to divert Church funds to endow an ambitious marriage for the miller's daughter, his own granddaughter.[8] Church law does not catch up with him in the tale, but Chaucer's intense sarcasm does – and by the end of the tale the parson's social ambitions have been severely crushed because his granddaughter's saved-up virginity has been taken by a rustic student.

At a higher level of society, the authority of the Church and its power to intervene are demonstrated when we read in the *Clerk's Tale* that it requires the semblance of a special dispensation from the pope for a regional overlord, the marquis of Saluzzo, to divorce his peasant wife Griselda. The Church held marriage to be indissoluble except where evidence of one spouse's involvement in a prior secret marriage or of an impediment such as consanguinity (too close a family connection between spouses) or impotence could be proved. The Marquis has the power, money and influence to obtain forged papal 'bulles' [edicts] authorizing a divorce and remarriage on the pretext of pacifying his people's discontent at his marriage to a commoner (IV 736–49).[9]

7 See R. N. Swanson's excellent account of the jurisdiction of the courts in *Church and Society in Late Medieval England* (Oxford, 1989), pp. 166–81.

8 Chaucer is up to date with this emphasis. Church authorities of his time were particularly concerned to prevent clerics who lived with mistresses ('concubines') from diverting Church property to them through bequests; Conor McCarthy, *Marriage in Medieval England: Law, Literature and Practice* (Woodbridge, 2004), pp. 44–7.

9 For papal intervention and manipulation of the Church judiciary to obtain divorce see McCarthy, *Marriage*, pp. 37, 40.

Corrupt officials from Church courts making bogus inquiries into sexual activity; parsons with illicit families; and forged papal documents available to get around the Church's own rules on marriage – we are in a fourteenth-century world of sleaze rather familiar to medieval historians, where Christianity's power of institutional intervention in sexual and marital matters betrays its unattractive side. We shall come back to marriage later in this chapter. First, let us consider how Christianity might have informed Chaucer's idea of love.

Love, Gender and the Doctrine of 'Grace'

What we would call 'heterosexual' love (a term, however, which did not exist until the nineteenth century) absorbed Chaucer's attention from early in his writing life, and in this he is typical of court poets of his time. His poetry acknowledges various subdivisions of love including 'celestial' (religious) love and 'affeccioun of hoolynesse' (emotion of a religious sort). However, he writes most often of that which he calls 'love of kynde' or 'love as to a creature' (natural physical love), and especially of 'love paramours' (passionate/romantic/'courtly' love).[10] With all of these, medieval Christian doctrine had an uneasy relationship. 'Natural' sexual love was a good thing only if carefully regulated within the framework of marriage. Otherwise it debased itself into animalistic copulation, devoid of the rational restraint which ought to characterize human activity. And there were two problems with passionate romantic love (to which, following Chaucer, this chapter will apply the term 'love paramours' rather than the modern 'courtly love'). First, love paramours upset the hierarchy by which Christian doctrine held man to be superior to woman, especially in rationality. Second, in its idealizing tendency it threatened the hierarchy of Christian worship that ought to place love of God above love of another human being; in other words it came close to idolatry, as we shall see in more detail further on.

Chaucer's writings often explore uneasy relationships between desire, love and Christian morality. Such exploration is already obliquely present in the *Book of the Duchess* and *Parliament of Fowls*. These poems exemplify many Christian resonances that were fashionable in the representation of love paramours. Love exerts over the individual – primarily over the well-bred male – the imperious power over life and limb of a formidable medieval lord. In fact Love is an alternative god, notable for his own stunning miracles and cruelty (*PF* 11). Since the onset of love is thought of as an outright mental and physical assault on a person's psyche, the only way to cope with it/him is submission, imagined either as a formal act of homage to an overlord, or as self-subjection to a deity: this submission constitutes a man's commitment to the *idea* of being in love.

Stretched to this pitch, love paramours makes a man (less often a woman) feel he is suffering torture or 'penance'. During a probationary period he must painfully demonstrate his sincerity and worthiness to the prospective beloved before there can be any thought of his love being reciprocated. However, if this love is accepted the lover experiences a form of resurrection ('Reysed as fro deth to lyve', *BD* 1278), into a state of ecstasy or paradisal bliss. The language of Christianity,

[10] For these categories see respectively *TC* I 978–9; *CT* I 1155, 1158–9, 2112, 3758.

then, is extensively invoked in Chaucer's explorations of elevated heterosexual love, as indeed it is in much court poetry of the period. The heaven of success; the hell of waiting or rejection; the reverential self-abasement of the male before the female (as also the lover's abasement to the deified principle of Love); the protraction of self-restraint and frustration while desperately pleading for 'mercy' and 'grace'; the perception of the beloved as the lover's everything ('suffisaunce') and even his goddess (*BD* 1038–40): these form a quasi-religious vocabulary for expressing in a heightened way the evolution of amorous desire and the emotional peaks and troughs of courtship.[11]

Within this model, a gender differentiation is implicit which habitually ascribes attentive pursuit to the male, and to the female a more passive role of listening and responding. That is in line with a deep-seated medieval physiological and theological hypothesis that gender roles divide fundamentally into active, thought of as masculine, and passive, thought of as feminine. Thomas Aquinas was one theologian who propounded the theory that in actual lovemaking masculine penetration, being (for various reasons) more 'active', typified a 'more noble' role; the notionally passive role of being penetrated was 'less noble'.[12] Normatively, males were 'doing' something to women; women merely received.[13] (These were crucial gender distinctions. In sex acts that would nowadays be called homosexual, a male who took the 'receiving' role was alleged to become 'effeminate'.[14]) Chaucer often discloses the underlying active/passive binary. A husband is imagined 'labouring' his wife (VII 108); a wife is imagined waiting to 'suffice' to a lover's desire (IV 1999); a mistress's will is imagined becoming the 'instrument' of her suitor's will (V 568).[15]

Nevertheless, this model of love paramours inherited by Chaucer appears to assign to the woman a certain effectively 'active' role, namely the decision to accept her suitor's obedient service or not, and considerable continuing emotional authority over him if she does. A model for describing this came (again) from Christian doctrine. The granting of 'mercy' or 'grace' which signals her acceptance is modelled on the immeasurable bounty of grace ascribed to God in Christian thought. Just as God's mercy towards humankind enacted through Christ's act of self-sacrifice was reckoned to exceed anything humankind could deserve, considering the original disobedience of the Fall, so a woman's 'mercy' towards a lovelorn suitor transcended any notion he might have of deserving her love through his merit or his attentiveness. Troilus, welcomed into Criseyde's arms, exclaims that considering how undeserving he is, the grace of Love has saved him (*TC* III 1264–7), and Criseyde's mercy has overcome his unworthiness: 'Here may men seen that mercy passeth right' (III 1282–4). Aurelius, Dorigen's would-be lover, is another who acknowledges that he cannot demand from her 'any thyng of right' but only pleads for her 'grace' – though this is a slimy speech in which the religious formulae of courtship thinly disguise the claim he is really making by

11 See Elizabeth Archibald, 'Chaucer's Lovers in Metaphorical Heaven', *Envisaging Heaven in the Middle Ages*, ed. Carolyn Muessig and Ad Putter (London, 2007), pp. 222–36.

12 Payer, *The Bridling*, p. 95.

13 See Karras, *Sexuality*, pp. 3–4, 67, 79–80.

14 Ibid., pp. 23, 27.

15 Some exceptions can be found: e.g. May is said to want to 'have' her lover (IV 2095).

stating that he has fulfilled the condition she has set on loving him (V 1324–33). Chaucer characteristically enjoys milking the slipperiness of what is meant by a woman's 'grace' in his writing. Will the granting of grace mean that she agrees to be nice to the man, or will it mean she agrees to go to bed with him? The numerous cries for amorous 'mercy' or 'grace' uttered by Chaucer's males stretch from aristocratic Arcite's in the *Knight's Tale* to urban Absolon's in the *Miller's*. Such reiteration dulls, though it does not eliminate, the power of the Christian analogy.

Godlike 'grace', the power to lavish love, appears to be a woman's prerogative in this idiom of love. But before we assume that this amounts to an empowerment of women, we might note that the religious analogy tends actually to create an *expectation* of response even if it does not assert a right. While Christianity held that a person's virtue could not compel God's mercy, virtue stood a better chance than vice. Virtuous behaviour did not coerce God, but it might cajole a sympathetic hearing. So, too, occasional reassurances are articulated for Chaucer's suitors. Surely a woman couldn't be beautiful and virtuous *without* mercy or 'pitee' being among her characteristics?[16] Wouldn't it be a 'vice' for a lady *not* to cherish a really worthy supplicant?[17] Thus – in courtly theory at any rate – a woman's room for manoeuvre was insidiously constrained by the notion that the truly noble heart must nurture compassion. We begin to see that the religious diction fashions a literary game played between writer and reader. That does not mean it may not take a turn where human love seems to tread either more philosophically or more disturbingly on religious territory. Moreover, we must set this element of 'game' in its larger perspective.

Reconciling Human Love with Providence

Chaucer also produces from the start a profoundly emotive sense of the harrowing unpredictability that attends the finding of a love-partner; of the roller-coaster of delight and painful frustration that may characterize courtship; of the soaring elation that can come with achieved love; and of the utter devastation in losing it. In the face of these, medieval Christianity with its advocacy of self-restraint and commendation of higher things seems to have rather little to say – threatens to be, as it were, beside the point. The *Parliament of Fowls* is not a straightforwardly Christian poem, but manages to speak eloquently of the disconnection between those 'higher things' and amorous love. Its narrator learns that this world is insignificant compared with the next, that working for the common benefit is the key to the afterlife, and he hears of the punitive afterlife awaiting lovers – but all this gives him 'something he doesn't want', apparently a cosmology indifferent to desire; and 'not what he wants', apparently constructive enlightenment about passion (*PF* 57–84).

Chaucer's poem goes on to touch on several dimensions of erotic love; but its main focus is on the basic impulse to mate, and on the emotional complications around this when besotted rival males (in this 'bird'-poem these are eagles) compete for a female who refuses, for the moment, to be interested in any of them.[18]

[16] *BD* 1195–1200; *TC* I 897–900.

[17] *TC* I 985–7. The idea is subjected to parody in IV 1986–97.

[18] The text insists on this dynamic: males choose partners they desire; the female choice is whether to agree: 'And ech of hem dide his besy cure / Benygnely to chese or for to take, / By hire acord, hys formel

The procreative drive is ostensibly 'given' by Nature who oversees God's design for the species; yet female desire seems not to be in Nature's hands, let alone amenable to logic or argument (534–7, 631–7). The female eagle wishes to opt out for a year, and after that 'to have my choys al fre' (647–9).

God, in this context, is a remote figure responsible for a mating lottery in which desire is only erratically reciprocated. As Nature contemplates her protégés' mating ritual she just has to shrug her shoulders and hope they can pair off satisfactorily:

> as youre hap is, shul ye wynne or lese.
> But which of yow that love most entriketh,
> God sende hym hire that sorest for hym syketh! (402–4)[19]

In fact according to *Troilus and Crisedye* only Venus, the life-force of desire, really understands the enigma so baffling to women and men – just why it is that 'She loveth hym, or whi he loveth here, / As whi this fissh, and naught that, comth to were' (III 31–5). This image of an unlucky fish trapped arbitrarily in a weir figures the desolate flip-side of love.[20] For Chaucer the enigma of unreciprocated love is not trivial or academic, and it is never far from being a serious philosophical question about divine justice.

Although such an objection is sometimes associated in Chaucer's writing with a position of pre-Christian un-enlightenment, and although we shall later see how the poetry intermittently tries to transcend such objection, the sheer difficulty of reconciling the myriad frustrations of human sexual desire with the idea of a beneficent godhead remains a strikingly recalcitrant strand in Chaucer's writing. It could be described as a strand of scepticism.[21] It is visible, for example, in the trauma of ideal marital love lost through death in the *Book of the Duchess*. Here any idea of traditional Christian consolation for bereavement is quietly left aside. Consolation for the death of the Black Knight's Duchess Blanche is not to be achieved through any strenuous reassurance that she has escaped to a better afterlife. Christian doctrine filters into the poem only in an oblique guise. In medieval Christendom a suicidal frame of mind (*BD* 577–88) is the sin of despair and, as the dreamer notes, it leads to damnation (723–5). Gently and indirectly the mourner and the reader are reminded of a bracing Christian antidote to misery and death – 'waking up', a return to mental and spiritual vigilance from the lethargy of melancholy. One must wake up from the suicidal gloom of bereavement (202). The poem's recurrent attention to 'waking' constitutes a warning.[22]

Here Chaucer typically invokes Christian means of escape rather obliquely as he focuses on the unpredictable or emotional effects of passionate love and its

or hys make [female or mate]' (*PF* 369–71). In *TC* II 607–9, Criseyde reflects that however ardently a man loves her, a woman need not *assent* to love.

19 So too Emily's hopes – if she has to be married – are no more ambitious than at least to get whichever knight loves her more (I 2325).

20 As in *PF* 138–40.

21 I differ here from John Burrow, who is confident that in English medieval literature 'the voice of religious scepticism never speaks'; *Mediaeval Writers and their Work* (Oxford, 1982), p. 86.

22 Compare the *Miller's Tale* where the carpenter thinking his lodger is 'in despeir', bids him 'Awak!' (I 3474–8). Chaucer's Friar makes the standard appeal, 'Waketh!', to his audience to preserve themselves from being snatched to hell (III 1653–6).

frustration. Neither an escape from desire into a passionless focus on 'the common benefit' nor an enforced 'rousing' from emotion into spiritual awareness appear to be particularly sensitive remedies: nor, on the other hand, are they wholly unattractive means of escape if the alternative (seen in the example of Aurelius in the *Franklin's Tale*) is chronic raving and a death-wish. Not surprisingly, therefore, Chaucer does engage quite extensively with a Christian encouragement to think of the most satisfying love as a phenomenon of 'peace' and 'rest'. Criseyde, welcoming Troilus as her lover, addresses him as 'my pees' (III 1309). At the beginning of the *Franklin's Tale* Dorigen's acceptance of Arveragus in a conspicuously mutual marital relationship brings them both 'in quiete and in reste' (V 760). Walter's marriage to Griselda in the *Clerk's Tale* enables him to live initially in 'Goddes pees' (IV 423). His obsessive testing of Griselda turns this peace into rancour, but ultimately they live again 'in concord and in reste' (1132). The paradox, however, remains: fulfilled human love may bring 'peace' to a couple temporarily, but as the eventual fate of Troilus (transcending his human passions) suggests, and as Gower's contemporary *Confessio Amantis* also signals, it might be a *release* from passionate love that provides a more profound version of 'peace'.[23]

Consent

Another concern launched in Chaucer's dream poems, as we have seen, is *consent*. True, the right of the female eagle to choose in the *Parliament of Fowls*, and the right of the lady in the *Book of the Duchess* to reject the Black Knight's first approaches before she eventually accepts his love, belong to the conventional fiction of female sovereignty in medieval love paramours. Yet the momentousness of female choice in the *Parliament* – delaying the mating process for an entire population – is very conspicuous and goes beyond convention to reckon with a woman's unreadiness to consent to *any* partner.[24] Such unreadiness is voiced also by Emily in the *Knight's Tale*, Cenobia in the *Monk's Tale* and even, fleetingly, by Criseyde.

The full definition of marriage in the regulations of the medieval Church varied over time, but the reciprocal, formally uttered spoken consent of the parties was always a key element in it, and in the last analysis might be practically the only necessary element. The ecclesiastical authorities sought to gain as much control over marriage as possible. They tried to insist that any formal consent should be uttered at the doorway of a church and in the presence of a priest, and not until after three separate announcements of the 'banns' which allowed parishioners to identify impediments to the proposed marriage. Nevertheless if a couple freely stated to each other without meeting all those technicalities, or even stated secretly, that they now accepted each other as husband/wife, this was of the greatest importance in establishing a marriage. Consequently medieval Church courts were full of cases in which people pleaded – or denied – the existence of verbal

[23] In Gower's poem a thwarted and elderly lover's decisive abandonment of sexual passion is marked by Venus's gift to him of jewellery inscribed *por reposer* ('to achieve repose'): *Confessio Amantis* VIII 2904–40, *The English Works of John Gower*, ed. G. C. Macaulay, II (Oxford, 1901).

[24] 'I wol nat serve Venus ne Cupide, / Forsothe as yit, by no manere weye' (*PF* 652–3).

consent as being tantamount to a marriage contract, even if a 'clandestine' one.[25]

It has sometimes been urged that Chaucer's *Troilus* explores the concept of a 'clandestine marriage' between its hero and heroine, on the basis that their statements of commitment to each other, crowned by consummation, amount to marriage. Against this, Conor McCarthy argues that their words nowhere incorporate an actual reference to marriage, whereas such precise verbal reference (not the vaguer issue of intention) dominated ecclesiastical law.[26] Perhaps neither view quite puts its finger on what Chaucer is doing in *Troilus* and several of his *Tales*, which is to respond to the *general* sensitivity of the 'consent-issue' in his period by focusing on the underlying principle of mutuality in heterosexual relations. Chaucer's poetry communicates a sense that female consent was a precarious and embattled concept, despite the medieval Church's technical endorsement of it. It was indeed pervasively still the case that a woman's freedom of choice, her consent, was usually at risk from other factors, especially the entrenched supposition that authority lay with males and that marriage was an instrument of family (or political) alliance. An heiress of Rome, Custance, is involuntarily married off to a Sultan of Syria in the *Man of Law's Tale*. A young sister-in-law, Emily in the *Knight's Tale*, whose private wish is to continue single and chaste, is designated by her brother-in-law Duke Theseus as a marital prize in a tournament, and then when the victor dies is donated in marriage by him and the parliament of Athens (with only nominal consultation of her wishes) to reinforce an alliance between Athens and Thebes.

Marriage as a basis for alliance was in fact acceptable to the Church as a means of peacemaking, even though such a perspective could be 'at odds with the canon law's insistence on the right of free consent'.[27] Chaucer keeps the emotive question of consent before us. We are made very aware that Dorigen freely consents to marry Arveragus in the *Franklin's Tale*, whereas the prospect of having to yield herself sexually to Aurelius is totally abhorrent. The *Merchant's Tale* tells us of May, a young woman 'apoynted' to be an old nobleman's wife, who lies on her bridal bed as still as stone (IV 1818). We are never informed whether she consented to the marriage. By withholding that information, the tale prepares its readers to sense hollowness in the ecclesiastical blessing trotted out at this wedding: 'Forth comth the preest, with stole aboute his nekke [. . .] And made al siker ynogh with hoolynesse' (1703–8). The Christian rites seem to be in uncomfortable collusion with a patriarchy that supports the sexual oppressiveness of an old lecher. Eventually the plot discloses that May has a mind of her own, and can manipulate the verbiage of marriage to her advantage. She swears her fidelity to January on the tender flower of her wifehood dedicated to him 'Whan that the preest to yow my body bond' (2192), just before she motions her lover into a tree in readiness for sex. Telling January what he wants to hear, she reminds us how easily the Church's championship of 'consent' slips into a confirmation of female subjection, the woman's body reckoned 'bound' to the husband by the priest.

25 McCarthy, *Marriage*, pp. 19–50; Sue Niebrzydowski, *Bonoure and Buxum: A Study of Wives in Late Medieval English Literature* (Bern, 2006), pp. 29–60. Brundage notes that recorded marriage cases coming before English Church courts in the thirteenth and fourteenth centuries 'almost always centred on issues involving consent'; *Law*, p. 454.

26 McCarthy, *Marriage*, pp. 47–8.

27 Ibid., p. 86, within an interesting discussion of the marital politics of the *Knight's Tale*.

Consent is pointedly, but quite differently, dramatized by Chaucer in the *Wife of Bath's Tale*. The rape of a girl by a knight prompts an almost obsessive focus in the subsequent narrative on choice or lack of choice. The implication may be that the tale constitutes, among other things, a powerful endorsement of the medieval Christian advocacy of consent in sexual and marital relationships. Because he has denied consent to his rape victim, the knight is put in a position where he must enter a forced marriage to someone he perceives as an ugly old peasant. He is formally 'constreyned' into it (III 1071) by the ethics of a promise, because he vowed to fulfil any request by the woman if she got him out of his potential death sentence for rape. He experiences a salutary lesson in reverse sexual coercion. In the end, the knight only retrieves something of his flawed nobility by handing over the right of choice to the woman who has become his educator.

In the *Clerk's Tale* we are made aware, both that huge pressure is piled on a humble peasant to agree to a marriage which her feudal lord directly proposes and which her awed father endorses; and at the same time (an interesting tiny modification by Chaucer of the detail of his source) an opportunity is formally left open for her to choose: 'Wol ye assente, or elles yow avyse?', asks Marquis Walter (IV 350). What Griselda then actually agrees in her formula of consent ('as ye wole youreself, right so wol I', 361) notoriously extends beyond the mere consent to marry that Christian law required, for it volunteers unresisting compliance with the Marquis's every whim. But the effect of the entire tale is to focus attention on Griselda's free *choice* to commit to this. Indeed, whereas in Angela Carter's tale of a commoner girl married to a sadistic marquis, the girl can only be rescued from the disastrous error of her consent by her mother galloping into the marquis's mansion as a feminized version of a knight in shining armour,[28] in the *Clerk's Tale* the heroine's voluntary self-dedication, her *unwavering* consent, becomes a force of resolute unconditional love which reduces the husband in the reader's eyes to a figure of futile malicious caprice.[29] Moreover, if at times Griselda's consent seems to exemplify an extreme version of that wifely obedience that was routinely urged in the Middle Ages (indeed urged by the Clerk, as exponent of Christian doctrine),[30] at other times her dedication to the Marquis is invested with the quality of solemn human reverence in the presence of godhead: 'bitwixen youre magnificence / And my poverte', she asserts, no person can 'maken comparison' (815–17).

Spiritual Love

Noticing this quasi-religious awe we might well go on to ask, how far is Chaucer interested in writing of a love which actually *is* a religious, spiritual love – writing of what he calls love 'celestial' or 'affeccioun of hoolynesse'? In the *Prioress's Prologue* he does show easy mastery of the idiom of devotional exaltation of the Virgin Mary. The Prioress draws with paradoxically abstract lyricism on the Church's repertoire for communicating the miracle of Mary's non-sexual impregnation by the divine spirit whom, as the Prioress puts it, the Virgin's sheer humility

[28] 'The Bloody Chamber', *The Bloody Chamber and Other Stories* (London, 1979, repr. 1995), pp. 38–40.

[29] See Alcuin Blamires, *The Case for Women in Medieval Culture* (Oxford, 1997), pp. 164–70.

[30] 'She shewed wel, for no worldly unreste / A wyf, as of hirself, nothing ne sholde / Wille in effect, but as hir housbonde wolde' (IV 719–21).

ravished from heaven (probably in the sense 'plucked down by force of feeling'):

> O mooder Mayde! O mayde Mooder free!
> That ravyshedest doun fro the Deitee,
> Thurgh thyn humblesse, the Goost that in th'alighte
> Of whos vertu [power], whan he thyn herte lighte,
> Conceyved was the Fadres sapience (VII 467–82)

A supernatural scenario of love here necessitates ambitious but precise language of devotion, which rises powerfully above the Prioress's surrounding protestations of her own unworthy and childish intellect. Chaucer is good at such hymns. However, what we do not find in his writing is an expression of 'mystical' yearning for God, the impulse towards transcendental communication through love that was by his time a part of the Christian culture in Europe. On the contrary, he makes a mischievous parody of mystic ecstasy in the *Miller's Tale* by devising a plot element where Nicholas isolates himself in his room and gapes exaggeratedly upwards in a pseudo-trance (I 3444–5, 3473): all this to fool his landlord into crediting him with revelatory knowledge of a new Noah's Flood. It is difficult to escape the conclusion that Chaucer felt that the contemporary practice of mystical devotion was open to abuse.

He cultivated instead the sonorous hymn to divine love, and few have written in that vein more powerfully than he. Yet the *contexts* for such writing are confusing, for they show a 'Renaissance' Chaucer who finds even in Venus an exemplar of divine love. The relevant passage is an extraordinary prayer addressed to Venus at the start of Book III of *Troilus and Criseyde* when the narrative is about to describe the fulfilment of the lovers' relationship. Venus is hailed as the root cause of well-being, her power over friendship and attraction (both as planet and goddess) felt throughout the universe, capable of inspiring Jupiter and Mars into amorous passion, and stimulating noble behaviour in her adherents. Any worries we might have (didn't Jupiter's susceptibility to desire turn him into an adulterer and a rapist?) shrink before the unassailable absorption of the Venus-principle into the wider Christian principle of love:

> God loveth, and to love wol nought werne;
> And in this world no lyves creature
> Withouten love is worth, or may endure (III 12–14)

Chaucer's study of Boethius' *Consolation of Philosophy* and his knowledge of Dante support expressions of awe in the presence of an all-inclusive phenomenon of love. Love is subsequently hailed as a holy bond, an ordering principle by which God encircles all hearts, and which unifies peoples and even the elements (III 1744–71).

It is a moot point (in fact is the most profound question of all about the poem) whether in *Troilus* as a whole the lovers' relationship is to be interpreted as a celebration of love in this inclusive sense, or whether their love affair is to be dismissed – as Troilus finally dismisses it in his post-mortem – as a debased variant of a God-centred love. It is the narrator of the poem who utters the hymn to Venus. We may sense that this narrator is an over-enthusiastic devotee liable to whitewash the goddess and overrate her, for he sees himself as Venus's 'clerk' (III

41). Yet the link made with God's love seems not negotiable, and gives an unusual reinforcement to the familiar religious diction pervading the representation of the love affair.[31] The problem for readers is how far some of the religious 'imports' are meant to trigger in us a suspicion that the lovers (especially Troilus) are *confusing* the bliss of human relationships with a bliss which medieval doctrine said human relationships could not give. To say that you find full satisfaction (*suffisaunce* III 1309) in a partner is romantic, but significantly neglects a Christian belief that only God can be a source of total sufficiency. Troilus, committing himself to the God Cupid with the words 'O lord, now youres is / My spirit' (I 422) seems to divert his spirit to the wrong deity – unless the deities are one and the same. And the poem's narrator makes us catch our breath with the conscious audacity of his wish that he could have *bought with his soul* such a night of bliss as the lovers enjoyed in their sexual consummation (III 1319).

Irreverence and Marital Sexuality: the Merchant's Tale

This audacious streak of what we might call conscious *irreverence* criss-crosses Chaucer's handling of Christian dimensions in matters of love, sex and gender. (Perhaps Boccaccio's conspicuously irreverent *Decameron* was something of a model here.) We shall extend this part of our discussion by examining Chaucerian irreverence, its nuances, and its possible impact on the reader in several of the *Tales*.

In the *Merchant's Tale* January has followed his sexual appetite unmarried until he is in his sixties, when he decides it is time to experience the reassurance of sanctified sex within the holy bond of matrimony. Ostensibly in praise of this decision, the tale's narrating voice immediately heaps up over one hundred lines as if from an ecclesiastical point of view (IV 1267–1392), alleging that extramarital sexual relations rest on nothing but short-lived animalistic anarchy of desire, whereas a married man lives in an assured, orderly state of marital bliss. The assumed origination of the 'sacrament' of marriage in the Garden of Eden is recalled, and the creation of the first wife Eve as 'mannes helpe' (Genesis 2: 18) is described with mock-sentimental enthusiasm. The speaker fantasizes that wives in general rush with fanatical zeal to enact their husbands' bidding: '"Do this," seith he; "Al redy, sire," seith she' (1346). The passage undermines through naïve extravagance its own commendation of marriage as a state of divinely ordained and guaranteed bliss, and overlays the supposed advantage (for a husband) of wifely support and obedience with dollops of derisory exaggeration.

For the reader, the impression is complex. Several of Christianity's foremost ideas about the origins and benefits of marriage are being trotted out in a snide, self-subverting way. In this corrosive atmosphere the sacredness of even so sacred an exhortation as that which the speaker finally offers to husbands, 'Love wel thy wyf, as Crist loved his chirche' (1384), borrowing directly from Ephesians 5: 25, seems endangered. As for God's intention, stated in Genesis, of alleviating loneliness by creating woman as a 'help' for man, the notion of a woman as a supportive

[31] On this diction see Barry Windeatt, *Troilus and Criseyde*, Oxford Guides to Chaucer (Oxford, 1992), pp. 231–4.

marital companion collapses into the overt cynicism of the suggestion that a wife may last somewhat longer than wanted (1317).

Yet the intelligent reader senses that behind its bleak sarcasm the tale is critiquing not so much the doctrines themselves, as the simplifications and exaggerations by which people appropriate such doctrines into shrill propaganda for or against singleness or marriage, and for or against one side or the other in gender debate between men and women. More particularly the tale seems to have set out to highlight an old man's self-serving delusion about the material and spiritual blessings of the wedded state. January himself is egotistically naïve about marriage. He supposes it to be a context for legitimized sex-on-demand with a nubile young wife. Such a marriage will belatedly contrive a Christian compensation for his previous life of promiscuity which, he suspects, may have endangered his soul. (He is right about the spiritual danger but too complacent in banking on belated reform. One of the Church's greatest authorities, St Augustine, had questioned whether salvation could be assured for someone aiming at an eleventh-hour amendment.[32]) Yet January has a high estimate of his doctrinal knowledge. He boasts his knowledge of the 'causes' – he means the formally approved Christian reasons – why people should marry: that is, for the lawful procreation of children in honour of God; to avoid lechery (as a legitimate rather than random outlet for sexual drives: 1 Corinthians 7: 2); for the yielding of the mutual 'debt' of intercourse (a widespread idea of a marital duty of reciprocal sexual compliance: from 1 Corinthians 7: 3–4); and for mutual support, even in the absence of a sexual relationship (1441–55).

Obsessed with his own virility, January scoffs at the very thought of a no-sex marriage. He would rather focus on whatever pieces of text will serve his erroneous conviction that he and his wife are entitled by Christian law to unlimited sex. January means to exercise what he supposes to be that 'right' at considerable length and with the aid of the medieval equivalent of viagra. It is left to his adviser Justinus to recall the more stringent small print of the Church – that Christian law requires moderation in 'using' the desires of one's spouse. One must not 'plese' one's spouse 'too amorously' (1678–80). While this reads as a bizarre notion in the twenty-first century, it was seriously propounded by Christian moralists in the fourteenth. Since the chief objective of intercourse within marriage was procreation, not orgasm for its own sake, frequent intercourse 'oonly for amorous love' for the satisfaction of 'brennynge delit' is deadly sin, according to the *Parson's Tale* (942).

Justinus has in mind the claim of medieval theologians that what should make marital sex superior to illicit sex with a mistress is precisely its more measured, less frenzied quality. Theologians were fond of such sayings as: 'The too ardent lover of his own wife is an adulterer' (meaning such a husband is effectively descending to a level of illicit passion with his wife).[33] January has no inkling that someone can sin in sex with their own spouse and specifically asserts that a man does not 'kill himself with his own knife' (1838–40). Chaucer's Parson offers the corrective:

32 See Alcuin Blamires, *Chaucer, Ethics, and Gender* (Oxford, 2006), pp. 89–90.

33 Payer, *The Bridling*, pp. 120–3.

> And for that many man weneth that he may nat synne for no likerousnesse that he dooth with his wyf, certes, that opinion is fals. God woot, a man may sleen himself with his owene knyf . . . Certes, be it wyf, be it child, or any worldly thing that he loveth biforn God . . . he is an ydolastre. Man sholde loven hys wyf by discrecioun, paciently and atemprely . . . (X 858–60)

While critics sometimes doubt whether we should accept the Parson as a voice of moral authority in Chaucer's work, the complementarity between the Merchant's view and the Parson's here suggests that Chaucer has assigned to January a half-baked recall of Christian doctrine, whose erroneousness he expects readers to be able to appreciate.

Chaucer sets us a teaser, however, when he goes one better than this and has January summon his wife with phraseology from the biblical Canticles (or Song of Songs) as he prepares to take her into his private garden of Eros one spring day (IV 2137–48). The erotic nuptial love-song found in the Song of Songs had long been interpreted by Christian theologians as an allegorical song representing the marriage between Christ and the Church. Many of its expressions in praise of the bride had also been appropriated as ways of eulogizing the Virgin Mary. Yet of course January's marriage to May conspicuously fails to model itself on Christ's love for the Church. The 'enclosed garden' symbolizing the bride's inviolate virginity in the Song of Songs has become a garden of sex for whose symbolic gate there is here a duplicate key letting in May's prospective lover. In any case there is stunning and rank incongruity in her pornographic husband's adoption of biblical lyricism to address May. In a sense it is the climax of the tale's representation of January's eagerness to appropriate whatever suits him from Christian lore to disguise his sordid desires – even from himself. But the passage is capped unexpectedly by the narrator's comment: 'Swiche olde lewed wordes used he' (2149). It is difficult to decide how to translate *lewed* here. Does it condemn the words as 'crude', or 'wanton'? And whose is this drastic opinion of the language of the biblical Song of Songs? Are we being pointed to something genuinely unsavoury about the eroticism of the biblical Song? While we might be comfortable with the idea that January has *debased* the language in quoting it, there seems to be another layer of cynicism here, perhaps belonging to the Merchant, complicating our reading by scorning even the biblical source itself. It is a kind of double whammy. No stone is to be left unturned by the tale in desecrating conventional Christian associations of marriage. The relentless cynicism is breathtaking, but ultimately, we may decide, still relies on stimulating the reader's residual respect for Christian expectations that are being slighted.

Irreverence and Marital Sexuality: the Wife of Bath's Prologue

In the case of the *Wife of Bath's Prologue*, audacity in manipulating Christian propositions on marriage, love and gender famously goes to new lengths and six hundred years later the jury is still out on how we are meant to respond. She brings infectious glee and witty opportunism to the arguments about remarriage and virginity which Chaucer puts into her mouth from Christian debate about these issues. Specifically, the Prologue plays fast and loose with a source that had achieved great popularity in the medieval West: a treatise written by the late-fourth-century Christian propagandist St Jerome against a monk named Jovinian. The latter, defying influential currents of thought in the early Church, had presumed to argue that marriage carried no less spiritual merit than virginity. (Today, one might conceive of discussing the relative 'personal advantages' of each status – but few would imagine they could be thought of in terms of religious merit.) Jerome, being a great champion of Christian virginity, set out to 'strike a blow for virginity' in retaliation in his *Against Jovinian* and to insist on the relative inferiority of the married state. His treatise, together with a divergent treatise *On the Good of Marriage* by St Augustine, came to constitute authoritative sources on these topics, quoted and excerpted for hundreds of years.

It was from *Against Jovinian* that Chaucer saw, with a stroke of genius, that he could dig out some of the pro-marriage (and hence pro-sexual intercourse) opinions which Jerome had ascribed to his enemy Jovinian, and make the Wife of Bath utter them. That ancient monk's scepticism about virginity, and his privileging of marriage could become the voice of a fictional much-married fourteenth-century woman. Jerome's arguments on behalf of virginity and disparaging marriage could become the arguments of the 'enemy'. Why did Chaucer produce this volte-face? Partly because he was forever thinking up new ways to use existing texts: but partly also, it might be suggested, because he saw – and has the Wife herself complain – that representation of the female point of view was rare in a culture where writing was male-dominated. There were few literary precedents that championed the status and life-choices of a sexually active *wife*, the status and life-choices that were the inevitable mode for the huge majority of women in the Middle Ages. Jovinian's protests were adaptable as groundwork for that; Chaucer had only to spice some of them up and he already had the basis of an absorbing female character creation.

As a result, it is an easy critical game to go from the Wife's (Jovinian's) arguments back to Jerome's objections to them, which Chaucer has silenced, and suppose that Chaucer wants his readers to recognize the Wife as a systematically flawed debater reliant on straw arguments that we are meant to see through. That might seem true when, for example, she produces – like Jovinian (Jerome, *Adversus Jovinianum*, I.5)[34] – Solomon as a precedent from the Old Testament for multiple marriage (III 35–43). The Wife's eagerness to emulate the sexploits of the famous wise biblical king is most engaging. However, as 1 Kings 11: 1–6 alleges, and Jerome later points out (*Adversus Jovinianum*, I.24), it was under the influence of the 'hundreds' of wives and mistresses Solomon acquired from distant cultures that he turned away from God. Hence Chaucer's fellow-poet Gower, writing about chastity, finds in Solomon a warning *against* sexual appetite since he 'forsook' God and lapsed into 'ydolatrie' when he took 'Saracen' wives and mistresses.[35] And yet, even Jerome has to admit that Solomon built the first great temple to God, and quotes extensively from his biblical sayings. Are we then to crow over the Wife for relying on an unsatisfactory witness, or are we to admire her spirit in sensing that if the great Solomon got away with it, why shouldn't she?

In other respects Chaucer allows her to draw more unambiguous strength from Jovinian's reported arguments. Virginity, she concedes, may be a state of

[34] *Adversus Jovinianum*, Patrologia Latina 23, ed. J. P. Migne (Paris, 1883).

[35] *Confessio Amantis*, VII 4493–7.

perfection for some. But Christ did not summon everyone to perfection – he only said that *if* a person wants to be 'perfect' they should sell all they have, give their wealth away to the poor, and follow himself (Matthew 19: 21). Alisoun insists, Christ 'spak to hem that wolde lyve parfitly', and 'that am nat I' (III 111–12). We could argue that the call to perfection is not an optional matter: in one of his letters Jerome insisted that 'not to aim at perfection, is a sin'.[36] But in *Against Jovinian* he accepted that Matthew's 'if' proves there is optionality; there are different roles for people within the Christian community.[37] In the same vein the Wife can borrow from Jovinian's use of 1 Corinthians 7: 7, which Jerome has to concede (albeit grudgingly, *Adversus Jovinianum*, I.8) implies that marriage is just one kind of 'gift', virginity another: 'every man hath his proper gift of God, one after this manner, and another after that'. Alisoun takes full advantage of Jerome's grudging concessions, and in effect uses them to turn the tables on him.

In an extra creative move Chaucer supplies Alisoun with further ammunition on gifts, drawing on a central passage in the first Epistle of Peter, about using for others' benefit whatever natural gifts one has received from God (103–4).[38] Mischievously, this becomes an implicit justification for bestowing her gift of female sexuality generously in marriage. 'In wyfhod I wol use myn instrument / As frely as my Makere hath it sent' (149–50).[39] While the reader is likely to make the mental reservation that Peter probably did not envisage the female genital 'instrument' as a divine gift to be liberally deployed, there is an inherent attraction in Alisoun's advocacy of generosity, and besides she is only doing what theologians had done for centuries – appropriating biblical authority to the needs of her argument.

That is a clue to much of the Christian allusion in her *Prologue*. She is entering the fray of debate, snapping up what she can in the knowledge that male religious scholars, the Jeromes of this world, have had a field day with complacent, male-centred, negative representations of women (wives in particular), while women have lacked the literacy to offer counter-perspectives. Her own selective arguments using scriptural sources can sometimes be found wanting, but to object to that is to object to her counter-strategy of innovative female-centred assertion. A case in point would be her partisan allusion to the sexual 'debt' in marriage. Paul had written that each partner in a marriage should render what was 'due' to the other: neither partner had 'power' over their own body – but instead had 'power' over their partner's body (1 Corinthians 7: 3–4). From this was developed a massively disseminated idea that each owed a 'debt' of sexual compliance to the other, as part of the fidelity of marriage. If one spouse asked for sex, the other was not empowered to refuse it. Alisoun sounds as if she has only noticed a one-way formula. She talks of her husband as her 'dettour', paying her his 'dette' on the basis that it is she who has 'the power durynge al my lyf / Upon his proper [own] body' – as the Apostle has 'tolde' her, to her great satisfaction (153–62).

36 Letter XIV.7 (To Heliodorus): www.newadvent.org/fathers/3001.htm, accessed 9 August 2007.

37 *Adversus Jovinianum*, II.6, www.newadvent,org/fathers/30092.htm, accessed 9 August 2007; Jerome pursues this again in Letter 130.14 (To Demetrias): www.newadvent.org/fathers/3001.htm, accessed 9 August 2007.

38 'Use hospitality one to another without grudging. As every man hath received the gift, even so minister the same, one to another, as good stewards of the manifold grace of God', 1 Peter 4: 9–10.

39 For further discussion see Blamires, *Chaucer, Ethics, and Gender*, pp. 138–9.

Cheekily, the Wife blots out the reciprocity – that wives too have a duty to satisfy marital 'debt' whereby their bodies are in their husbands' power. Once again we could hold this against her; we could 'spot the deliberate mistake'. Alternatively, we could reflect that, however egalitarian the medieval theory of the mutual 'debt' in marriage might be on the surface, in practice it could amount to a rationale for husbands to impose their desires on wives. Dorigen, in the *Franklin's Tale*, puts that side of the bargain with uncomfortable clarity when she reproaches her admirer Aurelius for presuming to love 'another mannes wyf, / That hath hir body whan so that hym liketh' (V 1004–5). Part of the 'debt' theory as elaborated by medieval Christianity was that wives (unlike Alison) would be too modest to 'seek' the husband's 'payment'. Husbands should therefore intuit wives' unspoken desires and render the 'payment' even if it were not specifically being asked for.[40] Chaucer's Parson perhaps betrays the prejudicial potential in this thinking when he states that a wife who 'yeldeth to hire housbonde the dette of hir body' when she would rather not, has 'the merite of chastitee' (X 940): no vice-versa is mentioned by the Parson. Given this context, a female-centred insistence on husbands 'paying the debt' at the behest of wives could amount to an observant corrective – were it not that Alison rather gives the impression that she is permanently ready (III 151). Further complicating the picture, she claims that in the case of her earliest, elderly husbands she looked for payment of a financial sort before she would let them touch her in bed. There was a 'ransom' to be paid before the sexual debt could be satisfied. It is a witty convergence of the financial and the sexual, laid on a crust of biblical allusion.[41]

Procreation, Sex, and Deviancy: Chauntecleer, Cenobia and the Pardoner

Turning now specifically to the topic of procreation, we find that the sexual practice of an uxorious cockerel on the one hand, and an Amazon queen on the other, are again measured quizzically against implicit Christian doctrine. In the *Nun's Priest's Tale* the narrator makes an appeal to Venus not to let her protégé Chauntecleer the cockerel die, considering that the cock has exerted himself so much sexually in her service 'Moore for delit than world to multiplye' (VII 3342–6). For one joyous moment, the reader contemplates chicken life being judged against the Church's formal condemnation of marital intercourse indulged for sheer pleasure rather than to multiply humanity through procreation. Common sense reasserts itself with the thought, which the tale elsewhere recognizes,[42] that cockerels serve neither Christian law nor Venus: they just tread whatever hen is to hand. Indeed cockerels (stallions too) in their indiscriminateness are taken by a contemporary of Chaucer to symbolize the potential sexual mayhem of human desire, which the Church has tried to temper through its regulations on marriage and sexuality.[43]

Bizarrely, an outlandish adherence to those regulations in Chaucer's writing appears in the Persian princess Cenobia (Zenobia), living outside Christendom, who from her youth rejects stereotypical feminine concerns and excels in

[40] Ibid., pp. 81–3.
[41] A similar convergence is played out in the *Shipman's Tale*.
[42] The hens are Chauntecleer's sisters *and* mistresses: VII 2867.
[43] *Confessio Amantis* VIII 144–63.

Amazonian military and outdoor life. Although she disdains to be 'bound' (in marriage) to any man and initially appears to embody an unusual female autonomy, she is eventually obliged to tolerate an arranged marriage (VII 2271–3). Within the marriage, her terms and conditions for having sex depend on an idea of exclusively procreative sex so rigorous that she allows no act of intercourse if she finds herself pregnant, and will not even allow an act of intercourse while she is waiting to see whether a preceding act of intercourse *might* have made her pregnant. Her rationale, the Christian one in this unexpected place, is the one not shared by Chauntecleer: that her sole intention in sex is 'To have a child, the world to multiplye' (2282). In her view it is 'lecherie and shame' for wives to let husbands have sex with them other than with that objective (2293–4). So, trying for a baby in her estimate means trying once, then forthwith waiting to check the result before trying again. Christian theologians had a range of opinions on the acceptability of marital sex within pregnancy. The extreme view, which she evidently and incongruously holds, was that it would be a sin if the wife were known to be pregnant – because if you had already achieved conception and still had sex, you must now be driven by basically sinful motives of sheer desire.[44]

Chaucer probably took from Boccaccio's book *Concerning Famous Women* (*c.*1359) his material on this pagan queen with her academic zeal for Christian regulations. For Boccaccio, this type of scenario tends to be a way of celebrating 'virile' pagan women for outdoing Christian men, as well as women, in self-control: 'women having similar moral scruples are rarely found'.[45] Chaucer by contrast supplies no interpretative framework. Cenobia attempts to bypass 'normal' womanly life as an Amazon, and then to exert super-strict control of her body in marriage: yet the final glimpse of her is as a captive in a conquering Roman emperor's procession, carrying a distaff (classic implement of the housewife). Should we admire her as a sort of proto-feminist who finds herself reeled back into masculine control; or are we to be critical of her adoption of Amazonian and then of extreme Christian strategies to escape conventional sexual expectations of women?

More decisive insinuations of 'deviancy' appear in two other contexts in the *Tales*. One is the culmination of the *Miller's Tale*, where the vengeful thwarted Oxford youth, Absolon, intends to ram a plough implement up the backside of the carpenter's wife after she makes a fool of him – but his weapon instead finds its target in the backside of her lover and his rival, Nicholas. The phallic associations of the plough were a commonplace, still used afterwards by Shakespeare. Since the *Miller's Tale* involves a parody of Noah's Flood, and since Noah's Flood was generally supposed to have been provoked by a descent into deviant sexual malpractices in Noah's time, we might justifiably take this narrative climax as a comic projection of the type of sex acts most demonized by medieval Christianity: that is, non-reproductive acts. Such sex acts – whether male–male or non-vaginal male–female or female–female (though the latter was rarely alluded to) – were severely condemned in Christian doctrine. There is no Christian nemesis in the *Miller's Tale*: but providence nevertheless puts an end to the sexual or

[44] Payer, *The Bridling*, pp. 103–4.

[45] Giovanni Boccaccio, *Concerning Famous Women*, trans. Guido Guarino (New Brunswick, 1963), pp. 226, 228.

quasi-sexual scandals of this night through flood – even if it is only a flood in the imagination of the carpenter, whose knee-jerk reaction to Nicholas's screams for 'water' brings everything to a crashing halt. In effect, flood does again intervene against sexual 'degeneracy'.

Does Chaucer come any closer to representing what we would identify as gay identity than the pseudo-phallic invasion of Nicholas's rear? Many readers have speculated that the Pardoner is 'outed' by the Host at the end of the *Pardoner's Tale*. Here the Pardoner's concluding sales pitch infuriates the Host, who retorts by referring pointedly to the speaker's balls. Many theories have developed around this conclusion, as indeed around the Pardoner's whole performance. He is referred to in the *General Prologue* as a 'geldyng or a mare', his masculinity evidently called into question. Yet he may be a demonstration not of homosexuality, nor of hermaphroditism or eunuchry (two other possibilities) but rather of the humiliation of an outsider by sexual insult. He preys on Christian society with bogus relics and cynical use of confessional and sermon techniques. The aspersions cast on his sexuality both by the *General Prologue* narrator and by the Host constitute a means of insulting an unbeliever who is parasitical on Christianity. Alastair Minnis suggests that 'he is deeply objectionable for reasons which have nothing to do with his sexuality, but reference to that sexuality . . . is an effective if crude way of expressing well-founded disapproval'.[46] The label 'mare' in particular amounted – at least in some parts of medieval Europe – to the most heinous insult that could be levelled at a man, identifying him as 'passive' sexual partner.[47] Moreover, unbelievers and so-called heretics of all sorts were casually vilified as sexual 'deviants' in medieval Christian sources. The case of the Pardoner lets us see these patterns of vilification emerging. It does not tell us whether Chaucer disapproved of gay people, or even whether 'gay' people (in our definition) existed: rather it shows to us the mechanisms by which a social doctrine based on Christian ideas of the time could demonize men by labelling them as passive/female.

Conclusion

Our discussion of the Pardoner, like that of the Wife of Bath, confirms something apparent throughout this chapter. Chaucer's talent was especially to show how people use, or misuse, or perhaps misunderstand, labels or doctrines or beliefs in the realms of gender and sexuality, as indeed in other realms. It is notable that the Christian commentary on the Commandments written in English less than a generation after the *Canterbury Tales* reports as 'common opinion' (despite the Church's teaching to the contrary) the supposition that intercourse between a single woman and single man is *not* 'deadly sin'.[48] Perhaps Chaucer's January,

[46] Alastair Minnis, 'Chaucer and the Queering Eunuch', *New Medieval Literatures* 6 (2003), 107–28, p. 123. A large literature on the Pardoner is reviewed by Robert S. Sturges, *Chaucer's Pardoner and Gender Theory* (New York, 1999); the most influential reading in relation to religious doctrine has been Robert Miller, 'Chaucer's Pardoner, the Scriptural Eunuch, and *The Pardoner's Tale*', *Speculum* 30 (1955), 180–99. For an application of queer theory that sets latent challenges to sexual 'normativity' (detected in the case of the Pardoner) within an argument that the *Tales* radically explore questions of individual and national identity, see Glenn Burger, *Chaucer's Queer Nation* (Minneapolis, 2003).

[47] Karras, *Sexuality*, pp. 19 and 131–2, cites evidence from Icelandic law.

[48] *Dives and Pauper*, I pt. 2, p. 76.

who has absorbed and regurgitates bits of Christian doctrine on sex and marriage without true comprehension of them, flags up Chaucer's penetrating sense of a similar mismatch between the doctrine and many people's perception of it. (As Karras, says, 'much of what we know about sexuality in the Middle Ages' comes from theological sources and does not let us know 'what the sexually active common people thought'.[49])

At the same time, it is evident that Chaucer presents the manipulation of doctrines by January and others in the expectation that the reader will enjoy bringing superior understanding of the same doctrines to bear on them. A readership is assumed to exist – an informed intelligentsia, as it were – that is fairly well attuned to the main lines of the medieval Church's regulations on these matters. We have discussed Chaucer's 'irreverence' but I would argue that it does not extend to mounting any unequivocal challenge to the Church's basic doctrines in this field, with one muted exception. That exception is the question of passionate love. The impression (as we saw earlier) is that Chaucer could not always square a sense of the sheer power or frustration of passionate love with the assumption that a providential hand guided the world. Because that is still a question for most of us, it remains a great point of empathy for modern readers of Chaucer's writings.

[49] Karras, *Sexuality*, p. 9; also p. 59.

2

Chauncer and the Bible*

GRAHAM D. CAIE

TODAY most people think they have a reasonably good idea of what is being referred to by 'the Bible' and, especially if practising Jews or Christians, they will have some knowledge of its contents. The Bible is generally described as containing the canonical books of Judaism and Christianity. There are, however, distinct differences in the definition of the canon and hence today there are different versions of the Bible in the various denominations and faiths, such as the Jewish Tanakh, the King James Bible, the New English Bible, the New Revised Standard Bible, the Jerusalem Bible, the Living Bible, etc. What is less well known is that these different versions do not all contain the same books: the Catholic Jerusalem Bible (1966) contains the Deuterocanonical books (books added later to the original canon), such as Tobit, Judith, Maccabees (1 and 2), Baruch and others, whereas the Protestant New English Bible excludes these in the canon but includes them in its expanded edition, which contains both the Old and New Testament Apocrypha books, also adding 1 and 2 Esdras and the Prayer of Manasses.

The Greek version of the Scriptures used by early Christians was the Septuagint, and the first Latin version was the *Vetus Latina* or Old Latin version, based on the Septuagint. St Jerome was commissioned by Pope Damasus I in the fourth century to prepare a Latin Bible, which became known as the Vulgate, the only authorized version for the Catholic Church until the Reformation. Consequently when 'the Bible' is mentioned in late-medieval literature, it is the Vulgate which is being referred to.

In the Anglo-Saxon period there had been a number of close translations and paraphrases of parts of the Bible into English, but such translations were forbidden in the later-medieval period in England.[1] It was not until John Wyclif (died 1384) that there was an English Bible closely translated from the Vulgate. The Wycliffite Bible was translated partially by Wyclif himself (probably the Gospels) while his associates were responsible for the other biblical books. Wyclif, a doctor of divinity of Oxford, was also a priest, who in his major work, *Summa Theologia*,

*An earlier version of this material, 'Lay Literacy and the Medieval Bible', appears in *Nordic Journal of English Studies* 3 (2004), pp. 125–44.

[1] Bede was said to have made a translation (now lost) of the first part of St John's Gospel; there are also many glossed Psalters, such as the Vespasian Psalter of the ninth century; also the Rushworth Version of the Gospels (manuscript Bodleian Auct. D.ii.9) and the West Saxon Gospels; in the early eleventh century Ælfric translated the Pentateuch, Joshua, Judges, Kings, Job, Esther, Judith and Maccabees.

questioned the temporal rule of the clergy and attacked clerical abuses and failings. In this he was supported by John of Gaunt during the 1370s, though Gaunt turned against Wyclif's theological opinions (especially about the eucharist, where Wyclif argued against transubstantiation) as dangerous, from around 1381. The group modern historians call the Lollard Knights included men known to Chaucer and, as Chaucer was also possibly supported by Gaunt, and later became Gaunt's brother-in-law, there has been speculation as to the extent of Chaucer's sympathies with Wycliffite thinking (see further Frances McCormack's chapter in this volume). The Wycliffite English Bible was 'widely distributed throughout England and equally widely condemned by the ecclesiastical establishment'.[2] We have no direct evidence that Chaucer used this Bible (see McCormack, p. 37) but it is commonly thought that he was influenced by current Lollard ideas. Chaucer's portrait of the Parson in the *General Prologue* is a tribute to Wycliffite ideals in the parson's poverty, unworldliness, learning, his stress on making the teaching of the Gospel the centre of his preaching, his readiness to chastize even powerful men, his charity and concern for his parishioners:A good man was ther of religioun,

> And was a povre persoun of a toun,
> But riche he was of hooly thoght and werk.
> He was also a lerned man, a clerk,
> That cristes gospel trewely wolde preche;
> His parisshens devoutly wolde he teche. (I 477–82)

It would appear that the vast majority of the population would not have first-hand knowledge of chapter and verse of the Vulgate or be able to distinguish either which material was canonical, apocryphal and legendary, or between the original biblical text and the centuries of the Christian Church's interpretation of it. Consequently, in this chapter I concentrate on what people meant by 'the Bible' and how they learned the biblical stories in the period before a vernacular Bible.[3]

The Vulgate would have been available only to the Latin literate, while the vast majority, including those who could read English texts, would have gathered their biblical knowledge from a wide variety of sources, such the popular compendia of biblical, patristic and legendary material woven into vernacular texts, such as *Cursor Mundi* (*c.* 1200); or from biblical scenes depicted in wall paintings, stained glass, sculpture, carvings and many other visual media; or from biblical material presented in sermons and orally delivered poetry, and in religious drama. In particular I wish to examine the nature of what appears to be biblical reference in vernacular literature, particularly in the works of Chaucer, to see what might be learned about the nature of this virtual medieval Bible. If Chaucer is to carry out his fictional device of pretending to 'reherce', or retell, what his characters say (I 732), then he would also wish to suggest their level of biblical knowledge and literacy.

2 *The Cambridge History of the Bible: The West from the Fathers to the Reformation*, ed. G. W. H. Lampe *et al.*, 3 vols (Cambridge, 1969), vol. II.

3 See R. and C. Brooke, *Popular Religion in the Middle Ages. Western Europe 1000–1300* (London, 1984); Beryl Smalley, *The Study of the Bible in the Middle Ages* (Oxford, Blackwell, 1952); David Fowler, *The Bible in Early English Literature* (London, 1977); David Lawton, 'Englishing the Bible', *Cambridge History of Medieval English Literature*, ed. David Wallace (Cambridge, 1999), pp. 454–82; Valerie Edden, 'The Bible', in *Chaucer: An Oxford Guide*, ed. Steve Ellis (Oxford, 2005), pp. 332–51.

There are over seven hundred biblical allusions or quotations in the *Canterbury Tales* and these include misquotations, partial quotations and paraphrases.[4] Some of Chaucer's characters acknowledge their biblical source and some do not, while others give incorrect references – especially by the standards of modern knowledge of the Bible text. The Parson, for example, conveys a sound knowledge of the Bible, although modestly admitting 'I am nat textueel' (X 57), but many others, like the Miller, appear to have a pretty shaky grasp of Scripture. Nicholas in *The Miller's Tale* bases his trick on John the carpenter on the sure knowledge that John would not know that the stories of Noah's wife were non-canonical legends. Men such as the Miller, and thus his character John, would have seen the enactment of the Noah story, replete with the argumentative Mrs Noah, in contemporary drama and art and appear to take it as 'gospel'. The Wife of Bath, the Man of Law, the Merchant and Pardoner are presented by Chaucer as having a better understanding of Scripture but as cleverly manipulating it and other authorities for their own purposes. However, Chaucer's main aim is not to teach the Bible: he is an author and creator of fictional characters and all books, including the Bible, were a means to a *literary* end. Edmund Reiss suggests that Chaucer's misquotations of Scripture are most likely intended and may be a literary method to portray his characters' limitations.[5] Chaucer is as interested in the *way* his characters use or manipulate their sources as in *what* they say. He is concerned more with the marriage of wisdom to rhetoric, of meaning to style, rather than with an accurate use of sources. He never openly criticizes a character for gross textual harassment of Scripture; rather he allows his readers to draw their own conclusions about the character from the way they apply biblical knowledge. He will have a sly character like the Pardoner congratulate the Wife of Bath on her preaching techniques, as he uses identical partial translation of the Bible or quotations out of context in his sermons.

Given that the Vulgate, as a written text, was not accessible in the fourteenth century to many of the same social and educational groups as those to which his characters belong, we might well ask how successful Chaucer was in reflecting the type of biblical sophistication (or lack of it) his various characters might be expected to possess. Turning the question round: is there anything to be gleaned in Chaucer's works about levels of literacy in the late fourteenth century, given that Chaucer intends to make his characters realistic? We have scant evidence of literacy at this time and have to rely on items such as wills or bankruptcy lists for information on book ownership. However, I cannot see why we should not look at literary characters too for clues about how the Bible is conveyed to the 'lewed' or laity and in what ways 'auctoritee' trickles down to those with little learning in the fourteenth century.

Many university teachers these days complain about the low level of biblical knowledge which our students have. Even those who profess to know their Bible and claim to have learned it at Sunday school are still shaky on details. How many today are convinced that the Fall of the Angels and Christ's Descent into Hell are

[4] See Edmund Reiss, 'Biblical Parody: Chaucer's "Distortions" of Scripture', *Chaucer and the Scriptural Tradition*, ed. David Lyle Jeffrey (Ottawa, 1984), p. 48.

[5] Ibid, p. 52. On lay literacy and the Bible see Janet Coleman, *The Bible in English Literature in History 1350–1400: Medieval Readers and Writers* (London, 1981), pp. 204–9.

actually narrated in the Bible itself and that the fruit eaten by Adam and Eve was an apple, just as many medieval people would, although all these three are later accretions to the tradition? However, detailed knowledge of the Bible by the laity is a post-Reformation phenomenon, much reduced in the last fifty years, and we today are perhaps nearer the medieval mentality, receiving our biblical knowledge from films and TV as well as fiction, just as medieval *illiterati* learned the Bible aurally and visually. We must not, however, underestimate the biblical knowledge of the *illiterati*, but at the same time we should be aware of the filters through which this knowledge passed and how it was integrated in a vast encyclopaedic understanding of the history of man and his universe.

Margery Kempe, for example, thanks the priest in Lynn who read to her the Bible, the writings of Hilton and St Birgitta and much more. She also mentions the paintings and sculpture and an Easter sepulchre, which sent her into a mystical state.[6] Visually and orally she would be totally immersed in the Bible and aware of the typological links between Old and New Testament, as the biblical scenes from both were invariably juxtaposed in art and literature. Whether she could distinguish between canonical and apocryphal episodes is unimportant, as all was wrapped up in what might be described as the medieval biblical experience or what Margaret Aston calls 'that vanished English library of "laymen's books"'.[7] All such information had a clear didactic aim, namely to help the laity lead good lives and understand the working and significance of the Church's sacraments, and whether the source was canonical or not was not so important.

In the Middle Ages, as today, there was a wide range of literate and illiterate population. Illiteracy today and then was often hidden and notions of literacy vague. Michael Clanchy demonstrates how *clericus* and *litteratus*, 'cleric' and 'literate', were practically synonymous, as were *laicus* and *illitteratus*, 'lay' and 'illiterate', in the early Middle Ages but the situation became more fluid and these terms no longer synonymous in the later period.[8] By lettered or literate people referred usually to Latin literacy and not vernacular but by end of the fourteenth century *litteratus* was used to describe not only persons of erudition in Latin but those with a minimal knowledge of Latin: this is the period of increasing numbers of *laici litterati*, laypeople who could read.

There were many English translations of parts of the Bible by the mid-fourteenth century; there were Gospel harmonies and commentaries, versions of the Pauline and Catholic epistles, as well as many other vernacular works which retold parts of the Bible. More important were the literary works, especially in verse, which paraphrased the Bible, and verse was important to attract the listener and to help the memory. A literal translation of the Bible was unnecessary, many thought, when more attractive renditions were easily at hand for the laity. The *Stanzaic Life of Christ*, for example, written in the mid-fourteenth century and

6 *The Book of Margery Kempe*, ed. Sanford B. Meech and Hope Emily Allen, EETS os 212 (Oxford, 1940) chapters 57–8, pp. 140–4. An Easter sepulchre was a symbolic representation of the Easter story in a church: the eucharistic host and often a crucifix were placed in a recess and covered, from Good Friday to Easter Sunday, representing Christ's burial in the tomb and Resurrection.

7 Margaret Aston, *Lollards and Reformers* (London, 1984), p. 121.

8 Ibid., p. 178; Anne Hudson, 'Laicus Litteratus: The Paradox of Lollardy', *Heresy and Literacy, 1000–1530*, ed. Peter Biller and Anne Hudson (Cambridge, 1994), pp. 222–36.

based on the Latin *Legenda Aurea* (a collection of saints' lives itself translated into the vernacular); the *Cursor Mundi* (*c.*1200), a history of God's loving relationship with humanity from the Creation to the Last Judgment; and the *Polychronicon* (mid-fourteenth century Latin, translated into English in 1387), were designed to present scriptural material to the laity. John Trevisa, the English translator of the *Polychronicon*, writes: 'A worthy person asked me to show certain things that he saw written in Latin, that he might know in the English tongue of Jesus Christ's nativity and his deeds in order, in which he might by good authority fully trust and know.'[9] Here are all the stories which John the Carpenter would know, some biblical but many apocryphal, such as narratives about Adam and Eve, Noah and his wife, and the Fall of the Angels, the life and death of Pilate, the legend of Seth and the post-lapsarian tree, the stories of Joseph of Arimathea, the Harrowing of Hell, the handkerchief of St Veronica, the midwives at the Nativity, the early (legendary) life of Christ, and the life, death and assumption of Mary. All these stories we find in church wall paintings, carvings, stained glass and, of course, the mystery plays. This medieval 'Bible of the laity' was not in any one book but an encyclopaedic synthesis of all the stories connected to the lives of the Old Testament patriarchs and the holy family, and gleaned from a wide range of sources.

It was also a pan-European 'virtual book' with the same themes and stories appearing throughout the continent in vernacular writing, paintings, carvings, frescoes, and so forth. A good example is found in the many frescoes in medieval Danish churches, which have the same details as in, say, the English mystery plays, such as the ale wife at Doomsday or the doubting midwife at the Nativity. All had a common purpose, not simply to narrate biblical scenes, but to influence the lives of the audience – especially towards understanding the centrality of repentance and salvation – as the cycle plays did, and to create an element of social control.

Much of Chaucer's own learning, including religious learning, would have come second-hand by this trickle-down effect – or, in Chaucer's case, cascade effect – not directly from the Latin Bible or patristic sources but from collections, *florilegia*, anthologies and miscellanies. We have the friars to thank for many of these compendia, from which Chaucer and many other vernacular writers gleaned Latin quotations, exempla and miscellaneous general knowledge. A good example of a very popular collection is John of Wales's *Communiloquium* of the late thirteenth century, used by priest and laity alike, and in which there were many biblical and classical quotations, all carefully listed with lemmata for quick reference. It is a work that Chaucer never mentions, but it would appear to have been used in his *Wife of Bath's Prologue, Summoner's Tale, Nun's Priest's Tale* and elsewhere: many of the exempla which the Pardoner uses in his model sermon are taken from this work, as Robert A. Pratt has shown.[10] Derek Pearsall writes of 'the magpie-like nature of his [Chaucer's] raids on scholarly texts', which were probably 'the product, more than we know, not of his indefatigable reading but of his conversations with more learned friends':

[9] Quoted from David Fowler, *The Bible in Early English Literature* (London, 1977), pp. 146–8 and 165–93.

[10] Robert A. Pratt, 'Chaucer and the Hand that Fed Him', *Speculum* 41 (1966), 619–42.

> Itemizing the sources of each tale does in fact give a misleading impression, since it misses that great body of writing in Latin anthologies, miscellanies, compendia and encyclopaedias, which is what gives the 'many storied' quality to Chaucer's writing in *The Canterbury Tales* . . . Echoes of sermons and sermon literature are everywhere, and of course the Bible and liturgy are plundered for some of Chaucer's most dazzling literary effects.[11]

One wonders how frequently the clergy went to the Vulgate even for biblical texts and exempla. 'Creative preachers must have been at a premium', states Janet Coleman: 'these handbooks may, in part, be the origin of frequent satirical complaints against a clergy illiterate in the Bible'.[12] As might be expected, these handbooks were severely criticized by the Wycliffites, who considered them stultifying for the spiritual growth of the laity. The Dominicans had been the first to collect exempla in handbooks for preachers. These were the work of important scholars such as the highly influential John Bromyard's *Summa Praedicantium* (*c*.1356), and Robert Holcot's *Liber de Moralitatibus*, containing moralized exempla – exempla whose messages are explained – a major source for Chaucer's *Nun's Priest's Tale*.[13] But this is not to downplay Chaucer's learning. Chaucer of course translated from Latin, as in his *Boece*, and he claims in the G Prologue to *The Legend of Good Women* to have translated Innocent III's *De Contemptu Mundi* (*LGW* G 414–15). In his translation of Boethius he relied heavily in the prose sections on Jean de Meun's French translation but he went back to Boethius' original Latin to check the French translation. He also used Nicholas Trivet's Latin commentary on Boethius to explain allusions. Indeed, the four works, Boethius' *De Consolatione Philosophiae*, Jean de Meun's translation, Nicholas Trivet's commentary and Chaucer's Middle English translation, appear in different combinations in a few fifteenth-century manuscripts, with the vernacular translation as a marginal or interlinear gloss.[14]

So, fourteenth-century lay authors, including Chaucer, can be shown to have had strong biblical and patristic knowledge, albeit much at second-hand, but how did they 'cascade' this to the next level, their lay audience who might or might not be literate in the vernacular? In the *Canterbury Tales* Chaucer creates characters who in real life would possess different degrees of biblical knowledge and understanding. The Parson is obviously well versed in Scripture, beginning his tale with the biblical reference for his text, Jeremiah 6, followed by the Latin Vulgate source, a close translation of it and then an explanation. Following exegetical practice he then gives patristic interpretations by Ambrose, Isidore and Gregory in his tale 'of moralitee and virtuous mateere' (X 38). In *Piers Plowman* the Vulgate plays a pivotal role. Latin Scripture naturally adds weight to the argument, but, as Janet Coleman suggests, 'the biblical, Latin quotations in *Piers Plowman* comprise a central principle of construction, from which the Middle English "divisions" fan

11 Derek Pearsall, *The Life of Geoffrey Chaucer* (Oxford, 1992), pp. 242–3.

12 Coleman, *The Bible in English Literature*, p. 176.

13 *Sources and Analogues of the Canterbury Tales*, ed. Robert M. Correale and Mary Hamel, 2 vols (Cambridge, 2002, 2006), vol. I, pp. 486–9.

14 See Pearsall, *Life of Geoffrey Chaucer*, pp. 163–5; *The Medieval Boethius: Studies in the Vernacular Translations of De Consolatione Philosophiae*, ed. A. J. Minnis (Cambridge, 1987). Examples include MS Cambridge University Library Ii.3.21 fols 13r-14v and MS Oxford, Bodleian Library, Rawl. G. 41, fol. 1.

out . . . [Langland] frequently began with a Latin quote and, using the aids of the medieval preacher, derived much of the substance of his poem.'[15] For example:

> And Salamon seide, þe same, þat Sapience made:
> '*Qui parcit virge, odit filium.*
> Whoso spareþ þe sprynge spilleþ his children'. (B V, 38–40)[16]

The biblical source is in this way amplified with allegories and examples, and much of this material has a source in Bromyard's encyclopaedic *Summa*. The Norfolk Fransciscan John of Grimestone (1372) uses the same technique: to provide notes for preachers he collected a vast range of patristic, biblical, classical and even contemporary authorities.[17]

A direct quotation from the Vulgate gives an English text authority, and Chaucer demonstrates how this method can easily be abused, for example by the hypocritical friar in his *Summoner's Tale*, who misapplies biblical quotations while claiming 'My spirit hath his fostryng in the Bible' (III 1845), and the Pardoner, who sprinkles or seasons his sermon with Latin, purely for effect: 'And in Latyn I speke a wordes fewe, / To saffron with my predicacioun, / And for to stire hem to devocioun' (VI 344–6). The Summoner delights in quoting phrases in Latin and indeed, when drunk, 'wold he speke no word but Latyn' (I 638). Such misapplication of the Bible is openly criticized in *Piers Plowman*. Langland's Lady Mede (and one meaning of *mede* was 'bribery') is angered by Conscience's argument against the abuse of riches and she defends gift-giving (implicitly bribes) with a biblical quotation:

> Also wroþ as þe wynde weex Mede in a while,
> 'I kan no Latyn,' quod she, 'Clerkes wite þe soþe!
> Se what Salamon seiþ in Sapience bokes:
> That þei þat ȝiuen ȝiftes þe victorie wynneþ,
> And muche worshipe haueþ þer-wiþ as Holy Writ telleþ,
> *Honorem adquiret qui dat munera.*' (B III 331–6)

Conscience points out that the quotation (from the apocryphal Book of Wisdom, attributed to Solomon) is unfinished. Mede, he says, is like the lady who quoted '*omnia probate*', 'test all things', but forgot the continuation, '*quod bonum est tenete*', 'hold that which is good', which she would have found if she had turned the leaf (V 337–43). Conscience says that 'a konnynge clerk', an intelligent cleric (347) should have pointed out her partial, misleading, quotation by turning the page and seeing the rest of the text. Conscience completes her Latin text and explains it in English: 'þe soule þat þe sonde takeþ bi so moche is bounde' (353): the Bible actually teaches that bribery is wrong.

Janet Coleman quotes a late-fourteenth-century sermon in which the preacher answers a parishioner's query about lay reading of the Bible, saying that the laity are not forbidden from reading Scripture, 'but itt is forbede anny lewde [uneducated] man to mysuse holywritte'. Coleman observes:

[15] Coleman, *The Bible in English Literature*, p. 194.

[16] Willliam Langland, *Piers Plowman: An Edition of the A, B, C, and Z Versions*, ed. A. V. C. Schmidt, 2 vols (1995), I 178. All Langland references are to this edition.

[17] Coleman, *The Bible in English Literature*, p. 181.

> This preacher seems to be saying that it is inappropriate for an unlearned man to misuse the Bible, but he who is able to read and go further in his education should do so, for it pleases Christ . . . It is not enough to read Scripture; one must understand its meaning . . . [i.e.] the traditional interpretations of the text.[18]

The clerical fear of vernacular translations of Scripture centred on the laity's lack of formal training in those traditional interpretations: *ennaratio*, the authorized interpretation of the Word. These interpretations of the Bible by the Church often maintained that a passage's true meaning was an allegorical message or an endorsement of some later Church doctrine or practice, rather than the literal sense of the words.[19] The pages of Latin Bibles often surround each passage of text massively with interpretations of this type: the 'glossing' (explanation). The many medieval texts that had traditionally provided the laity with biblical material, together with legendary, apocryphal and doctrinal additions, presented the Church's interpretation of the Christian message. In contrast, the plain, close, translation that Wycliffites attempted to produce obviously posed the danger – for conservatives – of freeing the text from such ecclesiastical control over its interpretation.

Surely the position of the most accomplished partial quoter in the Middle Ages must go to Chaucer's Wife of Bath. She has indeed a cleric to hand, namely her fifth husband Jankyn, the ex-cleric, who would have had a sound scholastic training, but Jankyn himself indulges in misapplication of Scripture for misogynistic reasons and Alisoun is simply copying his methods to prove her case for multiple marriages. The difference, however, between Lady Mede and Dame Alisoun is that the latter's misquotations and partial quotations are not picked up by a narrator or Conscience figure and the onus is on the reader to make of her biblical quotations what they will. Could this show that Chaucer has a more mature and trusting attitude to his readers, or does it reflect his greater interest in the *way* the Wife argues than the orthodoxy of her comments?

> 'I nyl envye no virginitee.
> Lat hem be breed of pured whete-seed,
> And lat us wyves hoten barly-breed;
> And yet with barly-breed, mark telle kan,
> Oure Lord Jhesu refresshed many a man.
> In swich estaat as God hath cleped us I wol persevere;
> I am nat precius.' (III 142–8)

The Wife of Bath confuses Mark and John in the passage about wheat and barley bread and totally misunderstands the traditional interpretation of this passage about the hierarchy of spiritual states (wheat representing chastity and barley incontinence) by confusing the literal and the anagogical (the 'spiritual') meanings: barley represents an inferior spiritual state in which we should not be content, but the Wife claims with mock modesty that she is happy as she is. She uses the same argument when partially quoting from 2 Timothy 2: 20–1:

[18] Coleman, *The Bible in English Literature*, pp. 204–5.
[19] On such interpretations, Wycliffite objections to it and discussion of Chaucer's engagement, see Edden, 'The Bible', pp. 332–51.

'For wel ye knowe, a lord in his houshold,
He hath nat every vessel al of golde;
Somme been of tree, and doon hir lord servyse.' (99–101)

She claims, again with apparent modesty, that she will be happy to remain a 'wooden vessel' in her Lord's house and not aspire to be golden; but the biblical text continues by comparing the gold and the wooden to honourable and dishonourable states, and encourages mankind to 'purge himself from these, [and] he shall be a vessel unto honour, sanctified and meet for the master's use.' (2 Timothy 2: 21). From the beginning of the *Prologue* the Wife has indulged in selective quotations, invariably choosing the part of texts about marriage which refers to the husband's responsibilities, while remaining silent on the mutual and reciprocal duties of the wife:

'I have the power durynge al my lyf
Upon his propre body, and nought he
Right thus the Apostel tolde it unto me,
And bad oure housbondes for to love us weel.
Al this sentence me liketh every deel'.
Up stirte the Pardoner, and that anon;
'Now dame, quod he, 'by God and by Seint John!
Ye been a noble prechour in this cas.' (160–7)

There is no Conscience figure here who pops up in alarm as in *Piers Plowman*: only praise for her rhetorical technique from the Pardoner, another expert in twisting his sources to prove his point. There is also a hint of ridicule when he possibly touches on the Wife's incorrect reference to St Mark by his oath 'by Seint John!' She seems a perfect example of the dangers of applying the Bible without expert theological help. But why does Chaucer allow her to go unchecked and does he not fear what can be called the new reading public of the fourteenth century, namely those who cannot read the Vulgate and have not been guided in their interpretations? Chaucer's motives are ambiguous, as he obviously wants the Wife to appear, not as the vindictive La Vieille in *Le Roman de la Rose*, but an attractive and well-armed adversary of the male, clerical interpretation of the Bible and Church fathers. I believe that the answer lies in the fact that he is more interested in her rhetorical techniques, namely her deliberate textual harassment, than her unorthodoxy.

There is, however, one controlling voice on the manuscript page. The majority of the earliest manuscripts have glosses, and there is no other section of the *Tales* more glossed than the *Wife of Bath's Prologue.* The glosses appear in the earliest manuscripts, Hengwrt and Ellesmere, written in the same hand and as large and prominent a hand as the text itself.[20] They are in Latin and visually appear to balance the vernacular text both physically and morally. They may be there

[20] See my detailed comments on the manuscript glosses in 'The Significance of Marginal Glosses in the Earliest Manuscripts of *The Canterbury Tales*', *Chaucer and the Scriptural Tradition*, ed. D. L. Jeffrey (Ottawa, 1984), pp. 75–88, and 'The Significance of the Early Chaucer Manuscript Glosses (with special reference to *The Wife of Bath's Prologue*', *The Chaucer Review* 10 (1975), 350–60; also Daniel S. Silvia, Jr, 'Glosses to *The Canterbury Tales* from St. Jerome's *Epistola Adversus Jovinianum*', *Studies in Philology* 62 (1965), 28–39.

to give weight and authority to the text, as most major Latin works of this time were glossed. Perhaps too that the glossator was afraid that the reader might not catch the pilgrim's distortion of the biblical text. There is a chance, I have argued elsewhere, that the author of many of these glosses was Chaucer himself, but if it were not he, then it was a contemporary 'editor' of the text keen to point out the original source.[21] A further, significant conclusion one can draw from the glosses concerns how Chaucer and thereby his characters have come by the text. Was it from the Vulgate or some intermediate source? Most of the biblical quotations do not quote the Vulgate directly, but are taken from paraphrases in Jerome's *Against Jovinian.* This is the text from which Jean de Meun found material for his character La Vieille and therefore a principal source of Chaucer's Wife. So what the wife is citing is Jerome's version of the text in *Against Jovinian*, in which Jerome builds a case against Jovinian's liberal views on the equal status of virginity and marriage. Jerome sees virginity, the state in which Christ remained, as symbolizing a spiritual perfection to which all mankind, married or not, should aspire. The Wife's examples and quotations, therefore, follow Jerome's and for this reason she includes texts which do not help her argument, including that of the Woman of Samaria (14–22).[22]

We must remember that we are dealing with a fictional character whom Chaucer could have endowed with any amount of learning, but it would appear a subtle authorial decision to make much of her learning come from her husband's book, the 'Book of Wikked Wives' (III 685).[23] Irrespective of her moral status, he makes the Wife one of the most successful rhetoricians, turning the anti-feminist and anti-matrimonial sentiments and exempla from his sources to her advantage. At the same time Chaucer is able to convey how such a lay person would acquire detailed knowledge of Latin sources, thereby demonstrating the 'trickle down' effect which must have been prevalent amongst the laity in the fourteenth and fifteenth centuries (conservatives were becoming increasingly alarmed by the end of the century both by a taste for discussing Scripture and doctrine by laypeople and, specifically, among women as well as men). Chaucer then uses a broad spectrum of applications of the Bible, apparently being less interested in teaching the Bible to his audience, as occurs in *Cursor Mundi* or *Piers Plowman*, than in investigating how specific characters and social classes in contemporary society might interpret the Bible and use it in their attempt to tell the best tale. At one extreme is the Parson quoting the Bible carefully and explaining it well, and at the other a character like the Miller who is verging on the pagan: 'I crouche thee from elves and fro wightes!', his 'night spel' (I 3478–9). At best he knows the popular renditions of the biblical narratives, for example the folklore element about Mrs Noah added to the Noah story. This knowledge of the biblical and legendary is that which is found in the cycle plays, popular art and literature, such as the *Cursor Mundi.* Between the two extremes are all those characters, keen to win Harry

21 See Caie, 'Significance of Marginal Glosses', pp. 76–7.

22 The glosses at lines 11, 13, 23, 28, 46, 50, 52, 54, 55, 57, 73 etc. are all attributed to Jerome's work.

23 Jankyn calls it 'Valerie and Theophraste', referring to Walter Map's *Epistola Valerii ad Rufinum de non ducenda uxore* (The letter of Valerius to Rufinus advising him not to marry), and the *Liber aureolus de nuptiis* (Golden Book on Marriage) by Theophrastus, a work preserved only in Jerome, *Adversus Jovinianum*.

Bailly's prize, who deliberately twist their biblical knowledge for their own ends. We have the Man of Law who seems to think that Daniel was not alone in the lions' den and that the others were eaten by the lion. Perhaps we are meant to view the rest of this character's statements as suspect if he is capable of such an error (see Helen Phillips's discussion of this passage, p. 70). Chaucer, then, skilfully conveys just the right amount of biblical knowledge and understanding to reflect a fictional character's educational and moral status. From such textual and intertextual material, we can glean much knowledge of the 'trickle down effect' of and grasp of theological texts amongst the late-fourteenth-century laity.

3

Chaucer and Lollardy

FRANCES M. MCCORMACK

THE EXTENT, nature and significance of Chaucer's connection to the Lollard movement have long been the subject of speculation and debate. Even before John Foxe, in his sixteenth-century *Actes and Monumentes*, referred to Chaucer as 'a right Wicklevian, or else there was never any',[1] Chaucer was already seen as providing a record of the dissenting voices of late-fourteenth-century England. In fact, in 1464 a copy of the *Canterbury Tales* belonging to one John Baron of Amersham was produced as evidence for the prosecution in a case of heresy.[2] Although, as Derek Pearsall asserts, the legend of the Protestant Chaucer faded in the seventeenth century 'when it was no longer historically relevant',[3] the interest in Chaucer's employment of Lollard ideas and motifs continues.

Why Chaucer's engagement with this movement continues to fascinate is clear. The theologian, John Wyclif, along with his followers,[4] provided a new challenge to the authority of the Church. This challenge was more potentially calamitous than the petty squabbles among the religious orders or the criticisms of the clergy that had stimulated ecclesiastical debate throughout the Middle Ages.[5] The Lollards challenged the foundation of the power of the medieval Church, demanding that it return itself to the state in which it was born of Christ in the Gospels. The subsequent questioning of papal authority, the challenge to ecclesiastical hierarchy and the condemnation of religious orders as superfluous to the operation of the Church were fuel enough, but the denial of the doctrine of transubstantiation was a step too far.[6]

1 John Foxe, *The Actes and Monumentes of John Foxe*, 8 vols., ed. Stephen R. Cattley (1843–9: New York, 1965). Foxe's mistaken attribution of *The Plowman's Tale* to Chaucer seems to fuel his idea that Chaucer was a heretic.

2 Anne Hudson, *Lollards and their Books* (London, 1985), pp. 125–40. Such a censorious attitude to the *Canterbury Tales* was probably inspired by suspicion aroused by the use of the vernacular – in particular for theological matter – at the time.

3 Derek Pearsall, *The Canterbury Tales* (London, 1985), pp. 305–6.

4 The use of the terminology of 'Lollard' and 'Wycliffite' is fraught with difficulties. Since Lollardy was a decentralized movement, existing and developing in a largely oral culture, it is unlikely that all adherents in all parts of the country shared the same beliefs. The distinction between Wycliffism and Lollardy is rarely made in scholarly works, and the terms tend to be used synonymously. For opposition to this approach, see Andrew Cole, 'Intermezzo: Wycliffism is not "Lollardy"', in his *Literature and Heresy in the Age of Chaucer* (Cambridge, 2008), pp. 72–3.

5 For the definitive account of Wyclif and Lollardy, see Anne Hudson, *The Premature Reformation: Wycliffite Texts and Lollard History* (Oxford, 1988).

6 This is the doctrine that during the consecration of the bread and wine their *substantia* (essence) becomes the *substantia* of the body and blood of Christ, while the accidents (the outward physical forms) remain bread and wine.

It seemed as though, by denying the miraculous power of the clergy, Wyclif and the Lollards were trying to usurp clerical authority and to return it to the lay person.[7] The call for vernacularity was therefore the ultimate threat, and the Wycliffite project of translating the Bible into English – so that every layman could engage with the one resource upon which his or her faith ought to be grounded – would arguably be the final straw. By promoting and facilitating access to Scripture, the Lollards were, in fact, empowering the laity to stand against ecclesiastical corruption and clerical misconduct. The Church reacted vehemently, with the contemporary chronicler Henry Knighton suggesting that in having facilitated access to Scripture, Wyclif had 'spread the Evangelists' Pearls to be trampled by swine'.[8]

This movement is likely to have been one with which Chaucer was quite familiar. His own former patron, John of Gaunt, had supported Wyclif in his quarrels with the Church (at least until Wyclif dared to deny the doctrine of transubstantiation).[9] Furthermore, Chaucer moved in circles of acquaintance with the so-called Lollard Knights[10] – a sub-coterie of the court of Richard II who had been associated with Lollardy by the contemporary chroniclers Thomas Walsingham and Henry Knighton. These men were influential in the movement at the levels of patronage and protection, and had been connected with Chaucer throughout his employment in the court and beyond.[11]

Chaucer is not to be expected to make substantial and explicit references to Lollardy, though. As a poet he is often seen to be apolitical, refusing to provide his readers with significant insight into the major conflicts, challenges and crises of his day. Helen Phillips sees this as symptomatic of his age, in which political commentary 'is often subsumed into religious or moral discourse'.[12] When Chaucer does present his readers with something that touches more explicitly upon contemporary socio-political concerns, though, it is a cause for great interest. When, for instance, the Parson of the *Canterbury Tales* is called a Lollard by the Shipman (for having censured Harry Bailly for swearing),[13] a number of particularly exciting lines of reading are presented. One may, like J. S. P. Tatlock, interpret this 'insult' as a throwaway remark,[14] or one may see it as an invitation to examine the Parson on suspicion of heresy.[15] If one takes the latter approach, then the results are very interesting indeed, especially in the light of the Parson's portrait, which

7 See William Kamowski, 'Chaucer and Wyclif: God's Miracles against the Clergy's Magic', *The Chaucer Review* 37 (2002), 3–25.

8 'et sic euangelica margarita spargitur et a porcis conculcatur', *Knighton's Chronicle, 1337–1396*, ed. and trans. G. H. Martin (Oxford, 1995), pp. 244–5.

9 Joseph H. Dahmus, 'John Wyclif and the English Government', *Speculum* 35 (1960), 51–8.

10 See Kenneth Bruce McFarlane, *Lancastrian Kings and Lollard Knights* (Oxford, 1972).

11 For a brief account of these relationships, see Frances McCormack, *Chaucer and the Culture of Dissent: The Lollard Context and Subtext of the Parson's Tale* (Dublin, 2007), pp. 22–38. For more detail, see Martin Crow and Clair C. Olson (eds), *Chaucer's Life Records* (Oxford, 1966).

12 Helen Phillips, 'Register, Politics and the *Legend of Good Women*', *The Chaucer Review* 37 (2002), 101–28, p. 101.

13 The practice of swearing was one to which the Lollards were opposed – both in the context of blasphemous swearing, and the swearing of legal oaths. Douglas J. Wurtele sees the Parson's objection to swearing as entirely orthodox: 'The Anti-Lollardy of Chaucer's Parson', *Medievalia* 11 (1989 for 1985), 151–68.

14 'Chaucer and Wyclif', *Modern Philology* 14 (Sept. 1916), 257–68, p. 267 n. 2.

15 See McCormack, *Chaucer and the Culture of Dissent*; Katherine C. Little, 'Chaucer's Parson and the Specter of Wycliffism', *Studies in the Age of Chaucer* 23 (2003), 3–25.

appears to depict him as a Lollard Poor Priest.[16]

Following this 'suggested mode' of reading, the *Parson's Tale* has not provoked unanimity from scholars, and even those who see suggestions of Lollardy in it do not generally perceive Chaucer to be taking a pro- or anti-Lollard stance, but rather to be exploiting the discourse and ideology of the movement for aesthetic, didactic or literary reasons.[17] Others, however, insist upon the *Parson's Tale*'s orthodoxy. Katherine C. Little, for instance, asserts that in the *Parson's Prologue* the teller takes pains to defend the orthodoxy of his meditation on penance – even going so far as to put it under correction of clerks who may find therein doctrine that displeases them.[18] Karen Winstead, however, asserts that the entire *Parson's Tale* seems designed to refute the accusations of Lollardy against it, and perceives in the *Tale* 'a richer, more liberal definition of orthodoxy'.[19] The extent to which a 'liberal orthodoxy' could coexist with a Church that was becoming increasingly threatened from within by a heterodox movement, however, remains to be seen.

Elsewhere I demonstrate that there is much more 'Lollardy' surrounding the Parson than has previously been detected.[20] Apart from the portrait that links the Parson with the Lollard Poor Priests, and apart from the accusations of Lollardy made against the Parson, the *Tale* itself is brimming with what Anne Hudson terms 'Lollard Sect Vocabulary'[21] – a distinctive use by the group of rhetoric and vocabulary in which the Lollards would set their depiction of themselves and their opponents (the orthodox Church), and in which they would ground their doctrine. Furthermore, there are instances in which Chaucer appears to have used the Wycliffite Bible to assist or influence him in his scriptural translations in the *Tale*.[22] Add to this points of doctrine on which Chaucer's Parson and the Lollards are clearly in accordance, and the results are certainly compelling.

The conclusions to be drawn from such data are not necessarily self-evident. Chaucer's employment of Wycliffite thought and discourse do not necessarily mean that he was a card-carrying Lollard.[23] Yet, while Lillian M. Bisson describes

[16] The Lollard Poor Priest was a peripatetic preacher who, having embraced apostolic poverty, travelled the countryside expounding Lollard doctrine and preaching Scripture to the laity. For an analysis of the Parson's portrait as a depiction of a Lollard Poor Priest, see Doris V. Ives, 'A Man of Religion', *Modern Language Review* 27 (1932), 144–8.

[17] For such a reading, see McCormack, *Chaucer and the Culture of Dissent*. Alan J. Fletcher, too, suggests that Chaucer employs Lollardy for various reasons in his writings, but that his primary loyalties are to the momentum of writing itself, rather than to orthodoxy or heresy ('Chaucer the Heretic', *Studies in the Age of Chaucer* 25 (2003), 53–121, p. 114).

[18] 'Chaucer's Parson and the Specter of Wycliffism', p. 244.

[19] 'Chaucer's Parson and the Contours of Orthodoxy', *The Chaucer Review* 43 (2009), 239–59, p. 241.

[20] See *Chaucer and the Culture of Dissent* (*passim*).

[21] 'A Lollard Sect Vocabulary?', in M. Benskin and M. L. Samuels (eds), *So Meny People, Longages and Tonges: Philological Essays in Scots and Medieval English Presented to Angus McIntosh*, Middle English Dialect Project (Edinburgh, 1981), 15–30. See Helen Barr, *Signes and Sothe: Language in the Piers Plowman Tradition* (Cambridge, 1994); Peggy Knapp, *Time-Bound Words: Semantic and Social Economies from Chaucer's England to Shakespeare's* (Basingstoke, 2000).

[22] Craig T. Fehrman compares Chaucer's scriptural quotations in the *Parson's Tale* to the Wycliffite Bible and the Vulgate, and draws the similar conclusion that Chaucer was influenced by the Wycliffite translation of the Bible: 'Did Chaucer read the Wycliffite Bible?', *The Chaucer Review* 42 (2007), 111–38. Andrew Cole, too, notes significant similarities between the General Prologue to the Wycliffite Bible and the Prologue to *A Treatise on the Astrolabe*: 'Chaucer's English Lesson', *Speculum* 77 (2002), 1128–67.

[23] Knapp writes that 'These echoes from Wycliffite discourse do not prove the *Canterbury Tales* a Lollard piece, but they do demonstrate its moral and doctrinal appeal to both mainstream and Wycliffite

the extent of Chaucer's connection to the movement as 'tantalizingly elusive',[24] the assigning of a Wycliffite image and voice to his idealized Parson (whose meditation on penance arguably inspires Chaucer to retract his sinful works) does seem to suggest a Chaucer not entirely opposed to the movement.

At other points in his writing, though, Chaucer treats the issue of Lollardy with much less solemnity. Both the Summoner and the Pardoner have been shown to appropriate Lollard discourse for the purposes of humour.[25] Paul Strohm, for example, analyses what he sees to be a Lollard joke in the *Pardoner's Prologue:*

> Thise cookes, how they stampe, and streyne, and grynde,
> And turnen substaunce into accident
> To fulfile al thy likerous talent![26]

Although Strohm demonstrates that this passage has a twelfth-century analogue, he sees it as being set into a Lollard frame of reference by its relation to the Lollard debate on transubstantiation – a debate in which the terms 'substance' and 'accident' first came to be used in English.[27]

Strohm insists on a certain ambiguity in the Pardoner's joke: rather than questioning whether substance and accident can in fact be separated (the essential point on which the Lollards and the Church disagreed), the Pardoner's reference insists on the alteration of one into another: 'turnen substaunce into accident'. The cooks, he asserts, 'could either be orthodox (in their belief that substance can be transformed, leaving only an accidental remainder behind), or heretical (in their obtuse overreliance upon the persistence of accidents in the form of brute matter)'.[28] Strohm concludes that even if one takes this joke to be a parody of Lollard doctrine, the very nature of the joke itself permits Lollardy to act within the tale as a dissenting voice – a voice which he refers to as a 'symptom of repressed unease',[29] providing not only a level of interpretative indeterminacy to the text, but by raising the latent to the level of the manifest in its hermeneutic importance.[30]

It is Chaucer's use of the doctrine of Lollardy in adding shading to the character of the Wife of Bath, though, that is perhaps most surprising. Alcuin Blamires demonstrates that the Wife of Bath's use of Scripture calls up another key point of

elements in fourteenth-century thinking': Peggy Knapp, *Chaucer and the Social Contest* (New York and London, 1990), p. 93.

24 *Chaucer and the Late Medieval World* (Basingstoke, 1999), p. 59.

25 For analyses of the Wycliffite resonances of the *Summoner's Prologue and Tale*, see Fiona Somerset, 'Here, There and Everywhere? Wycliffite Conceptions of the Eucharist and Chaucer's "Other Lollard Joke"', in Fiona Somerset, Jill Havens and Derrick Pitard (eds), *Lollards and their Influence in Late Medieval England* (Woodbridge, 2003), pp. 127–38; Alan J. Fletcher, 'The Summoner and the Abominable Body of the Antichrist', *Studies in the Age of Chaucer* 18 (1996), 91–117.

26 Chaucer, *Canterbury Tales*, VI. 538–40.

27 'Accidents' refers to the outward qualities of the Eucharistic bread which could be perceived by the senses – its whiteness, flouriness, and so on; 'substance', on the other hand, refers to the essential 'breadness' of the bread. The Catholic Church insisted that at consecration the substance of bread and wine was changed into the body and blood of Christ, while the accidents of the bread and wine remained. The Lollards, on the other hand, denied this as a philosophical impossibility and a blasphemy.

28 Paul Strohm, 'Chaucer's Lollard Joke: History and the Textual Unconscious', *Studies in the Age of Chaucer* 17 (1995), 23–42, p. 27.

29 Ibid., p. 41.

30 This interpretation is reinforced by Peggy Knapp, who sees authorized and Wycliffite meanings contending in the text: *Chaucer and the Social Contest*, p. 84.

Lollard doctrine.[31] The Lollard call to strip the Church of those things that were not 'grounded' in Scripture came to be one of the defining features of the movement (with 'groundid' becoming one of the key words in Wycliffite discourse). The literal level of Scripture, they asserted, was to be confirmed in importance as the primary level of interpretation, and they affirmed the plain truth of Scripture unadorned. What emerged, then, was an unusual dichotomy in the Lollards' perception of glossing – the practice of adding commentary to the text. While the Lollards themselves insisted that glossing was not necessary in order to facilitate the layperson's engagement with Scripture, they supplied their own glosses to explain points of ambiguity or to serve as moral commentary.[32]

It is in the context of this aspect of Lollard belief that the *Wife of Bath's Prologue* squarely places itself. The Wife of Bath is clearly seen (by herself and others) to have appropriated some of the duties of preacher. The Pardoner, for instance, praises her abilities, and calls her a 'noble prechour';[33] the Friar refers to her as dabbling in 'scole-matere',[34] and she receives what is essentially a licence from the same character to continue preaching.[35] Apart from the fact that Lollardy raised questions about who could preach and where, a number of female Lollards were noted not only for their skill in preaching, but also for their ability to reproduce scriptural text verbatim.[36] Furthermore, as Blamires demonstrates, the most common retort to such women was to tell them to go back to spinning – an occupation with which the Wife of Bath is associated in her portrait.[37] Her preaching style, therefore, has been of great interest to the critics. Lawrence Besserman asserts that through the Wife of Bath (and her appropriation and manipulation of Scripture for her own end), Chaucer raises questions of validity of biblical exegesis, and of the dangers of unmediated access to the Bible.[38] Knapp, too, lists the Wife of Bath's various references to glossing, and sees her as politicizing the issues of textual production and interpretation.[39] Carol Martin, however, goes one step further, and describes the Wife of Bath as a caricature of English fears of Lollardy.[40]

Elsewhere, Chaucer employs the trope of heresy (and accusations thereof) to draw attention to issues of textual production, authority and problems of discourse.

31 'The Wife of Bath and Lollardy', *Medium Ævum* 58 (1989), 224–42. As I have already mentioned, the Lollards saw Scripture as the basis for Christian belief and, therefore, undertook a translation project of the Bible into the vernacular in order to facilitate access for the layperson.

32 See Henry Hargreaves, 'The Marginal Glosses to the Wycliffite New Testament', *Studia Neophilologica* 33 (1961), 285–300; Henry Hargreaves, 'Popularising Bible Scholarship: The Role of the Wycliffite Glossed Gospels', in W. Lourdaux and D. Verhelst (eds), *The Bible and Medieval Culture* (Louvain, 1979), 171–89; Anne Hudson, *The Premature Reformation*, pp. 248–59.

33 *CT* III 165.

34 *CT* III 1271–2.

35 *CT* III 853–5.

36 See Shannon McSheffrey, *Gender and Heresy: Women and Men in Lollard Communities, 1420–1530* (Philadelphia, 1995); C. Cross, 'Great Reasons in Scripture: Women Lollards, 1386–1530', in David Baker (ed.), *Medieval Women*, Studies in Church History, subsidia 1 (Oxford, 1978), 359–80.

37 Blamires cites Hoccleve and Kempe as primary sources: 'The Wife of Bath and Lollardy', p. 230.

38 Lawrence Besserman, 'Biblical "Glossing" and Poetic Meaning', in his *Chaucer's Biblical Poetics* (Oklahoma, 1998), pp. 138–59.

39 Knapp, *Chaucer and the Social Contest*, p. 115.

40 Carol A. N. Martin, 'Alys as Allegory: The Ambivalent Heretic', *Comitatus: A Journal of Medieval and Renaissance Studies* 21 (1990), 52–71, p. 59. Blamires, 'The Wife of Bath and Lollardy', suggests that the 'wexe and multiplye' text employed by the Wife of Bath in her prologue (III 28–9) was a touchstone for heresy (p. 233).

Helen Phillips notes that in the G Prologue to the *Legend of Good Women*, the accusation of heresy against the narrator is laden with Wycliffite jargon, which she describes as politically provocative.[41] Chaucer's employment of Lollard register, according to such a reading, would have significant 'authorial' implications (if we may, anachronistically, use the idea of 'authorship' to signify the medieval maker's role), equating interpretative control with political authority.[42] Some of the terms employed in this Prologue certainly do resonate with the Wycliffite questions of translation and interpretation of the Bible, the clearest example being Chaucer's reference to the 'naked text' in the sense of an account free from interpretation (a phrase which is used both by and against the Lollards in contemporary discourse).[43] Phillips reads this lexical manoeuvre as typically Chaucerian: at once provocative and demure, suggesting dissent but refusing to endorse or condemn it. Language, here, becomes the site of political conflict, in which 'discordant registers and polysemy produce momentary fragmentation and multiplication of senses in certain words, within a passage's surface meaning and the dominant discourse'.[44] Helen Barr, taking a broadly similar view, argues further that the accusations of heresy against the narrator of the G Prologue (and the language in which they are couched) to be 'directly relevant to Chaucer's treatment of the politics of representation', perceiving this passage to be concerned with translation as the locus for meanings that conflict with those endorsed by dominant culture.[45]

These are merely a few of the elements of Lollard discourse and thought incorporated into Chaucer's writings. It seems as though the movement influenced the type of questions he asked through his characters, and created, in the very latency of Chaucer's references, a kind of unverbalized debate about the validity and relevance of these questions to late-fourteenth-century English society. Michaela Paasche Grudin observes that in such manipulation of discourse, 'Chaucer repeatedly explores the ways in which speech refuses to be prescribed and contained'.[46] The *Canterbury Tales* is, after all, about discourse, about the interplay of various social groups, about competition to be heard and validated, and by employing the dissenting voice of Lollardy in this text Chaucer permits engagement with the very idea of authorized and unauthorized discourse. Elsewhere in his writings, where similar concerns persist, Chaucer makes ample use of contemporary, highly charged rhetoric in order to convey the urgency with which the political dimension of language intrudes into all forms of discourse. Regardless of the reasons for, or, for that matter, the extent of Chaucer's interest in the movement of Lollardy, the incorporation of its doctrine and ideology into his writings permits him to reflect the disorder of his age, and to implicate the reader into the movement in the roles of inquisitor and collaborator all at once.

41 'Register, Politics and the Legend of Good Women', p. 104.

42 Ibid., p. 112.

43 Ibid., p. 109. This phrase again relates to the Wycliffite concept of the sufficiency of the literal scriptural text without gloss. See further Sheila Delany, *The Naked Text: Chaucer's Legend of Good Women* (Berkeley, 1994), which additionally relates the image to Chaucer's handling of the subjects of women and anti-feminist traditions.

44 Phillips, 'Register, Politics and the *Legend of Good Women*', p. 102.

45 Helen Barr, *Socioliterary Practice in Medieval England* (Oxford, 2001), p. 100.

46 *Chaucer and the Politics of Discourse* (Columbia, 1996), p. 20.

4

'Toward the fen': Church and Churl in Chaucer's Fabliaux

STEPHEN KNIGHT

Church versus Churls

The ironic dynamic of Chaucer's fabliaux is usually taken as anti-romance. The Miller is held to 'quite' the *Knight's Tale* (I 3127) by parodying his noble love-conflict, with a shared line to pin the joke (2779 and 3204), then the Reeve reverses the reversal on behalf of his trade; anti-romance can also be heard in the parodic voices and behaviour of Damian in the *Merchant's Tale* and Chauntecleer in the *Nun's Priest's Tale*. Yet the French fabliaux realized not ironic romance but louche battles between clerics and churls, and there is an insistent religious referentiality in the Oxbridge diptych, as indeed in the tales of Shipman, Friar, Summoner and Pardoner. It is a Monk whom the Miller displaces as a tale-teller, not a Knight (3118–19); Chaucer, like his French predecessors, may well be directing his humorous venom at the presumptions of the lower orders in both Church and town, with anti-romance vulgarity as only part of their general comic unacceptability.

Church on Churls

Inappropriate code-switching from Church to world is a recurrent motif in the presentation of the religious orders in the *General Prologue*. Loaded words like 'curteisie' and 'countrefete' (I 132, 139) position the Prioress as quasi-secular, and the language grows more cutting: neither 'conscience' nor 'Amor' have in her purview anything to do with God (142, 162). The rhymes in the Monk's description imply the disabling secularity of the man the Host will later address as 'My lord the Monk' (VII 1924): 'maistrie/venerie' (165–6), 'able/stable' (167–8), 'cloystre/oystre' (181–2), 'enoynt/poynt' (199–200), and 'estaat/prelaat'(203–4 – it is his horse's 'estaat', but the word implies the lordly property that so much interests the rider). Both language and rhyme proclaim the Friar a traditional sexual and financial predator with 'daliaunce and fair language' (211) and spectacular sequences, almost *laisses*, of romance rhymes at 218–24 and 244–51.[1] Brilliant as they are,

[1] On anticlerical satirical traditions see Jill Mann, *Chaucer and Estates Tradition: The Literature of Social Classes and the General Prologue to the Canterbury Tales* (Cambridge, 1973), 17–54, 128–37.

these satiric verbal manoeuvrings are not pursued in these characters' tales, which pose more elusive questions about the use and misuse of church discourse in saint's legend, tragedy and devil-fable.

Less marked in the *General Prologue* is the light sketching of a possible Christian characterization for the worst of Chaucer's churls, but this use of a disturbing discourse – post-colonialists call it abrogation, asserting difference through discursive challenge – is more productive in the churls' tales, where the words of God can be appropriated by characters for their own misuse, and their own consequent judgement.

Just as the secular satirizing of Prioress, Monk and Friar grows in sequence more florid, less restrained, so the clerical hints about the churls seem to become bolder as the Prologue continues. With the Miller the only verbal cue is that he is (*not* is like) a 'goliardeys' (560), a clever comic spoiled clerk. The image seems underlined by visual signs familiar from manuscript illustrations of negative humans in his porcine beard and black open nostrils implying a pig-snout: this is the bestial face found throughout the Queen Mary Psalter upon the executioners of saints, and on the face of Christ's torturers in medieval and even renaissance Christian art. His mouth, being like a 'greet forneys' (559), may have parallel hell-mouth associations, as Gray notes.[2]

Visualizations of this suggestive and negative Christian kind more assertively frame the Reeve, with at first his fringe 'dokked lyk a preest biforn' (590) and finally his gown: 'Tukked he was as is a freer about' (621). Medieval people, including travelling friars, tucked up long gowns for physical activity. A renegade priest turned outlaw known as Friar Tuck is recorded from 1417, and the sword just mentioned might support that connection,[3] but more certain is Chaucer's later development of these Christian leitmotifs from the *General Prologue*. The notion that this Reeve is in some way an angry false priest is expressed by the Host in response to his Headlink rant (3903), and his tale will make the churls more Church-linked than the scholars – a reflex of the *Miller's Tale*, where the clerks are goliardeys-like, semi-learned lechers.

Chaucer moved on in the *General Prologue* with Christian discourse, written and visual: the Summoner's 'fyr-reed cherubynnes face' (624) is red with disfigurations, implicitly syphilitic, not like a real cherub 'inflamed with divine love'.[4] This physical anti-image and his garbled Latin act as prologue to the Pardoner's double redirection of both Christian discourse and conventional masculinity. In all these churls it seems Chaucer has redeployed with characteristic inventive point the parodic grotesqueries so richly found in the margins of medieval psalters (but not in equally artistic but more devout context of church windows[5]). These figures often consciously parody – and so by their crudeness implicitly elevate – the sacred texts around which they cavort.

2 See the *Riverside Chaucer* note on this line by Douglas Gray; for traditions about churls as descended from Cain or Ham cursed by God, as a race apart and animal-like, see Paul Freedman, *Images of the Medieval Peasant* (Stanford, 1999).

3 Stephen Knight, *Robin Hood: A Complete Study of the English Outlaw* (Oxford, 1994), 263.

4 Gray, *Riverside Chaucer* note.

5 At Chartres, the most westerly but one of the north-aisle windows (as secular a situation as you find in a cathedral) does, very unusually, have marginal figures, but they are merely drinkers: people holding up cups, apparently in honour of the peasant-born bishop of Chartres St Lubin, the topic of the window; see Jean-Paul Deremble and Colette Manhès, *Les vitraux légendaires de Chartres* (Paris, 1988), p. 188.

Church–Churls Dialectic

Displacing the Monk's dull learning (as we later discover it will be), the Miller acts like any goliard. His reverse-clerical claim is made clear as he speaks 'in Pilates voys' (3124) and swears violently 'By armes, and by blood and bones' (3125) – as if Christ's 'armes' were weapons. The Host invokes the Miller's implicit infernal positioning with 'Tel on a devel way' (3134); he follows the instruction by degrading the important Christian genre 'a legend and a lyf' and then joking grossly over a sexualized 'Goddes foyson' (3165), with the especially tasteless and direly blasphemous *doubles entendres* in 'Of Goddes pryvetee, nor of his wyf' (3164) – it sounds like His wife, let alone what might be His 'pryvetee'.

As the Miller starts his tale we are already far, as the narrator notes, from 'storial thyng that toucheth gentillesse, / And eek moralitee and hoolynesse' (3179–80): the tale is not only, he warns us, romantic irony. But it is also that. As Jack Bennett has detailed,[6] setting the story in an Oxford tradesman's house is a deliberately multiple move, clerical and churlish. But the text adopts another discourse as the clever clerk Nicholas is committed to 'deerne love' (3200). Never alleged of the Clerk of the *General Prologue*, a description whose irony is limited to over-learning,[7] the idea of the sexy scholar thrived in medieval English songs and ballads, a prolepsis of the later gypsy rovers and rock stars as itinerant unattached males. When Nicholas sings '*Angelus ad virginem*' (3216),[8] he deploys a heavenly parallel of this long-favoured genre. And, closer to the Friar than the Clerk, Nicholas has on hand his own earthy version of the Prioress, an *amie* with hardly a hint of *daunger*. The big joke, apologized for already and omitted from many manuscripts, is of course the brutally elegant *rime riche* on 'queynte' and 'queynte' (3275–6), which Chaucer lets resonate twice more (3605, 3754).[9]

Both churls and clerks employ Christian adjurations in ironic-romance moments and other narrative engagements. The lost discourse of oath-naming, like the language of flowers, is often revealing. Alisoun commits herself to Nicholas 'by Saint Thomas of Kent' (3291) and John the Carpenter invokes St Thomas twice in his anxiety over Nicholas (3425, 3461), so referring to the enigmatically double secular-cum-religious Canterbury pilgrimage frame, but he also swears by the local St Frideswide (3449).[10] The genial and hard-working blacksmith Gervase swears by St Neot (3771) – Chaucer is much more likely to have known the East Anglian, now

6 J. A. W. Bennett, *Chaucer at Oxford and Cambridge* (Oxford, 1974).

7 The extent of the irony can be debated. When in the 1960s the new Macquarie University took as its motto 'and gladly teche', through its medievalist first Vice-Chancellor Alec Mitchell, staff at the senior Sydney University, led by the not unfabliauesque Leslie Rogers, liked to argue this was a jibe at boring pedagogues implying 'and obsessively teach'.

8 Bennett notes this was a student hymn, p. 31, and Gray comments on its erotic implications in his *Riverside Chaucer* note on this line.

9 After the emphatic phrase about clerkly abstract thinking, 'ful subtile and ful queynte', the rhyme with 'queynte' in a bodily sense in 3276 constitutes a drastic bathos both in the action and the word; Larry D. Benson shows how much the contemporary semantic range of 'queynte' itself, in the sense 'genitals', combines courtly and euphemistic registers, 'The Queynte Puns of Chaucer's Critics', *Studies in the Age of Chaucer* 1 (1984), 23–47.

10 As Bennett notes, p. 24, she was patronne of Oxford cathedral, i.e. Christ Church chapel. She remained alive in popular memory: among the many convivial societies of post-National Service Oxford in the 1950s was one called 'The Frideswide Boys': though based at Christ Church it was the social opposite of the ultra-posh Bullingdon Club. Her legend centres on her flight from a would-be seducer.

Cambridgeshire, location for this saint than the south-western one, and St Gervase has one of his few church dedications in Norwich Cathedral (on other *Canterbury Tales* oaths and their spiritual or moral resonances see also Sherry Reames's chapter, pp. 83–5). Closer to the discursive hybridity of the text is Gervase's coupling, among the phonic richness of his words to Absolon, the clerical 'benedicitee' with the demotic Romance of 'upon the viritoot' (3767–71) – his linguistic richness may relate to his surprisingly fancy name, popular mostly in France.

If Chaucer's language embeds a Church–churl dialectic in this comic romance, the plot also has its twists and turns. Fabliau traditionally has a 'target-figure', a male of low class or clerical caste who will be humiliated in sexual and/or excremental terms. While medieval aristocrats, like some modern scholars, seem to have enjoyed these sado-masochistic cartoons,[11] Chaucer refashions them interrogatively, as he does with all his genres: the target of the action is not the target of the text. True, John the carpenter is fooled by Nicholas and Alisoun, breaks his arm and is publicly humiliated, even isolated, but he is also the only person who shows faith in God or love of his partner. Yet while modern sentiment is inevitably invoked by what Chaucer shows as his touching fidelities, his garbled night-spell (including prosodically garbled) indicates he is at most a foot-soldier in medieval moral humanism:

> 'Jesus Crest and Seine Benedight,
> Blesse this hous from every wikked wight,
> For nyghtes verye, the white *pater-noster*!
> Where wentestow, Seine Peters sister?' (3483–6)[12]

If John is a willing target, one of Chaucer's wry approaches to Langland's patient poverty, Absolon is his opposite. Named for 'King David's comely son' as Kolve puts it,[13] from name to visual image he is the prat headed for a fall. Chaucer is both irritated and inspired by the wide range and narrow capacity of Church personnel, and pins the image to his page. When Alisoun, like her Bath namesake, goes to church for her version of 'cristes owen werkes for to wirche' (3308) – religion is never far from this story, and Bennett sees a joke on Alisoun and (Kyrie) Eleison[14] – Absolon is presented, in full mock-lover fig and in noisy action that is caricaturized by the comic rhyme 'rubible/quynyble' (3331–2). For him the censer is not the distributor of the odour of holiness: rather, he is, with a neat shift of verbal meaning, in sensual mode, 'Sensing the wives' (3341). The jokes flow – his voice is ladylike, 'gentil and smal' (a hint of the Prioress perhaps) – but Alisoun being a town girl, he offers her money as well as hot wafers: the garden of the rose and true love-service is far away in both class and tone. Expert in Church entertainments as he is, Absolon also plays Herod – and will try to replicate the part in furious reality later.

[11] The social context of the fabliaux has been a matter of some debate: Nykrog's argument for an aristocratic audience has been questioned by some scholars, see John Hines, *The Fabliau in English* (London, 1993), pp. 23–5. While the stories may have to some extent socially extended their popularity – as Chaucer's own usage implies – court culture seems their original and basic context.

[12] On contemporary encouragement, by conservative clerics, of simple devotional pieties, see Alan J. Fletcher, *Preaching, Politics and Poetry in Late-Medieval England* (Dublin, 1998), pp. 233–48.

[13] V. A. Kolve, *Chaucer and the Imagery of Narrative* (London, 1984), p. 164.

[14] Bennett, *Chaucer at Oxford and Cambridge*, pp. 42–3.

Church matters are marshalled towards the plot. Nicholas – named for the patron saint of scholars – energizes and debases his clerkly learning by imitating a mantic trance to produce the Noah plot, both suitable to the old husband with a wayward wife and, from his own theatrical persuasiveness, also a projection of Nicholas's own pre-diluvian world of sensual delight. But to the carpenter delight is now: his desire for stasis is so great he can be persuaded by any quasi-learned claims as Nicholas's ridiculous plot is elaborated with Chaucerian fun and clerical rococo.

The Church embraces the next move, in a less observed way. The carpenter goes to Oseney, that plain place out of complex, complex-ridden, Oxford, long known to locals just as Frogs' Island, to buy the abbey's timber (churls and Church had interests in common). Absolon goes to just the same place, but only 'to disporte and pleye' (3660), presumably at the well-known pleasure-ground Oseney Meadow:[15] he meets 'a cloisterer' (3661) there, but on this secular terrain the only guidance he draws from the holy man is about his planned romance.

If Absolon's fully sexualized scheme, like his sensual censing, starts in a church, it is first realized through another lecherous clerical appropriation, his version of a snatch from the Song of Songs – a droll reversal of St Bernard's own reclamation of the poem for mysticism. Absolon proclaims himself, unfortunately, and all too accurately, no better at this business than a bleating lamb seeking an udder, a cooing dove or an anorexic girl – he lacks the adult martial masculinity of the acceptable lover (3704–7). Alisoun remains with her own version of 'trewe love' (3715), but Absolon begs for a kiss, in deeply inappropriate terms, 'For Jhesus love', though he adds the would-be romantic clarification 'and for the love of me' (3717). Grotesque clericism points towards grotesque action, and Absolon receives the anal kiss that makes him the target of the successful clerical lover, but is also basically associated with the devil. At once, holding to his default clerical position, however degraded, he identifies the moment as diabolic: 'My Soule betake I unto Sathanas' (3750), and his play-acting as Herod tells him what to do.

Gervase, source of multiple discourse, ploughshares and for those who seek them weapons, identifies Absolon's infernal mood and mode: 'Ey, Cristes foo! what wol ye do therwith?' (3782), but Absolon hurries off on his stage-villain business, to deliver, as he thinks to Alisoun, a terrible unwomaning blow – a murderous mechanical rape long before science-fiction pornography. In wheedling her into his power he combines the courtly and the clerical, saying both God knows I am Absolon, and, so God save me, this is a ring my mother gave me (3792–7): this is the only love-discourse by Absolon that is not itself stylistically false. Behaving as a devil, he can quote true: it is his behaviour that speaks openly, as with his masculine identity in serious doubt he grotesquely, and like a grotesque, makes Nicholas the target of his hellish sodomization.

All three men are targets, just as all three in the *Franklin's Tale* could be the most generous, all three eagles in the *Parliament of Fowls* could each be the most suitable bird-husband. Alisoun's absence from targetude is less likely than Dorigen's non-evaluation to arise from a Chaucerian glimpse of structural misogyny: like the formel, Alisoun is basically an animal, like 'any wezele' (3234), wether,

[15] Ibid., p. 47.

kid or calf, to be tended, petted, and made productive. She has almost no religious discourse – she may even have got her oath by St Thomas from her husband. But with the three men churlishness and churchiness interrelate with, and even dominate, the terrain of ironic romance. John's verbal attachment to the faith is shown as deep if not wise: as they ascend the ladders Nicholas merely says in a moment of initial grandness 'Now, *Pater-noster*, clom!' (3638), but John when he arrives both 'seyde his devocioun' (presumably his rosary) and then 'biddeth his preyere' (no doubt the Lord's Prayer) (3641–2), proper actions at a time of danger. Absolon's perversion of his church learning is clumsier than Nicholas's scholarly fantasies, and less amusing, as is appropriate to his much lower role in the Church hierarchy as parish clerk, para-religious entertainer and sometime barber-surgeon.

Certainly a response to the *Knight's Tale*, with a range of possible political meaning in that connection, and as dazzling in its low-life complexity as Caravaggio or Robert Altman, the *Miller's Tale* is also a rich hybrid, attaching to the simple target-practice approach of the fabliau the mood of the clerical-lover songs, and then condensing the two modes to target in a way much fuller, more complex, more entertaining and ultimately more damming, the self-corruptions of members of the medieval Christian Church.

Church 1, Churls 0

As generations of students, and indeed lecturers, have discovered, at first with pleasure and then puzzlement, *The Reeve's Tale* is both like and unlike its predecessor. Sex, jokes, clerks and churls, certainly, but also difference. Even Bennett, who sees much linkage between the cities and their citizens in the tales, finally feels Chaucer separates them with 'uncanny instinct'.[16]

The Reeve responds to the Miller's story in the grip of the sin of wrath and its corollary, vengeance. But he claims wisdom with age and in distinctly sermonic mode, as Kolve puts it, borrows 'the voice of Christian authority':[17]

> 'Foure gleedes han we, which I shal devyse –
> Avauntyng, liyng, anger, coveitise;
> Thise foure sparkles longen unto eelde.' (3883–5)

He moves on to the equally preacheresque image of death drawing the tap of life, but as with the Miller, the Host senses the diabolic: 'The devel made a reve for to preche' (3903). The Reeve, again like the Miller, accepts the infernal terms and asserts in the spirit of negative reciprocity that 'leveful is with force force of-showve' (3912) and bluntly, and unchristianly, prays 'to God his nekke mote to-breke' (3918). If his tone and the Host's reference remind us of Absolon's devilish would-be vengeance, the purposeful note may recall that he is armed with a sword, and even the connections with the image of Friar Tuck (in his earliest appearances in Robin Hood tradition) as a fighting friar, whose habit is tucked up – to free his limbs for highly unclerical action.

[16] Ibid., p. 116.
[17] Kolve, *Imagery*, p. 229.

His miller carries even more weapons. Ironic romance is linguistically remembered as he has both a French 'panade' and a Yorkshire 'thwitel' (3929, 3933),[18] but then the tale separates from its predecessor by locating the major clerical connection in the churlish family, not in its clerical incursors. Crudely blunt as Symkyn is – and sharing the *General Prologue* Miller's bestiality in his ape-like shaven skull (apes were very common in the marginal illuminations, always up to sinful mischief) – his wife is a parson's daughter, brought up in a nunnery and by implication a nun's daughter: Chaucer cannot resist one of his glibly comic rhymes on 'nortelrie' and 'nonnerie' (3967–8). This goes beyond the Prioress's sentimentalities but the clerical daughter shares the Prioress's ladylike attitudes in a mundane way, being 'as digne as water in a dich' (3964) – a simile clearer in mocking implication than in specific meaning: Arthur Cawley offered 'stinking with pride', but it is a paraphrase, not a gloss.[19]

The daughter of this Church–churl pairing shares her father's physique but the pretensions of her maternal, clerical line are also marked on her, and she is to be the parson grandfather's heir: in one of those orally memorable underlinings Chaucer liked to use as foci, often in indirect speech, he stresses both the comic and the grossly improper elements of the parson's attitude:

> For holy chirches good moot been despended
> On holy chirches blood, that is descended
> Therfore he wolde his hooly blood honoure
> Though that he hooly chirche sholde devoure. (3983–6)

As the four phrases, *holy* plus noun, interweave in changing contexts, the first line is on its own innocent enough; the second grossly improper; the third deeply blasphemous; and the fourth line, which Kolve called 'mysterious and terrible',[20] predicts institutional collapse through sin. A half-line rhyming is set-up on 'good' and 'blood', but 'good' is lost in the last line, absorbed in the dark concept that he 'sholde', that is 'must', 'devoure' the Church, an image of Langlandian ferocity and bestiality, however euphemized by the general ironic tone.

After the Church–churl hybrids come the actual clerics, but for the men of Solar Hall their only guiding light is to avoid being cheated in commerce. For over thirty lines the scholars, their location and their superior are introduced without reference to the Church at all – they are, like Nicholas and Absolon, '[t]estif' and 'lusty' (4004), though neither has any of the sexual or ironic-romance meaning that saturated the carpenter's visitors, and they also lack the religious discourse the Oxonians manipulated variously. With pointed attention to their materiality, both John and Alan only use Christian discourse, dilute at that, to affirm their fidelity to their grain, respectively 'By God' (4036) and 'y-faith' (4044).

However, the miller – like the Reeve – is as much at home with clerical discourse as he is with a convent-bred wife. Speaking more like Nicholas or the Friar, he twits the scholars about 'al the sleighte in their philosphye' (4050) and asserts his own superior knowing with 'The gretteste clerkes ben noght wisest

[18] Bennett notes that, despite its northern character, 'thwitel' was actually used in a Trumpington legal record of the period, p. 5.

[19] *The Canterbury Tales*, ed. A. C. Cawley, rev. edn (London, 1978), p. 107, note.

[20] Kolve, *Imagery*, p. 254.

men' (4054). In this context the 'queynte crekes' (4051) he says that scholars make seem to have no sexual double meaning, but the story has some of this activity in mind for them. Symbolically at first, as the miller releases their horse: Chaucer has added the horse to the story as the symbol of male sexuality, as Kolve has outlined.[21] Showing he knows his role, the horse gallops 'Toward the fen, ther wilde mares renne' (4065): the internal part-rhyme, very unusual in the caesura position in Chaucer, emphasizes how the Reeve's narrative releases a frank and natural sexuality that his description and Headlink in different ways denied. The Miller's Headlink avowed such sexuality but his story acculturated it heavily, with clericism more than ironic romance.

But the natural sexuality of the roving clerk is yet the story's secret. The clerks lament their horse's absence, at first without anything approaching a Christian thought or exclamation – 'Harrow' and 'Weylaway' (4072) are decidedly secular. But in desperation they turn, in phrase at least, towards God: the sudden emphasis on Christian exclamation is as striking, and banal, as Christian discourse was elaborate and degradingly extended in the case of Nicholas and Absolon:

> 'Allas,' quod John, 'Aleyn, for Cristes peyne,
> Lay down thy swerd, and I wil myn alswa.
> I is ful wight, God waat, as is a raa;
> By Goddes herte, he sal nat scape us bathe!
> Why ne had thow pit the capul in the lathe!
> Ilhayl! by God, Alayn, thou is a fonne.' (4084–9)

Chaucer's language will always guide the reader, though sometimes into enigma. Horseless and swordless, they speak of God – but also they speak, in the first extended and emphasized way, in their northern accent. Like those other few from beyond the Fosse Way, the Shipman and the Wife of Bath, their knowledge of religion seems neither morally behavioural nor yet, as it is with the other clerical villains, a form of cultural manipulation. They may mention God in their distress, but they like their horse, run 'Toward the fen, bothe Aleyn and eek John' (4091): this time half-rhyme and assonance tie the suggestivity of 'fen' into the poetry.

This interface of gestural religion – the clerks – and devalued Christian discourse – the miller – is replayed as they beg for lodging just 'for the love of God' (4118) and he launches into another piece of mock scholasticism about learning 'art' and 'argumentes' (4123–4). All the scholars can offer is a rhyme-stressed reference to 'St Cutberd' (4127): Gray notes that this was a possible version of Cuthbert's name in the period, but in the mouth of an alleged scholar the usage is as clumsy and foolish as Tolkien originally suggested.[22] In the same unclerical way, to acculturate the scholars' situation John can only offer banal proverbs, emphasized by northernisms which, like their secular oaths, seem to suggest they are beyond the pale of civilized Christian society, even further than the Miller.

But they also have energy, and so does the story. Its brutal physicality is realized with drumming, action-oriented, monosyllabic Anglo-Saxon rhyming. Only a few rhymes remind us of the abandoned possibility of ironic romance, initially

21 Ibid., pp. 237–48.

22 See Gray's *Riverside Chaucer* note, Bennett, *Chaucer at Oxford and Cambridge*, p. 101.

'place' and 'solace' (4145–6), then in 'wyf' and 'jolyf' (4153–4), the English–French pairing reminds us of the wife's only part-genteel origin, and there is a droll excogitation of snoring in '*par compaignye*' and 'melodye' (4167–8). When the clerks debate their situation, their language is only elevated as far as the revenges of law, in 'amendement' and 'esement' (4185–6) and 'vileynye' (4191). Alan simply couples in silence with the daughter; the wife's 'nortelrie' is again briefly recalled as, sensing her notional error she mutters 'benedicite!' (4220). The story strides on in language and rhyme as vigorous and unelaborate as the actions of the scholars and their willing partners.

But Chaucer never maintains one tone for long. Dawn comes, and Alan and Malyne's exchange is as banal an *alba* as could be desired in ironic romance: he swears 'I is thyn owen clerk' (4239–Muscatine noted that the northern dialect adds to the irony[23]) and she tells her 'deere lemman' (4240) where to find their stolen meal, in the form of a great loaf – not unlike the *General Prologue* Miller's own jovial shield, with also a hint of Absolon's urban style of comestible wooing.

Like romance, religious language also returns in attenuated and ironic form to the action: Alan names God twice, in deeply irreligious mode, farewelling Malyne, and then in finding the cradle, and worse yet invokes 'Christes saule' and 'Seint Jame' (4263–4), as he mistakenly reports his sexual triumph. The miller responds, with his usual access to religious language, 'by Goddes dignitee' (4270), coupled, as at the start, with his family's elevated aspirations in 'disparage' and 'lynage' (4271–2).

But reality is in physical discourse: in their own true mode, they fight bestially like 'two pigges in a poke'; the wife may awake in nunnery language:

> 'Help! hooly croys of Bromeholm,' she seyde,
> '*In manus tuas!* Lord, to thee I calle' (4286–7)

but like a real miller's wife she grabs a staff and hits out. As fabliaux usually do, Chaucer's better than most, the final action offers both physical brutality and moral judgement: she mistakes the miller's pale shaven skull – a sort of secular tonsure – for a clerk's white cap and lays him out. His illusory clericality is his downfall; the scholars' lack of true churchly appearance is their salvation – physically at least. The miller finally exclaims, outside religion, as John did before, 'Harrow' (4307).

Clerks, horse, meal and loaf ride back to college, all none the worse for their adventures and the sentient ones at least having some gratifications to recall: not even Chaucer makes the grain more than an item of exchange value, though it has gained a romance context. The women are as usual silent, though they have not been inactive in their own exchanges. The miller, bereft of stolen corn, aspiration, wifely and daughterly honour, religious discourse and even consciousness, is left, a true target figure, with none of John the carpenter's remembered humble dignity.

Only in the final tag, where the Reeve speaks with the quasi-priestly and audience-enhancing ending common to popular poetry, is there any recognition of another world of Christian value:

[23] Charles Muscatine, *Chaucer and the French Tradition* (Berkeley, 1957), p. 203.

And God, that sitteth heigh in magestee,
Save al this compaignye, grete and smale. (4322–3)

Everyone has been small in this story, however great their muscles and fantasies. Parson, wife, miller – though, as with Alisoun, not the young woman – have degraded Church discourse; those who should uphold it have been as distant in faith as in accent from central standards. Where Nicholas and Absolon at least understood something of Church discourse, at varied levels, these clerks have only galloped towards the fen, with all its infernal implications.

The two fabliaux have occasionally been discussed in Christian terms. They were briefly touched by Robertsonianism in what Gray calls 'absurdly earnest symbolic and moralising criticism',[24] and this approach had no interest in the kind of verbal and behavioural detail this paper has explored. Kolve also found the detailed Christian references only 'local and limited',[25] compared with the patterns he revealingly explored of moral themes the fabliaux share with religious art. But grand and grandly referential though some of Chaucer's schemes may be, he is also one of the great masters of detailed work, where considerable complexity lies in the local effects of reference, language and rhyme and a rich sociocultural dialectics is found at the level of the signifier.

In this he is all the more like the master illuminators of his time and in these two tales Chaucer has perceived and memorably projected the possibilities of the marginal parodies of the great psalters; his language and prosody are at a level at least equal to the technical mastery and imaginative vigour of the great school of English illuminators of his time – and like them, by devious implication, he reminds us ultimately of the Christian majesty that remains within these comic, chaotic, but never unartful margins.

Church with Churls

It is hardly surprising that, after this exertion Chaucer, like John the carpenter and Symkyn the miller, is silent. The stump of the *Cook's Tale* indicates that even he could not follow that. Though it is tempting to think that if indeed he did have *Gamelyn* among his papers for reworking, as the *cd* line of manuscripts has been taken to suggest,[26] it was because the non-romance hero who goes from outcast

[24] Gray, *Riverside Chaucer* note to I 3718–22.

[25] Kolve, *Imagery*, p. 159.

[26] *Gamelyn* is located as a second Cook's Tale in the early Corpus manuscript (Oxford, Corpus Christi College 198) and its many dependants. On this basis Urry argued vigorously for the validity of Gamelyn as a second Cook's tale: see William C. Alderson, 'John Urry', *Editing Chaucer: The Great Tradition*, ed. Paul G. Ruggiers (Norman, OK, 1984), pp. 93–115, at pp. 105–6, and Skeat, seeming to agree in principle, printed it as an 'Appendix' to *The Canterbury Tales*; J. M. Manly and Edith Rickert refer to but are highly sceptical of the notion that *Gamelyn* was 'found in Chaucer's literary chest', *The Text of the Canterbury Tales* (Chicago, 1940), II. 172. The suggestion that it might have been meant for the Yeoman, which Urry mentions and was, before his work on *The Text*, supported by Manly (see his edition of *The Canterbury Tales by Geoffrey Chaucer* (New York, 1928), p. 503), is merely based on the poem's fairly brief forest-outlaw episode, and seems to ignore the way Chaucer tends to make his tales operate at a revealing distance from the apparent interests of the pilgrim narrators as described in the *General Prologue*. Modern editors, with their Hengwrt–Ellesmere focus, tend to dismiss the 'Gamelyn as potential source theory' – Ralph Hanna calls its presence in some manuscripts a 'bizarre supply', *Riverside Chaucer* textual motes, p. 1125, and Gray says it 'does not seem at all appropriate

quasi-churl to reinstated lord lays about him with his staff and knocks cold a whole congeries of corrupt clerics.

As the *General Prologue* proceeds to its end, Chaucer conflates negative portraiture of the churl with negative portraiture of ecclesiastical officers and abuses, in the Pardoner and Summoner. The comparisons with the animal world and the disgusting physical details frequently used of churls in literature and art, these two pilgrims' ignorance, and the slang permeating both portraits shows Chaucer drawing on anti-churl traditions to bolster anti-clerical traditions. Yet later, neither tells a fabliau and both are associated, in their tales and the prologues and link passages surrounding them not simply with satirical exposure of abuses in the Church but also with powerful moral teaching. The central moral target in the presentation of both is that of representatives of the Church who play fast and loose with people's spiritual well-being and salvation, for the sake of greed. The scatalogical and eschatological unite, with hell never far away in the sections of the sequence of tales associated with these two men, and with both their tales focused on the threshold between life, death and the afterlife. While the scatological language may, in the Pardoner's case, reflect homophobia, it also recalls Wyclif's repeated attacks on the worldliness of friars, particularly, as filth and on ecclesiastical venality as spiritual sodomy.[27]

It is also noticeable that the literally knockabout comedy of the first two fabliaux and the interweaving energies of their discursive hybridity are not repeated; the religious comedy of the following tales is less grotesquely creative, more generically investigative. In terms of character and meaning the churls become normative, like the old woman in the *Friar's Tale*, the rich peasant of the *Summoner's Tale*, the off-stage widow of the *Nun's Priest's Tale*; the clerics become more learned, whether morally like the Clerk, dully like the Monk, fancifully like the Nun's Priest, or seriously Christian like the Second Nun.

And Church and churl are not always at odds. Two men of peasant stock who are not realized physically in the *General Prologue*, but whose lives are enshrined there in positive Christian discourse, are the brothers Plowman and Parson.[28] They are as structurally and morally central to the *General Prologue* as they are to Christian community and continuity. With silence and sermon they assert that both churls and churchmen can stay far from the fen; they act as an anti-narrative frame to the whole work. Only later ages gave the Plowman a tale – for Chaucer his life is his story; and the Parson eschews literature for true preaching, in the sermon that in the true voice of the Church, in both moral and structural terms ends the churlish secular discourse of the *Canterbury Tales*.

for the Cook' (*Riverside Chaucer*, p. 853). But many early scribes were convinced that it fitted in, and its Church–churl links may be a reason for that.

[27] For example, 'Fifty Heresies and Errors of the Friars', *Select English Works of John Wycliffe*, ed. Thomas Arnold, 3 vols (Oxford, 1871), vol. III, 399–40. I am grateful to Helen Phillips for information about Wyclif's writings about commerce and the friars, and on growing peasant disillusion about worldly clerics.

[28] See Helen Barr, 'Wycliffite Representations of the Third Estate', *Lollards and their Influence in Late-Medieval England*, ed. Fiona Somerset, Jill C. Haven and Derrick G. Pitard (Woodbridge, 2003), pp. 197–216, at pp. 200–4.

5

'A maner Latyn corrupt': Chaucer and the Absent Religions

ANTHONY BALE

THIS ESSAY examines two egregious moments in the *Canterbury Tales* at which Christian identity comes under scrutiny and attack from non-Christians: firstly, in the Jewish–Christian encounter of the *Prioress's Tale*, and secondly in the triptych of faith communities, of Christian Rome, Saracen Syria and pagan Northumbria, envisaged in the *Man of Law's Tale*. My title, referring to 'absent religion', does not simply suggest that Jews, Muslims and pagans were absent from Chaucer's London.[1] Rather, 'absent religion' refers to the practice of non-Christian religion as represented in these stories, as ciphers of Christianity, within Chaucerian poetics, the larger project of the *Canterbury Tales* and Chaucerian criticism more generally. I am not primarily concerned with asking 'What did the terms "Jew" and "Muslim" mean to medieval people?' Instead, I am asking 'What do the terms "Jew" and "Muslim" mean within the *Canterbury Tales*?'

There was not a recorded Muslim community in medieval London, and the city's Jews had been expelled, along with the rest of the Anglo-Jewish community, in 1290.[2] However, we have long known that Jews, as well as Orthodox Christians from Asia Minor, Armenia and Russia, visited late-medieval England, and stayed there.[3] Whilst largely Christian, late-medieval English cities

[1] It is well known that both Jews and Muslims visited and lived in later-medieval London; but I want to stress the methodological issue that Chaucer was intimately acquainted with, for example, women but this does not account for, or help us understand, the *Wife of Bath's Tale*.

[2] On the history of the English Jewish community, established in the late eleventh century and expelled in 1290, see Anthony Bale, *The Jew in the Medieval Book: English Anti-Semitisms 1350–1500* (Cambridge, 2006), pp. 1–23; V. D. Lipman, *The Jews of Medieval Norwich* (London, 1967); Robin R. Mundill, *England's Jewish Solution, 1262–1290: Experiment and Expulsion* (Cambridge, 1998); Cecil Roth, *A History of the Jews in England*, 3rd edn (Oxford, 1964), pp. 70–98; *The Jews in Medieval Britain*, ed. Patricia Skinner (Woodbridge, 2001). On Jews in England between 1290 and their formal readmission in the seventeenth century, see Eliane Glaser, *Judaism without Jews: Philosemitism and Christian Polemic in Early Modern England* (Basingstoke, 2007). On Muslims in medieval England see Sheila Delany, *The Naked Text: Chaucer's Legend of Good Women* (Berkeley and Los Angeles, 1994), pp. 164–86, and Dorothee Metlitzki, *The Matter of Araby* (New Haven, 1977).

[3] The *Domus Conversorum* (house of converts) in London housed the children and grandchildren of English Jewish converts and was renewed in the fourteenth century by converts from Brussels, Spain and Turkey; see *The Religious Houses of London and Middlesex*, ed. Caroline Barron and Matthew Davies (London, 2006), pp. 191–5; the deposed king Leo of Armenia visited France and England and acted as a mediator between the French and English kings in the 1380s (see Nigel Saul, *Richard II* (New Haven, 1997), p. 153). It is likely that Muslims visited too; David Wallace's brilliant work on medieval

like Bristol, London, Lynn and York were not exclusively 'English' in terms of inhabitants or in terms of culture. In London, one might have bought pilgrims' travel guides to the Levant, or joined a pilgrimage to Jerusalem, Rome, Walsingham or Wilsnack.[4] One could buy furs too, traded through Novgorod, close to the pagan animists of the Baltic. Luxurious fabrics and clothing – damasks and tabbies or an acton jerkin, their very names attesting to an intimate connection with the Middle East – came to London brokers via Genoa, Lucca and Venice.[5] Spices and sweets – cinnamon (from the Hebrew *kinnamon*), juleps (from the Persian *gul-ab*, rose-water), caraway, saffron and sesame (the Arabic *karawiya*, *zafaran* and *simsim*) – were brought to London from the East, changing both the tastes and language of the English. London was part of the spatial and symbolic infrastructure of an emerging pan-European economy, one of several lynchpins in the inter-city network trading between the Baltic, the Low Countries, France, the Mediterranean and beyond. In London, as in Augsburg, Baghdad, Genoa, Samarkand and Venice, the world was at its smallest, for the city had 'global reach': people and goods from all over the globe passed through such cities, and from these cities one could depart, perhaps with a guide-book and a tour-party, to the edges of the known world.[6] It should no longer surprise us that the borders of Chaucer's Christian England were porous, and that trade, war and diplomacy facilitated both commerce and intellectual traffic. That many of these 'other' people – that is, those who did not conform to an idea of normative, English Christian identity – would have been known to Chaucer is not surprising and speaks more to a modern idea that the Middle Ages were a period of homogeneous, stable identity, than to the actuality of the late-medieval European city. David Wallace has recently shown how travel and intercultural contact could define the late-medieval urban experience, not only in terms of interaction but also in more intimate terms of borrowing, translation and miscegenation.[7] In their cultural artefacts and their laws against aliens, medieval Londoners had an active sense of self-definition – of who was in and who was out – but, on an everyday level, the medieval London society known to Chaucer can be described as heterogeneous and international, if broadly, but not exclusively, Latin Christian.[8]

It is axiomatic that the pilgrims who set off from Southwark in the *Canterbury Tales* are imagined as a kind of Christian polity – in as much as they are together

Genoa in *Premodern Places: Calais to Surinam, Chaucer to Aphra Behn* (Oxford, 2004), pp. 181–202, shows how this medieval city, visited by Chaucer in 1373, fused trading connections and cultures from Russia, Tartary and the Black Sea to the Canaries, in part through slavery (which included Jewish, pagan and Islamic subjects).

4 Such English guides include those of William Wey (Santiago and Jerusalem, 1456–62) and Richard Guylforde (1508); see *The Itineraries of William Wey*, ed. G. Williams, Roxburghe Club (London, 1857); *The Pylgrymage of Sir Richard Guylforde*, ed. Henry Ellis (London, 1851).

5 'Tabby' comes from the Baghdad suburb *attabi* where such fabrics originated; damask from Damascus; acton, a quilted cotton jacket, from the Arabic *alqutun* for cotton.

6 See Fernand Braudel, *Capitalism and Material Life 1400–1800*, trans. Miriam Kochan (London, 1973), pp. 309–24, on the relationship between the growth of trade and the expansion of travel.

7 See Wallace, *Premodern Places*.

8 See David B. Leshock, 'Religious Geography: Designating Jews and Muslims as Foreigners in Medieval England', *Meeting the Foreign in the Middle Ages*, ed. Albrecht Classen (New York, 2002), pp. 202–25; Wallace, *Premodern Places*, pp. 116–17, usefully discusses anti-Flemish violence in Chaucer's London, in terms of the exclusion of others and the growing cult of the Eucharist.

engaged in a pilgrimage to the shrine of St Thomas Becket at Canterbury. Explicit heterodoxy is absent from the pilgrimage band – there is, after all, no *Lollard's Tale*, *Saracen's Tale* or *Jew's Tale* and we could not expect there to be – although many of the pilgrims demonstrate the fallibility of religious office (we need look no further than characters such as the Friar, Pardoner and Prioress for satirical portraits of compromised religious authority) and Wycliffite controversies might be discerned, often implicitly, in the pilgrimage. But the borders of Chaucer's imagination in the *Canterbury Tales* are as porous as those of medieval London: the pilgrims' texts range from different degrees of the domestic – the secular London of the *General Prologue* and *Cook's Tale*, Oxford (*Miller's Tale*), Cambridge (*Reeve's Tale*) and Yorkshire (*Summoner's Tale*) – to commerce in medieval France (*Shipman's Tale*), riot and dice in Flanders (*Pardoner's Tale*), and *marriage à la mode* in Italy (*Merchant's Tale*), to a kind of mythical semi-Christian landscape of a vanished past, like the Brittany of the *Franklin's Tale*, the Rome of the *Second Nun's Tale* and *Physician's Tale* and the 'fayerye' land of the *Wife of Bath's Tale*. There is pagan antiquity (*Knight's Tale*), and universal moral history which traverses time and geography (*Melibee* and the *Monk's Tale*). There are also vagrant landscapes of Mediterranean travel (the *Man of Law's Tale*, *Clerk's Tale*) and a version of thirteenth-century Lincoln transplanted to, or dislocated in, a Christian Asia (*Prioress's Tale*). Within the first seventy lines of the *General Prologue*, with its famous paean to the pilgrimage to Canterbury, we are transported, with the Knight, to international travel in Egypt (I 51), Prussia (53), Lithuania and Russia (54), Spain (56), Morocco (57), Turkey (58, 65); more specifically, this travel is not concerned with 'felawshipe' (32) but the defeat of 'hethenesse' (49), of slaying one's 'foo' (63). The explicit declaration of properly directed Christian travel, the route 'toward Caunterbury' (27), with which the *Canterbury Tales* opens, gives way to an international perspective and to an awareness of the limits of the English and Christian world. Just as the Canterbury pilgrims and their stories wander from the straight path, down the 'croked wey' (VI 761), so too Chaucer's poetry is more often concerned with what was *not* within everyday experience rather than reflecting or reporting what was 'normal' in medieval London.

'Free and open at eyther ende': Chaucer's Jews of 'Asye'

The 'Jewerye' (VII 489) of the *Prioress's Tale* is part of an imaginative cityscape which acts as a kind of set or backdrop to the Prioress's story of moral contrasts and violent conflict:

> Ther was in Asye, in a greet citee,
> Amonges Cristene folk a Jewerye,
> Sustened by a lord of that contree
> For foule usure and lucre of vileynye,
> Hateful to Crist and to his compagnye;
> And thurgh the strete men myghte ride or wende,
> For it was free and open at eyther ende. (VII 488–94)

This description rhetorically separates Jew from Christian in the Prioress's characteristic immoderate diction – 'Amonges Cristene folk a Jewerye', 'foule', 'lucre of vileynye', 'hateful to Crist' – whilst showing the several levels of interconnectedness between Jew and non-Jew:[9] 'Amonges Cristene folk', 'sustened by a lord of that contree', 'thurgh the strete men myghte ride or wende', 'free and open at eyther ende'. These opening lines establish the paradoxical proximity of Christian to Jew which, by the close of the tale, has been transformed by the Prioress into separated communities of Church Triumphant and fallen Jewry. Moreover, it is made clear in these lines that 'men' enter and pass through the Jewry, elaborated in the next stanza: 'A litel scole of Cristen folk ther stood / Doun at the ferther ende . . .' (495–6).

In seeking to understand this cityscape we need not look to medieval maps or the facts of Jewish life in medieval European cities; the Prioress's description of the city develops a theme introduced in the *Prioress's Prologue*, in which Jewish forms are overlaid with Christian interpretation. Or, to put it another way, the closeness of Christian to Jew is simultaneously declaimed and repudiated. The first three of the five stanzas of the *Prioress's Prologue* are a paraphrase of Psalm 8 (a scriptural authority both Jewish and Christian) and a typological interpretation of the burning bush which appeared to Moses (Exodus 3: 2): the remaining two stanzas of the prologue address the Virgin, in a humility topos which focuses on the Prioress's scarce ability to narrate, 'My konnyng is so wayk, O blisful Queene, / For to declare thy grete worthynesse' (481–2). The prologue thus neatly encapsulates a poetics of supercession which is elaborated and carried through in the tale: Christian worship is based on, departs from and makes a new sense of Jewish Scripture. The burning bush, 'o bussh unbrent, brennynge in Moyses sighte' (468), does not mean something 'Jewish', but is, according to the Prioress and the medieval theological interpretation, a figure of the Virgin, she who was, like the bush, ravished but not consumed by the deity.[10] Indeed, the Prioress's rendition of the miracle of the boy singer is introduced by a range of Marian liturgical allusions from the Mass of Holy Innocent's Day or Childermas (28 December), a feast based on murdered boys (Matthew 2: 16–18) and marked by ceremonies involving children and therefore particularly appropriate as an intertext for the

[9] It is important to note that 'Jewerye' does not, and could not, mean 'ghetto': a 'ghetto', in terms of a lockable or isolated Jewish area made compulsory by Christians, only came about in sixteenth-century Iberia and Italy. Some European Jewish communities had become enclosed – partly through Jews' desire to live in a religiously observant environment and partly through persecution by local non-Jews. In Nuremberg, after the massacres of Jews which accompanied the 1348 plague, Jews returned to an unfashionable part of the city, building a synagogue, ritual bath and hospital around an enclosed great court, whilst in 1351 Pedro I of Castile attempted to separate the Jews of Valladolid from Christians. By 1391 Barcelona's Jewish *call* had gates, which were attacked by rioting Castilians. In Augsburg the Jewish community was enclosed by 1434 with ropes, although this may well have been an *eruv* (a Jewish ritual limit for Sabbath observances) rather than a boundary imposed by non-Jews. It is conceivable that Chaucer might have seen such enclosed Jewries, but he would have been familiar with the term 'Jewry' from English street-names, particularly in London and Oxford, where central streets remained named 'Jewry' long after 1290 (in Canterbury, London, Southampton and Winchester one can still visit roads named 'Jewry Street'; the London churches of St Lawrence Jewry and St Olave Old Jewry recall, in Christian space, the displaced medieval Jewish quarters. On medieval Jewish quarters more generally see Alfred Haverkamp, 'The Jewish Quarters in German Towns during the Late Middle Ages', *In and Out of the Ghetto*, ed. R. P. Hsia and H. Lehman (London, 1995), pp. 237–53.

[10] See Sherman Hawkins, 'Chaucer's Prioress and the Sacrifice of Praise', *Journal of English and Germanic Philology* 63 (1964), 599–624; Sumner Ferris, 'The Mariology of the Prioress's Tale', *Benedictine Review* 32 (1981), 232–54. The Holy Innocents were understood by medieval Christians typologically, as forerunners of Christ and his martyrdom.

Prioress's story of boyhood threatened, preserved and sainted.[11]

So just as the city of the *Prioress's Tale* starts as an admixture of Christian and Jewish and stages the separation of these elements, so too does the Prioress's scriptural interpretation *surpass* and *supersede* Judaism: the slain boy's mother described as a 'newe Rachel' (627), and the allusion to the story of Abel, 'the blood out crieth on youre cursed dede' (578), curses the Jews by their own traditions and shows Jewish Scripture to be in the possession, or at the behest of, the Christians.[12] At the same time, the interconnectedness of Christian and Jew has become a violent kind of separation in which patterns of repeated interpretation and behaviour are suggested (a kind of liturgical 'layering' noted by Beverly Boyd).[13] Lee Patterson has discerned in the Prioress's prologue and tale 'a range of imitative practices, including (but not limited to) ventriloquism, impersonation, reproduction, duplication, parody, and mimicry', producing a 'tension' between 'an absolutist desire for purity' and an 'obstinate historicity';[14] similarly, Steven Kruger has noted how Christian and Jewish communities each act as both persecutor and victim, in a reactive relationship of similarity and repetition.[15] Thus the 'moral' judgement inflicted by the Christian provost on the Jews – 'Yvele shal have that yvele wol deserve' (632) – is a retribution comprised of 'Jewish' law (Exodus 21: 33–4) inflicted with an unswerving and merciless literalism: 'Therfore with wilde hors he dide hem drawe / And after that he heng hem by the lawe' (633–4).[16] In sum, the Judaism depicted in the *Prioress's Tale* is an intensely familiar and enabling presence: it is used by the Prioress to confirm her religious interpretations and, at the same time, facilitates the magnificent funeral, shared by the tale's Christians, with everybody (except the Jews) united about the little boy's corpse and his 'tombe of marbul stones' (680).

The practice of Judaism, as articulated by the Prioress, is restricted to usury, Satan's residence in the Jews' hearts, the hiring of the 'homycide', and the Jews' toilet. Any medieval Christian audience would have been familiar with similar discourses of Judaism, which could be seen in stained glass and mural art, heard in exemplary Latin sermon texts, read in vernacular poetry, and performed in drama. Stories of satanic Jews, excreting Jews, Jews murdering little boys: this was the stuff of much medieval religious experience.[17] This is an important point, as many critical approaches have made much of the Prioress's stance towards Judaism without considering the cultural prevalence of such images in European popular

[11] See *The Prioress's Tale: A Variorum Edition*, ed. Beverly Boyd (Norman, 1987), pp. 4–6.

[12] Indeed, the story of Rachel weeping for her children is taken from Jeremiah 31: 15 and reiterated in Matthew 2: 13–18 as a typological figure for the massacre of the Holy Innocents.

[13] See Boyd, *Prioress's Tale*, p. 17.

[14] Lee Patterson, 'The Living Witnesses of Our Redemption: Martyrdom and Imitation in Chaucer's *Prioress's Tale*', *Journal of Medieval and Early Modern Studies* 31 (2001), 507–60, pp. 507–8.

[15] Kruger, 'The Bodies of Jews', p. 307.

[16] On this retribution see Archer, 'Structure of Anti-Semitism', p. 50. Literalism was itself, in many Christian writings, an essentially Jewish facet, following St Paul's redefinition of circumcision 'in the spirit, not in the letter' (Romans 2: 29).

[17] See, for instance, Bale, *The Jew in the Medieval Book*; M. Bayless, 'The Story of the Fallen Jew and the Iconography of Jewish Unbelief', *Viator* 34 (2003), 142–56; Claudine Fabre-Vassas, *The Singular Beast: Jews, Christians and the Pig* (New York, 1997). Many religious stories featuring Jews can be found in *Index Exemplorum*, ed. F. C. Tubach (Helsinki, 1969), which gives a good idea of the widespread nature of such narratives.

religion.[18] The Jews of such depictions cannot automatically be read to narrate a vicious or perverted bloodlust on the part of its proponents, although such representations did, in Europe, license violence against actual Jewish communities; rather, such depictions rewrite Scripture around a clear sense of judgement and retribution, and explore the nature of sacrifice, blood and death.

So what does 'Asye' mean here? There is nothing specifically Asian about the landscape of the *Prioress's Tale*, and, other than the description of the Jewry, the Jews' 'wardrobe' (572) and the 'covent' at the 'pavement' (677) there is almost no description of the city.[19] The setting of 'Asye' merely establishes at the outset an imaginative distance between the Prioress and her story, framing the story as foreign to England. This distance disappears at the tale's close, in the important closing coda of the Prioress's final stanza:

O yonge Hugh of Lyncoln, slayn also
With cursed Jewes, as it is notable,
For it is but a litel while ago,
Preye eek for us, we synful folk unstable,
That of his mercy God so merciable
On us his grete mercy multiplie,
For reverence of his mooder Marie. Amen (684–71)

'Hugh of Lyncoln' is the child-saint, Hugh of Lincoln, said to have been murdered by the Jews of Lincoln in 1255. There was a shrine to Hugh in Lincoln Cathedral, erected shortly after the expulsion of the Jews from England in 1290, which survived until the seventeenth century. The Prioress's reference to Hugh of Lincoln diminishes the distance between the Canterbury pilgrims and the Prioress's 'Asian' story, and suggests a repeated pattern of interaction between Christians and Jews ('slayn *also* / With cursed Jewes', emphasis added). Moreover, the reference to 'Lyncoln', 'but a litel while ago', indicates the familiarity, the proximity, of the story to the Prioress; her repeated begging references in this final stanza to 'mercy' for 'us', 'we synful folk unstable', show how the Prioress's story is a fiction which, as elsewhere in the *Canterbury Tales*, looks abroad or outward in order to look inwards.

This brief reading of the *Prioress's Tale* has approached the story as a fiction, as a piece of poetry based around religious imagery and interpretation, as an allusive rhetorical artefact to be scrutinized. What I have tried to avoid is considering the intentions of Chaucer, an obstacle upon which a great deal of literary criticism has stumbled regarding the *Prioress's Tale*. Late-twentieth-century critical sensibilities, in noting the stereotypes of murderous Jews in the tale, tended to be concerned with the extent to which one can 'blame' Chaucer for the tale (he is,

[18] See Ruth Mellinkoff, *Outcasts: Signs of Otherness in the Northern European Culture of the Later Middle Ages*, 2 vols. (Berkeley and Los Angeles, 1994), on the prevalence of such images in the religious and artistic worlds of medieval Europe.

[19] For this reason, the cityscape no more resembles Lincoln than Asia. Boyd makes a circumspect suggestion that the cityscape is based on the Flemish city of Bruges, although this too is without firm foundation: Boyd, *Prioress's Tale*, p. 21. Sheila Delany, 'Chaucer's Prioress, the Jews, and the Muslims', *Chaucer and the Jews: Sources, Contexts, Meanings*, ed. Sheila Delany (New York, 2002), 43–57, argues that we should think of the tale's 'Asian' setting as including Spain, Bulgaria and Hungary, and points out that cities like Baghdad and Damascus were major 'Asian' centres of Jewry.

after all, the person who wrote the story, although the miracle narrative on which it is based emerged in northern Europe in the early thirteenth century) and how much he can be attributed with its 'anti-Semitism'.[20] Lawrence Besserman, in an essay on the critical approaches to the tale, follows Alan Gaylord in discerning 'hard' and 'soft' critical approaches:[21] 'hard' approaches say that Chaucer did not intend the tale to be read as a satire, because 'anti-Semitism' was such an ingrained part of medieval culture. 'Soft' readings argue that both the genre of the tale and the Prioress are satirized, as blinkered and bloody-minded. All such readings are beating around an erroneous bush of authorial intentionality; nowhere else in his oeuvre would we apply to Chaucer such uncomplicated standards of authorial mediation. (Would we, for example, conflate the Pardoner with Chaucer? Would we suggest that Chaucer necessarily approved of the morality of the *Reeve's Tale* merely because he wrote it?) It is clear throughout the *Canterbury Tales* that teller and tale are intimately linked in meaningful and often ironic relationships, and this is particularly true (and illuminating) of the Prioress and her tale.

In giving the story of the boy-singer to the silly, shallow and misguided character of Prioress Eglantyne Chaucer signals the comprised cultural authority of this kind of popular religion. Not only is the Prioress imperfect in her observance of religion but, as Graciela Daichman has shown, the Prioress is within an established *literary* genre of wayward nuns.[22] Moreover, her choice of tale, with its 'litel' hero and heightened pathos and judgement, reflects late-medieval sentimental and popular religion: similar stories to the *Prioress's Tale* were frequently read by women, children and families, and, as Andre Vauchez comments, ritual murder cults were precisely the kinds of unofficial religion that was very popular and that the Church tried to stamp out.[23] Both misplaced mercy and popular religion are features of the portrait of the Prioress given in the *General Prologue*: her charity and pity are extended to mice and dogs (I 144–9), she wears a fashionable ring labelled 'amor vincit omnia' (162) quoting Virgil rather than Scripture, and both her vain care for her appearance and her presence on the pilgrimage away from her priory are at odds with her religious vocation. As I have argued elsewhere, Chaucer's representation of Judaism, through the exclamatory, sensationalist mouth of the Prioress, is affective and ardent, which means that it is of limited use in reconstructing Jewish (or Christian) life in the Middle Ages but is very useful in considering the construction of an exclamatory, emotional poetic subjectivity.[24] To 'hate' Jews in the schematic and culturally endorsed manner of the Prioress is neither 'irrational' nor 'illogical', even as what is being said about the Jews is

[20] On versions of the tale see Bale, *Jew in the Medieval Book*, appendix 1.

[21] Besserman, 'Ideology, Anti-Semitism, and Chaucer's *Prioress's Tale*', *The Chaucer Review* 36 (2001), 48–72, p. 57; Alan Gaylord, 'The Unconquered Tale of the Prioress', *Papers of the Michigan Academy of Science, Arts, and Letters* 47 (1962), 613–36.

[22] Graciela Daichman, *Wayward Nuns in Medieval Literature* (Syracuse, 1986).

[23] On the audience of such tales, see Bale, *Jew in the Medieval Book*, pp. 112–27. On the reaction of the institutional Church to boy-saint and ritual-murder cults see A. Vauchez, *The Laity in the Middle Ages: Religious Beliefs and Devotional Practices*, ed. D. Bornstein, trans. M. Schneider (Notre Dame, 1993), pp. 141–52.

[24] Louise O. Fradenburg, 'Criticism, Anti-Semitism and the Prioress's Tale', *Exemplaria* 1 (1989), 69–116, suggests that it is in itself an anti-Semitic move, on the part of the critic, not to consider the 'real' ritual murders, of pogrom and holocaust, inflicted by Christian on Jew. However, such a reading, whilst ethically engaged, understands the tale as a piece of writing worthy of blame, rather than as a satire.

patently untrue;[25] the ardour, emotion and empathy which sustain the *Prioress's Tale* is aesthetic and has an expressive logic and conventional devotional *sense* to it. In this way, the *Prioress's Tale* fits perfectly with the other stories of fragment VII of the *Canterbury Tales*, especially the *Nun's Priest's Tale*, *Shipman's Tale* and *Sir Thopas*, which demonstrate the prevalence and limitations of received fictions and the difficulty of discerning 'fruyt' from 'chaf' (VII 3443).[26]

'Infortunat ascendent tortuous': the Man of Law's Vagrant Poetics

The similarities between the *Prioress's Tale* and *Man of Law's Tale* are slight, but the tales make a neat pair for modern criticism in that they both disesteem non-Christians, the former Jews and the latter Syrian Muslims. Moreover, both are affecting stories in a Christian key with an eye to popular pathos and both use commerce – 'usurye' in the *Prioress's Tale* and 'chapmen riche' (II 135) in the *Man of Law's Tale* – to stage the encounter between Christians and non-Christians. In slightly different ways, both tales are exemplary: the 'clergeon' of the *Prioress's Tale* and suffering Custance in the *Man of Law's Tale* offer examples, taken from established and generic Christian narratives, of clear morality, Church Triumphant and the power of faith.[27]

The manner in which the *Man of Law's Tale* depicts the non-Christian world can be divided into four sections; the first (II 134–322) shows the devoutly Christian Custance and the noble Syrian sultan, himself open to conversion to Christainity; the second (323–441) shows the evil sultana and her obstinate, poisonous brand of Islam; and the third shows a blurred and doubt-ridden semi-Christian world, of Custance consigned to Fortune and of the lapsed-Christian and pagan world of Northumbria, presided over by King Alla (442–952). The final section of the poem (953–1162), with the return of the Syrians, mixes the three faiths. Throughout, the tale throws the three religions – Christianity, Islam and paganism – into an ambivalent and contiguous relationship. The tale is similar to many other romances – *The King of Tars*, *Sir Beues of Hamtoun* and *Reinbroun* – as well as the ubiquitous *Mandeville's Travels* in that it combines a broad condemnation of the non-Christian world with a fascination with, and an embrace of, this world as martial, desirable, ordered and governed along the same lines as the Latin West.[28]

As in the *Prioress's Tale*, the way in which the Islamic Syrian merchants come

[25] These terms are taken from Gavin Langmuir, *Toward a Definition of Anti-Semitism* (Berkeley and Los Angeles, 1990), pp. 333–40.

[26] On the relation to the rest of fragment VII see Mary Hamel, 'And now for something completely different: the relationship between *The Prioress's Tale* and *The Rime of Sir Thopas*', *The Chaucer Review* 14 (1980), 251–9; Patterson, 'Living Witnesses of Our Redemption', pp. 512–14.

[27] For roughly contemporary versions of the story, known as 'The Miracle of the Boy Singer', see Laurel Broughton, *Prioress's Tale, Sources and Analogues of the Canterbury Tales*, ed. Robert M. Correale and Mary Hamel, 2 vols (Cambridge, 2002, 2006), vol. II, pp. 583–48; the story was often found in sermons. The Man of Law's story of Custance, whilst clearly connected to medieval saints' lives, also has folkloric and exemplary origins.

[28] On these texts see Geraldine Heng, *Empire of Magic* (New York, 2003); C. F. Heffernan, *The Orient in Chaucer and Medieval Romance* (Cambridge, 2003); and Iain Macleod Higgins, *Writing East: The "Travels" of Sir John Mandeville* (Philadelphia, 1997); for more general treatments see Metlitzki, *Matter of Araby*, Richard Southern, *Western Views of Islam in the Middle Ages* (Cambridge, MA, 1962), and John Tolan, *Medieval Christian Perceptions of Islam: A Book of Essays* (New York, 1996), all of which are focused on intellectual, scientific and theological approaches to Islam.

into contact with the Christians of Rome at the outset of the tale suggests shared vectors of trade and leisure, rather than animosity.[29] The Syrian merchants are 'sadde and trewe' (135), trustworthy and 'thrifty' rather than villainous. The merchants travel from Syria to Rome in a journey resonant of pilgrimage, for an unspecified, but apparently benign, reason: 'Were it for chapmanhod or for disport, / Noon oother message wolde they thider sende, / But comen hemself to Rome. . .' (143–4). Likewise, the 'Sowdan of Surrye' (177) is a man of 'beningne curteisye', a lexical reflection of Custance, 'mirour of alle curteisye' (166). The tale immediately problematizes an easy narrative of Islamic expansion *versus* Christian meekness: the Syrian merchants sojourn happily in Rome, 'as fil to hire plesance' (149), whereas the language of the 'commune voys' of the Romans suggests power, and, with prolepsis, expansion and conflict:

> This was the commune voys of every man:
> 'Oure Emperour of Rome – God hym see! –
> A doghter hath that, syn the world bigan,
> To rekene as wel hir goodnesse as beautee,
> Nas nevere swich another as is shee.
> I prey to God in honour hire susteene,
> And wolde she were of al Europe the queene.
> In hire is heigh beautee, withoute pride,
> Yowthe, withoute grenehede or folye;
> To alle hire wekes vertu is hir gyde;
> Humblese hath slayn in hire al tirannye.
> She is the mirour of alle curteisye;
> Hir herte is verray chambre of hoolynesse,
> Hir hand, ministre of fredam for almesse.' (155–69)

This description of Custance is clearly reminiscent of descriptions of female saints and of the Virgin Mary, particularly in the description of her as 'verray chambre of hoolynesse';[30] however, we might note too the decidedly *territorial* and socio-political terms interwoven: 'commune voys', 'Emperour', 'of al Europe the queene', 'tirannye', 'ministre of fredam for almesse'. The terms of spiritual virtue are mixed with affairs of state and the language of advice to princes, a theme which is developed throughout the tale.

The distance in the tale between Christian and Muslim, and between European and Syrian, is not great; the sultan has a 'privee conseil' (204), and a coterie of wise men, capable of 'subtil resoun' (213), which sounds distinctly similar to models of fourteenth-century English government (this being one of the elements of the story added by Chaucer). The religion of 'mawmettrie', the 'lawe sweete / That us was taught by Mahoun' (223–4), is described in little detail or as having little substance other than it is *not* Christianity, and its adherents have not been

[29] Susan Schibanoff, 'Worlds Apart: Orientalism, Antifeminism, and Heresy in Chaucer's *Man of Law's Tale*', *Exemplaria* 8 (1996), 59–96, notes how Chaucer departs here from his sources, which generally stress the foreignness of the merchants.

[30] Later on, a similar and explicitly Marian formula is used regarding Custance: 'he myghte have grace/ To han Custance withinne a litel space . . .' (206–7). The formula of 'infinite riches in a little space' was used to describe the Virgin and her womb; here it is almost identical to the Middle English translation of St Bernard's *Laetabundus*. See G. K. Hunter, 'The Theology of Marlowe's *Jew of Malta*', *Journal of the Warburg and Courtauld Institutes* 27 (1964), 211–40, p. 223.

'ycristned' (240). In the first part of the tale, difference between Christian and non-Christian is constructed not through practice or belief but through rhetoric – 'the Barbre nacioun' (281) – and, here, an explicit proto-nationalism. The Man of Law, our narrator, calls to mind other great conflicts between states, rather than religions:

> I trowe at Troye, whan Pirrus brak the wal
> Or Illion brende, at Thebes the citee,
> N'at Rome, for the harm thurgh Hanybal
> That Romayns hath venquysshed tymes thre,
> Nas herd swich tendre wepyng for pitee
> As in the chambre was for hire departynge;
> But forth she moot, wher-so she wepe or synge. (288–94)

The allusions to the Trojan, Theban and Roman wars not only suggests a repeated pattern of European conflict, based on invasion and occupation, but that Custance's journey to Syria is an international and political, rather than or as well as a religious, journey. In a move reminiscent of the overlapping worlds of the *Prioress's Tale*, the Man of Law bemoans 'O Mars, o atazir' (305), combining the pagan and Arabic/Persian nomenclatures for planetary influence, as fate itself takes on a non-Christian complexion.[31]

The substance of Islam becomes yet further confused with the introduction of the wicked sultana, 'welle of vices' (323), a kind of antithesis to the Prioress's 'welle of mercy' (VII 656). The sultana articulates a remarkably cogent defence of Islam whilst the Man of Law mis-describes Islam as 'olde sacrifices' (325). The sultana reveres 'the hooly lawes of our Alkaron / Yeven by Goddes message Makomete' (332–3) and declares, like the Second Nun's St Cecilia, her willingness to die for her reverence to her faith, for 'Makametes lawe' (336). On the one hand, these lines show Chaucer's familiarity with an Islamic understanding of Mohammed as prophet and divine messenger. On the other hand, the sultana articulates a 'Jewish' antipathy to Christianity on the grounds of it being a 'newe lawe' (337) which will supersede her own.[32]

It is through an inverted commensality that the sultana celebrates the vengeful maintenance of her religion, ironically through the destruction of her own family and bloodline:[33] splendid Christian feasting and 'compaignye' (the word used in the first line of the tale (134), from *cum pane*, of breaking bread together), a wedding-feast of 'deyntees mo than I kan yow devyse' (419), becomes the swift

31 For a stimulating reading of Chaucer's learning in Arabic and Hebrew see Gila Aloni and Shirley Sharon-Zisser, 'Chaucer's "Lyne Oriental": Mediterranean and Oriental Languages in the *Treatise on the Astrolabe*', *Mediterranean Historical Review* 16 (2001), 69–77. The explanatory note in the *Riverside Chaucer* to these lines has a wealth of detail on the astrological allusions and sources of the *Man of Law's Tale*.

32 See Christine Rose, 'The Jewish Mother-in-Law: Synagoga and the *Man of Law's Tale*', *Chaucer and the Jews: Sources, Contexts, Meanings*, ed. Sheila Delany (New York, 2002), pp. 3–24. Rose notes how many of the images used to describe the sultana are taken from images of Synagoga, the personification of Judaism; the sultana is also described as a 'Semyrame the secounde' (359), a reference to a lustful Babylonian queen who, in some versions of her story, usurps her son (see *Riverside Chaucer* note). Again, the precedents and patterning of conflict is called to mind.

33 On the role of the family in medieval romances of Christian–Islamic conflict see Heng, *Empire of Magic*, pp. 205–8.

and literal sacrifice at the dining table:[34]

> For shortly for to tellen, at o word,
> The Sowdan and the Cristen everichone
> Been al tohewe and striked at the bord,
> But it were oonly dame Custance allone. (428–31)

The sultana's murder of the guests at the feast is an attack on the social articulation of Christian identity, of eating together, as shown in the repeated general group noun also used by the Prioress, 'Cristen folk' (380, 386, 416). That is to say, the expression of the sultana's power is an attack on the Christian group, its rhetoric of social grouping and its rituals.

These early parts of the tale have already thrown identity into a complex relief, 'bewildering, disorienting, and seemingly endless'.[35] In the voice of the Man of Law, in considering Islam, God is seen as the protector of other Others: the God 'that kepte peple Ebryak from hir drenchynge' (489), a countervailing foreshadowing of the Prioress's Satanic 'Hebrayk peple, allas!' (VII 560), and the God that protected 'the Egipcien Marie' (II 500), the reformed prostitute, St Mary of Egypt. Syrians convert to Christianity whilst Custance leaves Rome for Syria; Islam is seen to be at once a mortal threat to Christianity and part of a Christian plan of providence (470–6, with its prefigurative reference to 'Danyel in the horrible cave'). The *Man of Law's Tale* thus presents a kind of vagrant cosmopolitanism, of shared traditions and Mediterranean miscegenation, at least at the level of rhetoric and allusion.[36] This intermingled world is developed further when Custance reaches Northumberland, her 'Latyn corrupt' and so 'mazed', bewildered, by her sea-journey 'that she forgat hir mynde' (526–7); Custance is, in every sense, mixed up.[37] This is all the more striking when we consider how closely the story of Custance is to medieval hagiography, those stories of the saints' militant virtue and Christian triumphs.[38]

This Northumberland is in many ways a parallel to the Syria from which Custance has providentially travelled, again suggesting the repeated patterning of nationhood or the cultural imperative for religious conflict. The 'Cristen folk' (541, that distinctive formula again), have 'fled', 'thurgh payens, that conquereden

[34] On the meanings and etymology of 'company' in the Middle Ages, and on the importance of commensality in medieval social relations, see Gervase Rosser, 'Going to the Fraternity Feast: Commensality and Social Relations in Late Medieval England', *Journal of British Studies* 33 (1994), 430–46.

[35] Carolyn Dinshaw, *Chaucer's Sexual Poetics* (Madison, 1989), p. 88.

[36] Dinshaw, ibid., notes that 'sudden shifts in tone' and generic mixing are the hallmarks of the tale. There is an important gendered element, of conquest and incest, at work in the tale, which I have not covered here; Dinshaw's analysis of the tale remains a full and very stimulating reading of these elements.

[37] Indeed, many scholars, in particular Robert Bartlett's influential work, have seen flexibility and mutability as the defining facets of 'race' in the Middle Ages; see Jeffrey Jerome Cohen, 'On Saracen Enjoyment: Some Fantasies of Race in Late Medieval France and England', *Journal of Medieval and Early Modern Studies* 31 (2001), 113–45, pp. 115–17, for a critical overview of medieval work on 'race'.

[38] Michael R. Paull, 'The Influence of the Saint's Legend Genre in the *Man of Law's Tale*', *The Chaucer Review* 5 (1971), 179–94, and Paul M. Clogan, 'Narrative Style of the *Man of Law's Tale*', *Medievalia et Humanistica* 8 (1977), 217–33, see Custance as a representative heroine of late-medieval hagiographic romance. However, see John A. Yunck, 'Religious elements in the *Man of Law's Tale*' *English Literary History* 27 (1960), 249–61, which stresses how Chaucer made his version of Custance less militant that in his source, Trivet's *Chronicle*.

al aboute' (542), but a vestigial and potential Christianity remains; the kingdom of Northumberland, meanwhile, remains in conflict with the Scots (580). Custance starts, in earnest, evangelizing, in Geraldine Heng's words 'positioned now as a successful cultural contestant, seeking alliances and catechizing on behalf of her religion'.[39] Given the similarities between this Northumberland and Syria, of mixing and of conversion upon marriage, it is no surprise that the king of Northumberland is called 'Alla': this nomenclature makes perfect sense within this mixed tale as belonging at once to Ælla (r. 560–88), a northern English king, but has encoded within it a suggestive reference to Allah, the Arabic name of God. Precedents and repeated patterns mark the narrative – Custance's multiple suitors, her maritime journeys, repeated conflicts with the mothers-in-law – which collapse distinctions between the personal, national and religious. As Custance marks territory through its conversion to Christianity, her body is marked by attempts to guide, contain or own it, as seen in the incident in the tale in which the 'yong knyght' (585), an avatar of both the sultan and Alla, fails to woo Custance and then creeps into Hermengild's chamber to frame Custance for a murder she did not commit. As in Syria, Custance's new 'home' is shown to be decidedly hostile but providentially set for conversion, as Custance falls on her knees and recalls heroic female precedents from Jewish and Christian lore, Susannah and the Virgin Mary (639–44). The Man of Law employs similar precedents later in the tale, recalling the famous battles between David and Goliath (934–4) and Judith and Holofernes (939–40).

The *Man of Law's Tale* is not simply an account of *translatio imperii* – the ascension of the West over the East – but a tortuous story of the ways in which cultures define themselves against each other. The narrator is himself not only limited as a poet – his story wanders with the same lack of aim as Custance in her rudderless boat – but also limited as an 'accurate' authority: he reminds his audience several times of his fallibility, his poem is marked by abrupt transitions, and he signposts his clumsy narration (for example, 'But turne I wole agayn to my mateere', 581; 'I kan no bettre seye', 874; 'of which the name in my text noght I fynde', 905; 'Now lat us stynte of Custance but a throwe', 952; 'I wol no lenger tarien in this cas', 983; 'as I gesse', 1088).[40] In sum the *Man of Law's Tale* revels in miscegenation but, as in the *Prioress's Tale*, turns this into an ambivalent conquest: at the tale's conclusion, Mauritius (the only character in the tale with a conventional, Christian saint's name) becomes the emperor of a Christian Europe which now includes a Christian Northumbria.[41] As in the *Prioress's Tale*, the non-Christian must disappear as such, be it through extermination or conversion, but self-examination remains at the heart of this process of erasure. The tale concludes with Custance back in Rome, with Alla dead, where she 'fyndeth hire freendes hoole and sounde' (1150) and her father. Custance's virtue and providential protection has been shown, and the empire is enlarged, but remarkably little

[39] Heng, *Empire of Magic*, p. 197.

[40] On the Man of Law as 'character' see A. C. Spearing, 'Narrative Voice: The Case of Chaucer's *Man of Law's Tale*', *New Literary History* 32 (2001), 715–46.

[41] Chaucer does not draw out the legend of St Maurice, but he makes a particularly fitting exemplar for the story, not as the patron saint of Holy Roman Emperors and of kingdoms, but as the saint who was to have crushed a non-Christian revolt. St Maurice is usually depicted in armour, a popular image of the *miles Christi*, a soldier of Christ. See David Woods, 'The Origin of the Cult of St Maurice', *Journal of Ecclesiastical History* 45 (1994), 385–95.

has changed in Rome, and the tale's ending is retrospective, nostalgic and isolating. As Heng observes, Custance and her son, the emperor Mauritius, parallel the divine family of the Virgin and Christ, performing 'a myth of re-foundation'.[42]

As Steven Kruger writes, in medieval Europe 'Jews and Jewishness are everywhere, yet at the same time everywhere under erasure';[43] the same is true for Islam, or rather adherents to the law of 'Mahoun', in romances. Kruger calls this 'spectrality', and others have written of the 'virtual' Jew, the 'imaginary' Jew and the 'hermeneutic' Jew. What we see in the *Prioress's Tale* and the *Man of Law's Tale* is not a definition of Judaism or Islam, but a critical and ambivalent interrogation of Christianity, its definition and its precepts. Neither the Prioress's passive 'clergeon' nor the Man of Law's rudderless Custance appear as characters with much volition or prerogative, but are instrumental in turning those around them to faith. Yet in neither tale does Christianity emerge as coherent, or *total*: Christian is set into ironic and complex relationships with other religions, mediated through the fallible fictional narrators. Judaism, Islam and paganism are presented as corrupted versions of Christianity, which allow Chaucer's fictional narrators to probe their own religious identities.

The Jews and Muslims of such popular, vernacular writing might play threatening roles and be imagined as menacing to Christianity, but we might more accurately see these imaginary non-Christians as intensely familiar: not only in the sense that such images appear with a great frequency in medieval writing, but also in the medieval sense (*domesticare*) of the familiar: in Mary Carruthers's words, 'to make something familiar by making it a part of your own experience'.[44] These Jews, Muslims and pagans are versions not of Judaism and Islam but of Christianity and Englishness. In sum, the Judaism depicted in the *Prioress's Tale* and the Islam and paganism of the *Man of Law's Tale* is an intensely enabling presence: it is used by the narrators, the Prioress and the Man of Law, to confirm and domesticate their worlds whilst showing, as elsewhere in the *Canterbury Tales*, the ironies of self-identity and the patterns of human experience.

[42] Heng, *Empire of Magic*, p. 209.

[43] Steven Kruger, *The Spectral Jew: Conversion and Embodiment in Medieval Europe* (Minneapolis and London, 2006), p. xiii.

[44] Mary Carruthers, *The Book of Memory. A Study of Memory in Medieval Culture* (Cambridge, 1990), p. 164.

6

The Matter of Chaucer: Chaucer and the Boundaries of Romance

HELEN PHILLIPS

JEAN BODEL in the late twelfth century divided romances into three groups, reflecting their subject matters: the matter of France (concerned with Charlemagne and other French Christian leaders fighting Islam), the matter of Rome (classical subjects), and the matter of Britain (subjects related to the world of Arthur).[1] But romance is a varied genre and other discernable types include romances that celebrate particular dynasties, like *Guy of Warwick*; romances with oriental settings; and romances centred on conflicting love and loyalty, like the Lancelot or Tristan stories. Recurrent plot patterns include calumniated wives, abandoned noble babies, dispossessed heirs, Muslim maidens who convert and marry Christian heroes, and family romances in which relations, initially separated, are finally reunited.

Roger Ascham famously condemned romance as 'open manslaughter and bold bawdrye',[2] and romance typically deals with secular subjects at odds with the highest Christian ideals: glorification of warfare, revenge, extra-marital passion, worldly glory, luxury and magic or, in romances with classical sources, pagan gods. Yet many romances include Christian history, like crusades or wars against the pagan Anglo-Saxons, or motifs related to Christian spirituality, like the wise hermit or the grail, which from around 1200 is identified as the cup of the Last Supper, symbolizing a spiritual perfection taking knights beyond the Round Table's earthly chivalry. Some romances, including *Sir Gowther* and *Sir Gawain and the Green Knight*, centre on the Christian pattern of penitence, where a hero's success lies less in chivalric triumphs than contrition, confession and subsequent reconciliation with divine and human order.[3] The genres of romance and saint's life can be similar, as Chaucer's *Man of Law's Tale* illustrates. Nevertheless, Georges Duby argued, romance's most characteristic plot is the lone quest of a nobly born youth, leading, after adventures demonstrating his prowess, to an advantageous marriage and the acquisition of land.[4]

1 See Dieter Mehl, *The Middle English Romances of the Thirteenth and Fourteenth Centuries* (London, 1968), p. 31.

2 *The Scholemaster*, in Roger Ascham, *English Works*, ed. W. Aldis (Cambridge, 1904, repr. 1970), p. 230.

3 See Andrea Hopkins, *The Sinful Knights: A Study of Middle English Penitential Romance* (Oxford, 1990).

4 *The Chivalrous Society* (London, 1977), p. 119.

Chaucer's romances form a distinctive group, both like and unlike other medieval romances: the matter of Chaucer, we might say. Exemplifying a range of romance types, they treat romance self-consciously and raise questions about the cultural myths of aristocratic chivalry it celebrates. Little concerned with the classic plot of the noble hero's quest for land and bride, except in the absurd *Sir Thopas*, Chaucer's romances show recurrent interest in a group of essentially philosophical problems: free will and determinism; the moral status of sexual desire; and how adversity fits into a cosmic and human order created by a benevolent divinity. Their exploration of these is often through perspectives with classical origins or is innovative, looking outside the conventional paradigms of Chaucer's own period and not limited to answers supplied by Christian teaching. Yet though these problems are not distinctively Christian issues, like sin or the devil's wiles, they were questions that concerned fourteenth-century Christian thinkers: questions to which the fourteenth century had no ready or agreed answers or, in the case of sexual passion, no wholly adequate discourses or agreed terms for debate.

Which count as Chaucer's romances? The *Knight's*, *Man of Law's*, *Wife of Bath's*, *Squire's* and *Franklin's Tales*, *Sir Thopas*, and *Troilus* are obvious candidates. But themes characterizing the matter of Chaucer transcend genre boundaries, appearing also in the *Clerk's*, *Physician's*, and *Manciple's Tales* and the *Legend of Good Women*. The *Legend* stories, for example, problematize both *gentilesse* and the ethics of sexual love, as well as including characters – Dido, Jason, and Medea – who feature in classical romances like the *Roman de Troie* and *Roman d'Enéas*. Questions raised in Chaucer's romances also appear in his comedies: destinal forces in the *Nun's Priest's Tale*, for instance. The comedies depict Christian life and practices more often than the romances and sometimes incorporate major Christian themes, such as the Fall in the *Merchant's* and *Nun's Priest's Tales*. Chaucer's characteristically narrative imagination invades the lyric in *Anelida*, *Pity*, *Mars* and the *ABC*: these all, though based in non-narrative forms (ballade, lover's complaint and Marian prayer), imply a surrounding presence of adventures, danger, intrigue and emotional searching and longing, and are animated with narrative images of quest, peril, flight or rescue.[5] Many lyrics also explore philosophical ideas found in Chaucer's romances: see below on *Mars* and the *Franklin's Tale*.

For Chaucer the crises and dangers characteristic of romance plots trigger questions – especially questions about humans' experience in relation to secularity and suffering. One issue is causation, whether there is free will or all is determined; another the problem of evil; a third how emotions, especially sexual passion, should be evaluated, both ethically and ontologically. An exploratory approach to the genre of romance itself and its implicit ideologies appears both in Chaucer's parody romance *Sir Thopas* and the handling of ideals of aristocratic honour in the *Knight's*, *Wife of Bath's*, *Squire*'s and *Franklin's Tales*. *Sir Thopas* mocks typical romance motifs and vocabulary, as does the *Miller's Tale*, which also mirrors in non-*gentil* form the *Knight's Tale*'s plot pattern of love-rivals. The *Tales* miscellany itself challenges the cultural sway of genre and aristocratic assumptions by placing romances alongside religious and comic tales, and their

[5] See Helen Phillips, 'Chaucer and Deguileville: The *ABC* in Context', *Medium Ævum* 62 (1993), 1–19.

contrasting worldviews, and within the social melting pot, in terms of disruptions of hierarchy, taste and ethical norms, created by the pilgrimage frame-story.

That miscellaneity suggests one answer to the question of why Chaucer's crowning work was not a mighty romance on one of the genre's great subjects, for example a grail or crusade romance or one celebrating Arthur, England or a powerful dynasty. Such a decision would have involved subscription to one of the *grands récits* embodied in various types of romance, whether to a religious vision of a specific kind, to glorifying a dynasty, or the unequivocal, exclusive, celebration of the *gentil* class and its ideology. Contemporary historians were, moreover, expressing scepticism about Arthurian traditions,[6] and, though Arthurian adventures and prophecies had regularly been vehicles for contemporary rulers' politics, Richard II made an unlikely Arthur, not ruling particularly harmoniously with his magnates, not pursuing belligerent policies overseas or in the British Isles.

The *Tales* miscellany, social, moral and aesthetic, permits exploration of the romance genre but not within the confines of the great quest or princely heroic narrative. The absence of a great masculine quest seems to make more space for women's experiences, and the theme of suffering, masculine and feminine, and how suffering can be explained or met. Chaucer's romances exhibit more interest in endurance of adversity, or philosophical or religious contempt for it, than the triumphalist pursuit of victory and love that forms the trajectory of many romance plots.[7] This interest in suffering links with a trend Rosalind Field observes: the prevalence in fourteenth-century English romance of the 'short, often sentimental, tale of suffering, loss, and hardship transformed into restitution and reconciliation'; she suggests its popularity reflects a widening audience of readers, and it brings into prominence experiences often present in romances but not previously centre-stage, including childhood, motherhood, isolation and spiritual and emotional development.[8]

Certainties and Questions in the Franklin's and Man of Law's Tales

Non-Christian settings are common. The *Squire's Tale* is set in a Mongol court, the *Knight's Tale* and *Troilus* in pre-Christian Thebes and Troy respectively, with the planetary gods' powers prominent in their narratives, albeit in relation to ideas about Fortune and contempt of this world with well-established Boethian and Christian associations. The *Wife of Bath's Tale*, though set in Arthur's reign, tells a wholly secular adventure: no grail quest or wars against pagan Saxons. Chaucer gives the *Franklin's Tale* an ambiguous religious setting, with few Christian references and no religious condemnation of adultery or suicide when these become possible actions for its heroine. Yet Dorigen prays to, and protests against, a 'Lord'

6 Chris Given-Wilson, *Chronicles: The Writing of History in Medieval England* (London, 2004), pp. 3–5.

7 See Derek Pearsall's discussion in *The Life of Geoffrey Chaucer: A Critical Biography* (London, 1992), pp. 262–70.

8 'Romance in England, 1066–1400', *Cambridge History of Medieval English Literature*, ed. David Wallace (Cambridge, 1999), 152–76, p. 173; see Geraldine Heng's arguments about romances as expressions of national cultural fantasy and trauma (rather than historically engendered expressions of class and ideology), and the *Man of Law's Tale* as linking the family romance motif of the exiled mother to fantasies of nation and conquest, *Empire of Magic: Medieval Romance and the Politics of Cultural Fantasy* (New York, 2003).

(V 865–93) who, if never absolutely identified with the Judaeo-Christian deity, is described as a loving Creator; she asks how he could create so cruel and 'unresonable' a world (872). The magician, however, prays to Phoebus Apollo, and claims to be able to alter nature by astrology. Chaucer's narrative problematizes such claims, condemning them as 'illusioun', 'supersticious cursednesse', and what 'hethen folk useden in thilke dayes' (1134, 1272, 1293), yet showing ambivalence about the ethics of such beliefs and whether the magician produces a real change or an illusion.

Historically Chaucer's 'olde gentil Britouns' (719), Bretons, had been Christians. Chaucer disregards or may not have known that. In the *Franklin's Tale*, as in the *Knight's Tale*, *Troilus* and the *Legend of Good Women*, he seems to find settings free of the specific assumptions and prohibitions of Christianity opportune for examining philosophical and moral issues surrounding sexual desire, besides other questions, including the problem of evil. The latter is raised both in the *Franklin's Tale* and 'Philomela', which asks why God allows evil men like Tereus to exist (*LGW* 2228–37). The lyric, *Mars*, again amid pagan parameters, similarly asks why a loving God brings 'hardnesse' on his creatures, forcing them to love in a mutable world. The ending of *Troilus* is the most provocative treatment (paradoxically by bringing in explicitly Christian discourse) of Chaucer's interest in the gap between a pagan story and the standpoint of a modern Christian audience and author.

The *Franklin's Tale* is called a Breton lay. Marie de France, the twelfth-century inventor of this type of romance, depicted a Brittany where magic appears part of Nature, and which allows her to present moral ideals at odds sometimes with conventional Christian morality, in what can be seen as a humanist spirit, especially in her celebration of true, devoted love outside marriage. Marie's settings are lightly Christian, occasionally mentioning institutions like priests or abbeys in the background to her dramas of human goodness and evil, loyalty, love and selfishness, yet Christian criteria do not drive the crises, moral judgements or outcomes. The genre's tendency to set adventures in imagined worlds which are not bounded wholly or exclusively by Christian expectations (a tendency illustrated very clearly by the type of Other World depicted in *Sir Orfeo*) perhaps gave Chaucer not just license to deal with magic but stimulation for intellectual speculation – especially about the problematic relationships between love and marriage. The *Franklin's Tale* presents challenges to conventional assumptions about husbands' domination of wives and about female sexual honour (V 761–98, 1355–1456) yet its central conundrum seems to be the wider question of how to contain both love and lust within concepts of hierarchy, both marital and social. Unlike twelfth-century romances, the *romans antiques* and those of Chrétien de Troyes, where passages of debate, question and answer, and love casuistry mark the onset of desire, the *Franklin's Tale* begins with a marriage, rather than ending with it, and the agitated rhetoric of a passage discussing love paradoxes occurs here in relation to the subject of marriage, not – more conventionally – to that of desire.

Sometimes, as with his refusal to condemn Aurelius' designs on Dorigen as sin, Chaucer ignores obvious Christian answers to problems raised in his narratives; the *Book of the Duchess* provides another clear example. The *Man of Law's Tale* seems initially anomalous among Chaucer's romances in its dogmatic certainty about the benevolent design and protective love of God and the Christian faith of many of its characters. With affinities to a family romance, it also resembles a saint's life and a conversion narrative. Yet even here Chaucer's writing keeps readers intellectually on their toes, with challenging tensions within its structure and a tone which often presents religious certainties through a rhetoric of questioning and human speculation.

One tension is that between the tale's ascetic, unworldly values and its prologue's tirade against poverty: a 'hateful harm' that makes people blame Christ for distributing wealth unfairly (II 99–126). The prologue presents the tale itself as a product of international commerce, something brought to these shores by merchants, suggesting a parallel between travels that produce encounters between faiths, with spiritual conversions, and commercial travels, monetary exchange and profit. The tale's message resembles one proposed for the *Clerk's Tale* (IV 1145–62): 'suffraunce' of whatever adversities life sends, in obedience to God's 'governaunce' (1161–2). Compared with Trivet's tale of Constance, Chaucer makes his heroine more passive, more dependent on heaven and less on her own resourcefulness.[9] While showing her totally in the hands of earthly and heavenly fathers, and subject to other males' wills, he makes unusually explicit the oppression of helpless women under patriarchy (the daughter's lament when her father marries her off, II 274–87; the grim description of marital sex as female endurance of male pleasure, 708–14). The Law of the Father appears both cause of, and protection from, oppression, while the writing seems both to uphold and expose this.

Chaucer also introduces statements about the causative influences of destiny, the planets and Fortune (for example, II 190–6), beliefs potentially challenging the Christian principle of free will. Of course, Christian thought had to some extent assimilated these inherited concepts, asserting human freedom to act virtuously despite cosmic influences. The Aristotelian term 'firste moevynge' (295) appears, nevertheless, amid a description of celestial powers as 'cruel' (295, 301), in a fashion suggesting perhaps Chaucer found the availability of non-Christian models convenient for introducing into his narrative an acknowledgement that the world's ruling power(s) might not be wholly benevolent.

This tale's combination of firm Christian conviction with admission of difficult questions has parallels in its style. While proclaiming God's protection of his servants, Chaucer writes in terms of debate and human attempts to 'rede' (interpret) dilemmas and signs: many examples appear during his long passage about astrological omens and human decision-making (II 195, 202–3, 211–17, 228, 309–15); the writing often asserts belief through a rhetoric of asking questions (470–5, 484–5, 498–501, 932–42). As with Dorigen's readiness finally to leave 'disputison' over the dilemma of evil to 'clerkes' (V 890), or the *Nun's Priest's Tale*'s acknowledgement (VII 3234–50) of 'greet disputisoun' about predestination, the *Man of Law's Tale* links an openness to intellectual questioning with statements of faith: God is declared 'lord of Fortune' at II 448; 'Clerkys' know the answers (480); God will guide Custance's boat (511); he saves her (938–45) and Mary will ensure her safe return (950–2).

9 Helen Phillips, 'The French Background', *Chaucer: An Oxford Guide*, ed. Steve Ellis (Oxford, 2005), pp. 292–312, pp. 304–6.

Romance, with its plots characterized by vicissitudes and peril, seemingly provokes Chaucer to questions about how events are governed in a dangerous universe. His romances typically leave such questions open. But other romance conventions, of wondrous events and happy endings, enable him to steer towards happy closures (with, in *Troilus*, happy faith as the closure rather than happy union), though such narrative closure is not accompanied by fully adequate philosophical address or closure of the might questions raised within his narratives. In the *Man of Law's Tale*, the miraculous coincidences and happy ending typical of the genre double as justification of God's ways to man. Custance's perils and the allusions to destinal forces implicitly raise the question that Dorigen voices in the *Franklin's Tale*: how could a loving Creator make such a world? But this text supplies an orthodox answer: God protects his servants (470–504). The structures of Chaucer's romances show difficult issues raised in the middle of these texts concluded but not resolved.[10]

Linda Georgianna observes that modern critics often make Chaucer a sceptic, despising characteristic tenets and practices of the medieval Church, especially simple and superstitious beliefs.[11] And clearly Chaucer mocks 'lewed' carpenter John's mumbo-jumbo and complacent confidence in an unintellectual faith, yet the *ABC* and the Prioress's and Second Nun's prologues affirm with sophisticated poetry the power of a simple reverence and devout trust, together with certainty about Mary's power to provide a safe haven for the sinful soul, struggling through life's perils. That image (*ABC* 2–16, 41–8, 145–8, 183–4) recalls the structure of Chaucer's romances: they too move finally towards an ending which is a haven from ambitious questions as well as narrative dangers. This structure is not without strains and one obvious point of strain – submission to a highly paternal ruling power – appears acknowledged in several passages that convey women's subjugation in blatantly extreme terms: Chaucer's articulation of Custance's sexual subjection and Griselda's total resignation of her will are examples.[12]

Chaucer treats Custance's trials polysemically, sometimes evoking the deepest resonances of prayer and liturgy familiar to his audiences, sometimes as both Christian apologia and patriarchal exposé, but also as fictional events resembling those in political circles familiar to him. Thus the Man of Law's reference to Daniel (a fellow judge), II 470–6, plunges the narrative into the world of prayers for the dead: God's help for Daniel appeared in the Commendation of the Dying and often occurs in extant personal prayers for protection from enemies, spiritual and earthly.[13] In art Daniel's rescue symbolized resurrection from the tomb.[14] It is often cited in female martyrs' lives: this biblical reference is thus one of the points where this romance intertextually recalls hagiography.[15] Yet, just as the pale face

[10] Compare Sheila Delany's presentation of thirteenth- and fourteenth-century discussions about faith and logic in *Chaucer's 'House of Fame': The Poetics of Skeptical Fideism* (Chicago, 1972), pp. 14–21.

[11] 'The Protestant Chaucer', *Chaucer's Religious Tales*, ed. C. David Benson and Elizabeth Robertson (Cambridge, 1991), pp. 55–69, at pp. 63–6.

[12] Ibid., pp. 67–8.

[13] Eamon Duffy, *The Stripping of the Altars: Traditional Religion in England 1400–1580* (New Haven and London, 1992), pp. 267–8.

[14] Ann Eijenholm Nichols, *The Early Art of Norfolk: A Subject-List of Extant and Lost Art Including Items Relevant to English Drama* (Kalamazoo, 2002), p. 46.

[15] For example *The Life of St Katherine*, ed. Eugen Einenkel, EETS os (London, 1884), lines 1816–28.

at 645–51 makes its heroine's ancient, fantastical trials seem parallels to the contemporary audience's political world of the Appellants and Merciless Parliament ('Have ye nat seyn . . .?', the narrative appeals), so the royal lady's situation, like that of many *Legend* heroines, is an extreme parallel to the fate of many women of the contemporary ruling class, whose political importance and destiny was dynastic or strategic marriage: women who could be in Chaucer's audience like Anne of Bohemia, Constance of Castile, Philippa and Catalina of Lancaster. The appeal to royal ladies in his audience ('O queens . . .', 652), though it stresses their own secure 'prosperitee', suggests a recognition not only of parallels between them and her in piety (and in rank: Anne of Bohemia was also an 'Emperoures doghter', 655) but implicitly also the text's acknowledgement of the lonely courage such royal destinies might require from young royal women.

Sex and Marriage

Though some medieval romances dramatize Christian, even monastic, ideals, romance is the chief vehicle for secular fiction before Renaissance drama and the novel, and conflicts with Christian principles emerge most clearly in sexual matters. In Marie de France's lays the glorification of love challenges orthodox moral attitudes, particularly of the ascetic, often misogynistic, strand in medieval Christianity. Such celebration of love, expressed also, though more equivocally, in Chrétien de Troyes' *Lancelot*, prompted C. S. Lewis's famous 'rule' that Courtly Love was adulterous.[16] The apparent elevation of adultery, however, can alternatively be seen as asserting the power of mutual, freely given, love over other considerations and duties. Indeed, paradoxically, Marie's lays celebrate precisely that primacy of consent that the twelfth-century Church had established as the legal core of a true marriage (prevailing, in theory, over the wishes of families).

Chaucer's *Legend of Good Women* presents pagans, whose passions often lead to suicide, as 'goode wimmen': faithful, innocent and generous heroines, who disprove misogynists' condemnation of women; he provocatively labels their stories saints' legends. *Troilus* similarly makes fidelity a central ethical issue while disregarding sex outside marriage. Marriage is not idealized in Chaucer's writings: Criseyde values her freedom (II 750–6); Emily, like the tercel in the *Parliament*, would rather stay single; and Chaucer paints as unsentimental a view of marriage in the *Man of Law's Tale*, a romance, as in the *Wife of Bath's Prologue*, describing marriage as 'subjeccioun' to a man who may not be pleasant (II 270–3) and a bridal night as licensed abuse (708–13). Female reluctance over marriage may reflect patriarchal perceptions of marriage as something men do to women (see Alcuin Blamires' discussion, p. 8), besides recognition of the medieval widow's relative legal and financial independence. Chaucer's romances sometimes expose how far masculine sexual desire is also oppression, admitting into texts problems and contradictions which the discourses of love in his period could not encompass. Examples include the predatory imagery of *Troilus* III 1191–1211 (Criseyde as the lark caught in a sparrow-hawk's claw), disconcertingly mingled with chivalric

[16] *The Allegory of Love* (London, 1936), pp. 1–43.

language of courtly devotion (1277–1302) and comparison of Troilus' desire to celestial love (1254–67).[17]

Yet Chaucer takes every opportunity to portray his *Legend* heroines as wives; Alceste is an exemplar of 'wyfhod' and *fine amour* combined (*LGW* F 545), and the *Franklin's Tale* starts with the assumption, shared by many romances, that happy marriage is the goal of courtly love. It subsequently presents without apparent condemnation an equally intense passion, that of Aurelius, which is adulterous in intent yet here rendered beautiful by language that links his desire to high-minded and *gentil* tropes associated in romance with love (music, humility, knightly reputation and morality). The garden (V 902–24), an image with potential to condemn him, through associations with Eden, is described without verbal hints encouraging any such reading. The contradictions in this text are contradictions about women, passion and marriage present in medieval culture: it would be weakening Chaucer's powerful narrative to dismiss them, or iron them out, simply as his portrayal of a pre-Christian age. Such contradictions bring this romance to a point where a faithful, chaste wife is forced – through wifely obedience to her loving husband and his chivalric principles – to consent to rape. Dorigen is saved not by contrition, penitence or a miracle, as might arise within wholly Christian parameters, but the would-be rapist's combination of compassion for her and respect for another man, her husband, and his concept of *gentilesse*. A secular code, chivalry, substitutes for Christian rules here in this curiously God-free ancient Brittany.

In the *Wife of Bath's Tale*, 'Philomela' and 'Lucrece', rape – male assertion of power over women – is linked to questions about honour and *gentil* status, attributes credited to powerful males. Chaucer's writing more than once questions a rapist's *gentil* identity (III 1109–76; *LGW* 1819–24, 2330–9); and Arveragus problematizes '[t]routhe' (V 1479), as identical for women and men, contradicting patriarchal tradition that restricts woman's honour to her menfolk's ownership of her body. Chaucer's innovative move here is later complicated by his text's reversion to patriarchal perspectives, in Aurelius's wonder at a husband's generosity with the wife he owns, and Arveragus' fear of public shame. This romance interrogates what constitutes *gentilesse* and how far honour is gendered. And, beneath its beautiful, highly controlled, narration, it exposes contradictions in ideas about divine providence, upper-class honour, and in what is called love within a patriarchal society.

The Knight's Tale

Chaucer's Knight, despite fighting 'for oure feith at Tramyssene' (I 62), does not tell a crusade romance. The fourteenth century saw growing scepticism about crusades: some believed lords' efforts should be concentrated at home; the expense and taxation made military campaigns unpopular; and doubts increased after morally dubious crusades like the 1383 invasion of Flanders by the belligerent bishop of Norwich on behalf of the schismatic Avignon pope. Whereas Wyclif roundly condemned this expedition, Chaucer's allusion appears bland: his Squire

[17] See on marriage, power and the Church David Aers, *Chaucer, Langland and the Creative Imagination* (London, 1980), pp. 125–8, 153–60.

is credited, apparently approvingly, with participating in 'chyvachie / In Flaundres, in Artoys, and Pycardie' (I 85–6).[18]

The *Knight's Tale* story of love and war originated in Statius' epic, the *Thebaid* (*c.* AD 90), which was transformed into a chivalric romance in the *Roman de Thèbes* (*c.*1150). In that, written soon after the First Crusade, the war between Thebes and Argos has some echoes of contemporary conflict with Islam. Chaucer, however, like his immediate source, Boccaccio's *Teseida*, focuses on a story of Theban lovers, not the clash of nations. He abbreviates Boccaccio's descriptions of fighting, removes his sensual descriptions of characters and sex, and casts his narrative more as a philosophical meditation on power and order, earthly desires, mutability, and acceptance of the inevitability of loss in human affairs. Speeches by Egeus on mutability (I 2837–49) and Theseus on the cosmic harmony reigning beyond the appearances of loss and chaos in human life (2987–3057) draw on Boethius' *Consolation of Philosophy* (II metrum 8; IV prosa 6), to teach contempt for 'this wrecched world adoun' (2995). This romance offers Boethian ideas as consolations and explanations for pain and transience, answers which, though compatible with Christian worldviews, lack any distinctive Christian doctrines like atonement or salvation. The *Knight's Tale* makes no appeal to Christ's love as an alternative to human love and the pain it brings, like that which concludes *Troilus*.

Perhaps Chaucer presents Theseus' consolations as inadequate because they are based on the limited wisdom of pagan thought.[19] Alternatively, he uses, as often in his romances, a non-Christian setting and the genre's crisis-filled plots to raise questions about human misery and the design of the universe, yet finally moving abruptly into a narrative happy ending (another characteristic of the genre), which, while asserting belief in benign outcomes, attempts no philosophical solutions to the text's earlier conundrums, or the question of how its bleak philosophical outlook relates either to Christian faith or the powerful experience of human passions.

Even more than his lawyer's tale, this knight's tale celebrates, albeit with intermittent questioning, a vision of control and the Law of the Father, without the *Man of Law's Tale*'s insistence on the accompanying, protective *love* of God. Governance and submission are its principles, central to its conceptualization of harmony and love, as well as of war and politics. The imposition of harmony, i.e. order, by 'governour' (861) Theseus, whose earthly control parallels that of Jupiter, is a key motif signalled in the initial image of male domination over female power, just as in the concluding resolution of destructive passions by marriage at Theseus' command. The concept of harmony this model proposes is arguably an inauthentic, as well as an inadequate, response to the questions about desire, suffering and oppression raised in the course of Chaucer's text. That pattern of disjunction – philosophical conundrums raised but answered only in narrative fashion, by happy closure – is the characteristic structure in the matter of Chaucer. In this case, Chaucer's removal of Boccaccio's stronger acknowledgement of the body (for example Palemone's eagerness for his wedding night and his

[18] 'Fifty Heresies and Errors of the Friars', *Select English Works of John Wyclif*, ed. Thomas Arnold, 3 vols (Oxford, 1871), vol. III, pp. 366–401, at pp. 385–6.

[19] See Alastair Minnis, *Chaucer and Pagan Antiquity*, Chaucer Studies 8 (Cambridge, 1982), pp. 125–31.

sexual energy during it) seems judicious, aesthetically but also strategically. It helps to make his happy ending an acceptable (or not completely jarring) finale for this Boethian rendering of the love story: playing down the force of precisely those human experiences that are omitted from, yet potentially form a stumbling block to, Boethius' wholly transcendental model of what is worthy of thought and respect within human lives.

Gentil Ideals and Challenges

Chaucer sometimes presents knights in relation to commercial contingencies of his period. The Knight's portrait includes mercenary services.[20] Chaucer, however, probably does not intend condemnation; indeed, the portrait mentions expeditions associated with several aristocrats in circles familiar to him, including Henry, duke of Lancaster, in the Mediterranean (Algeciras, Cyprus and Rhodes), and with the Teutonic Knights; and Henry Bolingbroke in the eastern Mediterranean and with the Teutonic knights. The Knight's portrait celebrates traditional chivalric ideals yet records the moral and political complexity of modern warfare and its often commercial incentives. Such acknowledgement of contemporary complexities is not restricted to Chaucer's presentation of *gentils*: the Merchant's portrait (I 270–84) is analogously poised between traditional Christian attitudes (opposition to usury and the pursuit of profit) and Chaucer's readiness to record a modern world of more mixed ethics: almost all commerce now regularly involved systems of interest and credit, as the *Shipman's Tale* further illustrates.

Gentilesse and economics collide in the Franklin's sentiments rating the desirability of his son's learning *gentilesse* above forty pounds' worth of land. Though Chaucer's Franklin is sometimes read as satire against a *parvenu*, recent research into the economic, social and political/legal development of the gentry suggests that Chaucer is examining a rising class with sociological acumen rather than writing simple destructive satire.[21] The *gentil* ideal in Chaucer's presentation of the Knight, Wife and Franklin and their tales reflects its increasing prominence as a social *concept*, at a period when literal numbers of knights were declining and the landholding class was expanding to include 'new men', leasing estates rather than inheriting them. The *Wife's* and *Squire's Tales*, like *Anelida* and the *Legend of Good Women*, convey aspects of what *gentilesse* and *courtesy* mean (including courage, loyalty to oath, honour, compassion, respect for women), while often also demonstrating un*gentil* behaviour by nobly born men.

Medieval romance, however, also taught the conduct and ideals of upper-class masculinity. The *Squire's Tale*'s Camyuskan, though a non-Christian, exemplifies the virtues that 'longeth to a kyng, [a]s of the secte [here 'religion'] of which that he was born':

> hardy [courageous], wys, and riche,
> And pitous and just, alwey yliche;
> Sooth of his word, benigne and honourable (V 19–21)

[20] See Terry Jones, *Chaucer's Knight: Portrait of a Medieval Mercenary* (London, 1980), pp. 7–140.

[21] See Chris Given-Wilson, *English Nobility in the Late Middle Ages: The Fourteenth-Century Political Community* (London and New York, 1987), pp. 69–72.

also young, constant, strong, eager for arms, handsome, fortunate (an interesting addition), he always 'kept so wel roial estat' that he was unparalleled. This could be a mirror of Richard II's self-image. It certainly illustrates how knightly ideals appeared to transcend barriers between pagans and Christians. The Knight's *General Prologue* portrait adds to such ideals the piety, humility and crusading interests of a medieval Christian warrior, while the Squire's portrait illustrates how central to *gentil* ideals are skills in the arts, elegance and good manners. While magic and warfare might have dominated a completed *Squire's Tale*, its preoccupations as it stands are deeply compatible with Christian social values: fidelity to others, and, in Canace, a sober, kind and thoughtful approach to life.

Yet *gentilesse* and *honour*, and the question of who in class and gender terms deserves respect, are aggressively interrogated by the *Wife of Bath's Tale.* The crone's speech urges on a young aristocrat respect for the old and the poor, and implicitly for females and sub-aristocratic classes. It calls virtue true *gentilesse*, and includes arguments based on Christ's poverty, a controversial contemporary issue, used by Wycliffites to attack a worldly Church.[22] A typical Chaucer romance, its denouement manipulates closure through magic and happy marriage, without satisfactorily addressing these provocative points (the knight never has to tolerate and respect an old, ugly, wife; it is never clarified whether, if *gentilesse* really is virtue, that challenges inherited status). As in the *Franklin's Tale*, after a disruption of the idea that men of honour act within a coherent and reliable code of conduct, closure is forged from the optimistic hypothesis that individual humans will act generously, willingly abjuring rights due to them. Both tales' denouements release *gentils* from consequences of their actions, basically because less privileged persons voluntarily abjure the opportunities that events – and their own cleverness – hold out to them.

Rather than knightly adventure and quests, with the romance hero's often extensive journeying and warfare across a large terrain, Chaucer's romances often centre on enclosure and restraint, situations where characters are caught between forces or duties, with no freedom to move according to personal will: Palamon, Arcite and Emily forced to submit to ruling political and cosmic powers; Dorigen, Arveragus and Custance caught in moral impasse or helpless victimhood; the Wife's crass young knight, arrested amid his self-directed *aventure* and forced into self-restraint and reform – Chaucer's gender-centred version of a 'penitential knight' romance – and Canace's falcon, first bullied and then enclosed, for her own good, in a decorative cage. *Troilus* too – far more than its source, and far more than contemporary interest in aristocratic privacy fully explains (though that is certainly an important element) – depicts an internal emotional drama, located and captive within a sequence of enclosed spaces: little rooms, walled gardens, curtained beds, a parliament chamber and a besieged city. Its central depiction of happy love (Books III and IV) begins with entry into a private bedroom and ends with exit from one. Troilus' ultimate perception is of human experience itself as an enclosed place, this little spot of earth (*Troilus* V 1815–16), encircled by sea. The *Legend* stories climax in situations where their protagonists have no room for

[22] 'De Paupertate Christi', *Wyclif's Latin Works: Opera Minora*, ed. Johann Loserth (London, 1913), pp. 19–73.

manoeuvre except death; Custance and Griselda have imposed on them events that deny them free will, and their strength is to endure virtuously. This perception of life as prison or impasse recurs all over Chaucer's oeuvre, serious and comic. It might be dismissed as the limited vision of a pagan when Theseus speaks of the 'foule prisoun of this lyf' (I 3061), or the self-mockery of the hapless first-person voice, caught in the *Parliament* between alternatives, unable to move, and having to be *shoved* on into his adventure, or feeling 'walwed and ywounde' like a fish imprisoned in galantine (*To Rosamounde* 18). But the image appears too in Chaucer's writing about both moral and spiritual wisdom. In *Truth* the image is 'Forth, beste, oute of thy stal!', and 'Trouth thee shal delivere, it is no drede' (18, 21). Here virtue, loyalty and integrity can 'delivere': lead a way out from the impossible pressures of moral and career dilemmas in human society. In the *ABC* and in *Man of Law's Tale* the divine provides the ultimate safe haven for storm-tossed and otherwise helpless souls; human life as immurement in a rudderless boat or submission to tyrants' decrees are further narrative forms of Chaucer's imagery of enclosure and constraint.

Troilus

Chaucer did produce one mighty, self-standing, romance. But *Troilus* supremely illustrates his use of romance to raise philosophical questions rather than confirm chivalric ethos: here questions about free will, love, destiny and consolations or explanations for misery. It interleaves a love story drawn from Boccaccio's *Il Filostrato* with ideas from Boethius' *Consolation*, and adds a final episode, taken from Boccaccio's *Teseida*, where the hero's soul flies to the spheres, laughs at mourners down on earth, and condemns earthly desires (V 1820–5).[23]

One might rephrase that picture of the romance's design and see its philosophical challenge residing not just in using a tale of earthly love to explore transcendent ideas about the relation of this world to the next, but as provocatively transferring questions about free will and determinism out of the spheres of theology or Boethian philosophy, clerkly spheres where in Chaucer's intellectual culture they belonged, to the secular sphere of personal subjective and emotional experience. In so doing, *Troilus*, which so brilliantly captures in its style the world of delicate and evanescent feelings, sensibilities and reactions, poses the question of what value such feelings have. The narrative frequently conveys dramas of mood, its ups and downs, and the idea that the 'capacity to feel is something prized'.[24] It places within parameters of Christian and philosophical interpretations of life (and thus seriously interrogates) a human phenomenon, interior emotional consciousness, which Chaucer's age recognized as central to courtly ideas and to affective piety – and which also pervades the genre of romance – but which had not gained, particularly when allied to sexual passion, adequate discussion, or adequate discourses for discussion, within the worlds of late-medieval thought, theology and ethics.

[23] See J. M. Steadman, *Disembodied Laughter* (Berkeley, 1972).

[24] Barry Windeatt, *Troilus and Criseyde*, Oxford Guides to Chaucer (Oxford, 1992), p. 270; see his demonstration of how Chaucer extends the problem of free will to the spheres of narrative and audience, pp. 262–76.

Boethius's *Consolation of Philosophy* (written in 524) argues that random fortune and misfortune teach the need to trust only in the eternal certainties of truth and the freedoms of the mind. The chief source for the medieval idea of Fortune, it also debates fate, predestination and free will. Its consolation for adversity is that humans should turn from this world to that of the mind, that they always have free will to disregard Fortune's blows and embrace morality, rationality and spiritual ascent. It lacks – indeed avoids – any real consideration of human love, dismissing the expression of grief (the muses of tragedy) in its first scene. It does not mention God's redemptive love, though Boethius was probably Christian, but presents creation in its ordered working as expressing the love of the supreme being. Such a vision, as a kind of substitute for human desires and anguish, Chaucer's *Knight's Tale* employs both for Theseus' speech and to lead up towards the concluding marriage. Audaciously, however, in *Troilus* he quotes from one of Boethius' most august poetic expressions of this vision to praise sexual passion (III 1744–71).

Thomas Usk called Chaucer the 'noble philosophical poete', particularly because of his handling of the question of free will.[25] Chaucer's claim to that title, however, does not, I would suggest, inhere simply in his use of Troilus' story to illustrate Boethian ideas. Arguably, instead, *Troilus* raises ontological and moral questions, never resolved in the poem and perhaps unresolvable in contemporary culture, about human love and subjective personal experience. The *Consolation*'s philosophical argumentation, its bleak yet simultaneously consoling view of human experience and its griefs, depends on accepting an underlying proposition of the nullity and ontological insubstantiality of all earthly experiences, especially emotions. Much that is most powerful in Chaucer's narrative, however, strengthens our sense of the power and importance of inner, emotional experience. Many passages convey interior dramas; gesture, as Windeatt shows, constantly indicates the strength of internal feelings and reactions.[26] And the constant stress on private spaces and enclosed rooms creates an objective correlative to this insistence on the power and substantial presence of subjective experiences. Images of privacy and an enclosed subjective realm recur, and they are finally problematized in the concluding vision of the medieval geographical image of earth itself, 'This litel spot of erthe that with the se / Embraced is' (V 1815–16). They are countered by Troilus' final rational contempt for the little world of earth and for emotional experience, and also by the concluding prayer to both Trinity and Redeemer as divine images of reconciliation and union.

The narrative's previous evocation of an enclosed, discrete, interior realm of emotional subjectivity, dominating five long books of poetry, is striking in a culture whose conceptual models of interiority tend to be either as the Christian soul poised between temptation and grace, or as an arena – a psychomachia – where generic virtues and vices meet. Consequently, one of *Troilus*' genuinely original philosophical issues is the distinctly modern question of what the nature and epistemology of individual subjectivity and consciousness are. Troilus declares that the indestructible core of his inner passion, that subjective experience created at the birth of desire in Book I, will eternally survive (IV 456–76). That speech

[25] *Chaucer: The Critical Heritage*, ed. Derek Brewer, 2 vols (London, 1978), vol. 1, p. 43.

[26] Windeatt, *Troilus*, pp. 271–2.

marks a direct contradiction of core teachings in Boethius about earthly emotions. First, Boethius had claimed that nothing is real except to the mind; Troilus rejects the idea that he could merely demolish his painful love. Interior consciousness is ontologically irreducible (462–9): a challenge to Boethian tenets. Secondly, this speech takes the trope of descent to Hades, Boethius' powerful rewriting of Orpheus' descent to seek his beloved (*Consolation* III, metrum 12) as a condemnation of all attachment to earthly loves and desires, and uses it instead to assert the absolute power of Troilus' own love and desire.

Chaucer conducts here in Book IV not just a challenge to Boethius' ideas about the insubstantiality of earthly desires but implicitly also a philosophical argument about the relative degree of reality that experiences in this world have, in relation to the next world. There is an ontological issue as well as one about sexual passion. And the concentration, on so many occasions in the poem, on private rooms and private feelings has given the experience of earthly emotional consciousness a powerful palpability and force to Chaucer's readers during the long narrative – only for his death to become an occasion for expression of the opposite idea, that powerful emotion is ludicrously insubstantial, mere 'vanite' (V 1817–22).

It is not in dispute that Chaucer shapes *Troilus* to exemplify Fortune's power: its five-book structure (like the *Consolation*'s), with the middle book presenting the lovers' brief happiness on top of Fortune's wheel, is just one indication of this. And the concluding declarations, both Boethian and Christian, propose in tones of certitude that humans can avoid emotional pain and intellectual folly by seeing all earthly emotional desires as nugatory and contemptible. Yet the poem's writing seems designed more to raise discussion than teach and lead toward that certitude. The disjunction between the writing in the centre of this romance and the closure is all the sharper because of the explicit philosophical and religious concluding statements, rather than a simple happy ending. And here the emotional values of the centre of the narrative are the intellectually challenging element that Chaucer's closure does not adequately address. Meaning in literature lies in how we travel as much as where we arrive. *Troilus* uses five long books to build an experience that Chaucer's art renders challengingly powerful: as a subject calling for readers to take it seriously, and one embodying elements of morality and quasi-spiritual significance (and also chivalric ideals). In contrast, its final stanzas are dismissive of emotional consciousness – affect – in terms that seem less than adequate, at one point simply condemning what the poem has presented because of its pagan setting (V 1849–50).

The preceding narrative, however, is profoundly dialectic. Provocatively it describes sexual passion in religious language. Book III hymns Love, as Venus, as the 'Plesauce of love', but also as the Christian God himself (or perhaps more precisely his love permeating and creating Nature): 'God loveth, and to love wol nought werne' (III 1–3, 4, 12). Later the lovers' joy lying in bed produces references to 'God' as the giver of such bliss: for instance, Troilus thanks God 'of his grace' (1349), the narrative voice declares a wish to have bought such a 'blisful nyght' or the smallest of their joys, with his soul (1317–20); women are bidden 'For love of God' to emulate Criseyde embracing her lover (1224). Book III challenges readers with three highly poetic speeches which in their Chaucerian contexts identify Troilus' passion with the divine love that creates and sustains the world and offers grace to sinners: they are Troilus' hymns at 1254–74 and 1744–71 (the latter directly translated from Boethius), and a prayer based on a prayer by Dante to Mary at 1261–7. The first of these is particularly daring, addressing a power, 'O Love, O Charite', which is described simultaneously in words that convey both pagan and Christian ideas of deity: this is Cupid / Amor, the son of Citherea (Venus), yet also 'Benigne Love, thou holy bond of thynges' whose 'grace' passes the deserts of suppliants, vocabulary that irresistibly suggests Christian theology too.

In weighing the import of Christian discourses in *Troilus* it is surely important for critics to ponder the fact that, against all that seems to invite a consideration of *Troilus and Criseyde* in relation to Christian perspectives, Chaucer himself in his *Retraction* grouped the poem among his 'giltes': dialectic to the end, he groups it with the tales of Canterbury that 'sownen unto synne' and his 'leccherous' lays (X 1085).

For some critics, despite its dialectic mode, *Troilus* teaches that to dignify and prize sexual love is false, foolish and unchristian (Robertson calls Troilus' love 'idolatry'[27]): in short, that the whole long poem should be interpreted from the perspective in its final stanza, 'Lo here, thise wrecched worldes appetities'.[28] Other critics see separation between the attitudes of a fictionalized narrator, naively endorsing Troilus' own reverence for emotional experience, and the final condemnation, which they identify as Chaucer's own judgement.[29] Such interpretations, though rendering more consistent a poem whose presentation of love otherwise points in incompatible directions, raise enormous questions. Why should Chaucer labour through five long books to render so forceful and empathetic experiences which are to be dismissed as nugatory and derisory? Why create an elaborately misleading narrative voice and give it sublime poetry? Like the *Canterbury Tales Retraction*, the very abruptness of the ending, the disjunction between it and much of the preceding writing, perhaps has the effect of leaving disparate worldviews intact, likewise the ontological and ethical problems their presence raises. Barry Windeatt's subtle and even-handed 1992 study[30] gives full weight to the diverse themes and implications in Chaucer's poem and deftly quotes Boethius himself on what Windeatt characterizes as the 'openness' of its ending: 'of thing that ben withouten ende to thynges that han ende may be makid no comparysoun' (*Boece*, ii, pr. 7, 106–9). And those two observations together, by Windeatt and Boethius, though not, I think, tending to the same view of earthly experience, seem both to acknowledge the decisive authority of Chaucer's final appeal to the infinite divine love and yet recognize that such a perspective cannot provide terms for evaluating subjectivity and passion as existential concepts in time.

Boethius' *Consolation*, written in alternating prose and verse, is itself a text poised between the explanations poetry gives and those which philosophy gives. It is also an encounter between Christianity and pre-Christian, philosophical tradition. No wonder its translator, Chaucer, draws on it frequently in his probing,

27 D. W. Robertson Jr, *A Preface to Chaucer: Studies in Medieval Perspectives* (Princeton, 1962), p. 499.

28 For example Robertson, 'Chaucerian Tragedy' (repr. in *Chaucer Criticism*, ed. Richard J. Schoeck and Jerome Taylor, 2 vols (Notre Dame, 1961), vol. I, pp. 86–121).

29 For example Robert Jordan, *Chaucer and the Shape of Creation* (Cambridge, MA, 1962).

30 Windeatt, *Troilus*, 270–3.

speculative, romances. Yet, given Chaucer's romances' tendency to allow questions and disparities to co-exist with the expression of certainties, with regard to both chivalric and religious worldviews, it is not surprising that passages conveying transcendental philosophy should co-exist provocatively with the celebration of earthly love. Interpretations seeking in *Troilus*' final stanzas a consistent demolition of what went before ignore multivalences in the final stanzas themselves. For instance, after condemning 'payens corsed olde rites', Chaucer proudly announces 'Lo here, the forme of olde clerkis speche / In poetrie' (V 1854–5). Like his valedictory request for his own poem to 'kis the steppes' where Virgil, Ovid, Homer, Lucan and Statius process (1791–2), this suggests pride in his writing's intellectual and poetic affinities with the masters of pagan antiquity.[31] The final stanzas' multiplicities include conflicting views of heaven: first, appropriate for a classical pagan, appears the rational ascent of a disembodied mind to the spheres, with dualistic rejection of all embodied experience; but secondly a promise and a prayer that recognize the Christian model of a deity who is engaged with this world and humans, as loving Saviour.

Closure, of course, is the lie narrative tells. Experience is something else. It is no condemnation of the matter of Chaucer that it boldly raises questions – often born before Christianity, yet of importance to fourteenth-century Christians, and often involving conundrums Chaucer's age found it hard to articulate or conceptualize – to which it fails to give adequate answers, preferring to tie up his romances instead with narrative types of resolution or declarations of divine transcendence. The *Canterbury Tales*' own ending, not with a narrative closure – whether arrival at the shrine or return to the Tabard – but with two combative statements, the *Parson's Tale* and *Retraction*, about challenges lying beyond the realm of fiction (challenges of moral conduct and the soul's destiny), seems further proof of Chaucer's awareness of tension between narrative models of life and other models, philosophical or religious, that turn human minds back either towards society or heaven: duty towards neighbour or God. The philosophical questions whose disruptive tendencies are central to the matter of Chaucer lead, in the *Tales*, towards the rejection of all fictional narrative, 'fable', by the Parson.

[31] Helen Cooper demonstrates the serious assertion of the modern poet as successor to virtuous pagans in Chaucer's words, 'After Chaucer', *Studies in the Age of Chaucer* 25 (2003), 1–25, p. 16.

7

Mary, Sanctity and Prayers to Saints: Chaucer and Late-Medieval Piety

SHERRY REAMES

REMINDERS OF THE CULT OF SAINTS were omnipresent in Chaucer's society.[1] Saints' days far outnumbered other kinds of holidays, and churches celebrated the major ones with processions to an altar with the saint's image or relics, special hymns in the saint's honour and readings about the saint's life. These occasions were so embedded in the culture that both ecclesiastical and secular documents habitually dated events in terms of the nearest saint's day instead of giving the month and numerical day. Carved and painted images of the saints were everywhere, too – present not only in churches and private homes but even in secular public contexts like city gates – inviting the faithful to remember them and pay them homage. Modern readers, especially those of us from non-Catholic backgrounds, are often inclined to envision Chaucer as sceptically detached from all such manifestations of late-medieval piety. Given his satire against corruptions in the Church and his austerely reformist portrayal of the good Parson, we may even expect to find him agreeing with the followers of Wyclif, who urged the faithful to pray directly to God rather than any saint, condemned the veneration of relics and images as idolatrous and regarded the retelling of most saints' legends as a waste of time, or worse, because it distracted attention from sound, Bible-centred teaching.[2] Chaucer's actual treatment of these issues, however, is surprisingly nuanced.

Even the *Pardoner's Tale*, which vividly demonstrates the ways in which unscrupulous churchmen could exploit an ignorant laity's trust in the power of relics, does not quite close down the hope that the genuine relics of a saint might heal bodies and souls. The *Pardoner's Epilogue* not only ends on a charitable note, with the Pardoner being forgiven and accepted back into the group of pilgrims, but also makes two surprising allusions to specific relics and posthumous miracles of Thomas Becket which reinforce the implicit message that the pilgrimage itself is

[1] 'Cult' in this sense means 'veneration' or 'devotion', without the connotations of dangerous excess that 'cult' often has in modern English. The medieval Church defined saints as those who had lived and died with such exemplary holiness that believers could safely assume their souls were already with God in heaven, able to intercede on behalf of those who prayed to them. See Bernard Hamilton, *Religion in the Medieval West* (London, 1986), pp. 124–6.

[2] Anne Hudson summarizes the positions taken on these issues by Wyclif and his followers, *The Premature Reformation: Wycliffite Texts and Lollard History* (Oxford, 1988), pp. 301–9, 311–13. For a more in-depth discussion of their thinking about images in particular, see Margaret Aston, *Lollards and Reformers: Images and Literacy in Late Medieval Religion* (London, 1984), pp. 135–92.

worth making. When the Host angrily protests against the Pardoner's sales pitch for his fraudulent relics, knowledgeable medieval audiences would have recognized a parodic reference to the worn and filthy haircloth breeches, prominently exhibited at Canterbury, which showed that Becket had secretly been mortifying his flesh for years before his murder:

> 'Thou woldest make me kisse thyn olde breech,
> And swere it were a relyk of a seint,
> Though it were with thy fundement depeint!' (VI 948–50)

Although the image seems disgusting, it suggests the great contrast with the Pardoner's fraudulent relics: Becket's underwear was actually precious because it testified to the genuineness of his sanctity. Chaucer's medieval readers would also have recognized the Becket allusion in the Host's next crude insult to the Pardoner:

> 'I wolde I hadde thy coillons in myn hond
> In stide of relikes or of seintuarie,
> Lat kutte hem of, I wol thee helpe hem carie.' (VI 952–4)

Here the Host's brutal words obviously echo the narrator's comment in the *General Prologue* that the Pardoner seemed to be a eunuch (I 691), and they also recall the extraordinary miracle stories, memorialized in the breviary office for Thomas's feast days and in some of the cathedral windows at Canterbury, which claimed that several castrated men had actually had their testicles restored when they made pilgrimages to Thomas's shrine.[3] Even as the Host is verbally abusing the Pardoner, then, his words paradoxically suggest that there is still hope for a reprobate like the Pardoner (since God's power to redeem and heal is greater than the human power to do harm) and that his healing might occur at Becket's shrine (since God often works through genuine saints).

As with the Pardoner, so elsewhere in his writings, Chaucer offers both carefully qualified endorsements of devotion to saints and warnings about the potential for abuses in this area. Besides showing considerable knowledge of the traditions surrounding individual saints, he explicitly affirms his own authorship of 'legendes of seintes', including them in his *Retraction* alongside 'omelies, and moralitee, and devocioun' in the short list of works that he is glad rather than repentant to have written. On the other hand, he tends to treat saints' cults and legends very selectively – implicitly endorsing some uses of saints' names (but not others), some kinds of prayer to saints (but not others), some definitions of sanctity (but not others). Since full discussion of all his allusions to saints would require far more space than I have, the remainder of this essay will focus on a few key aspects of his practice, with suggestions for further reading.

[3] For English translations of these tales, see Edwin A. Abbott, *St Thomas of Canterbury: His Death and Miracles*, 2 vols. (London, 1898), vol. II, pp. 80–107. The related chant text is the eleventh responsory at Matins in the standard monastic version of the Office for St Thomas, or the eighth responsory in the Sarum version: 'Novis fulget / Thomas miraculis; / membris donat / castratos masculis, / Ornat visu / privatos oculis' (Thomas shines with extraordinary miracles: he gives genitalia to castrated men, he provides sight to those deprived of eyes). Three of the five window panels illustrating one of these stories are reproduced by Madeline Caviness, *Early Stained Glass of Canterbury Cathedral, c. 1175–1220* (Princeton, 1977), plate 167.

Brief Invocations of Saints in the Canterbury Tales

Modern students are sometimes taken aback by the frequency in the *Canterbury Tales* of oaths, curses, prayers for help and other invocations of the sacred, often in profane contexts (see Stephen Knight's examination of oaths in the first two fabliau tales, pp. 43, 47–8). The names and attributes of God and Jesus Christ are invoked by far the most often, but Chaucer's characters also call on a variety of saints, some of them so beautifully matched to the occasion that many studies of these references have focused narrowly on the appropriateness of the chosen saint.[4] Also interesting, however, are the ways in which Chaucer uses invocations of saints and other sacred entities to enrich the characterization of his speakers, heightening the drama of the moment or (more often) sharpening the satire.

Chaucer's satirical use of such invocations is especially clear when the speaker is obviously trying to deceive. For example, Chaucer exposes the shameless hypocrisy of the monk in the *Shipman's Tale* by having him swear in quick succession by God, two saints appropriate to the French setting and his profession as a monk that he is telling the truth as he starts to seduce his friend's wife, betray her husband and violate his own vow of celibacy at the same time (VII 148–57). The false canon in the *Canon's Yeoman's Tale* continually calls God as his witness while he is swindling the gullible priest and crowns his exhibition of impenitent deceit with an oath by St Giles, whose name in Middle English puns on the noun *gile* ('guile, treachery'): 'For of you have I pitee, by Seint Gile!' (VIII 1185).[5] In other cases Chaucer uses incongruously timed oaths to call attention to moral issues of which the speakers themselves seem unaware. In the *Friar's Tale*, for example, when the greedy Summoner refuses to have mercy on the poor old widow, he swears 'by the sweete Seinte Anne' (of all saints) to seize one of her few valuable possessions unless she pays the amount that he pretends she owes him (III 1613–17). In the *Miller's Tale* Alison invokes St Thomas Becket to witness her promise to have sex with Nicholas as soon as she finds the opportunity (I 3291–3). In the *Reeve's Tale* Aleyn invokes St James to witness his nasty boast about having 'swyved the milleres doghter' three times that night (I 4262–7).

Besides hypocrites and morally obtuse speakers who invoke the saints when up to no good, some sincere but misguided prayers also come in for satirical attention in the *Canterbury Tales.* Thus, to cite the most conspicuous example, Chaucer sums up the small-minded and superstitious piety of old John in the *Miller's Tale* by having him respond to an apparent emergency by immediately calling for help to St Frideswide, patron saint of Oxford, his home town (I 3449), and then – after pausing to congratulate himself on his own ignorance, which he considers his saving grace – recite a nonsensical charm that will supposedly confer on his household the protection of Jesus Christ, St Benedict, a mysterious entity called 'the white pater-noster' and the equally imaginary sister of St Peter (3480–6). There is a similar masterstroke of characterization in the *Reeve's Tale*, when the

4 Ann S. Haskell, *Essays on Chaucer's Saints* (The Hague, 1976), includes St Nicholas, St Joce, St Loy, the Pardoner's 'St Ronyan', and the Host's 'precious corpus Madrian'; Glending Olson, 'On the Significance of Saint Simon in the *Summoner's Tale*', *The Chaucer Review* 33 (1998), 60–5; Robert Boenig, 'Chaucer and St Kenelm', *Neophilologus* 84 (2000), 157–64.

5 See Ann S. Haskell, 'The St Giles Oath in the *Canon's Yeoman's Tale*', *The Chaucer Review* 7 (1973), 221–6.

ostentatiously religious wife of Symkyn the miller wakes up in the dark, startled and confused by the fighting around her bed, and spontaneously calls for help first to the 'hooly croys of Bromeholm', a relic famous in East Anglia for its purported powers, and second – apparently recalling her convent education – to God, in Latin: '*In manus tuas*! Lord, to thee I calle!'(I 4286–7).[6]

It is worth pausing to notice the complexity of the satirical targets in the passages just cited. Chaucer seems to have been amused by provincial loyalties to local saints and relics, but he holds them up for ridicule only when they are combined with pretension.[7] He does not suggest that there is anything inherently ridiculous about seeking help from a saint or even a relic. Significantly enough, however, when Chaucer wants to present an unambiguously solemn and trustworthy vow, he virtually always has the speaker swear by God or Jesus rather than a mere saint.[8] The only clear exception I have found occurs in the *Friar's Tale*, when the old widow invokes the Virgin Mary to witness that she is telling the truth about her poverty (III 1604–7), as she has earlier invoked Jesus (1590–2). The same pattern seems to hold for serious blessings and prayers for help. The most exemplary figures in the *Canterbury Tales* – and even less exemplary ones, in their better moments – address their prayers almost uniformly either to Jesus, to God the Father or to God's nearest human relative, the Virgin Mary.[9] Despite all Chaucer's references to lesser saints, that is, the Virgin Mary occupies a unique position in his work as the only saint whose cult seems to be held up for actual imitation. It does not necessarily follow, of course, that Chaucer endorses every contemporary form of devotion to Mary.[10] Just as his characters sometimes misuse

[6] The joke is enhanced by her choice of the particular Latin phrase 'in manus tuas', a quotation from Psalm 30/31 familiar to Chaucer's audience as the opening words of Christ's final utterance before he died (Luke 23: 46) and as part of the Office of the Dead. The miller's wife obviously has an inflated view of the danger she is in at this moment, and perhaps also of her own importance in the scheme of things.

[7] The Prioress's closing prayer to young St Hugh of Lincoln might be another instance of conspicuously misguided devotion, but her tale demands extended analysis before deciding why Chaucer had her pray to this minor and questionable saint. Chaucer may have been satirizing her notion of piety or raising more substantive questions by having her conclude with emphatic invocation of the supposedly martyred child whose killing launched the first anti-Jewish pogrom in England. See esp. Gavin Langmuir, 'The Knight's Tale of Young Hugh of Lincoln', *Speculum* 47 (1972), 459–82.

[8] For example Alla solemnly invokes both God 'and his halwes brighte' to support his explanation that he did not give the order to exile Custance and their son (II 1060–4); Griselda reaffirms her promises to Walter with oaths to God at least twice (IV 505–6, 820–6); Walter solemnly swears his veracity by God when he finally tells her the truth (IV 1062–4). Dorigen swears her intention to remain faithful by 'thilke God that yaf me soule and lyf' (V 983–4) and 'by heighe God above' (V 989). The Canon's Yeoman invokes God to witness his veracity (VIII 740–1, 865–7, and *passim*).

[9] The Parson prays to Jesus before starting his tale, asking for 'wit' to show his listeners the way to the heavenly Jerusalem (X 48–51). Custance prays to the Cross of Christ (II 449–62), God and Mary (639–44), and Mary alone (841–54). Griselda prays to Jesus, committing her child to his care (V 556–60). Most of the *Second Nun's Prologue* consists of an extended prayer to Mary. St Cecilia prays to God (VIII 126, 135–7), and 'hevene king' (542–6). Pope Urban prays to Jesus (191–9). Dorigen prays to God, begging him to keep her husband safe (V 865–93). In his one moment of apparently genuine sincerity, the Pardoner urges the other pilgrims to seek the best pardon, that of 'Jhesu Crist, that is oure soules leche' (VI 916–18). In the serious final lines of his tale, the Friar tells listeners to pray to Jesus, seeking grace to resist the devil's influence (III 1653–62). The preceding list excludes the prayers in the *Prioress's Prologue and Tale* because I have serious doubts (as suggested in note 10) that Chaucer intended the piety of the Prioress to be seen as exemplary.

[10] Critics who appreciate the traces of traditional Catholic piety in Chaucer sometimes overstate their case, as if Chaucer (having shown himself to be a good Catholic after all) could not possibly have made discriminations in this area. Thus, for example, Sister M. Madeleva uncritically accepts all the

the name of God, they may invoke Mary for unworthy reasons or pray to her in ways that Chaucer himself considers misguided. If we read closely, in fact, we will see that Chaucer gives us some criteria for distinguishing questionable expressions of Marian piety from more valid ones.

Chaucer's Extended Prayers to the Virgin Mary

The extended prayers to Mary in Chaucer's works comprise most of the *Prioress's Prologue*, most of the *Second Nun's Prologue*, the self-standing prayer generally known as Chaucer's *ABC*, and a prayer spoken by Custance in the *Man of Law's Tale*. Both admirers and detractors of these prayers have usually been inclined to emphasize what they seem to have in common – including the fact that they are all written in stanzaic forms and rather ceremonious language, with echoes of the liturgy – and the possibility that Chaucer composed them all as specifically feminine expressions of piety. The supposed gender link is actually quite tenuous, since for the *ABC* it rests entirely on a note added to its title in Speght's 1602 edition, some two hundred years after Chaucer's death: 'made, as some say, at the request of Blanche Duchess of Lancaster, as praier for her privat use, being a woman in her religion very devout'.[11] And in all probability Chaucer wrote both the prologue and the tale of the Second Nun for some earlier occasion and assigned them to the Second Nun as an afterthought.[12] The supposed common link with women remains an attractive idea, however, since it allows modern critics to find potentially feminist and progressive implications in these Marian prayers or to distance them from Chaucer's own beliefs, or both.[13] Critics who dislike their stylistic elaborateness have even argued that such artifice appealed specifically to women in Chaucer's time and that he (like the Parson, the Wycliffites and the critics themselves) preferred simpler expressions of faith.[14]

Instead of looking for evidence of either a feminist Chaucer or one who anticipated modern tastes in religious language, I would suggest that we need first to

prayers in Chaucer's works as 'evidences of a . . . sincere piety and devotion' that remained consistent throughout his life: *A Lost Language and Other Essays on Chaucer* (New York, 1951), p. 26. Hardy Long Frank adopts a similarly undiscriminating stance, contending in effect that modern readers must accept every aspect of both the Prioress's own personality and her tale that can be linked to the medieval cult of Mary: 'Chaucer's Prioress and the Blessed Virgin', *The Chaucer Review* 3 (1979), 346–62. Some critics distrustful of Marian piety and the Prioress in particular have taken all-or-nothing positions on the opposite side, concluding on very little evidence that Chaucer must have felt as they do about the whole tradition.

11 *Riverside Chaucer*, p. 1076.

12 The best evidence that the *Second Nun's Tale* predates the *Canterbury Tales* comes from Chaucer's list of his works in the *Legend* (F 426). The *Second Nun's Prologue* also bespeaks an occasion other than the Canterbury pilgrimage: it does nothing to identify the narrator as anyone other than Chaucer himself and refers to the tale as a text the narrator has already written (VIII 24–6, 78–84).

13 Carolyn P. Collette interprets the *Prioress's Prologue* and *Second Nun's Prologue* as women's utterances, empowered and authorized by the example of Mary but also threatened by authorities who want to silence such prophetic voices, 'Chaucer's Discourse of Mariology: Gaining the Right to Speak', *Art and Context in Late Middle English Narrative*, ed. Robert R. Edwards (Woodbridge, 1994), pp. 127–47.

14 Thus Alfred David lumps together the *ABC*, the *Prioress's Prologue and Tale* and the Prioress's portrait, as revealing 'a sentimentalized religiosity' that, although 'still dressed in the forms and symbols of orthodox Christianity . . . worships beauty as a version of truth': 'An ABC to the Style of the Prioress', *Acts of Interpretation: The Text in Its Contexts 700–1600*, ed. Mary J. Carruthers and Elizabeth D. Kirk (Norman, OK, 1982), pp. 147–57, at p. 157.

understand and evaluate the specific religious content of these Marian prayers. The prayer at the end of Chaucer's *Retraction* provides a helpful starting point, since it reminds us of the two most basic criteria that critical observers have used, in both medieval and modern times, to evaluate examples of Marian piety. Doctrinally, the *Retraction* elevates Mary above other saints but avoids the theological error of setting her in competition with the Trinity, as if she were a goddess, a supernatural being with power all her own.[15] Although this prayer asks her and the other saints for grace, it clearly subordinates and connects them all to Christ, to whom it refers as the true source of all grace: the sole redeemer, whose blood saved humankind, and the ultimate king, priest, and judge:

> [for the saints' legends and other writings not retracted] thanke I oure Lord Jhesu Crist and his blisful Mooder, and alle the seintes of hevene, bisekynge hem that they from hennesforth unto my lyves ende sende me grace to biwayle my giltes and to studie to the salvacioun of my soule, and graunte me grace of verray penitence, confessioun and satisfaccioun to doon in this present lyf, thurgh the benigne grace of hym that is kyng of kynges and preest over alle preestes, that boghte us with the precious blood of his herte, so that I may be oon of hem at the day of doom that shulle be saved. (X 1090)

Morally, this petitioner resists the temptation to presume too much on the mercy of Christ and the saints.[16] Instead of seeking an easier path to heaven, his prayer accepts the full rigour and discipline of the late-medieval penitential system (on which the Parson has of course just expounded at length) and asks for the grace necessary to fulfil all its demands in this life. Although it would be unreasonable to expect every valid prayer to be so austerely focused on penitence and on the ultimate issues of death and judgment, the prayer in Chaucer's *Retraction* serves to remind us of the fundamental Catholic principle that grace is given in order to evoke and assist human effort, not cancel out the need for it.

Measured against these criteria, the best of the extended Marian prayers composed by Chaucer is the one assigned to the Second Nun; the most deficient, the prayer of the Prioress. On the surface these two look very similar. They do not just use similar vocabulary and develop the same standard themes (praise of the Virgin, humble supplication before her, confession of the petitioner's own

[15] Jaroslav Pelikan summarizes the theologically sound position in the Middle Ages (and since): 'The countervailing force against what the Protestant Reformation was to construe as Mariolatry . . . was the recognition that [Mary] had been "exalted through [her] omnipotent Son, for the sake of [her] glorious Son, by [her] blessed Son", as Anselm put it in one of his prayers. It was, moreover, a consensus that Mary had been saved by Christ': *Mary through the Centuries: Her Place in the History of Culture* (New Haven, 1996), p. 133. Other historians of doctrine have suggested asking one basic question: whether or not the devotion to Mary leads the believer beyond Mary, to Christ; see, for example, Thomas O'Meara, *Mary in Protestant and Catholic Theology* (New York, 1966), p. 90.

[16] The central moral danger here is a kind of escapism, a longing for comfort and reassurance without concomitant responsibility. René Laurentin identifies the source of the problem as a twisted sense of Mary's maternal care that visualizes her only as a source of security: *Mary's Place in the Church*, trans. I. Pidoux (London, 1965), p. 108. As an antidote, Graef offers the reminder that '[Mary] is not only the never-failing help of Christians, she is also to be their example, and her assistance depends on men's conduct': Hilda Graef, 'Devotion to Our Lady', *Twentieth-Century Encyclopedia of Catholicism*, vol. 45 (New York, 1963), p. 44. Nor is this just a modern idea: Graef quotes a famous sermon by Bernard of Clairvaux: 'In dangers, in anxiety, in doubt, think of Mary, call upon Mary. Let her name not leave your lips nor your heart, and that you may receive the help of her prayer, do not cease to follow the example of her conduct', pp. 43–4.

inadequacy, and pleas for her help); more surprisingly, each includes some lines on Mary's virtues based on the same source and saying almost exactly the same thing.[17] When Chaucer placed both these prayers in prologues spoken by nuns, he clearly signalled his intention that readers should compare them, and it seems safe to assume that he wanted us to notice how different they are in religious content.

The theological core of the *Second Nun's Prologue* is provided by two stanzas on the Incarnation (VIII 36–49). This passage begins with familiar paradoxes about Mary, addressing her first as both 'Mayde and Mooder' and 'doghter of thy Sone', and describing her a few lines later as simultaneously 'humble and heigh over every creature' (39). Even when praising Mary as the pinnacle of human goodness, however, this prayer also emphasizes God's initiative both in choosing her (38) and in humbly descending to form the physical child in her womb: 'Thow nobledest so ferforth our nature, / That no desdeyn the Makere hadde of kynde / His Sone in blood and flessh to clothe and wynde' (40–2). And the poetically powerful stanza that follows celebrates the transcendent glory of God far more than it celebrates the creaturely greatness of Mary:

> Withinne the cloistre blisful of thy sydis
> Took mannes shap the eterneel love and pees,
> That of the tryne compas lord and gyde is,
> Whom erthe and see and hevene out of relees
> Ay heryen; and thou, Virgine wemmelees,
> Baar of thy body – and dweltest mayden pure –
> The Creatour of every creature. (43–9)[18]

The *Prioress's Prologue* includes a stanza on the Incarnation which begins with the same paradoxes and has also been praised for its eloquence.[19] This stanza, however, is far more exclamatory and less coherent than the corresponding passage in the *Second Nun's Prologue*, and it seems to be centred almost exclusively on Mary herself:

> O mooder Mayde, O mayde Mooder free!
> O bussh unbrent, brennynge in Moyses sighte,
> That ravyshedest doun fro the Deitee,
> Thurgh thyn humblesse, the Goost that in th'alighte,
> Of whos vertu, whan he thyn herte lighte,
> Conceyved was the Fadres sapience.
> Help me to telle it in thy reverence! (VII 467–73)

From a theological perspective the most noteworthy points here are the surprising verb 'ravyshedest' (469), which figuratively gives Mary the principal, active role in the Incarnation, as if God wanted to resist but was overcome by her attractions,

[17] The lines are VII 474–80 and VIII 50–6, both paraphrasing the same passage from Dante (see next note).

[18] The major sources behind this portion of the Prologue are Dante's prayer to the Virgin, *Paradiso* canto XXXIII (for lines 43–7 in particular), and Fortunatus' famous hymn 'Quem terra': for texts of both see *Sources and Analogues of the Canterbury Tales*, ed. Robert M. Correale and Mary Hamel, 2 vols (Cambridge, 2002, 2006), vol. I, pp. 500–3. On the traditions at work in Dante's prayer, see Erich Auerbach, 'Dante's Prayer to the Virgin (*Paradiso*, XXXIII) and Earlier Eulogies', *Romance Philology* 3 (1949–50), 1–26.

[19] Beverly Boyd observes that 'critical opinion has been consistently lavish', Introduction, Variorum Edition of the *Prioress's Tale* (Norman, OK, 1987), pp. 3–4.

and the ambiguity of 'whos vertu' (471), which ought theologically to refer to the power of the Holy Spirit but could be another reference to Mary's virtue.[20] Indeed, although the *Prioress's Prologue* actually begins with an invocation to God (453–9), it seems to get sidetracked by the first reference to Mary ('the white lylye flour / Which that the bar, and is a mayde alway', 461–2) and rarely mentions any member of the Trinity again, except as an afterthought (as in 466) or in an apparently passive relationship to the activity of Mary (as in 469, 472, and 480).[21]

The prayers assigned to the Second Nun and the Prioress also differ rather profoundly in their moral content. Each petitioner expresses a great sense of inadequacy, but not for the same reasons. In the *Second Nun's Prologue* the speaker repeatedly laments her (or his) tendency to sin, evoking the common plight of humanity since the Fall by calling herself (or himself) a 'flemed wrecche [banished exile] in this desert of galle' (58) and an 'unworthy sone of Eve' (62), and sadly confesses the way her/his soul is 'troubled . . . by the contagioun / Of my body, and also by the wighte [weight] / Of erthely lust and fals affeccioun' (72–4). When this petitioner calls on Mary for help in the 'werk' she/he is now undertaking, then, the work in question is not just retelling the saint's life that will follow, but (as in Chaucer's *Retraction*) the life-long human struggle against sin and the prospect of hell:

> And, for that feith is deed withouten werkis,
> So for to werken yif me wit and space,
> That I be quit fro thennes that most derk is! (64–6)

In the *Prioress's Prologue*, on the other hand, there is no mention of sin, repentance or moral struggle. In fact, nothing more seems to be at stake than the quality of the petitioner's literary performance in the Virgin's honour. Although she abases herself before the Virgin and seeks her help, the only kind of inadequacy she confesses is her own ignorance, and she seeks to excuse herself for that by claiming to be as helpless as an infant:

> 'My konnyng is so wayk, O blisful Queene,
> For to declare thy grete worthynesse
> That I ne may the weighte nat susteene:
> But as a child of twelf month oold, or lesse,
> That kan unnethes any word expresse,
> Right so fare I, and therfore I you preye,
> Gydeth my song that I shal of yow seye.' (481–7)

The Prioress will go on to tell a Marian miracle story of the kind which Lee Patterson has deplored because they 'celebrate not just prayer but prayer as a kind of charm', thus encouraging the simplistic idea that devotees of Mary can rely on a

[20] My reading of the Prioress's prayer is particularly indebted to the trenchant analysis by Marsha L. Dutton, 'Chaucer's Two Nuns', *Monasteries and Society in Medieval Britain: Proceedings of the 1994 Harlaxton Symposium*, ed. Benjamin Thompson, Harlaxton Medieval Studies VI (Stamford, 1999), 296–311. Also illuminating is Louise O. Fradenburg's critique of this prayer, 'Criticism, Anti-Semitism and the Prioress's Tale', *Exemplaria* 1 (1989), 69–115, pp. 90–5.

[21] Dutton, 'Two Nuns', pp. 302–3. Some critics find feminist implications in the Prioress's exaltation of Mary in this prayer, but such interpretations are both profoundly ahistorical and theologically naive. To promote a creature above the Creator is idolatry, not feminism.

quasi-magical set of words in her honour to save them. Patterson further suggests that the medieval cult of Mary in general 'foster[ed] a lack of spiritual struggle by short-circuiting the inwardness and penitential self-examination of true religious reformation'.[22] This analysis seems quite applicable to the Prioress's own prayer, as well as the tale she tells, but I would argue that Chaucer presents the Prioress as an extreme case, not a typical one. His remaining Marian prayers affirm the need for self-examination and spiritual struggle, and their theology is also less problematic than the Prioress's, although they do not reach the theological heights of the *Second Nun's Prologue*.

The *ABC* used to be dismissed as a very early work (because Speght's note would require it to be dated before the death of Blanche of Lancaster in 1369) and a mere translation of an alphabetical prayer from Guillaume de Deguileville's *Pèlerinage de la Vie Humaine*. This prayer also poses an unusual challenge for critics because it seems both repetitive and disjointed, with its 23 stanzas (in Chaucer's version) given unity and order only by the successive letters of the alphabet. In recent years, however, more appreciative studies have called attention to the mature artistry of Chaucer's style in the *ABC.* and the significant ways in which he changed his French source as he adapted it.[23] Georgia Ronan Crampton characterizes it as 'a poem which not by originality but by thoroughness of participation in its milieu bears the same relation to Marian penitential lyrics as *Troilus and Criseyde* does to medieval romance'.[24] Building on the work of George B. Pace, Crampton provides another valuable key to understanding the form of the *ABC* by pointing out its resemblances to the psalms which oscillate between praising God, confessing the speaker's failings, and pleading for help, sometimes in alphabetically ordered verses.[25]

The penitential aspect of Chaucer's *ABC* is emphasized by its tone, which conveys noticeably more urgency and moral intensity than Deguileville's version of this prayer to Mary.[26] The petitioner repeatedly confesses his own sinfulness, even

[22] Lee Patterson, '"The Living Witnesses of Our Redemption": Martyrdom and Imitation in Chaucer's *Prioress's Tale*', *Journal of Medieval and Early Modern Studies* 31 (2001), 507–60, pp. 517, 518.

[23] *ABC*, not in the octosyllabic couplets of Chaucer's early dream visions, but decasyllabic lines and the *Monk's Tale* stanza, might more logically be dated to Chaucer's 'Italian', rather than earlier 'French period'. Its style has impressed most recent critics as fairly mature.

[24] Georgia Ronan Crampton, 'Chaucer's Singular Prayer', *Medium Ævum* 59 (1990), 191–213, pp. 192–3. See also Kay Gilligan Stevenson, 'Medieval Reading and Rewriting: The Context of Chaucer's *ABC*', *'Divers Toyes Mengled': Essays on Medieval and Renaissance Culture*, ed. Michel Bitot *et al.* (Tours, 1996), pp. 27–42; Helen Phillips, '"Almighty and al merciable queene": Marian Titles and Marian Lyrics', *Medieval Women: Texts and Contexts in Late Medieval Britain, Essays for Felicity Riddy*, ed. Jocelyn Wogan-Browne *et al.* (Turnhout, 2000), pp. 83–99, William A. Quinn, 'Chaucer's Problematic *Prière: An ABC* as Artifact and Critical Issue', *Studies in the Age of Chaucer* 23 (2001), 109–41.

[25] Crampton, 'Singular Prayer', p. 193; Crampton cites Psalm 118/119, and other abecedarian poems in the Bible: Psalms 9/10, 24/25, 36/37, 110/111, 111/112, 144/155, plus Proverbs 31: 10–31 [the praise of a good woman], Sirach 51: 13–30, Lamentations 1: 1–22 and Nahum 1: 2–8. As Crampton and Pace note, medieval translations of the Bible often had ornamental Hebrew letters to point out the abecedarian form of these poems, as do some modern Bibles; see George B. Pace, 'The Adorned Initials of Chaucer's *ABC*', *Manuscripta* 23 (1979), 88–98.

[26] Crampton (pp. 195–7) notes increased intensity; Phillips points out that many features of Chaucer's *ABC*, including 'its tone of dramatic urgency, the sense of physical movement and flight, [and] the greater emphasis on death and penitence' (p. 1) – may reflect dramatic narrative in Deguileville's *Pèlerinage*, 'Chaucer and Deguileville: The *ABC* in Context', *Medium Ævum* 62 (1993), 1–19. Stevenson observes that Chaucer reflects Deguileville's pilgrim's desperate need for aid, 'Medieval Reading', p. 33.

calls himself wicked (44) and admits that he has been living in 'filthe' (157) and deserves to be damned (for example 18–24). Although he has some moments of optimism about the possibility of being saved (for example 116–20), he always falls back into doubt and anxiety, as in:

Queen of comfort, yit whan I me bithinke
That I agilt have bothe him and thee,
And that my soule is worthi for to sinke,
Allas, I caityf, whider may I flee? (121–5)

As Crampton notes, even the end of the prayer sounds less confident than the French version, leaving the petitioner's salvation still very much in question. The 'imperfect ring closure' in the last line echoes the first line's praise of Mary as 'al merciable' but splits *merciable* in two, asserting only that heaven is open to penitents who 'ben to merci able' – that is, those who have become fit candidates for mercy.[27] Nor does this prayer minimize the difficulty of such repentance and reform. The petitioner occasionally portrays himself as a frightened and guilty child, begging Mary to intercede with his angry father:

Glorious mayde and mooder,
. . . .
Help that my Fader be not wroth with me.
Spek thou, for I ne dar not him ysee,
So have I doon in erthe, allas the while,
That certes, but if thou my socour bee,
To stink eterne he wole my gost exile. (49, 52–6)

Besides praying for Mary's pity and her protection on the day of Judgment, however, he pleads throughout the prayer for her forceful intervention in his present life, using metaphors which suggest the direness of his spiritual state. At various points he begs her to protect him from the power of the devil and his own besetting sins (7–8, 15, 47–8), correct him in preparation for the Judgment (36–40), chastize him, judge him and heal his soul (129–34), cure him of the wounds caused by sin (147–52), and teach him how to obtain her grace (155–7). His apparent desperation at times approaches the tone of Donne's 'Batter My Heart, Three-Personed God', but Chaucer's prayer sounds more universal than Donne's. He expresses not only his own need for Mary's intervention but that of 'the seed of Adam' in general (182), praising her on behalf of every sinful soul whom she hauls out of error (67–8), brings 'out of the crooked strete' (70), cures of spiritual lameness (75–6) and washes clean (177–8).[28]

From a theological perspective, the praise of Mary in the *ABC* occasionally seems rather extravagant. The most obvious example is Chaucer's bold opening line: 'Almighty and al merciable Queene'. Since only God is truly omnipotent, calling Mary 'almighty' has struck some critics as excessive, even heretical (and cannot be blamed on Deguileville, whose first stanza says no such thing).[29] Phillips,

[27] Crampton, 'Singular Prayer', pp. 194–5

[28] Crampton suggests the poem's fluctuations between 'I' and 'we' encourage readers to appropriate the prayer for themselves, p. 206; see also Quinn, 'Problematic *Prière*', p. 136.

[29] On 'almighty' see Theodor Wolpers, 'Geschichte der englischen Marienlyrik im Mittelalter', *Anglia* 69

who provides the most extensive and helpful discussion of this line, suggests its apparent heterodoxy is an isolated and puzzling anomaly in Chaucer's poem, but also takes it seriously as a 'theological mistake [that] reflects the gap between popular understanding of Mary's power and theological definitions of her power as limited and dependent'.[30] It is worth asking, however, whether Chaucer and his audience might automatically have understood 'almighty' in a relative rather than an absolute sense when it was paired with a noun that implied subordinate status, as 'queen' did. Strengthening this possibility, Nature in Chaucer's *Parliament of Fowls* is carefully described as 'vicaire of the almyghty Lord' (379) but also called 'almyghty queen' (647).

Otherwise, the most extravagant-sounding language in the *ABC* is concentrated in the L-stanza, which stresses the pains of both Christ and Mary at the Crucifixion (83) and even suggests that Mary shared in the work of redeeming mankind ('that ye bothe have bought so deere', 86). The emphasis on Mary's share in Christ's pain was traditional by Chaucer's time, but her share in the redemption was not.[31] In this same stanza Chaucer calls Mary 'thou grounde of oure substaunce' (87), a phrase that can be read as an unorthodox claim that Mary played a part in the Creation, or – in Crampton's brilliant interpretation – as a rich metaphor that simultaneously suggests the supporting ground beneath the sinner's feet, the Virgin's own origins from the same earthly clay as Adam, and 'the ground in whom Christ planted himself' (p. 201).

Despite a few extravagant-sounding lines, I would argue that Chaucer actually strengthened the doctrinal orthodoxy of Guillaume's prayer by clarifying the theological status of Mary and her relationship with Christ. For example, the sources and limits of Mary's power are more carefully defined in Chaucer's version. In the O-stanza, where Guillaume simply gave Mary the titles 'de Dieu chanceliere' and 'de graces aumosniere' (God's chancellor and almoner of grace), Chaucer explicitly assigns her the role of an intermediary and specifies that God gave her that power: 'From his ancille he made the maistresse / Of hevene and erthe, oure bille up for to beede' (107–8). Mary's role is similarly clarified in the Q-stanza, when she is sought as a 'mene' to her Son (125) rather than as a refuge in herself, and in the N-stanza, when Chaucer adds the reminder that it is as 'Cristes mooder deere' (99) that she can be considered the source of human comfort.

As he moderates the portrayal of Mary's role in the scheme of salvation, Chaucer adds important reminders that her mercy cannot be divorced from the mercy of Christ and the larger intentions of God. In the H-stanza, where Guillaume personified Christ's pity and used an involved argument to prove that the petitioner could share in its benefits, if Mary so willed, Chaucer makes it clear that Mary's role is simply that of an intercessor, for Christ has already redeemed humanity – and done it of his own free will (57–62). On three occasions where Guillaume's petitioner invoked the mercy of Mary to protect him from God or from Christ,

(1950), 1–88, p. 29; Phillips, '*ABC*'; Quinn, 'Problematic *Prière*', pp. 131–2, 134–5.

30 As Phillips puts it, 'nothing else in Chaucer's poem suggests a taste for, or influence from, eccentric theological source-texts' ('"Almighty and al merciable queene"', p. 96).

31 Stevenson, 'Medieval Reading', pp. 36–7. As Graef points out ('Devotion', p. 52), the idea that Mary shared in the redemptive work of the Crucifixion was implicitly rejected by Aquinas, but promoted by other eminent medieval churchmen, including St Bonaventure.

Chaucer's version asks for protection against the devil or sin instead.[32] Occasionally – as in the lines quoted above where the petitioner sounds like a frightened and guilty child – Mary is asked to mediate between the sinner and the Judge he is afraid to face alone; but Chaucer does not go further than that.[33] In short, he resists the most serious excesses of Marian piety found in Guillaume's prayer, and also in the *Prioress's Prologue*: the temptation to set Mary against God, to glorify her at His expense.

Custance's prayer to Mary in the *Man of Law's Tale* (II 841–54), spoken as she prepares to board the ship that will carry her and her newborn son into exile from Northumbria, is obviously meant to be exemplary, and provides an illuminating contrast with both the Prioress's prayer and the *ABC.* Unlike the more fallible petitioner in the *ABC*, Custance never even suggests the possibility of splitting Mary from Christ. In a powerful moment at the beginning of this scene, Custance explicitly accepts the exile as part of Christ's will for her, saying, 'Lord, ay welcome be thy sonde!' (826), and explains to the weeping onlookers that although she does not know how he can save her this time, she trusts him to do so:

> 'He that me kept fro the false blame
> While I was on the lond amonges yow,
> He kan me kepe from harm and eek fro shame
> In salte see, althogh I se noght how.
> As stronge as evere he was, he is yet now.
> In hym triste I, and in his mooder deere,
> That is to me my seyl and eek my steere.' (827–33)[34]

Although Mary's role naturally becomes more prominent in the two-stanza Marian prayer that follows, this prayer – unlike both nuns' prayers and the *ABC* – focuses primarily on Mary's human experience rather than her subsequent power and glory. In sharp contrast with the Prioress in particular, Custance identifies herself with the Virgin as a mother who yearns to protect her child, taking the role of the responsible and compassionate adult rather than the helpless child in the mother's arms. More unexpectedly, at this moment of crisis in her life Custance expresses compassion for Mary, recalling her suffering at the Crucifixion, and concludes that her own current plight is as nothing in comparison:

> 'thy child was on a croys yrent.
> Thy blisful eyen sawe al [thy child's] torment;
> Thanne is ther no comparison bitwene
> Thy wo and any wo man may sustene.

[32] At the end of the K-stanza, where Guillaume visualized divine justice as a weapon that would destroy him, Chaucer transfers the fear to the devil. In the L-stanza Guillaume's wording suggests that Christ is threatening to shoot an arrow at the petitioner; Chaucer changes the threat to the devil's snares. In the Z-stanza Guillaume's petitioner urged Mary to defend him, lest 'Justice' kill him; Chaucer transplants the reference to death into a discussion of Mary's power over sin.

[33] Even some of the greatest medieval theologians went that far: Graef and Pelikan cite Bernard, Anselm and Aquinas, among others, on the role of Mary as the ideal mediator between sinful human beings and their Judge, Christ ('Devotion', pp. 44–5; *Mary through the Centuries*, pp. 130–3).

[34] Custance's earlier prayer to the Cross (II 451–60) is also exemplary in its Christological content. Barbara Nolan provides a particularly helpful analysis of this prayer in 'Chaucer's Tales of Transcendence: Rhyme Royal and Christian Prayer in the *Canterbury Tales*', *Chaucer's Religious Tales*, ed. C. David Benson and Elizabeth Robertson (Cambridge, 1990), pp. 21–37.

Thow sawe thy child yslayn bifore thyne yen,
And yet now lyveth my litel child, parfay!' (845–9)

As George Keiser has noted, by rejecting the temptation to wallow in self-pity here and presumptuously draw a parallel between her own sorrows and Mary's, Custance reveals a combination of 'humility, love, and moral courage' that actually strengthens her resemblance to Mary.[35]

A subtler contribution to the moral dimension of Custance's prayer occurs a few lines earlier, when she refers to Eve, whose sin brought about the Fall of humankind and made the Crucifixion necessary:

'Mooder,' quod she, 'and mayde bright, Marie,
Sooth is that thurgh wommanes eggement
Mankynde was lorn, and damned ay to dye,
For which thy child was on a croys yrent.' (842–5)

This allusion serves in part to call readers' attention to the parallel between Eve, the archetypal sinner who caused the suffering of Christ and Mary, and Donegild, the wicked mother-in-law who is responsible for the current ordeal of Custance and her child. But Custance herself does not yet know that the order for her exile came from Donegild rather than the king. Her reference to Eve underlines the crucial point that she does not envision herself as an innocent victim like Christ or even her own child, but as an heir of Eve, a fallen human being who accepts suffering as part of her earthly lot.[36] Although this reference is gendered female, one cannot miss the resemblance to the petitioners' self-portrayals in the *Second Nun's Prologue* and the *ABC* and their common distance from the Prioress's notion of humility.

Exemplarity and Saints' Lives

Chaucer seems to present Custance's Marian prayer as a model not only for prayers addressed to saints, but also for the reading and retelling of saints' lives. Ideally, it suggests, one should emphasize the human dimensions of the saints' experience, rather than the special gifts and powers that set them apart from ordinary people, and one should find inspiration and added perspective on one's own life in the memory of the saints' virtues and the trials they endured. None of this sounds very revolutionary today, but envisioning the saints chiefly as moral exemplars was not yet common in Chaucer's time, even among the clergy[37] – and Chaucer shows an

[35] George R. Keiser, 'The Spiritual Heroism of Chaucer's Custance', Benson and Robertson, *Chaucer's Religious Tales*, pp. 121–36, p. 131.

[36] This language sounds very gender-specific, especially in connection with Custance's earlier observation about women's lot, which clearly alludes to God's punishment of Eve in Genesis 3: 16: 'Wommen are born to thraldom and penance, / And to been under mannes governance' (II 286–7). But elsewhere the tale makes her analogous with biblical figures of both genders: protected like Daniel, Jonah and the Israelites crossing the Red Sea (II 470–90), and achieving improbable victories like those of David and Judith. Thus we are prompted to see her as a symbolic representative of God's chosen people throughout the ages, or the capacity of the individual human soul for both suffering and faithfulness to God. For an in-depth exploration of religious symbols in the tale, see V. A. Kolve, *Chaucer and the Imagery of Narrative: The First Five Canterbury Tales* (Stanford, 1984), pp. 297–358.

[37] Surviving Sarum manuscripts show that liturgical reformers in England made at least one concerted

even more uncommon selectivity with regard to the kinds of saintly exemplars he endorses.

The only actual saint's legend Chaucer retells at any length is the life of St Cecilia, which became the *Second Nun's Tale*. Although Cecilia is both a virgin and a martyr, her legend is markedly less sexualized and sensational than most medieval virgin-martyr legends. The typical legend in this genre features a saint whose desire to remain a virgin is repeatedly at risk, a persecutor who either wants to marry her off or desires her for himself, and a potentially prurient interest in the saint's body, which is usually stripped naked and publicly tortured at some point in the proceedings; the Cecilia legend, however, is almost entirely free of these motifs. In fact, it dispatches the only threat to Cecilia's virginity at the start, when she converts her bridegroom to Christianity and celibacy at the same time, and it pays surprisingly little attention to her body thereafter. Instead of promoting monastic asceticism, it presents an alternative model of marriage – one in which the wife has superior wisdom and exerts a saving influence on her husband, and the marriage becomes fruitful when Cecilia and Valerian convert his brother Tiburce, who proceeds with Valerian to convert Maximus and others, adding many spiritual offspring to the family of God. As critics have sometimes noted, then, this tale can be seen as part of the 'marriage debate' in the *Canterbury Tales*. The Second Nun's narrative also fits well into the *Canterbury Tales* as a response to the *Prioress's Tale* – most obviously because the central figure here is not a helpless child but a grown-up, rational, highly articulate and fruitful female saint.[38]

Chaucer's original reasons for retelling the Cecilia legend perhaps had nothing to do with the *Canterbury Tales*. His choice of sources suggests that he was particularly interested in Cecilia's trial and the example she sets there of fearlessly proclaiming truth to authority. As I have shown elsewhere, the tale begins as a close translation of the abridged account in the *Legenda Aurea* but changes sources around line 342 (right before Tiburce's conversion), from then on closely following the liturgical abridgement used by the Roman curia and the Franciscans, which radically condenses the middle of the narrative but gives a fuller account of Cecilia's trial.[39] Significant stylistic changes also occur in the second half of the tale. Chaucer handles the rhyme royal stanza with noticeably more fluency, efficiency and effectiveness from line 342 on, suggesting that the part of the tale based on his second source was probably written a good deal later

effort in Chaucer's lifetime to replace breviary lessons based on traditional saints' legends with consistently sober, restrained lessons that emphasized the exemplary aspects of the saints' behaviour; but breviaries with more sensational, miracle-filled lessons continued to flourish, presumably because most clergy preferred them; see S. L. Reames, 'Late-Medieval Efforts at Standardization and Reform in the Sarum Lessons for Saints' Days', *Design and Distribution of Late Medieval Manuscripts in England*, ed. Margaret Connolly and Linne R. Mooney, Proceedings of the Tenth York Manuscripts Conference (York, 2008), pp. 91–117.

38 See Dutton, 'Chaucer's Two Nuns', and C. David Benson, 'The Contrasting Religious Tales of the Prioress and Second Nun', in his *Chaucer's Drama of Style: Poetic Variety and Contrast in the Canterbury Tales* (Chapel Hill, 1986), pp. 131–46.

39 Had Chaucer just wanted a briefer version than the *Legenda Aurea*, he could have found one closer to home in a breviary of Sarum or English Benedictine use, but surviving manuscripts of those suggest they tended to omit or radically condense Cecilia's trial, presumably because her outspokenness violated the compilers' sense of how a female saint should behave; see S. L. Reames, 'The Office for Saint Cecilia', *The Liturgy of the Medieval Church*, ed. Thomas J. Heffernan and E. Ann Matter (Kalamazoo, 2001, 2005), pp. 219–42.

than the part based on the *Legenda Aurea* – either completing a work originally left unfinished or replacing the original ending with a revised version. And he makes a number of small changes that add rhetorical intensity to the trial scene itself.[40] All this evidence significantly complicates the traditional idea of the tale as an early and innocuous exercise in translation on Chaucer's part. He may not have completed it in its present form before the late 1380s, and he probably expected his readers to see contemporary relevance in Cecilia's bold speeches to the Roman prefect – speeches in which she scoffs at the imperial authorities' pretensions to power, ridicules the folly of their idol-worship and exposes the injustice and illogic of the policies they are using to persecute innocent Christians.[41] The tale's narrator, much more circumspect than Cecilia herself, claims in the *Prologue* to be emulating the saint's fruitful activity by the 'feithful bisynesse' of translating her legend. Given the nature of Cecilia's example, however, this emulation may mean not only avoiding the sin of idleness, which the *Prologue* explicitly mentions, but also taking a stand that could be dangerous if those in power recognize the subversive implications of retelling this particular pious legend at this moment in history.[42]

Although Chaucer's outspoken St Cecilia looks very different from the figure of the suffering Virgin Mary in the *Man of Law's Tale*, Chaucer is not endorsing two radically different definitions of sanctity. For one thing, Mary was not always envisioned as patient and long-suffering. Luke's Gospel presents her as one of God's great prophets against the arrogance of power, crediting her with the prophetic speech called the *Magnificat*, and the medieval Church daily recalled this facet of Mary's identity by repeating the *Magnificat* in the liturgy.[43] Second, both Mary and Cecilia are married women, as are nearly all the other saintlike figures in Chaucer's tales. This point deserves emphasis because the majority of recognized saints in the Middle Ages were celibate men, especially monks and bishops. Ignoring that paradigm entirely, Chaucer gives us saints without much institutional power, saints who were officially subordinate to their husbands as well as to their fathers, higher secular authorities, and all clergy. Again and again his tales revisit the New

40 See S. L. Reames, 'Artistry, Decorum, and Purpose in Three Middle English Retellings of the Cecilia Legend', *The Endless Knot: Essays on Old and Middle English in Honor of Marie Borroff*, ed. M. Teresa Tavormina and R. F. Yeager (Cambridge, 1995), pp. 177–99, at pp. 191–9.

41 The most ambitious attempts at a fully historicized reading of the tale are those of Lynn Staley [Johnson], 'Chaucer's Tale of the Second Nun and the Strategies of Dissent', *Studies in Philology* 89 (1992), 314–33, and Lynn Staley, 'Chaucer and the Postures of Sanctity', ch. 5 in *The Powers of the Holy: Religion, Politics, and Gender in Late Medieval English Culture*, ed. David Aers and Lynn Staley (University Park, 1996), connecting this tale with *Melibee*, the *Canon's Yeoman*'s and *Clerk's Tales*. Staley's position is that the tale is concerned primarily with the state of material corruption and political repressiveness into which the English Church had fallen by the 1380s. For other possible interpretations, see John Damon, '*Seinte Cecile* and *Cristes owene knyghtes*: Violence, Resignation, and Resistance in the *Second Nun's Tale*', *Crossing Boundaries: Issues of Cultural and Individual Identity in the Middle Ages and the Renaissance*, ed. Sally McKee, Arizona Studies in the Middle Ages and the Renaissance 3 (Turnhout, 1999), pp. 41–56, and the end of Reames, 'Artistry, Decorum'.

42 Staley develops this idea persuasively in 'Chaucer and the Postures of Sanctity', pp. 200–2.

43 In fact, the *Magnificat* was a standard text not only in the Daily Office, a complex Latin liturgy used primarily by members of the clergy and religious orders, but also the Little Office of the Virgin Mary, widely familiar to laymen and women because of its inclusion in both Latin Books of Hours and vernacular Primers. See *The Prymer or Lay Folks' Prayer Book*, ed. Henry Littlehales, EETS os 105 (New York, 1895), pp. 29–30.

Testament paradox in which apparent lowliness is turned into spiritual influence and the power to fulfil God's purposes. Thus Custance converts her second husband and his whole realm to Christianity. Prudence converts Melibee from vengefulness to wise forbearance. Griselda proves herself a better ruler than Walter and eventually overcomes even his irrational suspicions with her virtues.[44]

Despite such victories, however, there is little or no triumphalism in the kinds of hagiography Chaucer endorses. Although the saintly figures in his tales are ultimately vindicated in some way, their victories come very slowly and usually at great cost. Reminders of the human, vulnerable Virgin Mary keep recurring: not only in the sufferings of Custance, who prays to her and comes unconsciously to resemble her, but also the humble origins and later ordeals of Griselda,[45] the grieving mother of the Prioress's 'litel clergeon', and even the heroic Cecilia, whose legend is uncommonly sober and realistic for its genre. The most popular medieval saints' legends are full of reassuring scenes in which the saints confront fearsome challenges and defeat them with miraculous ease. St George, as everybody knows, kills a dragon. The young virgin saint Margaret overcomes two devils in her prison cell. St Katherine wins a debate against the fifty greatest philosophers in the world and later emerges unscathed from a wheel sadistically designed to tear her body apart. Some martyrs of popular legend, including George, survive a long series of preliminary efforts to execute them, humiliating and infuriating the persecuting authorities – and entertaining medieval audiences, no doubt – with their bodies' apparent imperviousness to pain and death. By contrast, the miraculous events in the Cecilia legend – crowns of flowers and angels that only believers can see, the small miracles at the end that delay Cecilia's death by a few days – are quite restrained. Cecilia foils her persecutor only in the sense that she survives long enough to preach – bleeding and in torment – for three days after the attempt to behead her, winning more converts and leaving her house as a legacy to the besieged Christian community.

In short, even when writing in a genre that was especially prone to simplify moral issues and theological questions, Chaucer rather consistently refuses to minimize the reality of evil, the suffering it causes, and the lifelong need to struggle against it. His hagiographic tales, like his prayers to Mary, are written for adults, not children who need simple answers and easy reassurances about their faith.

[44] Such brief characterizations cannot do justice to the complexity of the *Man of Law's Tale* and *Clerk's Tale*, or to the many ways in which these quasi-hagiographical narratives echo, rework, and call into question the various conventions of saints' legends. The most helpful critical discussions I have found are Michael T. Paull, 'The Influence of the Saint's Legend Genre in the *Man of Law's Tale*', *The Chaucer Review* 5 (1971–2), 179–94; A. C. Spearing, 'Narrative Voice: The Case of Chaucer's *Man of Law's Tale*', *New Literary History* 32 (2001), 715–46, especially pp. 737–42; and Jill Mann, *Feminizing Chaucer* (Cambridge, 2002), pp. 100–28.

[45] Although the humble setting of Griselda's early life reminds modern readers only of the Bethlehem stable, medieval images of Mary were heavily influenced by apocryphal works like the *Protevangelium of James* which emphasize the humility of Mary's life at the time of the Annunciation, when she was living in a very small house, spent part of each day weaving, and had gone out to draw water from the well just before the angel came; see Elizabeth Salter's edition of *Chaucer: The Knight's Tale and the Clerk's Tale* (London, 1962), pp. 42–6, 51–2; Francis Lee Utley, 'Five Genres in the *Clerk's Tale*', *The Chaucer Review* 6 (1972), 198–228; James Wimsatt, 'The Blessed Virgin and the Two Coronations of Griselda', *Mediaevalia* 6 (1980), 187–207.

8

'Th'ende is every tales strengthe': Contextualizing Chaucerian Perspectives on Death and Judgement

CARL PHELPSTEAD

IN THE *Knight's Tale* Egeus' reflections on the inevitability of death culminate in an image with particular resonance for the Canterbury pilgrims listening to the Knight:

> 'Right as ther dyed nevere man,' quod he,
> 'That he ne lyvede in erthe in some degree,
> Right so ther lyvede never man,' he seyde,
> 'In al this world, that som tyme he ne deyde.
> This world nis but a thurghfare ful of wo,
> And we ben pilgryms, passynge to and fro.' (I 2843–8)[1]

In the late Middle Ages experience continually brought the truth that Egeus enunciates to mind, but since the end of the Second World War people in the West have not had their mortal nature drawn to their attention quite so forcefully or frequently as in earlier periods. As Jupp and Walter remark,

> The twentieth century was healthier and safer for the English than all previous centuries. It saw radical changes in the visibility of death. Death is no longer all around us; plagues do not descend randomly on rich and poor, pious and sinful; most children now survive childhood without witnessing the death of a parent or sibling; it is now possible to grow up without direct experience of human mortality. . . . Most English people die in old age, out of sight, in hospital or nursing and residential homes.[2]

Death came to no larger a proportion of the population in Chaucer's day than it does now, of course, but it came to one's family, friends and neighbours sooner, on average, and much more visibly.

[1] Compare Theseus' words (3027–34) and later words of the Clerk (IV 36–8).

[2] Peter C. Jupp and Tony Walter, 'The Healthy Society: 1918–98', *Death in England: An Illustrated History*, ed. Peter C. Jupp and Clare Gittings (Manchester, 1999), pp. 256–82, at p. 278. Two chapters of this splendidly illustrated book cover death during the fourteenth century: Rosemary Horrox, 'Purgatory, Prayer and Plague: 1150–1380', pp. 90–118, and Philip Morgan, 'Of Worms and War: 1380–1558', pp. 119–46.

Death in the Late Middle Ages

After centuries of steadily increasing population the fourteenth century saw a significant decline. A series of cold wet summers near the beginning of the century led to poor harvests in 1315–17 and a famine that killed between ten and fifteen per cent of the population of England.[3] Then the plague, known in modern times as the Black Death, reached the south coast of England in the summer of 1348 and killed between a third and a half of the English population (at least) in the following eighteen months.[4]

It used frequently to be claimed that the Black Death, together with the famine and war that also characterized the fourteenth century, was largely responsible for an 'obsession' with death in the later Middle Ages, and for the ubiquity of grotesque death imagery in the period. While it is hard to imagine that such a catastrophe did not have a profound effect on those who were spared, historians have more recently warned against making too straightforward a connection between the plague and a fascination with the macabre. Horrox points out, for example, that the popular motif of the Three Living and the Three Dead arose before the plague.[5] Other macabre commonplaces did not appear until so long afterwards that it is difficult to see them as a direct result of experience of plague; representations of the Dance of Death, for example, were a fifteenth-century innovation that reached their height of popularity in the sixteenth century.[6] The conventional view of the late Middle Ages as characteristically macabre in fact seems largely to derive from Huizinga's classic *The Waning of the Middle Ages*, in which the late-medieval macabre is a metaphor for what he saw as the decline of a civilization.[7]

Chaucer's writings reflect the experience of death in fourteenth-century England. John of Gaunt's wife, Blanche of Lancaster, almost certainly commemorated in Chaucer's *Book of the Duchess*, died from the Plague on 12 September 1368, when her husband was just twenty-eight years old. The *Canterbury Tales* feature other common ways of meeting death in late-medieval England, including warfare, murder and public execution.[8] The *Summoner's Tale* (III 1851–72) provides an example of the common experience of child mortality when Thomas's wife tells the friar that her son has recently died.

3 Horrox, 'Purgatory', p. 91.

4 An even higher figure of 62.5% mortality among the general population of England has been proposed in Ole J. Benedictow, *The Black Death 1346–1353: A Complete History* (Woodbridge, 2004), pp. 342–79. There were further outbreaks in 1361–2, 1369, and regularly thereafter for more than three centuries. In addition to Philip Ziegler's classic account, *The Black Death* (London, 1969), see W. M. Ormond and P. G. Lindley, *The Black Death in England* (Stamford, 1996) and Colin Platt, *King Death: The Black Death and its Aftermath in Late-Medieval England* (London, 1996); a wide-ranging anthology of contemporary documents is provided in Rosemary Horrox, trans. and ed., *The Black Death* (Manchester, 1994).

5 Horrox, 'Purgatory', p. 115. This story, in which three men encounter three corpses who warn them that they too will die, introduced to England in the thirteenth century, became a popular subject in fourteenth-century manuscript illuminations and wall paintings (ibid. p. 93; also Paul Binski, *Medieval Death: Ritual and Representation* (London, 1996), pp. 134–8).

6 In the Dance of Death a personification of death (typically a skeleton) leads representatives of different classes and professions in a dance.

7 Binski, *Medieval Death*, p. 123; Morgan, 'Of Worms and War', p. 120. See J. Huizinga, *The Waning of the Middle Ages*, trans. F. Hopman (1924; repr. Harmondsworth, 1990); a more recent translation, *The Autumn of the Middle Ages*, trans. Rodney J. Payton and Ulrich Mammitzsch (Chicago, 1996), reveals ways in which the earlier English version misrepresented Huizinga's original.

8 See 'Death', *The Oxford Companion to Chaucer*, ed. Douglas Gray (Oxford, 2003), pp. 129–31.

The Medieval Christian View of Death

Like other religions, Christianity offers its adherents a way of understanding and coping with the inevitability of death. For Christians death is not the end of an individual's existence, but a point of transition to an eternity determined by the state of his or her soul at that moment. Christianity, in other words, understands death in relation to claims about what happens after death. By the late Middle Ages the Western Church had come to teach that with the separation of soul and body at death the individual is judged by God and his or her soul sent to hell, Purgatory or heaven until the Last Judgement, when the souls of all the departed will be reunited with their bodies to spend eternity in either heaven or hell. Of the three destinations to which a soul is sent at death, then, two are permanent, the third, Purgatory, only provisional: after a period there (and at the Last Judgement at the latest) the soul passes on to heaven. Purgatory was a medieval invention, but by Chaucer's time it had become absolutely central both to Christian thinking about the afterlife and to the elaborate range of practices and professions which that thinking produced.[9]

Late-medieval beliefs about death and judgement resulted from a process of doctrinal development over many centuries, and partly because of this they encompassed ambiguities and contradictions which provided grounds for their contestation (by the Eastern Orthodox churches and by Lollards and other heretics during Chaucer's lifetime, and by the Protestant reformers in the sixteenth century). The main part of this essay contextualizes Chaucer's treatment of death and judgement by considering the central doctrine of Purgatory and then looking at two consequences of medieval beliefs about death: the production of texts advising how to die well prepared, and the rise of professions devoted to provision for the faithful departed. These two themes come together in a discussion of the Pardoner and his tale.

Purgatory

In a prophecy concerning the Last Things, reported in Matthew 24, Christ foresees the imminent end of this world, and the early Church expected Christ's return in glory to occur within the lifetime of the first generation of believers.[10] When it became apparent that it would be normal for Christians to die before the world ended the state of the dead between death and the Last Judgement became a more pressing concern.

Saints, of course, went straight to heaven and could be petitioned to convey blessings on the living. The problem requiring a solution was the fate of those who were neither so reprobate that they would be damned eternally nor so saintly that they could go straight to heaven. Two scriptural passages acquired particular importance in formulating the doctrine of Purgatory: 2 Maccabees 12: 39–45 (which was believed to provide authority for prayer for the dead) and 1 Corinthians 3: 11–15 (which speaks of purgation by fire, a process which was eventually

[9] So Christopher Daniell claims that 'The key to medieval religion is the fate of the individual's soul after death': *Death and Burial in Medieval England 1066–1550* (London, 1997), p. 1.

[10] As is clear, for example, from 1 Thessalonians 4: 13 – 5: 10.

located in a place called Purgatory).[11] Prayer for the dead, which implies that their state can be improved and that the prayers of the living may help effect that improvement, is attested in early Christian funeral inscriptions and liturgical formulas, but it was some time before official teaching on the location and state of the souls of the departed was formalized; although Church Fathers were claiming from as early as the fourth century that certain sinners were saved by some kind of post-mortem ordeal, the noun *purgatorium* did not exist until the twelfth century.[12]

The concept of Purgatory was formalized during the twelfth century, defined by a pope for the first time in 1254 and promulgated by the Second Council of Lyons in 1274. The Church taught that although guilt (*culpa*) that otherwise leads to damnation can be pardoned after contrition and confession, punishment (*poena*) remains due and satisfaction must still be made by undertaking penance. In the treatise on penitence which constitutes his 'tale', Chaucer's Parson explains that 'verray parfit penitence' consists of three elements: 'Contricioun of Herte, Confessioun of Mouthe, and Satisfaccioun' (X 107–8); the last section of the tale is devoted to describing works of charity and forms of self-denial by which the penitent may make satisfaction (1029–80). The Second Council of Lyons declared that, if truly repentant sinners should die before making full satisfaction for their sins, 'their souls are purified after death by purgatorial or cleansing punishment; which punishment can be lightened by the prayers of the living'.[13]

Dissemination of the doctrine of Purgatory seems to have taken until well into the fourteenth century.[14] By the second half of that century, however, the concept was sufficiently well understood for Chaucer to be able to employ allusions to it for humorous effect: his Wife of Bath proudly claims of her fourth husband that 'By God, in erthe I was his purgatorie / For which I hope his soule be in glorie' (III 489–90). Similarly, Justinus warns January in the *Merchant's Tale* that his new wife may turn out to be his Purgatory (IV 1670).[15]

The doctrine of Purgatory arose to answer questions about the fate of the departed, their post-mortem location and the means by which they were prepared for admission to Heaven, but it in turn brought about significant changes in belief and practice. Purgatory was, for example, 'one of the main reasons for the

[11] Jacques Le Goff, *The Birth of Purgatory*, trans. Arthur Goldhammer (Chicago, 1984), pp. 41–4.

[12] Le Goff, *Birth of Purgatory*, pp. 3, 11. The story of poor Lazarus resting in Abraham's bosom while the rich man burns in hell (Luke 16: 19–31) provided the basis for an early belief that the righteous rested in the patriarch's protection until the Last Judgement. Two other post-mortem locations were the Limbo of the Patriarchs (where the souls of the righteous went who died before Christ, until it was emptied by him during the Harrowing of Hell) and the Limbo of Children, which, as Le Goff notes, was long an object of controversy (*Birth of Purgatory*, p. 220).

[13] Dogmatic statement of the Second Council of Lyons quoted in Binksi, *Medieval Death*, p. 186. Venial sins committed in ignorance accrue no guilt, but still require punishment which may be undergone in Purgatory.

[14] Horrox, 'Purgatory', p. 90; cf. Binski, *Medieval Death*, pp. 186–7. Christopher Harper-Bill argues that, although belief in Purgatory originated before the Black Death, it 'appears to have entered far more strongly into popular consciousness in its wake', 'The English Church and English Religion after the Black Death', Ormond and Lindley, *Black Death*, pp. 79–123, at p. 110. On English reception of the doctrine of Purgatory and its literary influence see Takami Matsuda, *Death and Purgatory in Middle English Didactic Poetry* (Cambridge, 1997).

[15] For an overview of Chaucer's references to heaven, hell and Purgatory see 'Heaven and Hell' in Gray, *Oxford Companion*, pp. 129–31.

dramatization of the moment of death',[16] because it involved belief in a personal judgement at the moment of death in addition to, and in advance of, the general Last Judgement. This created its own problems:

> the idea that the soul was immediately dispatched somewhere upon death sat rather uneasily with the older tradition that the dead would sleep until the Last Judgement and then be assigned to Heaven or Hell for eternity. The two versions could be reconciled by emphasising that what happened before the Last Judgement happened to the soul alone, which would not be reunited with its body until the general resurrection which would immediately precede that judgement, but illogicalities and contradictions remained.[17]

Partly because of such difficulties Purgatory was a controversial idea. Although they pray for the departed, the Eastern Orthodox churches have never developed a formal doctrine of Purgatory and the Greek Church refused to accept the Western doctrine when it became an issue in negotiations for reunion during the Middle Ages.[18]

Purgatory was also rejected by Protestant reformers in the early sixteenth century; Protestant unease with the doctrine of Purgatory focused on its tenuous foundation in Scripture.[19] The question of the basis for beliefs about the afterlife is also one that Chaucer raises in the fourteenth century, characteristically contrasting the authority of books with that of experience. This issue is addressed most explicitly in the opening lines of the *Legend of Good Women*, where the narrator agrees with the common proposition that 'there is joye in hevene and peyne in helle' (G 2) but points out

> That there ne is non that dwelleth in this contre
> That eyther hath in helle or hevene ybe,
> Ne may of it non other weyes witen
> But as he hath herd seyd or founde it writen. (G 5–8)

The fiend in the *Friar's Tale* (III 1515–20) informs the summoner that he will soon know hell better by experience than either Virgil or Dante, alluding to the journey to the underworld in Virgil's *Aeneid*, book VI, and to Dante's *Inferno*; the tale's narrator later briefly alludes to the biblical and patristic authorities for belief in the pains of hell (1645–50). The *Summoner's Prologue* tells of a friar granted a personal vision of hell in which, in accordance with the Summoner's anti-fraternal purpose, 'many a millioun' friars live in the devil's arse (III 1683–99).

Dying Well

Because one's eternal fate was determined by the state in which one died, the medieval Church placed a great deal of emphasis on dying well. A good death was

[16] Le Goff, *Birth of Purgatory*, p. 295.

[17] Horrox, 'Purgatory', p. 111.

[18] It was partly Greek resistance that led to the formal declaration of the doctrine at the Second Council of Lyons: see Le Goff, *Birth of Purgatory*, p. 52 and pp. 280–4.

[19] See Diarmaid MacCulloch, *Reformation: Europe's House Divided 1490–1700* (London, 2003), p. 580. Protestant rejection of 2 Maccabees, with other 'apocryphal' books, meant there was no longer any biblical precedent for prayer for the dead.

one for which the person was well prepared, and people therefore hoped for a slow end, allowing time for full preparation, rather than a sudden and unexpected death of the kind many hope for today.[20] Preparation for death involved sacramental confession and absolution, penance, extreme unction (anointing the body with holy oil) and a final act of holy communion, receiving the so-called Viaticum (literally 'provision for the journey').[21] There is an allusion to such deathbed preparation in the *Summoner's Tale* when the friar feigns a concern to ensure the dying Thomas makes as full a confession as possible (III 1815–18). If for some reason it was not possible to prepare properly, faith alone would be sufficient: as long as one had repented one's sins before death the necessary penance could be performed in Purgatory. It was, however, risky to put off making a proper confession. Chaucer's Parson acknowledges that 'he that synneth and verraily repenteth hym in his laste, hooly church yet hopeth his savacioun, by the grete mercy of oure Lord Jhesu Crist, for his repentaunce' but still recommends that one should 'taak the siker wey' of confession, absolution and penance (X 94).[22]

In the late Middle Ages manuals on how to die well became popular. The generic name for these manuals is *ars moriendi* ('the art of dying'), a term also used as the title for some individual examples. Some of these texts use a *memento mori* to encourage the living to lead better lives, reminding readers that because death comes to all and may come at any time one should always be ready for it.[23] Other texts focus on providing deathbed instructions for the sick. The moment of death and the sickness leading to it are seen as crucial because 'the death bed was the great battlefield where man's enemy, the devil, staked his last throw, and drew up all his strongest forces for one final and bitter assault'.[24]

The most important and substantial *ars moriendi* is *The Book of the Craft of Dying*. This is a translation of a Latin text called the *Tractatus* or *Speculum Artis Bene Moriendi*, which was probably written in the first quarter of the fifteenth century.[25] Though dating from a little after Chaucer's death the text elaborates on the traditional Office for the Visitation of the Sick, including the Last Rites, and so it is not inappropriate to read it as evidence of beliefs and practices with which Chaucer and his earliest readers would have been familiar.[26]

The *Craft of Dying* begins by claiming that ignorance of how to die well makes people fear death, and Chapter I is a plea to recognize the significance of death. The second chapter forms the core of the book and offers advice on how to overcome five temptations with which the devil makes his final assault: 'men that die, in their last sickness and end have greatest and most grievous temptations, and such

20 Hence the popularity of two acts thought to prevent sudden death on a particular day: looking at an image of St Christopher and seeing the elevation of the Host at Mass (Daniell, *Death and Burial*, p. 32).

21 See Daniell, *Death and Burial*, pp. 35–8 for an account of the Last Rites in medieval England.

22 He also approvingly notes Job's prayer for longer life to allow him a 'respit a while to biwepe and biwaillen his trespas' (179).

23 *Memento mori* means 'remember you will die', a warning presented in various forms in medieval art, poetry and devotional and homiletic writings.

24 Frances Margeret Mary Comper, *The Book of the Craft of Dying and Other Early English Tracts Concerning Death* (London, 1917; repr. New York, 1977), p. xl. Further references to this edition are given in parentheses.

25 Its writer was influenced by a section 'De arte moriendi' in Jean de Gerson's *Opusculum tripartitum*.

26 For a discussion of the *Craft of Dying* in relation to the *Ordo visitandi* see Eamon Duffy, *The Stripping of the Altars: Traditional Religion in England 1400–1580* (New Haven and London, 1992), pp. 313–27.

as they never had before in all their life' (pp. 9–10). Chapter III provides questions designed to establish an individual's saving faith, and Chapter IV encourages the dying person to imitate Christ's actions on the Cross, providing prayers focused on Christ's Passion. Chapter V emphasizes the responsibility of all Christians to help others die well, and the final chapter provides prayers to be said for the dying man by his companions. The whole work offers assurance and comfort rather than attempting to induce fear of death.

A rather different *ars moriendi*, sometimes called the *Art of Dieing*, circulated in England in Chaucer's lifetime. This short work is part of a much larger summary of the basics of Christian belief originally written in French and known as *Le Somme des Vices et Virtues* or *Le Somme le Roi*, a composite work compiled in the thirteenth century by Lorens d'Orléans. Most sections of *Le Somme*, including the *ars moriendi*, are found as separate texts in earlier manuscripts. The compilation was popular and circulated widely, being translated into several languages. The first English translation was the *Ayenbite of Inwyt* (1340), but the most widely attested in surviving manuscripts is the version known as *The Book of Vices and Virtues* (*c.* 1375).[27] The *ars moriendi* section of the *Book* describes great lords and princes lying in Hell lamenting that all their former wealth can now avail them nothing. Whereas riches and power make no difference beyond the grave, the Christian who lives a good life and dies well can look forward to death with eager expectation: 'For deþ is to goode men ende of al euel and a bigynnyng of alle goodnesse. Deþ is the brooke þt departeþ deeþ and lif, for deeþ is here and lif is þere.'[28] The reader is encouraged to visit heaven, hell and Purgatory in the imagination in order to see this life in the right perspective: 'go in-to helle while þou lyuest þat þou come not þere when þou art ded'.[29] Even more than in the *Craft of Dying*, the art of dying is seen to be the art of living: the reader is encouraged to amend his or her life by being reminded that it will have eternal consequences.

Other *ars moriendi* texts survive from late-fourteenth- and fifteenth-century England, and several examples were printed by William Caxton and Wynkyn de Worde between *c.* 1485 and 1507. The popularity of the genre leads Comper to argue that these treatises were 'translated and printed so frequently . . . that we can only conclude that they were of real service and help'.[30] The tradition also has affinities with the late-medieval morality play, *Everyman*, which provides instruction of the *ars moriendi* type through its allegorical dramatization of death.[31]

Chaucer's *Parson's Tale* comes close to the *ars moriendi* tradition in its frequent resort to reflection on the pains of hell and joys of heaven in order to stimulate repentance. A seed of grace is said to spring 'thurgh remembrance of the day of doom and on the peynes of helle' (118) and there is later a more extended reflection on the 'thridde cause that oughte moeve a man to Contricioun': 'drede of the day of doom and of the horrible peynes of helle' (158). As the Parson says,

27 *Dan Michel's Ayenbite of Inwyt or Remorse of Conscience*, ed. Richard Morris, EETS os 23 (London, 1866), pp. 70–5 for the *ars moriendi* section; *The Book of Vices and Virtues*, ed. W. Nelson Francis, EETS os 217 (1942), pp. 68–71 for *ars moriendi* section.

28 Francis, *Book of Vices and Virtues*, p. 70.

29 Ibid., p. 71.

30 Comper, *Craft of Dying*, p. xl.

31 *Everyman*, ed. A. C. Cawley (Manchester, 1961).

'whoso wel remembreth hym of thise thynges, I gesse that his synne shal nat turne hym into delit, but to gret sorwe for drede of the peyne of helle' (175). The Parson dwells rather more on the pains of hell than the joys of heaven, but they are not entirely neglected: 'the glorie of hevene, with which God shal gerdone man for his goode dedes' is advanced as a cause for contrition (283) and the tale ends (1076–80) with an eloquent description of 'the endeless blisse of hevene' (1076).

Handbooks on the art of dying were a late-medieval development, beginning in Chaucer's lifetime and gaining popularity in the fifteenth and early sixteenth centuries. This has been taken as indicative of a profound change in attitudes to death in the later Middle Ages, though there are certainly also continuities with earlier liturgical and devotional traditions. An unsympathetic view might see the books as an attempt by the Church to shore up its authority, using awareness of death and teaching on the Last Things as 'emotional bludgeons with which to combat ignorance, individualism, immorality and especially indifference'.[32] But this would be to underestimate the comfort which many people will have received, in fraught and uncertain times, from the reassurance that a good end could be made and the troubles of this world exchanged for a better life in the world to come. Texts and iconography of the late Middle Ages did sometimes elaborate in grotesque detail on 'deathbed horrors, putrefaction and punishments beyond the grave',[33] but a text such as the *Craft of Dying* did not dwell on such things, and instead offered the much more comforting message that whoever follows the book's instructions 'schal not dye everlastyngly'.[34]

The Professionals: Technocrats of Death in the Canterbury Tales

The medieval Church (unlike later Protestant churches) offered continuing assistance to its members after their death. After the Harrowing of Hell those consigned there were thought to be beyond assistance (with only very rare exceptions, such as the pagan Emperor Trajan, who, as Langland records, was believed to have been saved by the tears of Pope Gregory the Great),[35] but for those souls in Purgatory who had the benefit of help from the living the period of purgation could be shortened.

The most influential medieval understandings of how Christ's death on the Cross made salvation possible theorized the action in economic terms: Origen was followed by Latin Fathers, including Augustine, in understanding Christ's death as a ransom paid to Satan to redeem sinners over whom he had acquired a legitimate claim; in the late eleventh century Anselm of Canterbury influentially reinterpreted the death of Christ as the paying of a debt to God the Father on

[32] Nancy Lee Beaty, *The Craft of Dying: A Study in the Literary Tradition of the 'Ars Moriendi' in England* (London, 1970), p. 44.

[33] Ibid., p. 50.

[34] Although this tradition of instruction in the art of dying well is deeply alien to most modern readers, analogous texts exist in other religious traditions. A particularly striking parallel is provided by *The Tibetan Book of the Dead*, a text 'discovered' in the fourteenth century by Karma Lingpa: see the recent authoritative translation by Gyurme Dorje (London, 2005), and note especially how closely the section entitled 'A Masked Drama of Rebirth' (pp. 319–41) resembles the play *Everyman*. Stanislav Grof compares Egyptian, Tibetan, medieval European, and other traditions in *Books of the Dead: Manuals for Living and Dying* (London, 1994).

[35] William Langland, *The Vision of Piers Plowman: A Complete Edition of the B-Text*, ed. A. V. C. Schmidt, 2nd edn (London, 1995), XI, lines 140–58.

behalf of fallen humanity, a theory of the Atonement as an act of satisfaction later developed by Aquinas.[36] In both accounts the framework for understanding the nature of Christ's salvific work is economic: his death involves paying a ransom or redeeming a debt.

Economic models of the Atonement could easily be extended to other aspects of salvation, including what Binski calls the 'credit system' of indulgences acquired before death (see below) and the way in which praying for the dead ensured that 'The medieval view of the afterlife became "transactional", founded upon a covenant between the living and the dead'.[37] This 'economy of salvation' had quite literally economic consequences in the later Middle Ages, as a number of men came to earn their livings by performing works designed to speed the departed through Purgatory: they became what Binski calls 'a class of specialized technocrats of death'.[38]

The liturgy for the dead encompassed the Office for the Dead, comprising Vespers recited in the evening and Matins the next morning, and the Requiem Mass (so called from the opening of its introit: *Requiem aeternam dona eis domine*: 'Rest eternal grant unto them, O Lord'). Anyone could pray for the repose of the dead, asking God to shorten the time departed souls spent in Purgatory (so in the *Man of Law's Tale* the narrator asks for prayers for the soul of Alla (II 1146)), but of much greater benefit was the offering of the Mass on behalf of the faithful departed, which only a priest could do. Liturgical commemoration of the dead took place especially on the seventh and thirtieth days after burial, on the 'year's mind' or anniversary, and (for all the departed) on All Souls' Day (2 November).[39] There is an allusion to this liturgical provision in the *Summoner's Tale*, where the friar is said to have excited 'the peple in his prechyng / To trentals' (III 1716–17): a trental was a set of thirty Requiem Masses said for the repose of a soul in Purgatory (the term could also be used for a service on the thirtieth day after death or burial: the 'month's mind'). The friar's preaching is characterized as follows:

> 'Trentals,' seyde he, 'deliveren fro penaunce
> Hir freendes soules, as wel olde as yonge –
> Ye, whan that they been hastily ysonge,
> Nat for to holde a preest joly and gay –
> He syngeth nat but o masse in a day.
> Delivereth out,' quod he, 'anon the soules!
> Ful hard it is with flesshhook or with oules
> To been yclawed, or to brenne or bake.' (III 1724–31)

Funds could be bequeathed for Masses and the Office of the Dead to be said for a patron's soul over a given period; such an endowment was known as a chantry. By the fourteenth century space was set aside in churches for the performance

[36] For an overview of theories of the Atonement see *The Oxford Dictionary of the Christian Church*, ed. F. L. Cross, 3rd edn ed. by E. A. Livingstone (Oxford, 1997), under 'Atonement', pp. 122–4.

[37] Binski, *Medieval Death*, p. 24.

[38] Ibid., p. 32.

[39] The commemoration of All Souls began at Cluny in the late tenth century and soon spread throughout Western Christendom, preparing the ground for the formalization of the doctrine of Purgatory (*Birth of Purgatory*, p. 125). See Daniell, *Death and Burial*, pp. 20–5 for a description of liturgical provision aimed at freeing souls from Purgatory.

of such chantries and York Minster and St Paul's Cathedral, London, both had dozens of chantry priests engaged in praying for the dead.[40] If the apparently autobiographical passages in the C-text of *Piers Plowman* are to be believed, Chaucer's contemporary William Langland earned his living by praying for the souls of those who provided him with alms for this purpose:

> The lomes þat y labore with and lyflode deserue
> Is *pater noster* and my primer, *placebo* and *dirige*,
> And my sauter som tyme and my seuene psalms.
> This y segge for here soules of suche as me helpeth.[41]

The speaker's interlocutors, Resoun and Conscience, are critical of this way of earning a living, and in the *Canterbury Tales* the idealized Parson is praised for avoiding involvement in it:

> He sette nat his benefice to hyre
> And leet his sheep encombred in the myre
> And ran to Londoun unto Seinte Poules
> To seken him a chaunterie for soules (I 507–10).

His fellow pilgrim the Clerk is said to pray for the souls of those who fund him (I 299–301), though it is not entirely clear whether his patrons are dead or alive.[42] The duped priest in the *Canon Yeoman's Tale* is an 'annueleer' (VIII 1012), a chantry priest who sings Masses for the dead, living in London, where many such priests were attached to St Paul's Cathedral. The priest is conned only because he has an inordinate desire for money and riches, and the choice of a chantry priest as the covetous victim of the canon's deception implicitly suggests an inappropriately mercenary aspect to that profession as a whole.

The Pardoner and his Tale

The Canterbury pilgrim with the greatest personal investment in the late-medieval institution of death is the Pardoner. He depends for his living on acceptance of the Church's teaching about the afterlife even as he profits from his clients' confusion of forgiveness of guilt with remission of punishment.

As we have seen, the Church taught that penance that was not performed while the penitent was alive would be completed in Purgatory. It also came to teach that a 'treasury of merit' could be drawn on to remit some or all of the restitution required of a penitent. Being made up of the combined merits of Christ and his saints, this treasury provided more than enough merit with which to pay for the sins of all, but in practice it was to be distributed only selectively. As Christ's representative on earth, the pope was empowered to dispense from this treasury, and to transfer to

[40] Binski, *Medieval Death*, p. 116. Both Harper-Bill ('English Church', pp. 111–13) and Platt (*King Death*, ch. 7) relate the fourteenth-century growth in popularity of chantries to experience of the Black Death.

[41] *Piers Plowman by William Langland: An Edition of the C-Text*, ed. Derek Pearsall (London, 1978), V, 45–8. Vespers of the Dead was known as *Placebo*, from the first word of its introit (Psalm 114 (116): 9)), and Matins of the Dead as *Dirige* (from its antiphon (Psalm 5: 8)), whence modern English 'dirge'.

[42] A student living off alms was obliged to pray for the souls of his benefactors, living or dead: see Jill Mann, *Chaucer and Medieval Estates Satire: The Literature of Social Classes and the General Prologue to the Canterbury Tales* (Cambridge, 1972), pp. 81–2.

repentant sinners merits which would shorten their time in Purgatory.[43] This grant of merit was known as an indulgence; the period of punishment remitted by such an indulgence was commonly forty days, but a plenary indulgence secured full release from all the punishment due a sinner.[44] The system, and its rationale, were formally set out in Pope Clement V's bull *Unigenitus* in 1343.

In order to obtain an indulgence one had to repent one's sins, make confession of them to a priest and then undertake a prescribed act to which the indulgence was attached. Pope Innocent III, for example, offered an indulgence to those who (having repented and confessed their sins) prayed to the veronica, a representation of the cloth on which Christ's portrait miraculously appeared when St Veronica provided him with it to wipe his face on the way to the Crucifixion; such an image is among the equipment of Chaucer's Pardoner: 'A vernycle hadde he sowed upon his cappe' (I 685; a medal struck with an image of Veronica's veil was the badge of pilgrims to Rome).

In the fourteenth century opportunities to obtain indulgences in exchange for charitable donations increased, initiating what Binski calls 'the introduction of the cash nexus into this bookkeeping of the afterlife'.[45] A pardoner (Latin *questor*) was a priest, monk or layman authorized to sell indulgences. The financial payment was conceived as an alternative to other forms of penance, such as fasting. It was clear in theory that one could not simply buy forgiveness, but it is easy to see how misunderstanding could arise, and why it might be encouraged by unscrupulous sellers of indulgences: it was relatively easy to confuse the obtaining of the indulgence (which merely reduced the time to be spent in Purgatory paying for sins which had been confessed and forgiven) with actually obtaining pardon for one's sins; the latter, according to the Church's official teaching, was obtainable only by repentance and confession.

The theory of indulgences, and the confusion and abuses to which it could give rise, were the target of criticism in Chaucer's lifetime, which clearly informs his portrait of the Pardoner in the *Canterbury Tales*.[46] Lollard criticism of pardoners includes the following complaint that parish clergy allow pardoners to deceive people in order to obtain a share of the money they make:

> for whanne þere comeþ a pardoner wiþ stolen bullis & false relekis, grauntynge mo ȝeris of pardon than comen bifore domes day for ȝeuynge of worldly catel to riche placis where is no nede, he schal be sped & resceyued of curatis for to haue part of that he getiþ. [. . .] & þis pardoner schalle telle of more power þan euere crist grauntid to petir or poul or ony apostle, to drawe þe almes fro pore bedrede neiȝebouris.[47]

43 A Wycliffite writer argued that if this doctrine is true then the pope must lack charity if anyone is left in Purgatory, given that he has the resources to free everyone immediately: *The English Works of John Wyclif Hitherto Unprinted*, ed. F. D. Mathew, EETS os 74 (London, 1880), pp. 81–2.

44 The first plenary indulgence was granted to those taking part in the first Crusade (1095), though Purgatory was not yet a formalized doctrine. In 1300 Pope Boniface VIII granted a plenary indulgence to those who made a pilgrimage to Rome in the Jubilee year (or intended to make one but proved unable to do so); see Binski, *Medieval Death*, p. 187.

45 Binski, *Medieval Death*, p. 187.

46 Just over a century after Chaucer's death one particular scheme for selling indulgences provoked a reaction by Martin Luther which led to a schism within the Western Church that has lasted to the present: see MacCulloch, *Reformation*, pp. 115–32.

47 'How the Office of Curates is Ordained of God' in Matthew, *English Works of John Wyclif*, p. 154. The

Langland is also critical of pardoners in the Prologue to *Piers Plowman*:

> Ther preched a pardoner as he a preest were:
> Broughte forth a bulle with bisshopes seles,
> And seide that himself myghte assoillen hem alle
> Of falshede of fastynge, of avowes ybroken.
> Lewed men leved hym wel and liked hise wordes,
> Comen up knelynge to kissen his bulle.
> He bonched hem with his brevet and blered hire eighen,
> And raughte with his rageman rynges and broches. (B-text Prol. 68–75)

In Chaucer's *House of Fame* (2127) pardoners appear in the House of Rumour because of their penchant for spreading stories and telling lies.

The Pardoner among the Canterbury pilgrims exemplifies many of the faults for which his profession was notorious, including several which Langland refers to in the passage above: he is associated with the Hospital of St Mary Rouncesval at Charing Cross (I 670), an institution notorious for its scandalous attempts to raise funds from the sale of indulgences; he carries false relics (including 'pigges bones' (I 700)) and at least some forged bulls (those listed in the *Pardoner's Prologue* 342–3 cannot all be genuine); and (assuming he is a layman, as seems most likely) he exceeds his authority in claiming the power to absolve sins (VI 387–8; 906–14, 937–40).[48] In addition, he is a shameless hypocrite who preaches only to make a profit, has no concern about what happens to the souls of his hearers when they are dead (VI 400–6), and happily acknowledges that 'Thus kan I preche agayn that same vice / Which that I use, and that is avarice' (427–8).

In the *Pardoner's Tale* a 'technocrat of death', whose living depends on acceptance of the doctrine of Purgatory, tells a tale which emphasizes the inevitability, but unpredictability, of death. Plague provides the backdrop for the story: when the 'riotoures' at the tavern hear the bell being rung in procession before a corpse a boy informs them that this former companion of theirs has been suddenly slain by 'a privee thef men clepeth Deeth / That in this contree al the peple sleth . . . / He hath a thousand slayn this pestilence' (VI 675–6, 679). The boy has been educated in the *memento mori* tradition of the *ars moriendi* by his mother: 'Beth redy for to meete hym [Death] everemoore; / Thus taughte me my dame' (683–4). However, the young men betray their ignorance of Death's true nature and of Christ's having already defeated Death when they declare 'we wol sleen this false traytour Deeth' (699).[49] Their encounter with the old man who is prepared for, and even desires, death ('Deeth, allas, ne wol nat han me lyf', 727) fails to instil wisdom in them and he directs them to Death by indicating the way to treasure: their avarice leads them

text entitled 'Of Prelates' in the same edition contains a sustained attack on the doctrine of indulgences (ch. 13).

48 Evidence that Chaucer's Pardoner is a layman includes his lack of tonsure (I 675–9) and statement that he was about to get married (III 166). If a layman he also exceeds his authority in preaching 'lyk a clerk' (VI 391): see Alastair Minnis, 'Chaucer's Pardoner and the "Office of Preacher"', *Intellectuals and Writers in Fourteenth-Century Europe*, ed. Piero Boitani and Anna Torti (Tübingen and Cambridge, 1986), pp. 88–119 (esp. pp. 100–1).

49 Several characters in the tale understand the personification of death literally. Death was hardly ever personified in visual (as opposed to literary) art of this period (except as one of the Four Horsemen of the Apocalypse: see Revelation 6); artists instead created images of the dead: see Horrox, 'Purgatory', p. 93.

to murder one another, so that Death finds them when 'No lenger thane after Deeth they soughte' (772) and each of them dies in a state of mortal sin.

This exemplum is designed to produce the contrition which normally leads the Pardoner's audience to offer payment in exchange for his absolution (cf. VI 906–8). The Pardoner is quite open about this straightforwardly financial transaction:

> Into the blisse of hevene shul ye gon.
> I yow assoille, by myn heigh power,
> Yow that wol offer . . . (912–14).

When, however, he invites his fellow pilgrims to avail themselves of his services his having exposed the tricks of his trade earns him a powerful rebuke from Harry Bailly. In the *Pardoner's Tale* the *momento mori* of the *ars moriendi* tradition collides with, and is undercut by, contemporary criticism of corrupt pardoners who turn fear of Purgatory to personal profit.

Epilogue: 'Th'ende is every tales strengthe'

In *Troilus and Criseyde* Pandarus tells his niece that 'th'ende is every tales strengthe' (II 260). A long rhetorical tradition ascribing particular importance to the end of utterances and texts is precisely paralleled in the medieval understanding of the importance of death, a life's end, as the point at which that life is judged. The end of a text is likewise the moment at which a complete view and verdict is possible: it is thus figurative of the end of life, or of the world.

Chaucer's endings are famously inconclusive (or non-existent).[50] *Troilus* itself seems to end several times, with attempts at closure repeatedly undermined by a further attempt.[51] *The House of Fame* and *Legend of Good Women* both tantalizingly break off just as resolution and closure appear to be promised.[52] At the end of the *Canterbury Tales* the Parson is invited to 'knytte up' the proceedings (X 28). Critics of the *Parson's Tale* are divided between those whose approach Wenzel characterizes as 'perspectivist', seeing it as one tale and one view of the world among many, and those who take a 'teleological' approach that, partly because of the tale's terminal position, sees the Parson as offering an authoritative statement in terms of which to judge what has gone before.[53] But even if the tale is read as authoritative its relationship to the other tales remains open to interpretation: does it fulfil, resolve, transcend, contradict or cancel out what has gone before?[54] Whereas medieval Christianity looked to a day of final and incontrovertible

[50] On the open endings of Chaucer's narratives see Rosemarie P. McGerr, *Chaucer's Open Books: Resistance to Closure in Medieval Discourse* (Gainsville, 1998).

[51] Barry Windeatt, *Troilus and Criseyde*, Oxford Guides to Chaucer (Oxford, 1992), pp. 298–313 provides a good discussion of the ending(s) of the poem and critics' responses.

[52] The parallel between the end of a text and the Last Judgement may be hinted at in the *House of Fame*, which ends just as an apparently authoritative figure ('he semed for to be / A man of gret auctorite', 2157–8) appears as if to bring knowledge and certainty, as Christ will pronounce judgement at doomsday.

[53] Siegfried Wenzel, 'The Parson's Tale in Current Literary Studies', David Raybin and Linda Holley, *Closure in the Canterbury Tales: The Role of the Parson's Tale* (Kalamazoo, 2000), pp. 1–10.

[54] See Judith Ferster, 'Chaucer's Parson and the "Idiosyncracies of Fiction"' in Raybin and Holley, *Closure*, pp. 115–50.

judgement, Chaucer's texts resist closure: is this resistance a fear of the end? Or does it put the reader in the position of Judge, leaving to him or her the final verdict? Or is it a recognition that *all* merely human judgements are provisional and imperfect?

As the pilgrims approach Canterbury at day's end, the Parson picks up Egeus' image of life as a pilgrimage from the first of their tales:

> Jhesu . . . wit me sende
> To shewe yow the wey, in this viage
> Of thilke parfit glorious pilgrymage
> That highte Jerusalem celestial. (X 48–51)

He goes on to offer a discourse on penitence that is clearly appropriate both to the end of the Canterbury pilgrimage and to any sinner preparing for his or her death; Patterson says of the tale that 'its very nature is terminal'.[55] Yet it is not the ending envisaged at the text's beginning: there was to be, as Helen Cooper points out, a return to the Tabard, 'where judgement would be pronounced not on the pilgrims but on the stories'.[56] After the Parson has spoken there can be no question of ending with supper in Southwark: 'The pilgrims are not going back to London, but forward to death and judgment' as Ferster puts it.[57] Harry Bailly's verdict on the tale-telling is of no significance besides Christ's at doomsday.

The last word is not the Parson's, though. His voice gives way at some point – perhaps where the Ellesmere manuscript says 'the makere of this book [takes] his leve' – to that of Geoffrey Chaucer, whether the fictional pilgrim of that name or the historical individual who wrote the *Canterbury Tales* (or both). Listing his works in a way that seems to end, and close, a literary career rather than a single text, the poet prepares to die well by repenting of those of his writings that 'sownen into synne' and praying that 'I may be oon of hem at the day of doom that shulle be saved' (X 1086, 1092). The end of a text, and especially of this one, reminds a reader that the moment will come when a verdict on the whole of his or her life will be possible.

55 Lee Patterson, 'The "Parson's Tale" and the Quitting of the "Canterbury Tales"', *Traditio* 34 (1978), pp. 331–80.

56 Helen Cooper, *The Canterbury Tales* (Oxford, 1989), p. 397.

57 Ferster, 'Chaucer's Parson', p. 140.

9

Chaucer and the Saints: Miracles and Voices of Faith

LAUREL BROUGHTON

IN CHAUCER'S ENGLAND saints gave their names to churches and monasteries, to towns and villages. Their shrines and relics affirmed their continuing presences. Their names pepper the *General Prologue* and the tales. Chaucer tells a saint's legend in the *Second Nun's Tale*, a miracle of the Virgin in the *Prioress's Tale*, and creates a hybrid of the two genres in the *Man of Law's Tale*. Within the narrative structure of the saint's legend, Chaucer gives voices to those often unheard: women and children. Cecilia, the little clergeon and Custance use their voices at crucial moments in their tales to instigate change and establish their relationship with the divine.

Painted on church walls, carved in stone and wood, depicted in brilliant glass, saints surrounded the faithful when they walked into not only monumental cathedrals but their local parish churches, often adorned with images of titular saints, local saints and the Virgin Mary. That these held significance for the ordinary medieval person is witnessed by bequests made to images in medieval wills.[1] Chaucer and his audience would also have been familiar with saints through the liturgy. Almost every day in the Sarum liturgical calendar commemorates a saint or a feast of the church. Individual communities expanded the calendar by celebrating saints of local importance. Propers (specific service elements) for saints' feast days appear in the Sarum breviary, the service book used to celebrate the daily canonical hours. Even if they did not own a breviary, members of the increasingly literate middle class could have access to or own these calendars as well as litanies and other devotions to saints found in books of hours.[2] For those who could afford them, decorated books of hours provided portable images of the saints.[3] More elaborate books of hours frequently incorporate images of the original owner, demonstrating individual personal connection with the devotional object.

'The hooly blissful martir for to seke'

Chaucer builds the *Canterbury Tales* framework on a pilgrimage to the shrine of St Thomas Becket. Becket, born around 1118, served Theobald the archbishop of

1 Richard Marks, *Image and Devotion in Late Medieval England* (Thrupp, 2004), esp. pp. 2–3, 7–8.

2 See Roger Wieck, *Time Sanctified* (New York, 1988), p. 45; Eamon Duffy, *Marking the Hours: English People and their Prayers 1240–1570* (New Haven and London, 2006), p. 4.

3 Duffy, *Marking the Hours*, pp. 3–22.

Canterbury and Henry II, who appointed him successor to Theobald. Consecrated in 1162, Becket staunchly defended the authority and jurisdiction of the Church, bringing him into sharp conflict with Henry, once his close friend. Their disagreements led to Becket's exile to France in 1164. After reconciling with Henry, he returned to England in 1170, only to outrage the king once again. At Henry's instigation, the knights Reginald fitzUrse, Hugh de Morville, William de Tracy and Richard le Breton left the king's court in Normandy and, on 29 December 1170, surprising Becket in the cathedral, killed him.

Becket's body, dressed in his hair shirt, monk's habit and shoes, and covered by his consecration vestments, was buried the day after his murder in the cathedral crypt. The doors to the crypt were locked until 17 April 1171. Almost immediately after the public gained access, Becket's burial site became associated with miraculous healings, many of which form the narratives of the stained glass windows in the cathedral's Trinity Chapel. Becket was canonized in 1173. King Henry did penance at his tomb on 12 July 1174, in a dramatic public show of remorse. On 5 September 1174, much of the east end of the cathedral burned, although Becket's tomb in the crypt underneath survived unscathed and continued to accommodate pilgrims during the extensive rebuilding of the damaged choir. The rebuilding included an elaborate shrine for Becket's relics. On 7 July 1220, Becket's remains were translated to their new resting place, where they remained until the shrine was destroyed by reformers in 1538.[4]

Becket's shrine evolved from a local site to one of international importance.[5] While many commentators focus on the wealthy who could afford to travel in relative comfort, Ronald Finucane provides this vivid description of a likely scenario at Becket's tomb:

> A modern visitor, magically transported to the darkened crypt of this ancient church, would probably be astonished if not repelled by the sight of wretched cripples writhing on the floor at Becket's simple tomb, by the screams of fettered madmen straining at their bonds and the low moans of lepers and the blind, and by the characteristic odour of the Middle Ages, the stench of poverty and disease.[6]

Witness to Becket's miracles derives mostly from evidence collected by two monks, Benedict and William, in the years directly following Becket's murder.[7] Only about half of the cures recorded by Benedict and William occurred at the shrine. Other pilgrims gave thanks for long distance cures, wrought either by prayer to Thomas, or possession of a portable relic such as a vial of St Thomas's water. The murder site had been carefully cleaned, all remaining parts of his body preserved and his blood collected: the holy water might be conserved washing water, water that came into contact with his tomb, or water mixed with a drop of his blood.

[4] See John Butler, *The Quest for Becket's Bones* (New Haven and London, 1995), pp. 1–33; John Keates and Angelo Hornak, *Canterbury Cathedral* (Florence, 1980), pp. 35–45.

[5] Ronald C. Finucane, *Miracles and Pilgrims* (New York, 1995), p. 121.

[6] Ibid., p. 9.

[7] Becket's Miracles constitute the largest extant collection, according to Benedicta Ward, *Miracles and the Medieval Mind* (Aldershot, 1987), p. 89; for texts see *The Materials for the History of Thomas Becket, Archbishop of Canterbury*, 7 vols., ed. J. C. Robinson (London, 1875–85), vols. I–II.

In the tradition of those healed away from the tomb, and that of giving thanks, the *General Prologue*'s opening describes the motivation for pilgrimage:

> from every shires ende
> Of Engelond to Caunterbury they wende,
> The hooly blisful martir for to seke,
> That hem hath holpen whan that they were seeke. (I 16–18)

Some of Chaucer's pilgrims might be journeying to render thanks for healing already effected; others might be seeking healing for a condition currently endured (the Cook with his 'mormal' comes to mind); some on behalf of a sick relative or friend.

Lydgate's prologue to his *Siege of Thebes* picks up Chaucer's story and describes dinner at Canterbury with a group of pilgrims. *The Tale of Beryn*, found in the Alnwick manuscript of the *Canterbury Tales*, describes the Chaucerian pilgrims visiting Becket's shrine and the rituals involved in the visit. They make offerings of silver brooches and rings. After a monk sprinkles them with holy water, 'The Knyhte went with his compers [companions] toward the holy shryne / To do that they were come for' (145–6). The Pardoner and the Miller argue over the meaning of the stained glass windows until the Host shames them into making their offering. They

> Kneled adown tofore the shryne, and hertlich hir bedes
> They preyd to Seynt Thomas, in such wise as they couth.
> And sith the holy relikis ech man with his mowth
> Kissed, as a goodly monke þe names told and taught.
> And sith to other places of holynes they raughte
> And were in hir devocioun tyl service wer al doon. (164–7)[8]

This description omits other pilgrims and the writhing cripples, the blind, lepers or fettered madmen postulated in Finucane's vision of the shrine.

Other popular shrines included those of Walsingham, Bromeholm, William of Norwich, St Edmund of East Anglia and Simon de Montfort.[9] These names and a host of others would have been familiar to Chaucer. The *General Prologue*, with its references to St Thomas and a range of other saints gives us an understanding that he situates the *Canterbury Tales* firmly within the cultural context of medieval Western Christianity. Chaucer has been associated with Wycliffite sentiment (see Frances McCormack's essay in this volume, and references there). However, a close examination shows his hagiographical writing to be in the mainstream.[10] His references to things liturgical, in addition to his translations of *Boece* and the *ABC*,

[8] *The Canterbury Tales: Fifteenth-Century Continuations and Additions*, ed. John M. Bowers, TEAMS (Kalamazoo, 1992), p. 64; this includes the *Siege of Thebes* prologue.

[9] See Finucane, *Miracles*, pp. 11–12; Samantha Riches, 'Hagiography in Context: Images, Miracles, Shrines and Festivals', *A Companion to Middle English Hagiography*, ed. Sarah Salih (Cambridge, 2006), pp. 25–46. Marks also explores a number of local shrines and cult sites, *Image and Devotion*, pp. 64–85, 186–227.

[10] Elizabeth Robertson argues that the *Man of Law's Tale*'s radical 'difference' resides in Custance's gender, and that it engages aspects of orthodox Catholicism in opposition to Lollard views, 'The "Elvyssh" Power of Constance: Christian Feminism in Geoffrey Chaucer's *The Man of Law's Tale*', *Studies in the Age of Chaucer* 23 (2001), 143–80, p. 149.

a conventional prayer to the Virgin Mary, show religious thought to be integral to his understanding of the world around him.

Saints' Miracles

Saints' lives usually have three components: the life, the passion and miracles. Frequently these were formal documents originating as part of the canonization process. However, legendary lives of saints also become part of the oral and anonymous written traditions. Of the latter, many tell stories of holy persons who may in fact never have existed but whose legends were very real to the faithful in the Middle Ages. Miracles of the Virgin take these legends a step further by presenting Mary in hundreds of situations, ranging from healing and salvific interventions in the lives of the faithful to stories of visions and mystical betrothals.

These narrative forms have a long history in England. Arguably the most popular collection, the *Legenda Aurea*, the *Golden Legend*, compiled by the Dominican Jacobus de Voragine in about 1260,[11] circulated widely and was translated into Middle English.[12] Other Middle English collections of saints' legends include the late-thirteenth-century *South English Legendary*.[13] Collections of miracles of the Virgin appear even earlier than the *Golden Legend*: in addition to Marian stories included in works like Caesarius of Heisterbach's *Dialogue on Miracles* and Vincent of Beauvais's *Speculum Historiale*, discrete collections of miracles appear in manuscripts, including British Library Cotton Cleopatra C.X and Oxford Balliol 240, both from the late twelfth century.[14]

Some argue that Chaucer shows little concern for things beyond this world. Many feel more comfortable seeing him as celebrating the secular, and some would have us think him, if not a fledgling Lollard, at least a strong critic of a corrupt Church. And he does provide scathing portraits, particularly of the Pardoner and Summoner, but he balances these with the Parson. Despite these observations, Chaucer's choice of situating his tales within the framing pilgrimage and his inclusion of three tales we can consider saints' legends, in addition to moral tales like the *Clerk's Tale* and *Physician's Tale*, suggest that he, like many in his audience, understood the expression and power of faith.

The *Second Nun's Tale*, the *Prioress's Tale* and the *Man of Law's Tale* can be seen as centred on miracles. To medieval people, miracles constituted those events in which God directly intervened in the lives of individual humans in ways that went above or beyond what was considered natural. In Cecilia's case, the miracles concern her death. First, she continues to live, despite being placed in a scalding bath.[15] The second miracle occurs when she continues to speak even though her

11 William Granger Ryan, *The Golden Legend*, 2 vols (Princeton, 1993), I, p. xiii.

12 Caxton published a direct Middle English translation from Latin; the Middle English *Gilte Legend* was translated from a French version. See Ryan's introduction, p. xiv, and *Gilte Legende*, ed. Richard Hamer, EETS os 327 (Oxford, 2006), p. xi.

13 *South English Legendary*, ed. Charlotte D'Evelyn and Anna J. Mill, EETS os 244 (Oxford, 1959).

14 R. W. Southern, 'The English Origins of the Miracles of the Virgin', *Medieval and Renaissance Studies* 4 (1958), 176–216, argues that miracle collections first appeared in England and were then exported to the continent.

15 V. A. Kolve, accepting Fisher's definition of Cecilia's bath as a Roman hypocaust, points out that the church of St Cecilia in Rome has such a room, 'Chaucer's *Second Nun's Tale* and the Iconography of

throat has met the executioner's axe three times. The miracle told in the *Prioress's Tale* also involves a use of voice that goes beyond the ordinary: the little clergeon continues to sing after his throat has been cut to the neck-bone. Voice also plays a key role in the miracles found in the *Man of Law's Tale*. The miracles in Constance's life occur after she prays; these are God's or the Virgin's direct response to Constance's entreaties. This divine intervention does not merely thread the tales together; it stands as witness to the active working of God in Chaucer's world.

The Second Nun's Tale

The Second Nun tells the legend of St Cecilia, a Roman virgin martyr whose feast was established by the fourth century. Cecilia's sanctity is constructed by her dedication to virginity and refusal to sacrifice to false gods at the demand of the Roman prefect. Cecilia speaks throughout the tale and cannot be silenced, even when her throat has been cut three times; her voice becomes a crucial element of the narrative.

After invoking the Virgin in her prologue, the Second Nun begins with an account of Cecilia's marriage to Valerian, during the Roman persecution of Christians. On their wedding night Cecilia tells her new husband that he must honour her chastity:

> I have an aungel which that loveth me,
> That with greet love, wher so I wake or sleepe,
> Is redy ay my body for to kepe. (VIII 152–4)

When Valerian wants to see the angel, Cecilia sends him to be baptized by Pope Urban. When he returns, he can see the angel, who presents the couple with crowns of lilies and roses.[16] Thus, from the first encounter in which we see Cecilia conversing with another human being, she functions as an instrument of conversion.

The theme of conversion continues. When the angel asks Valerian what he most desires, he responds 'I pray yow that my brother may han grace / To know the trouthe' (237–8). Valerian's brother Tiburce goes to Urban for baptism, after Cecilia instructs him in the faith. The converted brothers, refusing to sacrifice to the Roman gods, greet their martyrdom, kneeling and with 'humble herte and sad [solemn] devocioun': 'Hir soules wenten to the Kyng of grace' (397, 399).

Conversion becomes exponential: the brothers convert Maximus, who converts other members of the prefect Almachius' retinue. Herself called before the prefect, Cecilia refuses to sacrifice and scathingly puts Almachius, and the language of secular power, in their place:

> every mortal man's power nys
> But lyk a bladdre ful of wynd, ywys.
> For with a nedles poynt, whan it is blowe,
> May al the boost of it be leyd ful lowe. (VIII 438–41)

Saint Cecilia', *New Perspectives in Chaucer Criticism*, ed. Donald M. Rose (Norman, OK, 1981), pp. 141–2.

[16] These crowns appear also within the context of chaste marriage in 'De Juliano Abbato, qui per Beata Virgine Marie multa fecit miracula', in Cambridge, Sidney Sussex MS 95, book five, chapter ten.

He condemns her to a scalding bath, and when that fails to kill her, sends an executioner to finish her off. Although struck thrice in the neck, Cecilia continues to speak.[17] After three days, Cecilia commends her followers to Urban, asking that her house be maintained as a church (VIII 551–3). This, consecrated by Pope Urban at the tale's end, is believed to be the church of St Cecilia in Rome's Trastevere section. Why choose to tell this particular legend, given the number of saints' legends available to Chaucer? Chaucer may originally have composed this legend for an occasion, the appointment in 1381 of Adam Easton as Cardinal Priest to Santa Cecilia in Trastevere.[18]

Her story, as found in the *Passio S. Caeciliae*, dates in writing from the fifth century. Chaucer's tale follows closely versions found in earlier texts. Sherry Reames (see p. 81 here for details) has demonstrated that Chaucer spliced two versions of the Cecilia legend: part from *The Golden Legend*, part from a Franciscan abridgement. Although the *Second Nun's Tale* has its detractors (among them David Aers, who sees the tale as 'a conventional form of sentimental piety'[19]), many believe it to be an exemplar of its genre: Kolve calls it 'the finest work in this genre to survive in Middle English'.[20] Chaucer himself calls it a translation (VIII 25), suggesting he has done little to alter his sources. The tale does, however, lead us to some possible conclusions regarding Chaucer's view of the sacred and the role of the saint within that sacred context. Since Reames's discovery of the Franciscan abridgement, much earlier discussion of Chaucer's use of sources needs reconsidering: the translation is a close one. However, as Grossi points out, small changes and omissions subtly change the direction of the story: he argues that Chaucer's minor changes heighten the absurdity and impotence of the pagan Roman gods in the face of Christian faith.[21]

Grossi, however, neglects one subtle change: Chaucer's description of Cecilia's discourse as preaching (VIII 342, 539), rather than merely the 'teaching' found in the Franciscan abridgement, has implications for the way in which the audience understands the tale, particularly Cecilia's role and by extrapolation the role of women in instruction on things divine. For many in Chaucer's audience, the idea of women adopting the authoritative role of preaching would have been a vexed concept. Paul's first letter to Timothy clearly outlines woman's role: 'Let the woman learn in silence, with all subjection. But I suffer not a woman to teach, nor to use authority over the man: but to be in silence' (1 Timothy 2: 11–12). Yet, as Blamires points out, some medieval theologians made the case that in certain circumstances, women were bound to preach/teach, and he shows the hair-splitting arguments produced around this issue.[22] Some commentators drew a

[17] Julian of Norwich mentions Cecilia's three neck wounds in her Short Text, additional evidence that the saint's story was known in Chaucer's time: *The Writings of Julian of Norwich*, ed. Nicholas Watson and Jacqueline Jenkins (University Park, PA, 2006), pp. 64–5.

[18] Helen Cooper notes this connection, *Oxford Guides to Chaucer: The Canterbury Tales* (Oxford, 1986), p. 358. See also John Hirsh, 'The Politics of Spirituality: The Second Nun and the Manciple', *The Chaucer Review* 12 (1977), 129–46.

[19] *Chaucer* (Brighton, 1986), p. 51, 54–7.

[20] Kolve, 'Chaucer's *Second Nun's Tale*', p. 139. See also Carolyn Collette, 'Critical Approaches to the *Prioress's Tale* and the *Second Nun's Tale*', *Chaucer's Religious Tales*, ed. C. David Benson and Elizabeth Robertson (Cambridge, 1991), pp. 95–107.

[21] Joseph L. Grossi Jr, 'The Unhidden Piety of Chaucer's St Cecilie', *The Chaucer Review* 36 (2002), pp. 298–309.

[22] Alcuin Blamires, 'Women and Preaching in Medieval Orthodoxy, Heresy and Saints' Lives', *Viator* 26

distinction between private instruction and public preaching. By Chaucer's time, we have examples of real women preaching, Hildegard of Bingen and Birgitta of Sweden among them, perhaps an indication that more women preached than we might acknowledge. The term *preach* was clearly loaded. The archbishop of York harasses Margery Kempe for preaching. Margery carefully disassociates what she does from preaching: 'I preche not, ser, I come in no pulpytt. I vse but comowny-cacyon & good wordys, & þat wil I do while I leue.'[23]

Cecilia preaches first to Tiburce, when she explains the Trinity to him, using the metaphor of man's three 'sapiences': memory, imagination and judgement (VIII 337–40). The narrator says that 'gan she hym ful bisily to preche' (VIII 342), glossed in the *Riverside Chaucer* as 'preach'. Chaucer here translates 'predicare' in the *Golden Legend.* This first instance of Cecilia's preaching falls into the private, personal sphere defined by Aquinas as acceptable for a woman.[24] Her audience is limited to family members, within the confines of her house and her aim is the spiritual good of her limited audience. Chaucer leaves his source in his second characterization of Cecilia's discourse as preaching: she preaches to the community gathered to watch her die. She

> nevere cessed hem the feith to teche
> That she hadde fostred; hem she gan to preche. (VIII 538–9)

This becomes public preaching. Although situated in her house – which will become a church – Cecilia preaches to those beyond her domestic circle. In this way, Chaucer places Cecilia in a masculine if not sacerdotal role (though in doing so he has the precedents of not only legendary but real holy women). Through her evangelizing, just as Valerian and Tiburce embrace Christianity, Maximus and the tormentors abandon their false gods, and the Christian community she had 'fostred' continue to learn the faith.

Cecilia's voice, then, becomes a primary instrument in this tale of martyrdom. If many of the elements we appreciate in the tale – Cecilia's eloquence, her nimble mind's ability to undercut Almachius in his pompous institution of power – can be found in Chaucer's two major sources, in what aspects of his tale do we see Chaucer's genius? Firstly, he has rendered his prose sources into verse form; Reames finds Chaucer's translation from the Franciscan abridgement much more energetic in style, especially through its use of rhyme royal.[25] Craig Fehrman has discussed Chaucer's style of translation in the *Astrolabe* in relation to the Wycliffite Bible and the theory of literal vs. 'opin' translation.[26] Chaucer's treatment of his two sources here may well present an example of both types within one tale.

If the *Second Nun's Tale* is an early example of Chaucer's hagiographical work, in his two other hagiographical ventures we see him giving more free play to

(1995), pp. 135–52.

23 *The Book of Margery Kempe*, ed. Sanford B. Meech and Hope Emily Allen, EETS os 212 (Oxford, 1940), p. 126.

24 Blamires, 'Women and Preaching', pp. 145–6.

25 S. L. Reames, 'The Second Nun's Prologue and Tale', *Sources and Analogues of the Canterbury Tales*, ed. Robert M. Correale and Mary Hamel, 2 vols (Cambridge, 2002, 2006), vol. I, pp. 491–528, at p. 496; see also Stephen Knight, *Geoffrey Chaucer* (Brighton, 1986), p. 146.

26 See Craig T. Fehrman, 'Did Chaucer read the Wycliffite Bible?', *The Chaucer Review* 42 (2007), 111–38.

his ideas, rather than 'translating' a source, and this tale introduces concerns that Chaucer explores more extensively in his other miracle stories.

Incarnational Piety and the Prioress's Tale

Although not a close translation of an identifiable source, the *Prioress's Tale* relies heavily on Marian legends popular in the late Middle Ages. A retelling of the widespread miracle, 'The Child Slain by Jews', it emphasizes the protagonist's use of his voice and the miracle of his ability to sing after his throat has been cut. Just as Cecilia continues to preach after axe strokes to her neck, the little clergeon sings *Alma redemptoris mater* after he is murdered. The shared Marian emphasis in these tales' prologues further indicates they are closely related in Chaucer's mind.[27] Some see no doctrinal significance in the *Prioress's Tale*.[28] However, close examination within the context of its analogues shows us how well Chaucer understands the incarnational piety and Marian devotion of his time and puts his knowledge to creative use. By the late Middle Ages many English devotional practices focused on the physical reality of Christ, as witnessed by, among others, the works of Julian of Norwich and Margery Kempe. The *Prioress's Tale* also invokes the incarnate Christ, by playing on a complex network of allegory and association to embody an artful celebration of sacrifice and redemption. At the centre of that network sounds the voice of faith, articulating the Word. The significance of the boy's song can be understood more fully by first defining incarnational piety as expressed in Bernard of Clairvaux's sermons on the Annunciation; second, by showing how the Miracles of the Virgin known as the lily miracles enact the devotional practices Bernard recommends in his sermons; and third, by establishing the *Prioress's Tale* as a lily miracle to suggest a reading for the perplexing 'greyn' that allows the little clergeon to voice his song after death.

Bernard's Sermons

Bernard of Clairvaux (b. 1090) most influentially expresses the foundation of incarnational piety in his four sermons on the Annunciation.[29] These do not expound any radical new ideas about Mary; however, they emphasize the value of Christians saluting the Virgin as did the angel Gabriel and thus became a blueprint for popular medieval incarnational piety.[30] Bernard articulates two ideas crucial to our analysis: firstly, he combines flower imagery with the concept of the Word, and secondly, he emphasizes individual participation in the incarnational moment. In doing so, he fuses into a cohesive whole the importance of Mary hearing and accepting the word as understood in John 1; Marian flower imagery; and a Marian interpretation of the Song of Songs. These elements work together to establish

27 See Carolyn Collette, 'Chaucer's Discourse of Mariology: Gaining the Right to Speak', *Art and Context in Late Middle English Narrative*, ed. Robert R. Edwards (Woodbridge, 1994), pp. 127–47.

28 Collette, 'Critical Approaches', pp. 95–107.

29 Bernard of Clairvaux, *Four Homilies in Praise of the Blessed Virgin Mary*, trans. Mary-Bernard Said (Kalamazoo, 1993), pp. xiii–xxiv. See also Laurel Broughton, 'Ave Maria: The Incarnational Aesthetic and Mary Miracle Collections', *Studia Mystica* (1999), pp. 1–14.

30 The Word/Christ equation begins with John 1: 1, an equation Augustine emphasizes in *Confessions* XI.

the importance of the Annunciation to individual salvation, defining a devotional practice through which anyone who repeats the angelic salutation ('Ave Maria', 'Hail Mary') actively participates in the Incarnation.

Bernard maintains that Mary's grace and apprehension of Christ result from her willingness to incline her ear (Psalm 45: 10) to the word. He connects flower symbolism with the concept of the word, saying that 'Nazareth' means 'flower' and 'It was at Nazareth therefore that Christ's birth was first announced, because in the flower lies the hope of the fruit to come . . . I think no one doubts that the Word is the fruit and the Word is Christ' (1.3).[31] Later he explains that the flower shall grow out of Jesse's root (Isaiah 11: 1), that the rod symbolized the Virgin and the blossom the virgin birth (2.5).[32] Bernard and others associate the blossom with the lily of the Song of Songs; thus the lily represents Christ, not just the purity of the Virgin.

Individual participation in the incarnational moment becomes the focus of Bernard's message. He draws his reader's eye to Mary's room, 'the private chamber of her modest room where, I suppose, having shut the door she was praying to the Father in secret' (3.1).[33] He exhorts his audience to enter this room:

> Gather round this virginal chamber and, if you can, enter your sister's chaste inner room. Behold, God has sent down for the Virgin. Behold, Mary is spoken for by the angel. Put your ear to the door, strain to listen to the tidings he brings. (2.2)[34]

Putting his ear to the door allows the reader not only to eavesdrop on the incarnational moment, but to take part as Bernard himself participates in the event. In his powerful closing image, he puts himself in both the place of the angel Gabriel, who brings Mary the word, and Mary herself, as she accepts the word. He, like the angel, waits poised for the answer:

> The angel is waiting for your reply . . . We, too, are waiting for this merciful word, my lady . . . Give your answer quickly, my Virgin. My lady, say this word which earth and hell and heaven itself are waiting for. The very King and Lord of all, he who has so desired your beauty, is waiting anxiously for your answer and assent, by which he proposes to save the world. (4.8)[35]

Bernard stresses the critical relationship between the Incarnation and the climax of salvation history. Without the Virgin's acceptance, salvation through the Crucifixion becomes impossible. Therefore, the faithful should emulate Mary, who by her perfect faith and complete acceptance of Christ becomes the first Christian and sets the example for all the faithful who follow, as Bernard emphasizes by putting himself in Mary's place when he uses her language to offer himself to God: 'May the Word . . . deign to be in me, deign to be to me according to your word. Let it be for the whole world, but let it be to me uniquely 'according to your word' (4.11).[36]

[31] Bernard, *Four Homilies*, p. 8.
[32] Ibid., p. 19.
[33] Ibid., p. 33.
[34] Ibid. p. 16.
[35] Ibid., p. 53.
[36] Ibid., p. 58.

Bernard, with his audience in tow, projects himself into the two major personages of the Annunciation scene. With Gabriel he brings Mary the word, articulated in the greeting, 'Ave Maria', and like Mary he accepts the word in saying with her, 'Be it unto me according to thy word'. In other words, participation in the incarnational moment can be achieved by anyone reciting Ave Maria, and Bernard and all the faithful can thereby become actors in this simple but potent drama.

In these sermons, Bernard identifies the Annunciation as the heart of what Gail McMurray Gibson has called the incarnational aesthetic, the fascination with the human physicality of Christ:

> In fifteenth-century devotion . . . it is the Incarnate Son rather than the Godhead who is ever fixed in the eyes of the beholder . . . the relevant central image for the late Middle Ages is a suffering human body racked on a cross.

She goes on to say

> The insistence on particular, corporal religious images perceived in the world is extended as far as, quite literally, the human eye can see. The spiritual object of meditation is held earthbound for as long as human ingenuity (and pious curiosity) will permit. Thus it is the fourteenth and fifteenth centuries which first produced images of the Annunciation with the conceived Lord already visibly present to the human worshipper on fecundating beams of light sent from God's hands.[37]

Like Bernard in his sermons, many visual depictions of the Annunciation encompass the whole cycle of salvation and redemption within the scene. The vase of lilies represents more than the Virgin's purity. As defined by Bernard and noted by both Schiller and Mâle, the lily represents Christ himself, who becomes a living, physical presence in the vase of flowers between Mary and Gabriel.[38] The crucifixion windows at Long Melford, Suffolk and Westwood, Wiltshire, showing Christ impaled on a cross of lilies, make explicit the connection between the lily and Christ and the flower's association with the sacrificial cycle of redemption set in motion at the moment of the Incarnation.[39]

The lily is not the only element common to both the tales and the visual representations of the Annunciation. Often depictions fuse 'word' with 'the Word': in many paintings the words 'Ave Maria' actually appear in the scene. Artists choose to spell them out, sometimes on a scroll, as in the manuscript Cambridge Fitzwilliam 242, sometimes on beams of light emanating from Gabriel's mouth, as in the Cortona Altarpiece by Fra Angelico. Jan van Eyck, in the Washington Annunciation, presents Mary's response, 'Ecce ancilla', upside down, presumably so God the Father can clearly read the words.

[37] Gail McMurray Gibson, *Theater of Devotion* (Chicago, 1989), pp. 6–7.

[38] Gertrud Schiller, *The Iconography of Christian Art*, trans. Janet Seligman (Greenwich, CT, 1971), I, p. 51; Emil Mâle, *The Gothic Image*, trans. Dora Nussey (1913, repr. New York, 1958), p. 244.

[39] Clopton Chantry Chapel, Holy Trinity Church, Long Melford; Brian Coe, *Stained Glass in England, 1150–1550* (London, 1981), Westwood crucifixion, p. 80. According to Sarah Brown, this association of the lily and the cross, a uniquely British motif, occurs as early as 1391, in the painted vault of St Helen's Church, Abingdon; she also cites an alabaster tablet in the Victoria and Albert Museum: *York Minster: An Architectural History c 1220–1500* (Swindon, 2003), chapter 6, n. 41.

The Lily Miracles

Bernard's blueprint became the plot vehicle for the lily miracles. As didactic proponents of the incarnational aesthetic, these legends contain two key components: first, a prayer or hymn, usually but not always 'Ave Maria', that commemorates Mary's conception of Christ; and second, the miraculous manifestation in the mouth, the symbol of Christ incarnate. Like Bernard, who impatiently urges the Virgin to respond to Gabriel's message, lily miracle protagonists actively participate in the cycle of redemption that begins with the Annunciation. They unite themselves with the angel in repeating 'Ave Maria' to Mary, but also emulate Mary in that their faith enables them to bear Christ in the form of the lily that springs from their mouths.

The basic lily miracle plot involves a protagonist who faithfully repeats Ave Maria. When he dies, a flower, usually a lily, springs from his grave and is discovered to be rooted in his mouth. The version in British Library Additional 39,996, 'The Clerk Buried outside a Churchyard', presents the basic lily pattern with some embroidery.[40] A clerk suddenly becomes ill in a field and dies unshriven, but before he dies, he recites 'Ave Maria'. He is buried in the field because, having died unshriven, he cannot be buried in a churchyard. The third day after his burial a lily appears on his grave, with 'Ave Maria' written on the leaves. The parson and community ask the bishop for permission to remove the body and bury the clerk in holy ground.

The implications of the miracle narrative go beyond the promise of the Annunciation to suggest the fulfilment of that promise in the Resurrection. The lily, the manifestation of Christ, springs from the unshriven clerk's grave three days after his death. This emphasizes the promise of everlasting life: just as Christ died and on the third day rose again, the clerk dies and on the third day the living symbol of Christ rises from his grave and causes a kind of physical resurrection of the clerk, in that his remains are removed from unholy to holy ground. As noted earlier, we find the scope of this story pattern echoed in stained glass. The Annunciation in York Minster's Bowet window depicts the usual scene but places a crucifix within the lily. the Long Melford Crucifixion window, mentioned before, shows Christ impaled on a cross of lilies.

The Prioress's Tale

The Prioress's Tale echoes key elements of Marian devotion defined by Bernard's sermons on the Annunciation and enacted in these lily miracles, most specifically the child's veneration of Mary and the Incarnation, and his compulsion to use his voice in repeatedly singing the antiphon. If Chaucer's version is a lily miracle, it must contain the two major lily pattern elements: the prayer/hymn and the miraculous manifestation. The tale's hero, the little clergeon, sings in praise of the Virgin, and when he dies, a miraculous manifestation appears in his mouth. The major components of the pattern, 'Ave Maria' and the lily, have been replaced by *Alma redemptoris mater* and the 'greyn', but neither change alters the pietistic basis of the tale, and Chaucer's tale complies with the lily pattern.

40 Text in Ruth Wilson Tryon, 'Miracles of Our Lady in Middle English Verse', *Proceedings of the Modern Language Association of America* 23 (1938), 365–7.

Alma redemptoris mater is fairly common throughout the tale's closest analogues, identified by Carleton Brown as the 'C' group. *Alma redemptoris mater* celebrates the Annunciation and the Incarnation. The antiphon praises Mary as the instrument of redemption. The closing lines directly refer to the Annunciation:

> Virgo prius ac posterius
> Gabrielis ab ore
> sumens illud 'Ave'
> peccatorum miserere.
>
> (Virgin before and after
> from Gabriel's mouth
> taking that 'Ave'
> have mercy on [our] sins)[41]

So the little clergeon commemorates the Annunciation and its implications as made explicit in the text of the hymn he sings. He learns this hymn as an addition to other devotional habits: whenever he sees an image of Mary he kneels and says an Ave Maria (VII 506–8).

'Ave Maria' does not appear in any of the other C tales; including it may be coincidence, arising out of Chaucer's search for something to emphasize the child's piety. However, given the popularity of the lily miracles and Chaucer's keen observation and knowledge of the society in which he lived, we may conjecture that he knew the legends and was aware of the implications of using 'Ave Maria' in this context. Chaucer varies the second element of the lily pattern by substituting 'greyn' for the more appropriate flower, a change that gives rise to varying interpretations. The slain clergeon explains his posthumous singing as follows: Mary

> bad me for to synge
> This anthem verraily in my deyynge,
> As ye han herd, and whan that I hadde songe,
> Me thoughte she leyde a greyn upon my tonge.
> Wherefore I synge, and synge moot certeyn,
> In honour of that blisful Mayden free
> Til fro my tonge of taken is the greyn;
> And after that thus seyde she to me:
> 'My litel child, now wol I fecche thee,
> Whan that the greyn is fro thy tonge ytake.
> Be not agast; I wol thee nat forsake' (VII 656–9)

This use of 'greyn' seems to be Chaucer's invention. The Latin C versions early enough to have influenced Chaucer only mention the child's ability to sing (the pebble and gem found in C9 and C10 are, by their manuscripts' dates, too late to have affected Chaucer, although these may have been derived from earlier versions, now lost). The Middle English analogue, 'The Child Slain by Jews', in the Vernon manuscript, puts a lily in the boy's mouth.[42]

41 John Harper, *Forms and Order of Western Liturgy from the Tenth to the Eighteenth Century* (Oxford, 1991), pp. 274–5.

42 See Broughton, 'The Prioress's Tale', *Sources and Analogues of the Canterbury Tales*, vol. II, pp. 583–647.

The meaning of Chaucer's ambiguous 'greyn' has long been debated by scholars, ranging from plausible liturgical readings to the absurdly pharmacological: Brachter goes so far as to suggest that the grain of Paradise completes a scatological pattern used by Chaucer to satirize the legend.[43] A ridiculous object for the Virgin to place in the schoolboy's mouth would mean Chaucer knowingly perverts the theological structure of the tale. It is more probable Chaucer intended to tell this miracle seriously and chose a symbol his audience would recognize as appropriate to the lily miracle's structure. Skeat and Beichner may have been on the right track when they interpreted 'greyn' as seed, although neither for the best reason.[44] Hawkins comes even closer when, reading the tale as an allegory of Church against Synagogue, he identifies the 'greyn' as either a pearl or a grain of wheat and links both symbols to the concept of Christ as logos.[45] Maltman's association with the liturgy of Becket's feast also comes close. However, reading the greyn in the context of the lily miracles encompasses these various interpretations.

Chaucer's use of 'greyn' derives from a commonplace image of the Incarnation. Seed, grain and green imagery have long been associated with the conception of Christ. Early Christian writers like Tertullian, Clement of Alexandria, Hippolytus, Anthanasius and Ephrem the Syrian use agrarian metaphors to describe the Incarnation, going back to the prophecies of Isaiah, particularly 11: 1: 'And there shall come forth a rod out of the root of Jesse and a flower shall rise up out of his root', and 45: 8, 'Drop down dew, ye heavens from above, and let the clouds rain the just: let the earth be opened and bud forth a saviour: and let justice spring up together: I the Lord have created him'. These, when combined with the various New Testament references to sowing seed, make the agricultural metaphor for the Incarnation particularly rich and resonant. Jesus himself glosses the parable of the sower: 'But he that received the seed upon good ground, is he that heareth the word, and understandeth, and beareth fruit' (Matthew 13: 23) And when one considers 'word' as it appears in John 1, the agricultural images take on more levels of meaning. The early Church fathers recognized and incorporated this many-layered metaphor into their works, as Gambero shows: Tertullian says: 'The second Adam, as the apostle said, had to come forth from a virgin earth'; Clement of Alexandria: 'But when the Father, full of goodness and love for men, rained down his Word upon the earth, this same Word became the spiritual nourishment for virtuous men'; Ephrem the Syrian: 'This earth is Mary's body, the temple in which a seed has been deposited. Observe the angel who comes and deposits this seed in Mary's ear'.[46] Bernard himself uses the metaphor, saying 'Not without reason do we understand Christ to be the fruit of the flowers sprung from this seed' (1.3)

43 See Sister Nicholas Maltman, 'The Divine Granary of the End of the Prioress's Greyn', *The Chaucer Review* 17 (1982), 163–70; James T. Brachter, 'The Greyn in the Prioress's Tale', *Notes and Queries* (December 1963), 444–5.

44 *The Complete Works of Geoffrey Chaucer* (Oxford, 1894–7), ed. W. W. Skeat, V, p. 491; Paul E. Beichner, 'The Grain of Paradise', *Speculum* 36 (1961), 302–7.

45 Sherman Hawkins, 'Chaucer's Prioress and the Sacrifice of Praise', *Journal of English and Germanic Philology* 63 (1964), 599–624.

46 Luigi Gambero, *Mary and the Fathers of the Church*, trans. Thomas Buffer (San Francisco, 1999), pp. 67, 71, 114.

The grain image has visual counterparts. The grain Virgins of Eastern Europe wear a dress decorated with a golden wheat pattern.[47] In the West too, the Rohan Master paints Mary on a bed of corn; the Virgin and Child with kneeling knight scene found in the manuscript Cambridge, Trinity College B.11.7, fol. 20r, shows Mary wearing a blue cloak embroidered with her name and grain-like vegetation.[48]

Sowing seed (Matthew13: 3–23, Mark 4: 3–33, Luke 8: 5–15) then becomes an metaphor the Incarnation, as seen in *The Myroure of Our Ladye*, the Middle English service book for the Brigittine convent at Syon:

> Blyssed be thow moste worthy sower that haste sowen a grayne of the beste whete in the best lande. wette wyth the dew of the holy goste. whyche grayne deed ys meruelously multyplyed. wherwith aungels are fedde. wherby deade men lyue agayne. by whyche sycke men ar heled. wherby all thynges are restored. Thys sower ys the father of heuen. the grayne ys the sonne. the erthe ys oure Lady. The grayne was sowen in the erthe by hys incarnacyon. yt was dede by hys passyon.[49]

In Matthew 12, Christ provides his own gloss for the parable of the sower, defining the seed as the Word of God. *The Myroure of Oure Ladye* imputes the same meaning to the 'word' in the parable as is given to 'word' in John 1. Thus the 'grayne'/word becomes the son, who is Christ, and the good earth upon which it fell, the Virgin. The English *Beata viscera* uses the seed metaphor, as does the late-thirteenth-century carol, 'Edi beo thu, hevenes quene', which describes Mary as 'erthe to gode sede'. Dunbar's 'Hale sterne superne' calls Mary 'Spice, flour, delice of paradys / That baire the gloryus grayne'.[50] Agrarian images from Isaiah and other references to seed pepper Sarum liturgy.

Chaucer has taken this multifaceted symbol of the Incarnation and used it to create a tale richly resonant with incarnational meaning. The seed is a manifestation that properly reflects the hero's celebration of the Annunciation and Incarnation. Like the lily, it signifies that praise of the Virgin brings forth the actual presence of Christ in the mouth of the praiser. Chaucer's choice of 'greyn' over the flower is logical because of its medicinal powers; by it dead men live again, the sick are healed, and all things are restored. This makes the symbol particularly fitting for the little schoolboy's predicament: he lives again to sing his song; his wound is healed in that it does not hamper his ability to sing; and he is restored to his earthly mother and ultimately to his heavenly mother.

Not only does this tale resonate with other miracles of the Virgin, it connects with seed images Chaucer uses in the *Second Nun's Tale* and the *Parson's Tale*. In the Cecilia legend, Pope Urban exclaims:

> 'Almyghty Lord, O Jhesu Crist,' quod he,
> 'Sower of chaast conseil, hierde of us alle,

47 For example Virgin Mary with the Garlands, St Nicholas Church, Bor near Tachov, Jiri Fajt, *Gothic Art and Architecture in Western Bohemia* (Praha, 1995), p. 77. My thanks to Lorraine Stock for bringing these grain Virgins to my attention.

48 For the Rohan Master see Anne Baring and Jules Cashford, *The Myth of the Goddess* (New York, 1991), p. 576, figure 17; Marks reproduces the Trinity manuscript illustration.

49 *The Myroure of Our Ladye*, ed. John Henry Blunt, EETS ES 19 (London, 1873), p. 201

50 *Middle English Marian Lyrics*, ed. Karen Saupe (Kalamazoo, 1998), pp. 52, 170.

The fruyt of thilke seed of Chastitee
That thou has sowe in Cecile, taak to thee!' (VII 192–6)

This use of seed, sower and fruit, found in Chaucer's *Golden Legend* source, plays on the commonplace symbol of chastity, especially in combination with the crowns of lilies and roses the angel gives Cecilia and Valerian in celebration of their chaste marriage. The 'greyn' also anticipates the seed of repentence and tree of the cross used by the Parson (and found in his source) as a metaphor for penitence.[51] I would not argue that Chaucer deliberately chose these images to link these three tales as much as that the imagery of green and growing things, deeply imbedded in his culture, provides a wider continuity between the tales.

Like Cecilia, the child uses his voice insistently to articulate his faith. Following the pattern Bernard establishes in his sermons, the clergeon participates in the incarnational moment with a voice that controls the action of the tale. Indeed, Chaucer emphasizes the idea of the mouth/voice beginning at the first stanza of the *Prioress's Prologue*: 'by the mouth of children thy bountee / Parfourned is' (VII 457–8). Beginning in the stanza that introduces the child, he uses his voice in devotion to the Virgin (VII 505–8); this devotion motivates him to learn *Alma redemptoris mater.* Learning the song's meaning, he asserts: 'I wol it konne Oure Lady for to honoure' (VII 543). Once he has learned the song he sings it 'wel and boldely'. Walking through the Jewish neighbourhood, 'Twies a day it passed thurgh his throte' (VII 548). He delights in the song which expresses his devotion:

The swetnesse his herte perced so
Of Cristes mooder that, to hire to preye,
He kan nat stynte of syngyng by the weye. (VII 555–7)

His mother uses her voice to express her anxiety and despair, and devotion to Mary. Searching for her missing child, 'evere on Cristes mooder meeke and kynde / She cride' (597–8). As if in response,

Jhesu of his grace
Yaf in hir thought inwith a litel space
That in that place after hir sone she cryde,
Where he was casten in a pit bisyde. (VII 603–6)

Significantly, just as she has inspired her son's devotion to the Virgin, the poor widow uses her voice to trigger divine intervention that manifests the miracle: the next thing we learn is that even with his throat cut, the child sings *Alma redemptoris mater* so loudly that 'al the place gan to rynge' (VII 613) and the community discovers his body. Mother and son become allied with the heavenly Mother and Son, the weeping widow calling to mind the weeping Virgin at the foot of the cross, while the martyred child reminds the audience of that ultimate sacrifice.

The Man of Law's Tale, Hagiography and Marian Miracles

Chaucer's *Man of Law's Tale* combines aspects of both the saint's legend and the

[51] See Richard Newhauser, 'Parson's Tale', *Sources and Analogues of the Canterbury Tales*, vol. I, pp. 530–613.

miracle of the Virgin. Like many saints, Custance is patient in the face of adversity, effects numerous conversions, and instigates a miracle or two. In addition to the elision of the two genres, Chaucer develops in this tale thematic elements like these found in the *Second Nun's Tale* and *Prioress's Tale*. Like Cecilia, Custance uses her voice as an instrument of conversion; like Cecilia and the little clergeon, she uses her voice to establish her connection with the divine. Thus in the *Man of Law's Tale* Chaucer presents both generic and thematic concepts that link the three tales under discussion.

Like the *Prioress's Tale*, the *Man of Law's Tale*, has received mixed critical reception. Readers are often tempted to see Custance as 'pale and passive', if not spineless.[52] Carolyn Dinshaw, while deriding what she sees as the tale's excessive length, characterizes Custance as having 'limited self-consciousness' that 'serves patriarchy'; more usually, critics and scholars avoid the tale, A. S. G. Edwards, notes, particularly neglecting the character of Custance and her role in the tale.[53]

While not defining it as preaching, the narrator places Custance in a relationship similar to that of Cecilia to her household and converts. By her very being, Custance elicits a number of conversions, beginning with the Sultan. In Northumbria Custance's presence creates the same effect in Hermengild, who through lovingly observing Custance in prayer and weeping, accepts Christ (II 538–9). Hermengild's conversion manifests itself when the blind Christian Briton asks her for healing, and Custance 'made her boold' to work the miraculous healing.

Perplexed by his wife's power, the constable questions Custance who tells him 'Sire, it is Cristes myght', and

> fereforth she gan oure lay declare
> That she the constable, er that it was eve,
> Converteth, and on Crist maketh hym bileve. (II 572–4)

Although Chaucer does not call this 'preaching' as he does in the *Second Nun's Tale*, clearly Custance teaches the constable the elements of the faith, as Cecilia teaches Valerian and Tiburce. Chaucer plays down this aspect of Custance's character as found in Trivet, the main contender for Chaucer's immediate source, where she clearly preaches.[54] The domestic, personal circumstances of Custance's instructing the constable echo the acceptable venue Blamires ascribes to Aquinas and others for a woman preaching/teaching.

In conjunction with conversion, many miracles occur in the tale. Presenting Custance as one of the significant mothers in the tale, Chaucer allies her with the Virgin Mary, as a reflection of Mary's divine motherhood, by three means: his echoing of Marian lore and devotional texts in descriptions of Custance; her relationships with her fiendish mothers-in-law and the men who attack her chastity;

[52] Stephen Manning, 'Chaucer's Constance, Pale and Passive', *Chaucerian Problems and Perspectives*, ed. E. Vasta and Z. P. Thundy (Notre Dame, 1979), pp. 13–23.

[53] Carolyn Dinshaw, *Chaucer's Sexual Poetics* (Madison, 1989), p. 112; A. S. G. Edwards, 'Critical Approaches to the *Man of Law's Tale*', Benson and Robertson, *Chaucer's Religious Tales*, pp. 85–94.

[54] Trivet uses 'precher' when she first preaches to and converts the Syrian merchants and when she and Hermengild convert Olda and his household. Gower, without using the word 'preach', conveys a sense of this activity: 'She hath hem with hire wordes wise / Of cristes feith so full enformed' (ll. 606–7); see Robert Correale, 'The Man of Law's Prologue and Tale', *Sources and Analogues of the Canterbury Tales*, vol. II, pp. 297, 307, 330.

and Custance's prayers to the Virgin and Mary's subsequent intervention in the Custance's and Mauricius' lives.[55]

By making Custance a mirror of Mary, Chaucer also refashions her story as a miracle of the Virgin, an element not found in Trivet and Gower.[56] These enhanced Marian references connect Chaucer's version to its more distant analogue, the Chaste Empress story.[57] By including these, Chaucer affirms Custance as an example of Marian piety, one that his immediate audience would have recognized and perceived as a positive example.

From the beginning, the Man of Law surrounds Custance with an aura of sanctity, stressing her purity and goodness. He extols her beauty, youth without folly, and humbleness (II 162–5). She is 'mirrour of alle curteisye' (II 166), 'Hir herte is verray chambre of hoolynesse' (II 167), words which could well be applied to the Virgin, who in *Pearl* is the 'queen of courtesy'.[58] Ambrose and Bernard of Clairvaux among others extol Mary's humility.[59] Other verbal connections between Custance and Mary include line 477: 'God list to shew his wonderful myracle / in hire'. Custance, selected by God, becomes a vehicle for God's glory, just as through Mary he worked the miracle of the Incarnation. When Alla weds Custance at Jesus' instigation (Chaucer's addition), she is 'This hooly mayden, that is bright and sheene', (II 690) common Marian epithets, and 'thus has Crist ymaad Custance a queene' (II 693), a statement recalling the popular image of Christ's coronation of the Virgin. Further language reminiscent of the Virgin includes 'unwemmed' (II 924) and 'mayde, ne of wyf' (II 1026).

Custance's relationships with her evil mothers-in-law inversely reinforce her alliance with the Virgin. These unnatural women, devoid of qualities associated with proper maternal feeling, emphasize the opposite in Custance. Chaucer's descriptions of the Sowdanesse and Donegild ally them with Satan. She is called a 'serpent under femynynytee',

> Lik to the serpent deep in helle ybounde!
> O feyned womman, al that may counfounde
> Vertu and innocence. (II 360–3)

She is linked to the devil:

> O Sathan, envious syn thilke day
> That thou were chaced from oure heritage,
> Wel knowestow to wommen the olde way!
> Thou madest Eva brynge us in servage. (II 364–7)

This outburst recalls Eve's sin, the sin that Mary reverses through the Incarnation. As an instrument of devil, this unnatural mother plots the death of her son and

55 Dinshaw, *Chaucer's Sexual Poetics*, pp. 109–11

56 Correale, 'Man of Law's Tale', pp. 277–350.

57 See Nancy Black, *Medieval Narratives of Accused Queens* (Gainesville, 2003), esp. chapters 1, 5 and 6.

58 Part VIII of *Pearl* develops this idea: *Pearl*, ed. E. V. Gordon (Oxford, 1953), lines 421–540. Medieval lyrics, including 'I sing of a maiden' and 'Edi beo thu hevenes quene', link Mary with courtliness: Saupe, *Middle English Marian Lyrics*.

59 See Ambrose, *Three Books concerning Virgins*, A Select Library of Nicene and Post-Nicene Fathers, Second Series, vol. X, pp. 374–87; Bernard, *Super missus est*, ed. J. P. Migne, Patrologia Latina 183 (Paris, 1871), pp. 70b–71a.

his converted courtiers, thus inverting the image of Mary mourning her son at the cross.

Similarly, the Man of Law employs language referring to the devil to describe Donegild:

> And therefore to the feend I thee resigne;
> Lat him enditen of thy traitorie!
> . . . .
> Fy, feendlych spirit, for I dar wel telle,
> Thogh thou heere walke, thy spirit is in helle! (II 780–4)

Setting Custance in direct opposition to these devilish women, Chaucer re-enacts through her the age-old duel between Mary and Satan, a popular plot element in miracles of the Virgin.[60]

Thirdly, Chaucer connects Custance not only with Mary but with Marian miracles through her direct prayer-appeals to the Virgin (see Sherry Reames's discussion of prayers to Mary, pp. 85–92).As her tribulations become increasingly heavy, her prayers increase their intensity of Marian devotion. When first exiled, she prays to the cross (II 451–62), the outcome of Mary's divine motherhood, perhaps a reference that places Custance like Mary at the foot of the cross.[61] Put in the boat by the Syrians, she asks the cross, red with the Lamb's blood, to keep her from the 'fiends claws'. This prayer emphasizes the Crucifixion, the ultimate result of the Incarnation, and again calls the reader's attention to original sin, 'the olde inquitee' reversed by Mary.

Custance's second prayer, when falsely accused of Hermengild's murder, says:

> thou, merciful mayde,
> Marie I meene, doghter to Seint Anne,
> Bifore whos child angeles synge Osanne,
> If I be giltlees of this felonyé,
> My soccour be, for ellis shal I dye! (II 640–4)

Custance's words here delineate a mother–daughter relationship (perhaps recalling her false mothers-in-law), as well as that of mother–son. And a miracle results: a hand smites the false knight, while a voice declares that he has slandered a daughter of holy Church. The justice-wielding hand and the voice, perhaps the voice of God, signal divine intervention, not unlike that seen in Cecilia's extended life and the clergeon's persistent song.

Custance's most intense prayer to the Virgin occurs as she faces her second exile, this time with her baby Mauricius. Chaucer plays on his audience's heartstrings, describing the child on Custance's arm weeping, even as she declares her acceptance of God's will. Her tender gestures recall images of the Virgin holding the infant Jesus and her prayer reinforces this image:

[60] I have identified approximately fifty miracles featuring this conflict, including the widely disseminated 'Pilgrim of St James', 'Theophilus' and 'Devil in beasts' shapes'.

[61] Charles Muscatine briefly made this connection: *Chaucer and the French Tradition* (Berkeley and Los Angeles, 1964), p. 193. See George Keiser, 'The Middle English *Planctus Mariae* and the Rhetoric of Pathos', *The Popular Literature of Medieval England*, ed. Thomas Heffernan (Knoxville, 1985), pp. 167–93; Robert Correale, 'Chaucer's Constance and the Sorrowing Mary', *Marian Library Studies* (1998–2000), pp. 287–94.

'Mooder', quod she, 'and mayde bright, Marie,
Sooth is that thurgh wommanes eggement
Mankynde was lorn, and damned ay to dye,
For which thy child was on a croys yrent.
Thy blisful eyen sawe al his torment;
Thanne is ther no comparison bitween
Thy wo and any wo man may sustene.
Thow sawe thy child yslayn bifore thyn yen,
And yet now lyves my litel child, parfay!
Now, lady bright, to whom alle woful cryen,
Thow glorie of wommanhede, thow faire may,
Thow haven of refut, brighte sterre of day,
Rewe on my child, that of thy gentillesse
Rewest on every reweful in distresse.' (II 841–54)

A sorrowing mother desperate to save her child's life appeals to the ultimate mother who willingly sacrificed her son. This, like the previous prayer, brings results: although Custance and the child drift in the boat for five years, they come to no harm. And Mary miraculously protects Custance, when they reach land, from rape by a 'theef', keeping her 'unwemmed', a word, as noted earlier, used of Mary's virgin state (II 920–4). After the boat passes through the straits of Gibraltar, Mary 'Hath shapen, thurgh hir endelees goodnesse / To make an ende of al hir hevyness' (II 951–2).

Chaucer's emphasis on her enemies' Satanic qualities and Custance's Marian virtues underscore Custance's alliance with the blessed Virgin. Despite the positive outcome of the tale, some have argued that Custance's alliance with the Virgin diminishes Custance as a character and denies her agency.[62] This position may say more about current ways of reading Chaucer than it does about how the *Man of Law's Tale* might have been understood by Chaucer's immediate audience. For such an audience, Custance's sanctity and alliance with the Virgin place her among the many holy women described in saints' legends and other narratives. Moreover, Chaucer's Marian interventions also place his tale firmly in the genre of miracles of the Virgin.

It strongly resembles the Chaste Empress legend, a popular miracle found in many collections and languages, including Middle English.[63] An emperor of Rome goes on a journey, leaving his brother in charge of his kingdom and his chaste wife. The empress rejects the brother's advances; when he refuses to leave her alone, she locks him in a tower and rules the kingdom until the emperor returns. The brother falsely accuses the empress of promiscuity. The emperor commands his men to take her to the woods and behead her. They try to lie with her first; her cries bring a lord, who slays her executioners and takes her home, where his wife makes her nurse to their young son. His brother desires her but she rejects him. While she sleeps he cuts the baby's throat and puts the knife in her hand. The warm blood running in the bed wakes her. She cries out; the lord and lady come to find their baby dead. The lord exiles her, giving her to shipmen, who want to lie with her, but she refuses. They decide to drown her but change their minds and

[62] See Dinshaw, *Chaucer's Sexual Poetics*, pp. 110–11.

[63] I summarize from the Middle English version in *An Alphabet of Tales*, EETS os 126, 127 (London, 1904), pp. 447–50.

abandon her on a high rock in the middle of the sea. There Mary appears to her, comforts her and shows her a herb lying under her head with which she can heal lepers. Finally a ship takes her to port, where she effects her first cure. The baby-killer contracts leprosy; the lord asks her, unrecognized, to heal his brother. She forces him to confess his sins. She reveals her identity and heals him. Returning to Rome she finds her brother-in-law a leper. Again, he confesses the plot against her. She reveals her identity, and heals all the lepers in that city. The emperor being dead, she takes a vow of chastity.

This story includes many elements found in the Custance story, including prayers to the Virgin in time of extreme need and the Virgin's intervention. Both heroines' alliance with the Virgin becomes a source of power, rather than a deprivation of agency. Although both Mary and Custance are praised for humility, the Mary of miracle stories possesses a strong mind and displays it often, arguing like a lawyer for those she wishes to save, putting the devil to flight (she is, after all, empress of hell) and negotiating with Christ himself when she thinks he is out of line. For Custance and many real women living in the real medieval world, the Virgin provides the example of negotiating between marriage, motherhood and commitment to the divine.

Trivet and Gower's versions lack Chaucer's Marian emphasis. Chaucer probably knew the Chaste Empress miracle story, recognized the similarities and capitalized on the affective and pathetic aspect to add greater appeal to his version. This argues for Chaucer's Marian knowledge, if not his own Marian piety, as well as his artistry as a story teller who knows well that 'Thus kan Oure Lady bryngen out of wo / Woful Custance' (977–8).

Conclusion

Individually, these three tales show us Chaucer's artistry in deploying his understanding of medieval English piety. Each allows him to engage specific issues in the manifestation of faith: Cecilia maintains chastity in marriage and embraces martyrdom by refusing to acknowledge pagan gods. The little clergeon rejoices in his love of the Virgin, yet in doing so ignites the anger of the Jewish community and thus brings on his own martyrdom. Custance faces assault on her honour and person and through steadfast prayer, surmounts them. While each tale raises issues that might be considered to test the boundaries, each manages to stay within, if not emphasize accepted pietistic practices.

Collectively, these tales show many of Chaucer's abiding concerns. All three protagonists demonstrate their faith through confrontation with the Other, that which resides outside orthodox belief: pagan, Jew, Muslim. Chaucer's narrators portray these indiscriminately as murderous. The protagonists all use their voices to promote action and response from the divine. Each shows a tendency to preach, or in the case of the clergeon to sing, in proclamation of his/her dedication. All three demonstrate Marian piety (although this is less evident in the Cecilia story itself, the Second Nun's prologue predisposes the reader to a Marian view of Cecilia).

These tales, while not shying away from difficult questions, such as that of women preaching, tend to affirm a spiritual perspective much in keeping with the tenor of Chaucer's time. Although it may be tempting to argue that these tales subvert the standard beliefs, none crosses the boundaries or promotes a potentially heretical view of the world. We might consider that it is possible to see and acknowledge individual faults, even to agree with certain viewpoints critical of the institutional Church, without rejecting the entire institution. After all, if that flawed vessel, the Pardoner, can bring sinners to true repentence, is it not possible to navigate the flaws in the Church, which is itself made up of humans, none of whom is perfect? Is it not possible for Chaucer to read and use some of the ideas of Wycliffe without becoming a committed Lollard?

Taken both individually and collectively, these tales show a writer capable of sophisticated theological thought, who uses his craft and his intelligence to tell stories that weave the stuff of his culture into tales that may provoke the modern reader but most likely pleased his early audiences. The individual and anthologized afterlives of these stories speak to their initial popularity: the *Man of Law's Tale* was the first to be printed separately;[64] five separate copies of the *Prioress's Tale* exist outside manuscripts of the *Canterbury Tales*, second only to excerpted copies of the *Clerk's Tale*.[65]

In these three narratives Chaucer describes miraculous, divine intervention. By choosing these tales, presenting them in rhyme royal and using a serious tone, Chaucer establishes his understanding of a world permeated with sacred possibilities. Enclosed within the framing pilgrimage, he collects many of those possibilities: the bawdy body, the bleeding, martyred body, the otherness of Jew, Muslim and pagan, the perfect (or close to) manifestations of faith and the corrupt individuals who serve the institutions of that faith. In Chaucer's created world these all live side by side, just as they must have in the real world Chaucer inhabited. In the end it may matter less that Chaucer was orthodox or reformist than that he absorbed the world around him and used it to create a world in words as delighting and at the same time perplexing as the world through which he moved.

[64] Edwards, 'Critical Approaches', p. 85; Cooper, *Canterbury Tales*, p. 125.

[65] Cooper, *Canterbury Tales*, p. 287.

10

Chaucer and the Communities of Pilgrimage

DEE DYAS

At nyght was come into that hostelrye
Wel nyne and twenty in a compaignye,
Of sondry folk, by aventure yfalle
In felaweshipe, and pilgrimes were they alle,
That toward Caunterbury wolden ryde. (I 22–7)

Introduction

The mention of community in the context of pilgrimage probably conjures up for students of medieval literature the kind of company which Chaucer depicts assembling at the Tabard inn one spring evening or the parties of travellers described by Felix Fabri[1] or Margery Kempe:[2] groups, assembled by prior arrangement or happenstance, brought together by the common purpose of seeking of a shrine and the benefits which such a journey were considered to bring. Chaucer's 'compaignye' of 'sondry folk', fallen into 'felaweship' provides a very useful narrative frame; it must also have often been a reality, as pilgrims from differing social backgrounds and varying spiritual aspirations formed a temporary community on the road for company and mutual protection.

However, behind any such group of pilgrims, historical or fictional, lie other communities which also need to be taken into account. Those engaged in pilgrimage to a holy place lie at the centre of a series of concentric circles, multiple communities which interact with one another and which must be considered together. It is therefore instructive to consider the dynamics and roles of these other communities before attempting to assess the functioning and characteristics of the central group.

The Community of Pilgrims through Life

The first and most broad-based community which needs to be considered is formed by those engaged in the 'pilgrimage of life', in other words the entire medieval Christian community at work and play, the community to which Chaucer's

[1] *The Book of the Wanderings of Felix Fabri*, trans. A. Stewart, Palestine Pilgrims Text Society (London, 1892).

[2] *Book of Margery Kempe*, ed. Sanford B. Meech and Hope Emily Allen, EETS os 212 (Oxford, 1940).

original audience all belonged. Shaped by New Testament[3] and patristic[4] writings, the idea that all Christian believers are pilgrims en route to the heavenly Jerusalem is a commonplace of medieval sermons and poetry.[5] This wider community not only provides an important backdrop to particular pilgrim expeditions but also functions as a dynamic component within them.

This is a view which runs counter to much discussion of pilgrim groups over recent years,[6] strongly influenced as that has been by the work of Victor and Edith Turner and their stress on concepts of *liminality*[7] and *communitas*.[8] The Turners argue that pilgrimage is *antistructural* in its effects, temporarily freeing participants from the hierarchical roles and relationships which characterize them in everyday life before returning them, changed by their experience, to their previous setting. It therefore subverts, they argue, rather than reinforces normal social patterns.

There are three problems with the application of Turnerian approaches to medieval pilgrimage. The first is that the Turners drew their data largely from twentieth-century manifestations of pilgrimage and it is inappropriate to attempt to read back their observations into medieval experience in the way that has sometimes been attempted.[9] Secondly, their conclusions, and in particular the way in they which have been applied, have recently been strongly contested by other social anthropologists. Eade and Sallnow comment that the 'Turners' model has been subjected to a number of theoretical critiques . . . and has been tested in a variety of field settings. . . In none of these cases did the investigator find support for the theory; to the contrary, a recurrent theme throughout the literature is the maintenance and, in many instances, the reinforcement of social boundaries and

3 For example 1 Peter 2: 11: 'I beseech you as strangers and *pilgrims* (*tamquam advenas et peregrinos*) to refrain yourselves from carnal desires which war against the soul'; Hebrews 11: 13 'All these died according to faith, not having received the promises, but beholding them afar off and saluting them, and confessing that they are pilgrims and strangers (*peregrini et hospites*) on the earth'.

4 The *Letter of St Clement* (bishop of Rome *c.* 90–9) to the Corinthians opens with the greeting, 'The Church of God which dwells as a pilgrim in Rome to the Church of God in pilgrimage at Corinth', *The Apostolic Fathers*, trans. Francis X. Glimm, Joseph M.-F. Marique and Gerald G. Walsh, The Fathers of the Church 1 (Washington, DC, 1969). In *The City of God* Augustine describes Christians as those who 'enjoy their earthly blessings in the manner of pilgrims (*tamquam peregrina*) and they are not attached to them, while these earthly misfortunes serve for testing and correction' (I.29). Citizens of the heavenly kingdom should use earthly things 'like a pilgrim in a foreign land, who does not let himself be taken in by them or distracted from his course towards God' (XIX.17), Augustine, *Concerning the City of God against the Pagans*, trans. Henry Bettenson (Harmondsworth, 1972), pp. 41, 877.

5 For example, 'Ich gode cristen man oweth to be a pilgrime goinge into hevenly Ierusalem', from a sermon by Richard Alkerton (1406), G. R. Owst, *Literature and Pulpit in Medieval England: A Neglected Chapter in the History of English Letters and of the English People*, rev. edn (Oxford, 1961), p. 104.

6 For example Julia Bolton Holloway, *The Pilgrim and the Book: A Study of Dante, Langland and Chaucer* (Bern, 1987), pp. xix, xx; Frederick Jonassen, 'The Inn, the Cathedral and the Pilgrimage of the *Canterbury Tales*', *Studies in Medieval Culture* 29 (1991), 1–35.

7 Defined as 'the state and process of mid-transition in a rite of passage. During the liminal period the *liminars* (the ritual subjects in this phase) are ambiguous, for they pass through a cultural realm that has few or none of the attributes of the past or coming state', Victor and Edith Turner, *Image and Pilgrimage in Christian Perspective* (Oxford, 1978), p. 249.

8 In Turner's model, *communitas* 'trangresses or dissolves the norms that govern structures and institutionalised relationships', Victor Turner, *The Ritual Process* (London, 1969), p. 128.

9 Eamon Duffy argues for a more nuanced use of liminality as a tool, suggesting that there are 'crucial aspects of late medieval pilgrimage that it obscures rather than illuminates', Eamon Duffy, 'The Dynamics of Pilgrimage in Late Medieval England', *Pilgrimage: The English Experience from Becket to Bunyan*, ed. Colin Morris and Peter Roberts (Cambridge, 2002).

distinctions in the social context, rather than their attenuation or dissolution'.[10]

Thirdly, and most importantly, they do not appear to square with the evidence we actually possess about the nature and complexity of medieval pilgrimage. A range of factors, theological, historical and social, all seem to point to a closer connection between the wider community and the central group than is often allowed.

Theological Perspectives

Many literary critics and historians have displayed a strong tendency to treat the twin concepts of life as pilgrimage and the pilgrim identity of all Christian believers as interesting but not terribly important metaphors, often meriting no more than a passing reference. A closer study of Christian theology, history and spirituality, however, shows that it is in fact the process of journeying through life, rather than travelling to holy places, which constitutes the primary meaning of pilgrimage in the late-medieval thinking and preaching, just as it did in earlier centuries. Sermons, anchoritic and mystical texts, the writings of Chaucer, Langland and many others reflect the conviction, evident from the New Testament onwards, that Christians are to consider themselves pilgrims and strangers in this world. Their daily lives are to be characterized by obedience to the commandments of God, resistance to the deadly sins of which St Peter warns in his first letter (1 Peter 2: 11), love of neighbour, service to their community, responsibility and stability (not just a monastic virtue).

So how does this broader concept of pilgrimage relate to the experience of those who travel to holy places? Crucially it provides a set of goals and standards which functions, implicitly and explicitly, as a commentary on the motivation, behaviour and spiritual progress of what can be termed 'place' pilgrims. Pilgrimage to holy places has always been problematic for the Christian Church. In the New Testament and the writings of the early Church there was a clear theological shift away from the pilgrimage practices of the Jews towards an emphasis on the omnipresence of God.[11] From the development of Christian holy places in the fourth century onwards, questions have been raised about the necessity and efficacy of such journeys by figures of the stature of Jerome[12] and Gregory of Nysssa,[13] and concern and opposition expressed by Church leaders and councils.

[10] *Contesting the Sacred: The Anthropology of Christian Pilgrimage*, ed. John Eade and Michael J. Sallnow (London, 1991), pp. 4–5.

[11] See W. D. Davies, *The Gospel and the Land: Early Christianity and Jewish Territorial Doctrine* (Berkeley, 1974); Joan Taylor, *Christians and the Holy Places: The Myth of Jewish-Christian Origins* (Oxford, 1993).

[12] 'When the Lord invites the blest to their inheritance in the kingdom of heaven, He does not include a pilgrimage to Jerusalem among their good deeds . . . O ye who fear the Lord, praise Him in the places where ye now are. Change of place does not effect any drawing nearer unto God' (Epistle 2), *Select Writings and Letters of Gregory, Bishop of Nyssa*, ed. William Moore and Henry Austin Wilson, trans. Schaff and Wace, Select Library of the Nicene and Post-Nicene Fathers 5 (Grand Rapids, 1954).

[13] Though often positive about the benefits of visiting the 'Holy Land', Jerome also warned 'What is praiseworthy is not to have been at Jerusalem but to have lived a good life while there . . . The city which we are to praise and to seek is not that which has slain the prophets and shed the blood of Christ, but that in which [the apostle] rejoices to have his citizenship with the righteous. I do not presume to limit God's omnipotence or to restrict to a narrow strip of earth Him whom the heaven cannot contain . . . Access to the courts of heaven is as easy from Britain as it is from Jerusalem: 'for the kingdom of God is within you.' Nothing is lacking to your faith although you have not seen Jerusalem . . . I am none the better for living where I do' (Letter 58.2, 3, 4), *Letters and Selected Works*, trans. Philip Schaff and Henry Wace,

Standard objections included the core theological paradox of believers journeying to encounter a God who was believed to be present everywhere, together with the practical issues of possible abdication of responsibilities at home by both lay people and cloistered religious, waste of resources and exposure to temptation. Place pilgrimage carried an in-built element of physical and moral danger, thus exposing those who undertook journeys to holy places to linked accusations of irresponsibility, instability and immorality.

Lollards alleged that such journeys were not only an excuse for self-indulgence and sin but a waste of time and resources which should be used to support the community,[14] but they were not alone in their concerns. Orthodox preachers, including the fiercely anti-Wyclif Dominican John Bromyard, complained of those who 'sin more freely when away from home' (away from the watchful eye of the community).[15] Place pilgrimage could only be justified if it contributed to that longer journey through life which Christians hoped would lead to the heavenly Jerusalem – and, crucially, if it was seen to follow the same guidelines: a desire to seek God and avoid sin; a willingness to embrace penance and sacrifice and self-discipline. A twelfth-century sermon, *Veneranda dies*, emphasizes that the physical journey should be accompanied by spiritual and moral reformation. It is framed by, and must function as, a microcosm of the pilgrimage of life. Before departure, forgiveness must be offered to others in the sending community, amends made to any who have grievances, permission obtained from all to whom the pilgrim has obligations. For this preacher, 'place pilgrimage' is not a detour or excursion but a section of the main route, and he borrows words from Matthew 7: 13–14 and from 1 Peter 2: 11 which speak of the Christian life as a whole: 'The pilgrim route is the best way, but the most narrow. The road is, in fact, narrow that leads man to life, and the road is wide and spacious that leads to death. The pilgrim route . . . tames lust, it suppresses carnal desires which militate against the soul.' On his or her return the pilgrim must abstain from wrong behaviour and persevere in good works 'until the end'.[16] This alone is 'legitimate' pilgrimage, requiring continuity and consistency of attitude and behaviour. In this context, a 'place pilgrim' is not escaping from his or her daily journey but seeking to resource and enhance it. That at any rate is the theory, even if in practice (as this preacher also notes) it is often honoured as much in the breach as in the observance.

I want to suggest that this is also an understanding which is reflected in Chaucer's account of the pilgrim group in the *Canterbury Tales.* Chaucer's selection

Select Library of the Nicene and Post-Nicene Fathers of the Church 6 (Grand Rapids, 1954).

[14] William Thorpe, for example, stressed the importance of Christian life as a pilgrimage but condemned the ignorance, worldliness, frivolities and immorality which he said were characteristic of place pilgrims travelling to shrines; see *Two Wycliffite Treatises. The Sermon of William Taylor, 1406 – The Testimony of William Thorpe, 1407*, ed. Anne Hudson, EETS os 301 (Oxford, 1993). A Wycliffite preacher declared 'now pilgrimage is mene for to do lecherye', *English Wycliffite Sermons*, ed. Anne Hudson (Oxford, 1992), p. 355.

[15] *Summa praedicanti feriae*, 1, 6, cited in J. D. Davies, *Pilgrimage Yesterday and Today. Why? Where? How?* (London, 1988), p. 83.

[16] In *The Miracles of Saint James*, ed and trans. Thomas F. Coffey, Linda Kay Davidson and Maryjane Dunn (New York, 1996), p. 26. Compare: 'Enter ye into the strait gate: for wide is the gate, and broad is the way, that leadeth to destruction, and many there be that go in thereat. Because strait is the gate, and narrow is the way, which leadeth unto life, and few there be that find it' (Matthew 7:13–14) and 1 Peter 2: 11 (see n. 3 above).

of a pilgrimage setting is clearly a useful device which allows him to assemble a wide (though not complete) range of representatives of different social groups on a single stage. Yet, as I have argued elsewhere,[17] it does not appear that his object in so doing is to *distance* them from their social roles and daily lives. In fact, the converse is nearer to the truth. Chaucer uses the pilgrimage frame to enable the pilgrims to relate to one another but in such a way as to *highlight and reveal* their callings within their home community and the responsibilities which they bear. The combined effect of the *General Prologue* descriptions and the pilgrims' self-revelations is to suggest not so much an escape from everyday life as an implicit analysis of everyday reality.

Some of Chaucer's pilgrims, notably the Parson and the Plowman, appear to serve the wider community well; some such as the Monk appear to place self-gratification above service alongside their peers; others, including the Friar, Summoner and Pardoner, actively damage communities, cheating, seducing and exploiting. It seems therefore, that Chaucer implies a close correlation between life and place pilgrimage, the Canterbury pilgrimage offering not merely a *pre-text* for gathering together a group of disparate characters but also a *context* in which they, their daily lives and relationships to their home community can be assessed.

So what should we make of the way in which a number of the pilgrims Chaucer presents argue, squabble, swear, overindulge and often exhibit a questionable degree of piety and penitence? Compared to the some of the activities and conduct portrayed in real-life pilgrimage texts: the hooligan behaviour of Felix's Fabri's noble companions in defacing the Church of the Holy Sepulchre,[18] the uncharitable (if understandable) responses of many of Margery Kempe's fellow travellers,[19] and the insistence of the German traveller Arnold von Harff that male pilgrims should be able to say 'Woman, may I sleep with you?' in at least four languages – it seems that in fact Chaucer doesn't show the half of it.[20] And yet in the background, for both real and fictional pilgrims, are the standards and requirements of that other lifelong journey, constantly challenging notions of escape, exposing disobedience, and, like the Parson, suggesting that pilgrimage to an earthly shrine needs to be integrated into that perfect pilgrimage 'that highte Jerusalem celestial' (X 51). They remain, whether they remember it or not, members of that of that wider community.

The Local Nature of Much Pilgrimage

A second factor which argues against an over-emphasis on the concept of liminality as a defining element in the pilgrimage experience is the local nature of much medieval pilgrimage.[21] Evidence from miracle collections indicates that 'the catchment areas of virtually all shrines were local or at most regional' and that 'a

[17] See Dee Dyas, *Pilgrimage in Medieval English Literature 700–1500* (Cambridge, 2001), chapter 10.

[18] 'Some nobles were led by vanity to write their names . . . on the walls of the church [of the Holy Sepulchre] . . . on the pillars . . . on the slab which covers the tomb of our Lord', *Wanderings of Felix Fabri*, p. 86.

[19] *Book of Margery Kempe*, pp. 64, 84.

[20] *The Pilgrimage of Arnold von Harff*, trans. Malcolm Letts (London, 1947), pp. 77, 91, 131, 220.

[21] Diana Webb, *Pilgrimage in Medieval England* (London, 2000), pp. xiii–xvi, 153–8, 215–17.

statistical majority of [Becket's] known pilgrims came from the southerly parts of England'.[22] Eamon Duffy suggests that 'for many medieval Christians, going on pilgrimage was . . . not so much like launching on a journey to the ends of the earth, as of going to a local market town to sell or buy geese or chickens' with shrines functioning as a 'local rather than a liminal phenomenon'.[23]

Intention rather than distance seems to have been the defining factor of a pilgrimage. Margery Kempe was a prodigious traveller but she also classed as a pilgrimage a trip to the church of St Michael Archangel which stood in a field just two miles from where she lived (and displayed the same degree of emotional intensity in her response).[24] Yet for most pilgrims the distance travelled must have had implications for the degree of detachment experienced. Moreover these shorter, local pilgrimages would often have taken on the character of a group outing, as villagers or townspeople made their way *together* to a shrine. Diana Webb gives examples of this kind of group, their pious excursion an extension of their daily communal life and the roles and relationships which it encompassed, rather than an escape from it.[25] The *House of Fame* (114–17) also makes reference to a two-mile 'pilgrimage', in this case to the shrine of St Leonard.

The Pilgrim's Community of Origin

The second community which requires attention is the pilgrim's own community of origin. The decision to embark on a pilgrimage to a holy place was not just an individual matter but one which customarily involved the pilgrim's home community in a number of ways. Members of that community played a significant role in commissioning and controlling pilgrimages, in dispatching *and* re-integrating pilgrims.

Commissioning

There was of course much pilgrimage which was not entirely voluntary. Penitential pilgrimage (to which the Parson refers, X 105: 'Commune Penaunce is that preestes enjoynen men communly in certeyn cas, as for to good peradventure naked in pilgrimages, or barefoot') could be imposed for a wide range of spiritual, moral and temporal offences, the latter category including slander, poaching and homicide. Being made to walk barefoot and sometimes in clothing which was both inadequate and humbling (as in the Parson's 'naked' above) were not uncommon elements in pilgrimages undertaken with a penitential purpose.[26]

Penitents were sent, not only, as is often envisaged, to distant goals such as Jerusalem and Rome, but to regional shrines, where they and their offences were exposed to local notice, a practice which Eamon Duffy sees as 'designed

22 Webb, *Pilgrimage*, p. 61.
23 Duffy, 'Dynamics', pp. 165–6.
24 *Book of Margery Kempe*, p. 200.
25 Webb, *Pilgrimage*, pp. 185–7.
26 Diana Webb notes that in 1281 the archbishop of York sent a group of penitents (guilty of trespass and poaching) to walk a distance of thirty-three miles barefoot and clad only in shirts, carrying candles, *Pilgrimage*, pp. 238–9.

to endorse and enforce rather than dissolve the values of the local community'.[27] There is also pilgrimage which could be called 'semi-voluntary, the vicarious pilgrimage attested to in wills and other documents, carried out by professionals, by friends (Margery Kempe is shown being given money in return for praying for the donor at the appointed goal)[28] or by family members who may or may not have been enthusiastic about the task. Pilgrimage was also undertaken for the living and Susan Morrison has noted how women pilgrims, in particular, travelled for the sake of family concerns, carrying petitions for fertility, childbirth and the health of surviving children.[29]

Control and Consent

Mobility was a serious issue during the late fourteenth century. Disapproval of mobility and praise of stability had political, social and also religious dimensions. Movement of money and other resources abroad was strictly regulated but there were also statutes which sought to restrict the mobility of labourers and servants, especially the Statues of Labourers, 1351. Criticism of mobility in late-medieval literature also assumes the existence of false pilgrims.[30] Almost all pilgrims, lay or clerical, were supposed to seek permission from their superiors, certainly for any lengthy absence. Married women, as in the case of Margery Kempe, needed the permission of their husbands.[31]

This pattern of consent in a sense formalizes the deeper obligation to serve the community which is inherent in the concept of life pilgrimage and expressed in ways which vary with the individual's calling and situation. Against this background it is, I think, valid to ponder the extent to which Chaucer portrays pilgrims who are potentially breaking those patterns of consent and obligation such as the monastics, and possibly, as Robert Swanson has suggested, the Parson. Of course in practice, there would have been significant variation in the degree to which those in religion were actually restrained from going on pilgrimages, and Diana Webb has commented that the presence of Chaucer's Prioress on the pilgrimage 'would not in practice have raised too many eyebrows'.[32] Moreover Chaucer's general presentation of the Parson is unusually unequivocal in its emphasis on this man's unworldly and dutiful clerical virtue.

The Wife of Bath, however, is another matter. The issue of consent is highlighted in her *Prologue* as she complains that one of her husbands (vainly) attempted to prevent her frequent involvement in pilgrimages and similar religious events:

> 'my visitaciouns
> To vigilies and to processiouns,
> To prechyng eek, and to thise pilgrimages
> To pleyes of miracles, and to marriages.' (III 555–8)

27 Duffy, 'Dynamics', p 174.
28 *Book of Margery Kempe*, p. 106.
29 Susan Signe Morrison, *Women Pilgrims in Late Medieval England: Private Piety as Public Performance* (London, 2000), pp. 16–19.
30 See Dyas, *Pilgrimage*, pp. 147–53.
31 *Book of Margery Kempe*, p. 22.
32 Webb, *Pilgrimage*, 240.

She is frank about her motives for joining in these occasions: to see and be seen by prospective lovers in her fashionable clothes, 'my gaye scarlet gytes'. The unabashed description of these outings reveals a degree of wifely disloyalty, since it was her husband's absence 'at Londoun al that Lente' that gave her the 'bettre leyser for to pleye, / And for to se, and eek for to be seye' (559, 550–1). The allusion to Lent, a season for penitence and punishment of the flesh, throws into sharp relief the Wife's incorrigibly worldly approach and disregard for the spiritual activities designed to increase laypeople's self-discipline and devotion. The Wife's appropriation of religious occasions as opportunities for flirtation becomes unambiguously irreverent when at her husband's funeral Chaucer depicts her focusing on Jankin's attractive legs while her neighbours, rather more appropriately, mourn the deceased (III 594–9).

The Wife of Bath's self-determination, coupled with her mobility, make her an ideal repository both of anti-feminist sentiment in general and of all the anxieties which have been mapped onto female pilgrims since Christian pilgrimage began in the fourth century.[33] Margery Kempe was widely travelled and the suspicion and criticism she generated is clear. Margery went to Jerusalem once, William Wey and Felix Fabri both went twice, while the Wife of Bath is said to have gone three times (I 463), raising the suspicion that a woman who so frequently takes herself off on pilgrimage is likely to be a very loose cannon indeed.

The narrative emphasis that the Wife of Bath's participation in pilgrimages, far from being carried out with her husband's consent, is actually achieved in the face of his opposition is, I suggest, highly significant. Since this appears to be illustrative of her whole approach to marriage, she is, in contemporary terms, clearly failing in a key aspect of her pilgrimage through life. Is it not intriguing, therefore, that she should at the same time be presented as the most experienced 'place' pilgrim by far of the whole *Canterbury Tales* 'compaignye'? Is this indicative of a critique of pilgrimage in general, of women pilgrims in particular, or simply an opportunity for Chaucer to draw on an additional rich vein of satire, by merging elements of misogynist tradition with the particular suspicion reserved for women who left their homes and communities for ostensibly spiritually motivated journeys.

Similarly intriguing in this context is the *General Prologue* comment that the Wife 'koude muchel of wandrynge by the weye' (I 467), an apparent aside which is in fact sandwiched neatly between the impressive list of holy places she has visited and a description indicating her predisposition to lechery. This could be read literally but in the context a metaphorical reading seems more likely, with her 'wandrynge' signifying her straying from the path of morality and godliness,

[33] Jerome was appalled by the behaviour of an anonymous female traveller: 'I have lately seen a most miserable scandal traverse the entire East. The lady's age and style, her dress and mien, the indiscriminate company she kept, her dainty table and her regal appointments bespoke her the bride of a Nero or a Sardanapallus' (Letter 54.13, Schaff and Wace, *Letters*). Gregory of Nyssa wrote 'it is impossible for a woman [pilgrim] to accomplish so long a journey without a conductor; on account of her natural weakness she has to be put on her horse and lifted down again; she has to be supported in difficult situations . . . the proceeding cannot help but be reprehensible . . . whether she leans on the help of a stranger, or on that of her own servant, she fails to keep the law of correct conduct', Epistle 2, *Select Writings and Letters*, Schaff and Wace, Library of Nicene and Post Nicene Fathers, second series, 5 (Grand Rapids, 1954).

since wandering functions as a negative spiritual marker in a number of medieval texts.[34]

Dispatch and Reintegration

The community of origin featured in both practical and spiritual preparation for pilgrimages to shrines of any distance. Lengthy absences would require the settling of debts,[35] the making of wills and arrangements for the protection of assets left behind. Place pilgrimage was not inherently a one-way process, as some studies have suggested,[36] but usually a round-trip with the community looking forward to return, reintegration and transferable benefits. The *Service for Pilgrims* in the *Sarum Missal* includes no fewer than five separate references to the home-coming of the prospective pilgrim.[37] Lincoln Guild records show that guild members were not only required to support those who went on pilgrimage but also to welcome them back.[38] Returning pilgrims might bring relics, which symbolized the transference of the power of the saint back into the home community, or even seek to recreate their experience through building churches or chapels modelled on holy places which they had visited such as the Church of the Holy Sepulchre in Jerusalem, imitated in the construction of the 'Round Church' in Cambridge and the Temple Church in London.

The nature of Chaucer's plan for the *Tales* necessarily remains uncertain. Some critics assume that Canterbury, pilgrimage and metaphorical pilgrimage to heaven are envisaged by Chaucer as not only the true closure of the narrative but are anticipated in earlier parts of the narrative in a coherent enough way as to make the *Tales* present an overall Christian message.[39] In Chaucer's text as we have it, however, it is unclear whether Chaucer would have described the pilgrims' arrival at Becket's shrine and the return journey to the Tabard, and eventually to their home communities or whether the Parson's treatise on Christian conduct in society, would have remained Chaucer's method of bringing his narrative to an end.[40] Either, in fact, would have served to point the message that the wider pilgrimage and ultimate pilgrim goal indicated by the Parson,

> thilke parfit glorious pilgrymage
> That highte Jerusalem celestial (X 50–1)

would for most of his audience only be achieved by obedient Christian living back in the communities from which they came and to which they remained accountable.

34 On 'wandering' in *Piers Plowman*, for example, see Dyas, *Pilgrimage*, Chapter 9.

35 *Book of Margery Kempe*, pp. 149–50.

36 For example Donald R Howard, *The Idea of the Canterbury Tales* (Berkeley, 1976), p. 30.

37 *Sarum Missal in English*, ed. Vernon Staley (London, 1911), pp. 167, 168, 169, 173.

38 *English Gilds*, ed. Lucy Toulmin Smith, EETS os 40 (London, 1870), p. 172.

39 For example Ralph Baldwin, *The Unity of the Canterbury Tales*, Anglistica 5 (Copenhagen, 1955).

40 See discussion of critical readings of the relationship between the *Tales* and pilgrimage in Dyas, *Pilgrimage*, pp. 187–204.

The Community of Place Pilgrims

Finally I want to return to the group which occupies the central position within the concentric circles under discussion here. Pilgrimages in Chaucer's England clearly did function as alternative, temporary, social milieus, and membership of multiple communities – 'fellowships' – was a central experience for many in contemporary life, as David Wallace's *Chaucerian Polity* makes clear in his examination of structures of power and identity.[41] Yet those on pilgrimage to holy places still carried with them their essential connectedness to their home community and their lifetime membership of that greater band of Christian pilgrims *en route* to heaven. And it is that connectedness which I wish to emphasize here. Far from moving into a state of *communitas* which 'transgresses or dissolves the norms that govern structures and institutionalized relationships', it is clear that many pilgrim expeditions were made up of friends and neighbours and that even those broader groups experienced by Margery Kempe and Felix Fabri display characteristics which support Eamon Duffy's assertion that 'most late medieval pilgrims were consolidating not dissolving their social and religious world'.[42] When we read Fabri's account of some pilgrims scornfully deriding those overcome by pious emotion in the Church of the Holy Sepulchre,[43] or consider Margery's frequent problems with her travelling companions, it does not seem that pilgrimage automatically created fellowship, sympathy or mutual care. There is a certain 'togetherness' as one group of Margery's companions sit down to remove their lice together in Germany[44] but one does not really get the sense that Margery experienced this as *communitas*. In fact Margery herself, as Tony Goodman has pointed out, for all her piety, remains intensely aware of her own privileged background and alive to small markers of social status during her pilgrimages – maintaining, in fact, the identity she carries from her home community.[45] Pilgrimage does not appear to have freed people from hierarchies, especially gender hierarchies. Social background influenced where one travelled, how one travelled and who one travelled with.[46] Gender affected freedom to travel and even the shrines to which one could gain admission.

What then of Chaucer and the clear social distinctions, the tensions and the disputes which he highlights in constructing his pilgrim group? Is he playing against a received idea of *communitas* or is this, rather, simply the way real-life pilgrimages were? In dealing with Chaucer it is, of course, usually safest to say both. He never takes a simplistic view of anything – why should pilgrimage be an exception? This, it seems, is how many pilgrimages were, yet there is also a sense of something lacking, both in the journey towards Canterbury and (by inference, I would want to argue) in the life journeys of some of those involved. It is a group assembled primarily as a Christian fellowship, yet that fellowship seems to be largely superficial, a togetherness, if such it is, which expresses itself in contest.

[41] David Wallace, *Chaucerian Polity: Absolutist Lineages and Associational Forms in England and Italy* Figurae: Reading Medieval Culture (Stanford, 1997), p. 381.

[42] Duffy, 'Dynamics', p. 177.

[43] *Wanderings of Felix Fabri*, pp. 284.

[44] *Book of Margery Kempe*, p. 237.

[45] Anthony Goodman, *Margery Kempe and her World* (Harlow, 2005), p. 54.

[46] See Webb, *Pilgrimage*, p. 85

Within it there are smaller, long-term groupings; there is also, with the appearance and disappearance of the Canon, an indication of the fluidity of pilgrim alliances and the varying trustworthiness of chance-met companions on the way which we also see in Margery Kempe's experience. We can certainly tell our churls from our *gentil* folk and when it comes to it a ploughman is still a ploughman and a knight is still a knight. Each has roles and responsibilities to which they must eventually return, forming an appropriate audience, therefore, for the Parson's teaching on Christian living within the wider community.

The communities of pilgrimage in Chaucer's England were, I have sought to argue, a series of concentric circles – circles which overlap and interact – with more continuity, more integration, more homeliness (in the English sense of the term) than we often allow for. When we look at any pilgrim group, Chaucer's included, we need also to be aware of the wider communities from which they came and to which the vast majority fully intended to return.

11

Classicizing Christianity in Chaucer's Dream Poems: The *Book of the Duchess*, *Book of Fame* and *Parliament of Fowls*

STEPHEN KNIGHT

The Book of the Duchess

To ask whether Chaucer's dream visions operate within a consciously and hortatively Christian context has rarely been seen as a credible procedure. Though Robertson and Huppé[1] offered an energetic exegesis of the *Book of the Duchess* and the *Parliament of Fowls* and Koonce[2] applied the Princeton approach to the *Book of Fame*,[3] the domain of the poems has generally been seen as insistently secular. The earliest of the poems, so far always agreed to be the *Book of the Duchess*, initiates such a position with some determination, startlingly excluding any thoughts of afterlife for the dead duchess and finding immortality only in her literary memorial, an especially curious procedure since it seems that the underlying purpose of the text is to rationalize the duke's selection of a new wife. To feel assured that his last duchess is in heaven might have been an easy path to rationalizing a successor.

This chapter will argue that while these three dream visions are effectively secular, they recurrently raise the possibility of a spiritual domain, but where Dante and Petrarch, Chaucer's contemporary thematic influences (Boccaccio is a textual influence), transcend the secular with the spiritual, especially love, Chaucer consistently juxtaposes the secular and the spiritual, the classical and the Christian in complex tension, where the classical and the secular is the essential domain of the poetry, but is put under question by recurrent reference to the implicit, even off-stage, voice of Christianity.

Though it is true that the *Book of the Duchess* is firmly, even obsessively, secular, it should be recalled more than is usual among Chaucerians that the source of the secular amatory vision, *Le Roman de la Rose*, is also a major source of Christian learning and devotion, at least as it is massively completed by Jean de Meun,

1 D. W. Robertson Jr and B. F. Huppé, *Fruyt and Chaf: Studies in Chaucer's Allegories* (Princeton, 1963).

2 B. G. Koonce, *Chaucer and the Tradition of Fame: Symbolism in The House of Fame* (Princeton, 1966).

3 This was, as J. A. W. Bennett comments, 'Chaucer's final title', *Chaucer's Book of Fame* (Oxford, 1968), p. ix. The commonly used title *The House of Fame* merely refers to only one feature of the poem: it is a wide-ranging study of fame, rather than a shrine or fortress related to it.

and Chaucer must have been well aware from there as well as from his reading in Dante and Petrarch that secular devotion can readily be the path to an even more transcendent form of love. But the *Book of the Duchess* seems to set its face firmly against such heavenly recidivism. While Robertson and Huppé imagined the text full of improbable reverence – fastening on a slender link between Christ and the number eight they made the dreamer's 'eyght yere' (37) malady a reference to 'Christ the Physician' and 'Octovyen' (368) as 'eight coming' an image of the resurrection[4] – annotators searching the actual surface of the poem for references, even partial or implicit, have brought little from the Bible or Christian commentary to bear on this text. From the latter domain only Boethius is glanced at, as late as 210–12; from the Bible minor references are made to Joseph (280), Delilah (738), Esther (987), Achitophel (1118) and Lamech (1162). This is no more than a set of Old Testament spear-carriers (though the locations of some will prove of some interest). Excitingly for Huppé and Robertson, St John is the last to appear (1319), but this possibility of apocalypse appears negated by the fact that the reference merely encodes John of Lancaster's name into the text.

Possible secondary references to the biblical text, though occasionally of interest in terms of position, are few and not of great force: for Phillips, line 368 suggests 'a revelation by the Sybil of Christ's birth', 574–6 on the search for pity in a man's heart are 'slightly reminiscent' of Christ's reproaches from the cross[5] and the scorpions of 636–41 relate to the same creatures in Revelation.[6] There is rather more in the link between 'The formest was alway behynde' (890) and Matthew 19: 30, and between the outstandingness of White 'amonge ten thousande' (972) and the Song of Songs 5: 9–10. The presence of these two biblical echoes is interesting, because, as will be discussed later, the language of the text itself has only in this sequence any sign of Christian awareness in its use of vocabulary.

At the start, the force behind human life is no more than the physical one of Kynde/Nature, invoked in both English and Latin form (16 and 18), without any trace of the Neoplatonic projection of them towards divinity, though this was clearly known to Chaucer. Similarly, it is a romance that the dreamer reads 'to dryve the nyght away' (49), not the Bible, just as the glazed windows of his chamber mediate only medieval romantic adventure, not Christian symbology (335). When he asks 'grace' it is only to sleep (118), and the 'Gode of Slepe' is the comic pagan Morpheus (137). Some notionally Christian language is used: the cave is as dark as 'helle pitte' (171) but this is a physical, not spiritual, connection with the links only made to Ovid and Statius;[7] it is a pagan who says 'I pray God' (210), and he speaks only to relieve his widow's misery; the narrator says 'A Goddys halfe' (370), but just to encourage hunting, and then uses 'By oure Lorde' and 'God helpe me soo' (544, 550) as mild imprecations to clarify his relation with the man in black: the ultimate appeal in this context is not to Christian verity but the

4 Robertson and Huppé, *Fruyt*, pp. 33 and 49. Texts are quoted from *Chaucer's Dream Poetry*, ed. Helen Phillips and Nick Havely (London, 1997); Phillips edited the *Book of the Duchess* and *Legend of Good Women* selection, and Havely the *Book of Fame* and the *Parliament of Fouls*: references to notes and introductions are here made in the name of the separate editors.

5 *Chaucer's Dream Poetry*, p. 76.

6 Phillips, *BD*, notes to these lines, p. 79.

7 Ibid., note to lines 163–5, p. 58.

secular morality of 'by my trouthe' (553).

After this trivial deployment of Church vocabulary, between 665 and 690 there is a higher number of Christian references, though themselves of little intrinsic weight – 'God wolde' (665), 'Before God' (677), 'be God' (680), 'as wys God' (683) and 'Be oure lord' (690) – also not in the source. This is, it seems not accidentally, directly after the clearly Boethian statement by the Man in Black of his betrayal by 'False Fortune'. But if a quasi-Christian critique has begun to emerge in the poem, it is swiftly deferred in a list of classical sufferers, first Tantale and Socrates, then a flow from Medea to Narcissus: these are in some cases drawn from *Le Roman de la Rose*,[8] but not the last case, Samson, who provides a surprising biblical terminus which could indeed, in a more supportive context, prefigure the Crucifixion, as Robertson and Huppé improbably claim it does here.[9]

Yet the poem does not quite abandon the Christian possibility: before the two credible biblical references mentioned above ('The formest' and Matthew, 890; White and the Song of Songs, 972) there is a steady and not completely trivial deployment of Christian phrases: 'A Goddys halfe!' (758), 'God wolde' (814), 'By God' (831) and 'As helpe me God' (838), and after those come the more specifically Christian pointers 'by the Roode' (924) and 'by the masse' (928), themselves followed by a firm indication of absent Christianity in 'I durste swere – thogh the Pape hit songe' (929). Most interestingly, as Wimsatt has noted,[10] the eulogy of White involves two images that are frequently linked to the Virgin, as a 'toure of yvoyre' (946) and as 'The soleyne Fenix of Arabye' (982). While Robertson and Huppé note the Marian connection they do not see it as any more forceful than the other links they ingeniously excavate from patristic commentary, and prefer to link the phoenix with the Resurrection.[11] This Christian development is overtly linked to 'Hester in the Bible' (987) and the unmalicious nature of White's wisdom is attested 'by the Rode' (992). That she is a main residence of 'Trouthe hymselfe' (1003) is closer to Christian allegory than classical philosophy, as may be her virtues of grace, perseverance and governance (1006–8).

This apparent incrementalization of a compatibility between White and Christian virtue seems to come to a climax, signalled with very Chaucerian wordplay in a summary:

> Ryght on thys same, as I have seyde,
> Was hooly al my love leyde;
> For certes she was, that swete wife,
> My suffisaunce, my luste, my lyfe,
> Myn happe, myn hele and al my blysse,
> My worldys welfare and my goddesse,
> And I hooly hires, and everydel. (1035–41)

Chaucer will later, through Petrarch in the *Clerk's Tale*, reflect on the possibility of marriage as the image of Christ's relationship with the human soul and, as in

8 Ibid., note to lines 726–39, p. 83.

9 Robertson and Huppé, *Fruyt*, p. 64.

10 J. I. Wimsatt, 'The Apotheosis of Blanche in *The Book of the Duchess*', *Journal of English and Germanic Philology* 66 (1967), 26–44, pp. 35–7.

11 Robertson and Huppé, *Fruyt*, p. 77.

medieval readings of the Song of Songs, that idea seems to haunt the language of this passage, with an apparent double meaning of 'hooly' at start and finish. It is hardly surprising then that the narrator responds 'By oure Lord' (1042), nor perhaps that one scribe may have had difficulty with this surprising, even shocking, statement.[12] Then, however, the text moves back into its comfort zone of classical secularity, though the misunderstanding narrator describes the black knight's position both callously and, in terms of a possible Christianicity in the poem, teasingly, as 'shryfte wythoute repentaunce' (1114) – a startling idea without parallel in the sources. And, while the bereaved lover immediately reverts to classical losses, as he moves to stating his real position a clear appeal to the Christian God recurs: the dreamer asks 'For Goddys love, telle me alle' (1143) and the Man in Black replies 'Before God' (1143–4). In the following self-explanation of his feeling, God and Lord recur more often than anywhere, except the flurry around line 900, as in 1175, 1178, 1205, 1235, 1237, 1277: this referentiality is emphatically doubled in 1307 and 1310 as he comes to state that 'She ys ded (1309).

Christianity seems to die as well. The text reverts to normal aristocratic life and hunting; the dreamer wakes at a bell which strikes hours that appear merely temporal, not monastic; there is no final reference to the Christian world. The possibility has been raised through Chaucer's elegant manipulation of language that White had aspects of truly Christian purity, that the appropriation of the language of worship for the human beloved might be to some extent reversed and an avatar of Mary found on earth.[13] But the secular thrust of the poem seems to silence that possibility: she is not grieved for beyond secular loss, nor seen to be in heaven, nor even on the way there. But the performative force of the poem's varying language, at times quite clear, at times almost unnerving in offering a religious possibility, must alert us to Chaucer's characteristic power to write at more than one level, to ask another question while answering a first. This power to double the meaning and inquiry of a vision, including in a super-secular mode, will be profoundly developed in his other dream poems.

The Book of Fame

That the *Book of Fame* precedes the *Parliament of Fowls* has usually been assumed: in a metrical version of the Whig theory of history it has been felt that Chaucer moved through French octosyllabics via Italian stanzas to the English perfection of the iambic pentameter. His work and temperament, not to mention those of most great artists, were almost certainly a good deal more volatile than such simplicity, and those few who have studied the poem's dating have placed them very close together, even overlapping, and a number of scholars, including most recently Marion Turner, have argued the *Book of Fame* may be later than has often been thought.[14] There are reasons both for considering the *Parliament* earlier

12 Phillips *BD*, p. 110, notes that the word 'Lord' is added in a later hand in the Fairfax manuscript.

13 Something similar seems part of the inspiration for Alceste in the *Legend of Good Women* but there Chaucer never shows how, in some culminating vision perhaps, he would have reconciled the heavenly and earthly female ideals, since the poem is unfinished.

14 Larry D. Benson, *Riverside Chaucer*, pp. xxii–xxv, dates the *Book of Fame* to '1378–80' and the *Parliament* to '1380–2', while Phillips and Havely see *Fame* as 'late 1370s or early 1380s' and

than the *Book of Fame*, and for coming to the opposite conclusion, and these are summed up later in a sequence which concludes, or rather provisionally accepts, that thoughtful analysis confirms the simplistic assumptions of a metrics-centred chronology.

Few works of art have been so variously interpreted as the *Book of Fame*. Its enigma, changes of tone and wide range of reference, and not least its absent ending, have led it to be seen variously as unedited draft, parody, nervous comedy, literary self-obsession, post-modernism well *avant la lettre*, Christian exegesis, or prologue, real or implied, to the *Canterbury Tales*. It is as if the poem's coded thematic clues can only be made coherent from a particular assumed viewpoint.

But to reflect on its relation to Christian thought and writing suggests that the poem is less labile, and that it shares an underlying structural and argumentative pattern with no less than Chaucer's acknowledged greatest works, *Troilus and Criseyde* and the *Canterbury Tales*. Both start with a Christian reference that could seem merely customary, both explore at great length secular conflicts and contradictions with occasional reminiscence of the conventional Christian position, and both end with a specific Christian statement which directly, even abruptly, rejects the secular textual experiences that reader, and it would seem author, have long been sharing and valuing. The endings of those two texts have often been described as palinodes, but they can also be read as making overt the recurrently implied underlying meaning that should have been nagging at the reader throughout. The end confirms the doubts and sense of error that secular conflicts have generated. Or, as a recent secular moralist, Dr Leavis, put it, the text enacts its own morality.

While the *Book of the Duchess* can itself be read in this way as a performative lesson, that lesson is couched primarily, in spite of its occasional use of Christian imagery and occasional emphasis, in secular, physical, natural terms: the opening reference to Nature and Kynde eventually leads to the notion of a naturally regenerating second marriage for the bereaved Duke. *The Book of Fame* starts differently. The opening line is 'God turne us every dreme to goode' (1), and this conceivably routine remark is spiritually emphasized in the rhyme on 'by the roode'. The excursus on human dreams thus juxtaposes religious and secular, just as *Troilus and Criseyde* in its opening elides the God of Love into an apparently Christian God, and the *Canterbury Tales* enigmatically doubles human and spiritual meanings of pilgrimage. The following dream discussion is about the physical and secular context of dreaming; the spirits mentioned in line 41 are far from holy, and though the next lines state a 'soule, of propre kynde' may be so 'parfit' it can 'forwote that ys to come' (43–5), this seems to have no emphasis greater than all the other supposition of this prologue – though a Dantean parallel of this comment (*Purgatorio* IX, 16–18) is textually close to the eagle who will be deployed later, and this may well be a referentially coded Christian emphasis.[15] More overt is the fact that however secular the opening discussion may seem to be, it is concluded by repeating the opening statement with the same emphatic

Parliament 'perhaps early 1380s', *Chaucer's Dream Poetry*, p. 3; Marion Turner summarizes the debate about the date of *Fame* in *Chaucerian Conflict: The Language of Antagonism in Late Fourteenth Century London* (Oxford, 2006), p. 13.

15 *Purgatorio* IX, 16–18.

rhymes, as the narrator decides to wish only 'that the holy Roode Turne us every dreme to goode!' (57–8)

Awareness of, but also lack of overt discussion of, a Christian structure is the opening manoeuvre of this winter dream. The date of 10 December is a clear rejection of the natural and positive spring–summer context of the usual love vision, but hardly an allegorical affirmation of Advent, as Koonce argues, buttressed with patristic references.[16] The text turns to classical gods with Morpheus (77) and a subsequent formally Christian prayer for good outcome is uncertain in religious and rhyming diction, beginning: 'pray I Ihesus God / That – dreme he barefote, dreme he shod' (97–8).

Withdrawing further from a Christian position, the opening book, though said to be in a 'chirche' (473), and one that Bennett feels is much more gothic than classical,[17] nevertheless collocates Virgil and Ovid on Fame, focusing on the story of Dido but avoiding any of the Christian possibilities of either the fourth of Virgil's *Eclogues*, which was taken as prophesying Christ, nor the commentary tradition that the first six books of the *Aeneid* represent a journey through Christian life, and certainly never linking Dido's Africa to the great African Christian, St Augustine. It is rather a thoroughly secular exposé of human conflict in a world full of pagan gods, but in Christian terms godless: it operates not unlike the first four tales of the *Canterbury Tales* as an initial engagement with a world without spirituality.

The narrator, characteristically and Chaucerianly unreliable, is impressed: he reads the images as displaying 'noblesse' and 'richesse' (471, 472), secular totems which for him are not misplaced in 'this chirche' (473). His negative positioning is somatized as he merges into 'a large felde' that 'nas but sonde' (482, 486), and though a glossator speaks of a 'field of sand',[18] 'felde' here just means flat region. Though there are clear links to Dante's 'diserta' and an in-text simile to a desert in Dido's 'Lybye' (488) it is in fact only some sand-plain of the imagination. Much like the opening Christian dream-frame, the narrator's instinct, or perhaps more exactly the possibility of grace, speaks:

> 'O Criste,' thoughte I, 'that art in blysse –
> Fro fantoume and illusion
> Me save!' and with devocion
> Myn eyen to the hevene I caste. (492–5)

The heavenly sense of 'blysse' rhymes, with typical Chaucerian ironic point, with the narrator's failed aspiration 'to rede or wisse' (491). Knowledge is the result of faith, not of reason, as St Anselm had clarified in his famous slogan 'credo ut intelligam'.

The narrator's heavenly cry and gaze is answered, but not simply. He sees the grand eagle – 'Hyt was of golde and shone so bryght' (503) – and this must suggest the eagle of St John, but it is mediated more closely by Dante (*Purgatorio* IX, 13–33), a passage that embraces the earlier reference to spirits capable of

16 Koonce, *Chaucer*, pp. 67–9.
17 Bennett, *Book of Fame*, pp. 12–13.
18 Havely, *HF*, p. 145.

foreknowledge. And yet the eagle is not only a possible spiritual allegory: like the ongoing text, it also has natural status; it is like a second sun of heaven (506). The possibility of the religious lying hidden beneath the context of the secular is a recurrent motif of this poem.

In that spirit Book 2 marches off with mixed Old Testament and classical dreamers from Isaiah to Elcanor, and with a rationalist emphasis in the book's primary invocation of thought in the context of classical Parnassian inspiration. Christianity is within cognition, but not in positive terms: the eagle in a de-authorizing rhyme like 'Jesus God' / 'dreme he shod' complains 'Seynt Mary, Thou art noyouse for to cary!' (573–4) and then asks 'God' in terms of merely physical anxiety 'Shall I noon other weyes dye' (585) and refers, again, to Old Testament and classical figures as if they were equal (588–9), as dreamers who rode up 'To hevene with Daun Jupiter' (591).

In what follows, the discourse of Christian faith remains barely recognized – the odd 'God me blesse' (629), 'that God made'(646) and 'helpe me God so wys'(700) are phatic Christian references, indicating a religious presence on the margins of this discourse of science, sounds and the construction of earthly fame. That this argument is in itself a Christian theme is marked by a firmly non-phatic Christian statement – '"O God," quod y, "that made Adame – Moche ys thy myght and thy noblesse!"' (970–1), and the development introduces a summary of Boethius's para-Christian position on worldly grandeur, ending with an enhanced Christian statement of faithful humility. The dreamer is baffled about his whereabouts and identity 'but, God, thou wost!' (982): the fact that 'wost' rhymes with 'gost' nails the amplified signifance of this new piece of coded statement.

The eagle, now neither John's nor Dante's, but belonging more to the material wing of neo-Platonism, launches into new science and the mechanisms of sound. Fascinating for historians of science, and potentially for historians – Fame brings a feudal insouciance to her castle-based power – the following sequence deals with physical possibilities and conflicts like the potent pages of the alleged 'marriage group'. But we are alerted to another range of possible values as the eagle offers a distinctly Christian farewell to the narrator: 'And God of heven sende the grace / Some goode to lerne in this place' (1087–8).

That this is not in fact a place of grace or good will become increasingly clear. Not at first: Chaucer begins Book 3 by invoking Apollo, but as Bennett has stated and Havely has clarified,[19] there are markers to the opening of the *Paradiso*: 'devyne vertu', 'in my hede ymarked' and 'entreth in my brest' (1101, 1103, 1109) invoke Dante's final ascent specifically (*Paradiso* I, 13–36) and Christian ontology in general. Very notably, this, itself somewhat coded, is our only Christian guide for some time as Fame exposes her secular power. But the text itself disavows its topic. The ice of the mountain may well imply impermanence; the clamour of the poets may well represent secular argument rather than serious debate: the descent into conjuring implies its own critique; the architecture seems a blasphemous parody of the great cathedral west fronts;[20] the splendour and volatility of the whole effect

19 Bennett, *Book of Fame*, pp. 100–1; Havely, *HF*, pp. 170.

20 Stephen Knight has argued that the west front of San Michele in Lucca inspired Chaucer by its representation of pillars actually borne up on human – or superhuman – shoulders; see 'Places in the Text: A Topographicist Approach to Chaucer', *Speaking Images: Essays in Honor of V. A. Kolve*, ed. R.

creates its own implied opposite, darkly cued by the resemblance of shape-shifting Fame to her dialectical relative Boethius' Lady Philosophy. Thematic structures like these implicitly evaluate the cacophonous world of secular honour, but more subtle – and testimony to Chaucer's closely coded verbal detail – is his management of the few instances of even marginally Christian discourse.

As the argument becomes dramatic, Fame is created as a random evaluator, a cruel, secular para-deity. People 'pray' to her 'grace' (1537, 1550) and she will even justify a rejection with 'Be God' – though not in rhyme (1561), but as she deals randomly with the first three troops, neither phatic nor reversed Christian discourse enters the text. But then, as in the eagle's farewell, the word of God jumps into focus: the fourth troop has hidden their names 'For Goddys love' and 'for bounte' (1697, 1698) and the fifth more searchingly have done good works 'for contemplacioun / And Goddes love' (1710–11). Fame's brutal whimsicality leads her to accept the first and deny the second in their equal quests for anonymity, and then she accepts the plea for fame of the hypocritic sixth troop who have done nothing but seek glory in the self-contradictorily jingling line: 'For goddes love, that sit above' (1758).

Reminding us, as these three troops do, of the force of Christian morality and also its vicissitudes in secular society, they do not themselves control the action: Fame continues to lay about her with further troops and fame-discrediting exhibitions. The only specific dissent is the narrator's intriguing statement to an anonymous 'Frende' that he is only here for some 'newe tydinges for to lere' (1886) – the mission of secular media investigation up to the present – and that he does not care about personal fame:

> 'I wote my self best how y stonde
> For, what I drye or what I thynke
> I wol my selfe al hyt drynke.' (1878–80)

While modern readers might be tempted here to identify bourgeois individualist Chaucer, or independent writerly Chaucer, such a rootless individualism can have in the medieval context only a position of no authority, like that of Will in *Piers Plowman*: he rejects secular fame, and (in spite of recent critical positions) the value of mere intellectualism: being alone, he is adrift.

The eagle returns to help and flies him to the 'Domus Dedaly' – itself through Icarus' story an emblem, among other things, of overweening – where in a world without social structure or moral evaluation rumour emerges to be canonized as fame, and the two locations offer respectively a parody of feudal appropriation of both peasant and mercantile productivity.[21] The world of rumour is even worse than that of fame in that there are no grand writers – though there are, as often in the *Canterbury Tales* and occasionally in *Troilus and Criseyde* – and the mystery plays as well – some fine strains of comic realistic vigour. From Manly on, commentators have seen Chaucer here foreseeing the Canterbury project, but it will be a development, not a departure: that collection of materials also has a Christian frame and close secular reportage. But it did close the frame with assertive Christianity, and

F. Yeager (Asheville, NC, 2001), pp. 445–61, at p. 452.

[21] See Stephen Knight, *Geoffrey Chaucer* (Oxford, 1986), pp. 21–2.

this is what *The Book of Fame* does not offer, or at least not complete.

The whirling wicker is not a separate house of rumour, as it is almost always called, but another part of the mediating mechanism of Fame, less reputable through being less aristocratic-connected and less literary-historical, but not therefore more unreliable. It becomes, like Fame's castle, more and more chaotic until a stampede occurs to hear someone who 'semed to be / A man of grete auctoritee' (2157–8). Here Chaucer, with both characteristic incompleteness and pre-post-modern aporia-ness, stops.

The verb 'semed' might appear to set a problem: so much has been seeming in this poem, from the value of dreams and Aeneas's honour to the grandeur of the up-to-date architecture of Fame's hall and the vigour of the whirling wicker world. Is this another illusion? But in fact 'semed' is ontologically valid, meaning to bear the external appearance of, therefore have public credit as – to medievally be. It is moderns who like the idea that identity is inward, an individual secret. Whether knowing this or not, few have been able to resist giving a name to the man. Some are predictably and undramatically text-linked like Boethius or Virgil; others improbably external, like the mundane historicism of Schoeck's 'Constable-Marshal of the Christmas revels'[22] or the jocularity of Minnis's Lollius.[23] Some are grandiose like Koonce's concept of our Lord himself, a Chaucerian hijack of the Beatific Vision; some feel it could be anyone in authority like a sheriff or a king.[24] But to be an 'auctorite' in such a context depends on being an 'auctor',[25] and the best candidate is surely the one who is implicit throughout and whom Lydgate believed to be behind the poem when he called it 'Dante in Englysh'.[26]

Koonce is surely over-egging the exegetical pudding to make *The Book of Fame* have as its three books an Inferno, Purgatorio and Paradiso (what a strange Paradiso that would be, even for a wag like Chaucer) and Jesus himself as the final man.[27] But Koonce is merely over-religious, not religiose: he is not in the wrong mode. There can be little doubt, as the recurrent references have shown, that the spirit of Dante pervades the whole, and he, perhaps accompanied by Virgil, would be fine authority to present a brisk palinode that made us readers recognize what we should have realized all along and what the coded references, and the sudden lack of them for lengthy periods, should have confirmed – that Boethius was right, that Fame is trivial, that poets themselves are implicated in its mediation, and for all the fun they can have and can create, they have also a higher duty. Chaucer knew that because he believed that, and regularly returned to it, however curious he was about exploring, even celebrating, its secular opposites. But he also had another model for the Christian resolution of the threatening structures of Fame.

22 R. J. Schoeck, 'A Legal Reading of the *Hous of Fame*', *University of Toronto Quarterly* 23 (1954), 185–92, p. 190.

23 A. J. Minnis, with V. J. Scattergood and J. J. Smith, *Oxford Guides to Chaucer: The Shorter Poems* (Oxford, 1995), pp. 236–7 and 224–5.

24 Koonce, *Chaucer*, pp. 266–73.

25 Bennett comments 'What little we are told of this commanding figure suggests an *auctor* with the prestige of the Africanus of the *Parliament*', *The Parlement of Foules: An Interpretation* (Oxford, 1965), p. 186.

26 See John Lydgate, *The Fall of Princes*, ed. Henry Bergen, 4 vols., EETS ES 121–4 (Oxford, 1924–7), vol. I, Prologue, 303.

27 Koonce, *Chaucer*, uses 'Hell', 'Purgatory' and 'Paradise' as titles for his sections on the poem's three books.

Fame and Petrarch's Trionfi

Petrarch's *Trionfi* offer a view of the underlying dynamic of *The Book of Fame*, before Chaucer realized it in the French metrical and structural forms of the mid fourteenth-century dream vision. Started after the death of Petrarch's beloved Laura in 1356, and still being reworked on his own death-bed in 1374, it is not credible that Chaucer did not encounter the poem when he was, just before that, in Italy, including Petrarch's Florence. The *Trionfi* offer a powerful Christian transcendence of human love and aspiration, a mediation of a Boethian position both through romance and explicit Christianity. After Laura's death she and her name become transcendent and are the foci for a parallel heaven-oriented understanding of the detailed secular world. While commentators assert that Chaucer replaced Boethius's Fortune with his own and Ovid's Fama, Petrarch was ahead of him. The 'Triumph of Fame' shows the splendour of earthly Fame but the succeeding Triumph of Time searchingly reveals the fading of Fame. The negative is here not simply as in Chaucer the fickleness and contextual triviality of Fame, but its actual failure to endure at all: the final Triumph, that of Eternity, transmutes this unreliable delight and that of love, even that for Laura, into its heavenly transcendence.

There are clear contacts between the two texts. The 'Triumph of Fame' like Chaucer's Book 3 has separate sections on heroes and (in its final revised edition) poets; there is a clear concept that winter, when the day is 'Nubil' e brev' e freddo'[28] ('cloudy and short and cold'), is the season of this disenchantment of the secular; fame melts like 'neve' (129, p. 376: 'snow'); there is also a specific originary date, April 6th, when Petrarch met Laura. But the essential connection is that the mix of Boethius and Petrarch provides a referential structure that is, as in the *Canterbury Tales* and *Troilus and Criseyde*, allowed to shadow the text through recurrent references, at a more or less fugitive level of coding. Chaucer does not, like Petrarch, extend into the final Triumph of Eternity but his recurrent reference to *The Divine Comedy* installs that domain of value in his poem.

The contact with Petrarch's *Trionfi* has a suggestive focal point, and revealing Chaucerian difference, in the elucidation of the coded message of *The Book of Fame*. Where Boethius made very clear his authoritative voice, in Lady Philosophy, Petrarch only hears announce Time's destruction of Fame: 'Udi' dir, non so a chi' (100, p. 372: 'I heard speak, I do not know whom'). If that matches the unidentified 'man of gret auctorite', the Chaucerian narrator's own unduly limited knowledge seems a conscious restriction of the moment when at the start of 'Triumphus Eternitatis' Petrarch's narrator 'mi volsi al cor, e dissi: – In che ti fidi?' (3, p. 391: 'I turned to my heart and said "In whom shall you trust?"'). His heart, like Langland's Conscience as the voice of God in man, answers: 'Nel Signor, che mai fallito / non ha promessa a chi si fida in lui' (4–5, p. 391: 'In the Lord: he who stumbles / has not promised his faith to him'). Consistent with his own secular emphasis and his coding of the Christian into the implied, Chaucer refrains from anything like religious triumphalism – and in his succeeding great works the Christian message will be austere, painful, and final only in the sense of closure, not bliss.

[28] Francesco Petrarca, *Triumphi*, ed Marco Aniani (Milan, 1988), 'Triumphus Temporis', 62, p. 367.

Perhaps that fascination with the intriguing negative, that reluctance to speak like a saintly *auctor*, is what conditions Chaucer's evident reluctance to name and realize the 'man of grete auctoritee' but the critical silence cannot conceal the insistent, subliminal and deeply serious trend of the poem's own self-creation. It may be Chaucer was undecided whether his authority was to be the classical Virgil or Boethius, or the contemporary Dante or Petrarch. The architectonics, reference, and above all the telling silences of the poem locate all four in the position of authority and it may be that what the final aporia points to most clearly is Chaucer's frequently expressed unwillingness to advocate a single voice, even a positive religious one. That power was not held by the narrator, and in the *Canterbury Tales* not by Chaucer the story-teller nor the prosaic and peremptory Parson; here it is not expressed by the constructed but unrealized man of silent, but unquestionably Christian, authority.

The Parliament of Fowls

Much shorter than its predecessors, written in a much tighter verse form – the rime royal derived from Boccaccio's *Teseida* – and performed with remarkable elegance, if not yet the prosodic liberty of *Troilus and Criseyde*, the *Parliament of Fowls* appears to be the first poem where Chaucer's art is complete in every feature, the confident, almost arrogantly casual, work of a poet in total control of his art. Such poise emanates from the opening lines, 1–5, where Chaucer hijacks Ovid's balanced words on Art on behalf of Love, and then, as if to realize that shock, destabilizes the flow of his line with two drastic enjambments to disavow any force to 'felynge' and 'worchyng' (4,5). Such dextrous flamboyance is then almost ostentatiously laid aside as the narrator reflects on the link of 'olde bokes' and 'new science' (24, 25) and paraphrases, in a stanza by stanza plodding tone one of the great Christianized classics, Macrobius's lengthy *Commentary* on Cicero's much brisker *Dream of Scipio*.

Linking Roman splendour with early Christian anti-worldly dissent, the book and Chaucer's account of it are more rigorously Christian than anything in the previous two poems: Affrican says 'oure present worldes lyves space / Meneth but a maner dethe' (53–4) and continues to mention heaven, the divinely made harmony of the spheres and the ultimate return of all the cosmos to its starting place. The text does not link this stasis to the moment of final judgement, as others do, and its recommendation for access to heaven is also unconventional: if 'thou werke and wysse To comune profyte' (74–5) you will surely come 'unto that place dere That ful of blysse ys and soules clere' (76–7). Robertson and Huppé take 'common profit' as the full Christian and Christ-focused virtue of charity,[29] but while that may indeed be a possible sense, it is not one that the poem will pursue at all, seeming to debate the possibility of secular commonality – and its difficulty.

Just as Affrican as an adviser to Scipio must call up Dante's guide Virgil, so the text will shortly quote Dante's *Inferno* (II, 1) as 'The day gan faile' (85) and the dream will begin–about an earthly paradise like that found towards the end of the *Purgatorio* (XXVIII, 1–33). Yet this text will not follow into a *Paradiso*, but

[29] Robertson and Huppé, *Fruyt*, p. 102.

rather revert to a troubled world, as if the insertion of Scipio's Roman concept of the common profit of social order (in Latin) acts as a relocating focus for Dante's deeply orthodox Christian scheme, a surprising extrusion from the opening just as fame became the theme emerging from the *Aeneid* in the *Book of Fame*.

This deliberate difference is pursued when Chaucer's gate adds to Dante's sombre message in *Inferno* (III, 1–3) the notion that you could equally pass to 'the welle of grace / There grene and lusty May shal ever endure' (129–30). But this 'grace' is less than divine. Chaucer's earthly paradise is not, as it develops, a purgatorial passage: though Robertson and Huppé make it the walled garden of Paradise,[30] its reference will be generally to the walled garden of love in *Le Roman de la Rose* and specifically to the dangerous domain of pleasure in Boccaccio's *Teseida*. The physical beauty of the world is realized, especially through trees and birds, but the text does not take the Neoplatonic path of seeing this as the gift of god's omnipotence to humankind. Rather, things are acculturated with 'Array and Lust and Curtesye' (219) and worse yet with 'Messagery' and 'Mede' (228): the pillars of this temple of delights are of beautiful but frail jasper (not Boccaccio's Venusian copper), while the building itself is of valueless and impermanent brass.

A more positive and certainly Neoplatonic figure, and world, is that of Nature, into which this dream world transforms: Alanus de Insulis and his *De Planctu Naturae* are referenced directly – and unusually for Chaucer's references, quite unironically – so that Nature is seen in the full splendour of twelfth-century Chartres, in poetry matching the eloquence of that other Carthusian, St Bernard, and with the emphatic stressing characteristic of Chaucer's English admirer Dryden:

> Nature, the vyker of th'almyghty lorde
> That hoot, colde, hevy, lyght, moist and drye
> Hath knyt be evene nombre of accorde. (379–81)

It looks as if the structure Bennett implies is working: Scipio's antithesis is followed by that of the Venusian garden, followed by that of Nature acting as a resolving thesis.[31] But Chaucer is never close to the Aquinan model of conflict-resolution, and he withdraws into the negatives of a set of unharmonized and painfully natural conflicts played out through the double image of the animal world and the contemporary parliament. Where Dante loved lucid teleological structure, Chaucer deals in dialectics.

In Neoplatonic terms the birds on St Valentine's day ought to symbolize the beautiful, progenerative, harmonic creation, like the spheres on earth. But a para-courtly best-of-three choice for the young lady eagle degenerates into an unseemly squabble, with characteristic Chaucerian – again dialectical – auto-validation through the vigour of its language and the underlying elegance of the verse form. Where the *Book of Fame* moved subtly towards an unspoken rejection of the secular, and the *Book of the Duchess* glimpsed and dismissed the sacred as it moved inside the secular world, the *Parliament of Fowls* works in religious reverse – which nay be the reason why Robertson and Huppé's treatment is so much shorter than that

[30] Ibid., p. 110.

[31] In his rather intricate presentation, Bennett exposes his understanding of the antithesis–thesis structure in *Parlement of Foules*, pp. 66 and 112.

of the *Book of the Duchess*. A classical-Christian Macrobian opening in poetic *sermo humilis* that restricts human valued action to the social world of common profit is followed by a steady sequence of desanctification: Dante's nightfall, the gate's message, the role of the earthly paradise, the divine physicality of Nature, all steadily turn towards the worldly, chaotic, and – the twist of the Chaucerian knife – insistently vigorous failure to achieve anything like common profit.

There is no sign here of a palinodic resolution, nor indeed any figure 'of grete auctorite' who might offer it, or even fail to. Nature, properly read, is only the nature of the birds (Chaucer for once is as true an allegorist as Langland always is), a world of nature beautiful, vivid, varied, and liable to disorder. Affrican departed as the dream started, as did Virgil towards the end of the *Purgatorio*, both leaving dreamer and text to resolve their own themes without help. But where Beatrice and divinity enlightened Dante's comedy, here, as in the *Book of the Duchess*, we have a secular palinode: there the clock alerted us to the present, here the birds finally sing a beautiful simple rondel about the changing seasons, so enacting their own roles, and their own meaning. Though Robertson and Huppé find in the voices of the birds the heavenly harmony of the Song of Songs 2: 12,[32] there is in fact no real harmony in the avian sphere, just a musical closure. There may be in that a little more of aesthetic value than most have seen: the rondel has been expanded in varied ways, especially in the manuscripts. But if it is expanded in standard French form, the poem comes out to have 700 lines, as David Chamberlain argued,[33] to a world deaf to his thoughts and their implication, for an image of aesthetic completion in the equivalent of one hundred stanzas, not unlike the hundred and one of *Sir Gawain and the Green Knight*. Much more finely written than either of the octosyllabic poems, showing in its stanza and its syntax an understanding of the *dolce stil nuovo* as it was physicalized by Boccaccio, the poem may finally use the power of art as its apology. In his neo-Neoplatonic mode, Chaucer withdrew to imply, on this occasion at least, that poetry itself may be the only thing of common profit, rather than pursue the Christian worm in the bud of the love-focused dream vision poem.

That sense, that this ending is a deliberate withdrawal from the challenge of the opening, a return to the simpler world of the *Book of the Duchess*, is what makes it seem persuasive that the *Parliament of Fowls* comes after the *Book of Fame*. The challenging practice of structural juxtaposition there, where set-pieces did not align in a thematic development, where anti-thesis follows anti-thesis, is here both used and not permitted to point to a spiritual pattern behind the complexities of the world; but the poem can remain relishing its splendidly realized secularities. The resolution of the dramas confronted but not finally evaluated in the *Book of Fame* await the great later works.

32 Robertson and Huppé, *Fruyt*, p. 137.

33 David Chamberlain, 'The Music of the Spheres and *The Parliament of Foules*', *The Chaucer Review* 5 (1970), 32–56, p. 49.

12

Morality in the *Canterbury Tales*, Chaucer's lyrics and the *Legend of Good Women*

HELEN PHILLIPS

Which Morality?

The variety of Chaucer's writings and the multiple ideologies current in late-medieval England – Christian, chivalric, patriarchal, Senecan, Boethian and others – make for a diverse presentation of virtue; that is one of his great strengths. *Melibee*, and, more briefly, the *Book of the Duchess* and *Fortune* contain moral debate; other texts, particularly *Troilus and Criseyde*, the *Knight's Tale*, the *Parliament of Fowls* and the *Legend of Good Women*, include passages of moral counsel – answers – but with only partial or guarded articulation of what moral questions they raise. Yet everywhere Chaucer's writing in complex and implicit ways incites its readers to moral questioning: about what constitutes correct action, about the criteria informing judgements and assumptions, and how discourses and literary traditions carry implicit or explicit ethical perspectives. How, for example, do courtly, Christian and Boethian moral assumptions interact in *Troilus* or medieval readers' expectations abut love and hagiography in the *Legend?*

What constitutes morality is rarely simple, constant or uncontested in Chaucer's writings. Questions arise most obviously when a text's ostensible message offends modern ethics or where devices in the writing – structural, verbal or intertextual – militate against smooth acceptance of a single moral judgement or where it is unclear how far the ethic of a source persists in Chaucer's composition. Griselda's trials and Virginia's beheading exemplify all these. The *Canterbury Tales* frame story increases the impression of ethically dialogic narratives, often leaving it unclear where, or in whom, moral perspectives are located; examples are the evil Pardoner's telling of a moral tale and the question of whether the *Prioress's Tale*'s anti-Semitism is attributable to Chaucer or his fictional construct, the Prioress. A text's morality might also reflect patrons' attitudes: perhaps, for example, the anti-Semitism of the *Prioress's Tale* reflects the same Lancastrian connection we seem to find recurrently in his oeuvre: anti-Semitism was rife in Castile (see Anthony Bale's essay, p. 176): did Constance of Castile favour such attitudes?

The last century of criticism raised three large questions about Chaucer's aesthetics and ethics. First, how far does medieval Christian teaching about virtue and sin guide the presentation of character and action? A related question is whether the earlier Canterbury tales are harmonized with the Christian penitential teachings of the final *Parson's Tale*. In answer, some critics have attempted analysis of the *Tales* based on the seven deadly sins: pride, avarice, envy, anger, sloth, gluttony and lechery;[1] another, more widely accepted, approach sees tensions between earthly and heavenly values, finally resolved in favour of the latter by the last tale and the *Retraction*.[2]

A second major question has been to ask how far the medieval tradition of using stories didactically as *exempla* is relevant to the *Tales*.[3] A third is whether Chaucer anywhere presents a secular ethic or whether all concepts of morality in his writings are rooted in Christian ideology.

Signs of a developing secular ethic can be read as topical and political responses to socio-economic and philosophical changes. Thus pride, the sin that led Adam and Eve to rebel against God, was traditionally considered the worst sin, yet the developing commercialization of English society produced by Chaucer's time great emphasis on avarice.[4] Certainly the upwardly mobile pride attributed to the *Reeve's Tale* miller has more to do with socio-economic phenomena – increasingly wealthy and assertive sections of the peasant class in the post-Black Death economy and after the 1381 Rising – than with spiritual rebellion against God. Another influential change is increasing late-medieval acceptance of the notion of righteous pagans.[5] Thus Chaucer, presenting evidence for good women from history, comments that they were 'hethene al the pak' (*Legend* G 299), deriving their virtue not from 'holinesse' but 'verray virtue and clennesse' (G 296–7), a concept of virtue and chastity as apparently independent of culture and religion – and as inherent in women (compare the *Squire's Tale*, V 484–7). The presence in Chaucer's writing of good pagans and moral ideas with classical sources derives also, however, from Christian intellectual traditions from Augustine onwards, which sought to subsume pagan, especially Stoic, ethical principles to Christian precepts.[6]

Morality and its relationships with literary forms and historical contexts have been central to critical debates over the last half century. Whereas in the 1960s and 1970s the Princeton critics declared all medieval literature was written 'for our doctrine', Alfred David's *The Strumpet Muse* argued for a Chaucer who begins with faith in the moral purpose of writing but ends seeing the limitations of art along with the limitations of the physical and social world that art – with so much brilliance in his own narratives – imitates.[7] David Aers suggested that Chaucer's question about the Monk, 'How shal the world be served?' (I 188), is provocative and topical, signalling engagement with contemporary arguments that the secular world required educated administrators, overturning that older ascetic condemnation of worldly monks to which superficially his question appears to

1 See the useful discussion of critical approaches in Richard Firth Green, 'Morality and Immorality', *A Concise Companion to Chaucer*, ed. Corinne J. Saunders (Oxford, 2005), pp. 199–217, at pp. 199–205.

2 For example, in Helen Storm Corsa, *Chaucer, Poet of Mirth and Morality* (Notre Dame, 1957).

3 See Larry Scanlon, *Narrative, Authority and Power: The Medieval Exemplum and the Chaucerian Tradition* (Cambridge, 1994); J. Allan Mitchell, *Ethics and Exemplary Narrative in Chaucer and Gower* (Cambridge, 2004).

4 See Lester K. Little, *Religious Poverty and the Profit Economy in Medieval Europe* (Ithaca, 1978).

5 See Frank Grady, *Representing Righteous Heathens in Late Medieval Literature* (Basingstoke, 2005).

6 Blamires, *Ethics*, pp. 7–9; also A. J. Minnis, *Chaucer and Pagan Antiquity* (Cambridge, 1982), pp. 50–60.

7 See D. W. Robertson Jr, *Preface to Chaucer* (Princeton, 1962); David, *The Strumpet Muse: Art and Morals in Chaucer's Poetry* (Bloomington, 1976).

belong.[8] The orthodox Christian closures to the *Tales* and *Troilus* prompt continuing debate about how secular values earlier in those texts can be evaluated ethically. Critics who reject the endings as directives to overall interpretation often do so on the texture of Chaucer's preceding writing. Thus Aers dismisses as merely 'moralistic' the language of the conclusions of *Troilus*, compared with what he considers the true moral force of the poem's earlier handling of faithful love.[9] Lee Patterson argues that the *Parson's Tale* replaces the fiction-like relics and pardons of the *Pardoner's Prologue* with true morality yet negates in its act of closure that deferral which is essential to all language and story-telling. Negating the preceding *Tales*, it cannot therefore evaluate it.[10]

Princeton 'patristic' criticism was reductive, narrowing down understanding of how literature handles moral judgements. Yet it was timely, challenging mid-twentieth-century tendencies to read Chaucer ahistorically and by criteria rooted in realist narrative – focused on 'character'. D. W. Robertson Jr insisted on the vast religious and scholarly hermeneutic heritage that often informed medieval reading and writing. Robertsonian criticism is a hermeneutics that wields heavy moral judgements, usually condemnations. For Robertson Chaucer's tragic heroes are always morally culpable; for Kathryn Heinrichs, the women of the *Legend* must be interpreted in line with earlier traditions that condemned them as exempla of sins.[11] Her readings challenge the surface moral import of Chaucer's text, which praises them. But they also prompt further questions. How much did Chaucer's audiences actually know of earlier negative judgements? Were Chaucer, and other late-medieval poets who praised Medea or Cleopatra, perceived as innovative? Patristic readings privilege only certain types of intertextuality, ignoring, for example, the moral complexities and diverse intellectual background of the highly influential *Roman de la Rose*, as well as the more respectful and confident handling of pagan classical material by late-fourteenth-century poets who include Froissart, Machaut and Chaucer.

Historical contexts have confronted criticism with moral questions in other ways. For example, V. A. Kolve's iconographical research points to classical and Christian traditions of portraying passion and reason as a horse and rider.[12] Should that affect readings of the loosing of the horse in the *Reeve's Tale* and, if so, is the religious analogy just a sophisticated enhancing of an already obvious joke (parallels between the palfrey and the lusty students) or does it invite moral condemnation rather than tolerant laughter? Another instance of historical research threatening to reverse moral judgements is Terry Jones's contention that, because the military operations mentioned in the Knight's portrait include cynical, commercial and brutal enterprises, the portrait should be read as ironically couched condemnation.[13] Analogously, post-colonial perspectives can reposition villains as

[8] *Chaucer* (Brighton, 1986), pp. 17–18.

[9] See also my argument about the ontological and existential philosophical issues raised by disjunctions between Chaucer's handling of the narrative and the conclusions, pp. 77–80.

[10] *Chaucer and the Subject of History* (Madison, Wis., 1991), pp. 316–17, 420–1.

[11] 'Chaucerian Tragedy', *English Literary History* 19 (1952), 1–37, p. 91; Heinrichs, *The Myths of Love: Classical Lovers in Medieval Literature* (University Park, Pa., 1990).

[12] V. A. Kolve, *Chaucer and the Imagery of Narrative: The First Five Canterbury Tales* (London, 1984), pp. 217–56.

[13] *Chaucer's Knight: The Portrait of a Medieval Mercenary* (London, 1980).

victims; obvious cases include the Jews of the *Prioress's Tale*, vilified as Satanic and cursed (VII 558–44, 574). Queer theory, which shifts – queers – views of texts away from positions presented as normative, also raises questions about texts' moral perspectives and about assumptions about veracity and authenticity. Thus Glenn Burger argues that Chaucer, by admitting the Pardoner's non-reproductive sexual identity into his *Tales*, also points to the way the *Physician's Tale* destroys the female through its drive to impose the 'will of the Father', the 'proper reproduction of masculine identity and authority'.[14] One of the most brilliant queer insights into Chaucer's narratives about morality and punishment is Pasolini's rewriting of the *Friar's Tale*:[15] his relocation of the main character as a homosexual, hounded by forces of surveillance and punishment, both reflects medieval church courts' jurisdiction over sexual behaviour and reconceptualizes the elements of hidden guilt, undetected danger, blackmail and punishment dramatized in Chaucer's tale.

Morality and History

Stephen Knight, Alcuin Blamires and Richard Firth Green all argue for the political and socio-economic contingency of much of Chaucer's deepest and most striking writing about moral issues. All three examine growing fourteenth-century individualism, in personal consciousness and economic practices. Knight interprets *Troilus* as exploring developments in social values through individuals' internal experiences, 'structures of feeling' (in Raymond Williams's famous term), at a period when socio-economic change was making a private sphere not only a lifestyle luxury but a possible self-concept. Analogously he sees the *Parson's Tale* advocating mastery of a turbulent and threatening social environment through individual moral consciousness, a personal relation with God, fostered by contemporary developments including lay literacy and *devotio moderna*.[16] Blamires argues that Chaucer acknowledges the inadequacy of Stoic *mesure* in relation to individual emotional suffering in his poetry and present in his society, particularly in relation to political violence and female suppression.[17] Green perceives a late-fourteenth-century shift away from mutual to documentary concepts of 'truth', and from a communally supportive – feudal – model of Christian society, to values which reflect increased individualism, commercialization and bureaucratization.[18]

Some tales' moral standpoints alienate modern readers. Examples include the dictates of Roman family honour in the *Physician's Tale* and wifely obedience in the *Clerk's Tale*, both entailing acceptance of child-murder. Chaucer's pilgrimage frame-story, with its links, comments and interpretations, problematizes the moral perspectives of both tales: Chaucer himself explicitly acknowledges the pastness of the *Clerk's Tale*'s moral assumptions (1163–82); analogously Cooper discusses the problems of relating the morality of Virginia's slaughter to Christian

[14] 'Doing what comes naturally: The *Physician's Tale* and the *Pardoner's Tale*', *Masculinities in Chaucer: Approaches to Maleness in the 'Canterbury Tales' and 'Troilus and Criseyde'*, ed. Peter G. Beidler (Cambridge, 1998) pp. 117–30, esp. p. 125.

[15] *I raconti di Canterbury / Canterbury Tales*, dir. Pier Paolo Pasolini, 1972.

[16] *Geoffrey Chaucer* (Oxford, 1986), pp. 33, 155.

[17] Alcuin Blamires, *Chaucer, Ethics, and Gender* (Oxford, 2006), pp. 152–82, 202–3, 237–8.

[18] *A Crisis of Truth: Literature and Law in Ricardian England* (London, 2002).

fourteenth-century attitudes, let alone modern ones, while Patterson sees Virginia's innocence betrayed by the patriarchy of Chaucer's text, as well as that of Appius, Virginius and the frame's Host.[19]

Yet the *Pardoner's Tale*'s passages of straight moral teaching of a distinctively medieval cast, to the effect that sins, which include gourmet cooking, swearing and drunkenness, are a form of death (VI 472–588), demonstrate how assumptions unfamiliar to many moderns can nevertheless offer a brilliantly illuminating moral analysis – here of sin, materialism and desire.

Some of Chaucer's most adventurous writing occurs when moral systems clash. For example, in the *Franklin's Tale* Arveragus, in bidding his wife act on the same criteria of 'trouthe' that constitute masculine knightly honour, rather than the traditional and purely sexual honour of women, represents a daring, non-traditional moral equality between man and wife, a clash of chivalric and patriarchal value systems. Yet by dictating that command, weeping and demanding her secrecy, he simultaneously voices the earlier system.

Many details in the *General Prologue* are fictionalizations of historical trends, not just moralistic character-creation. Thus the Shipman's ruthless fighting (I 397–400), rather than simply painting a shockingly callous individual, reflects the contemporary prominence of English piracy, deeply mixed up with – and important to – both England's Bordeaux trade and Anglo-French military relations. And Chaucer's pairing of pilgrims (Plowman with Parson, Lawyer with Franklin, and Pardoner with Summoner), instead of merely constructing imagined friendships or kinship, symbolizes topical perceptions of linked elements – whether good or bad – in contemporary society: an ideal of dutiful, peaceable priest and labourer (a synergy much desired after 1381); the increased interactions of county gentry and lawyers in Ricardian regional administrative policy; and concern over abuses tainting both the penitential and disciplinary duties of the Church. The pairing of the Parson and Plowman, whose virtues proceed out of Christian discipleship and dutiful churchmanship, also combines conservative political principles of the period (like the *Nun's Priest's Tale*'s contented peasant widow) with distinctly Wycliffite perspectives on the clergy (see Frances McCormack's essay, pp. 37–8). The first paired portraits, the Knight and Squire, provide both a conservative statement about the primacy of lineage as a social principle and also potential mitigation of any moral criticism of the pleasure-loving young soldier: father and son can be read together as figures exemplifying the medieval model of the Ages of Man, whereby preoccupation with love is an appropriate quality of Youth: it suggests that Youth moves by process of Nature and time to the *gravitas* of Middle Age.

Chaucer's writings read back moral preoccupations from his own era into history, producing anachronistic, often thought-provoking, Christian allusions amid classical contexts. Examples include the affinities between Cleopatra's tomb and medieval *memento mori* teaching.[20] Chaucer also applies medieval models of virtuous kingship and knighthood to ancient heroes. Thus a Theban widow (I 918–21) begs Theseus for 'pite' as a concomitant of his 'gentillesse', a contemporary (but

[19] Helen Cooper, *The Canterbury Tales* (Oxford, 1989), pp. 250–6; Patterson, *Chaucer and the Subject of History* (London, 1991), pp. 367–71.

[20] See V. A. Kolve, 'From Cleopatra to Alceste: An Iconographic Study of the *Legend of Good Women*', *Signs and Symbols in Chaucer's Poetry*, ed. J. P. Hermann and J. J. Burke Jr (Tuscaloosa, 1981), pp. 130–78.

also very Chaucerian) ideal that 'pite rennethe soone in gentil herte' (V 479–80).

The most adventurous treatments of virtue, and of a question Chaucer's writing often raises, 'What counts as virtue?', occur in texts set in a pre-Christian world. Thus the *Legend*'s 'Hypermnestra' raises questions about what counts as female virtue and shows a woman caught between different moral imperatives: patriarchal duty, a female stereotype of mercy, and a higher moral imperative forbidding murder. Yet it demonstrates what virtue is most powerfully in the texture of Chaucer's depiction of the lone moral courage of a girl calmly awaiting death as the consequence of her independent decision for humane action, and in Chaucer's brief but chilling picture of the recipient of her act saving his own skin and abandoning her.[21] The pity is in the poetry and so are the ethics.

Even Chaucer's unambiguously Christian writing can disconcert modern readers by alien assumptions, even about good deeds. The medieval prioritizing of transcendental penitential purpose over social ethics produces in the *Parson's Tale* a statement that good deeds done while in a state of sin or followed by sin are 'lost': 'mortefied and astoned and dulled', utterly 'dede' in terms of achieving 'the lyf perdurable in hevene' (X 230–5). Today, service to others in this world for their own sake is central to ethical thinking, Christian as well as secular.

The *Parson's Tale* is designed so that the transcendental, penitential purpose forms its frame (using passages drawn mostly from Raymond of Pennaforte), enclosing the tale's exposition of sins and virtues, derived mostly from William Peraldus and the thirteenth-century *Summa virtutum de remediis anime.* Towards the end, in accordance with the parable of the bridegroom, comes the teaching that Christians will 'heren at the day of doom' of their charitable acts (X 1030). The eschatological significance of good deeds remains uppermost.

Yet Chaucer's wording in this tale gives more value to earthly good deeds than that framework suggests. For example, his condemnation of pride (415–20) includes the cost to the poor of luxurious fashions, and the section on mercy defines mercy as an impulse 'stired by the mysese [distress]' (805) of others to give them alms and release them from obligations. Chaucer, however, ties that impulse to the overarching transcendental imperative by comparing it to the mercy of Christ, who gives himself and releases humans from hell.

Chaucer's portraits, showing sociological alertness as much as moral judgement, often convey professional outlooks with their own priorities, jargon and potentially their own duties. A disconcerting double moral vision in many portraits makes the pilgrim outstanding in his/her profession, regardless of absolute good or evil: the Friar is the best beggar, the Physician the 'parfit praktisour' (I 422), the Manciple brilliant in his cheating (I 574–5). This device, creating disparate effects simultaneously for the reader, seems to imply (among other things) competing perspectives in the world of work. The acknowledgement of credit (debt) in the Merchant's portrait and of interest on loans in the *Shipman's Tale* seem analogous: recognition of commercial requirements in late-fourteenth-century England which defy the Church's traditional asceticism and prohibition on usury, with which they co-exist.

[21] This Ovidian tale's exploration of moral causes is emphasized in an added passage about planetary influences on virtue and suffering (2276–99).

Some Secular Principles?

Richard Firth Green argues that, though Chaucer never shows virtue wholly independent of Christian values, his terminology distinguishes between concepts of sin and virtue as these were taught and judged by the Church and what he calls *moral virtue.* That, virtuous action within the human world, is a concept 'with overtones of Christian virtue . . . but [inhabiting] a realm conceptually distinct from those modes of behaviour indisputably subject to Church disciplines'.[22] Perhaps the Clerk, whose words were 'sownynge in moral vertu' (I 307), represents a secular parallel to the Parson, whose social moral acts are anchored in spirituality: love of God, reading the Bible and eagerness to follow Christ. Other details support such a parallelism: in both these clerks, the parish priest and university teacher, theory is backed by practice: the university scholar as happy to teach others as study himself (I 308); both demonstrate contented poverty; both are learned, with their learning the basis for service to others and indifference to materialism.

Medieval culture formulated several major concepts round which cluster moral ideas about this world, which do not fall wholly within Christian presuppositions. One is Nature or 'Kynde' (the supreme example of how twelfth-century Christian thinking refashioned Neoplatonic ideas and negotiated between classical and Christian philosophies and between secular and spiritual outlooks). Nature provides a way of imaging divine order ruling the lower, physical realm of creation. The word *kind*'s later semantic evolution to denote gentleness and charity witnesses to the moral force that was part of the medieval concept. Medieval Nature encompasses religious and ethical complexities, even inconsistencies.[23] So does another major concept, Fortune. In theory, Fortune's power discourages interpretations of events based on moral culpability. Yet in the *Monk's Tale* Chaucer vacillates over how far victims of Fortune appear innocent like Cenobia or culpable like Nero (VII 2463–550). The following *Nun's Priest's Tale*'s allusion to Bradwardine introduces into that tale contemporary theological debate about predestination and free will.[24] Concepts of Fortune and free will always involve moral questions and their recurrence in Chaucer's writing is unsurprising, especially given the centrality to all story-telling of issues of cause and effect, decision-making and moral assessment. *Troilus*, after a narrative filled with allusions to Fortune, leaves undecided whether Troilus' misery is caused by moral failings or simple blindness to the fact of mutability. The *Physician's Tale*'s extraordinarily inconsistent moral perspectives include the Host's statement that Fortune and Nature – rather than evil men – caused Virginia's death (VI 295).

'Trouthe', another major concept, epitomizes traditional values for social morality: loyalty to lord, fellow and promise, a value associated particularly with chivalric honour. The *Knight's Tale* shows loyalty threatened by the individualistic forces of passion; the *Friar's Tale* shows ostensible 'brothers' breaking the principle through predator-like eagerness for gain.

Common profit and fellowship are related concepts. Corsa, Wallace and

[22] Green, 'Morality and Immorality', p. 1.

[23] Well brought out in Hugh White's *Nature, Sex and Goodness in Medieval Literary Tradition* (Oxford, 2000).

[24] VII 3241–50; see *Riverside Chaucer* note.

Blamires, in different ways, argue that medieval structures and ideals of fellowship are central to the *Canterbury Tales*.[25] In the *Parliament of Fowls*, 'Commune profit' (75) enables Chaucer to adapt for a medieval Christian audience the Roman civic ethics of *Somnium Scipionis*, as preface to his love dream's conservative vision of order in Nature, the cosmos and marriage.

Morality for Specific Groups

Chaucer sometimes lists virtues appropriate to particular social groups: ideals for knighthood, for example, in the *General Prologue* (I 45–6, 67–72) and for kings in the *Squire's Tale* (V 12–27) and *Legend* (F 373–414). *Troilus* promulgates the notion that passion engenders virtues in *gentil* lovers. Troilus is improved across many qualities: service to his lady, protection of her reputation, fidelity, secrecy, humility, sensitivity and courtesy; becoming 'the frendlieste . . . gentilest . . . mooste fre', 'thriftiest [most successful]', courageous and popular, without cruelty and haughtiness (*Troilus* I 1072–84). These are not the seven Christian virtues showcased in the *Parson's Tale*, but secular and social qualities, qualities of a reliable and pleasant aristocrat, or the sort of consort a noble woman might be supposed to value (qualities itemized in the *Complaint of Venus* as 'manhod', 'worthynesse', 'trouthe', 'stidfastnesse', 'bounte', 'wisdom', 'governaunce', 'suffisaunce' and 'humblesse', 3–18).

Young women are another group associated with clusters of virtues. The praises of White, Virginia and Canace include beauty, modesty, *mesure*, sobriety and compassion, yet the first two show Chaucer's ideal not entirely one of a silent cloistered virtue: White is the life and soul of the party, while naturally drawn to goodness, wise, totally sincere, and, like Virginia, eloquent in speech (*Book of the Duchess* 826–34, 848–1016). In Prudence and Cecilia *speech* is a female virtue and a female power. Cecilia exemplifies the common hagiographical model of the undaunted female Christian martyr, upbraiding her accuser and teaching others.

Melibee (VII 1555–1675) advises on conduct for the wealthy, including the counsel to be generous in cases of need but not foolishly open-handed. Going further, Chaucer sometimes adventures into territory usually uncharted in medieval literature: the practices and duties necessary for successful businessmen. The contexts make this topic, when it arises, easy to dismiss merely as satire. Yet even Chaucer's most obvious satire can raise questions about what rules and advice pertain in the pragmatic, commercial world for working lives, and also implicitly the urgent contemporary question of how prudential conduct in commerce relates to received teaching about Christian conduct. Wyclif is dismissive of commerce, credit and usury; Langland, though admitting that there can be blameless aspects of *meed*, largely ignores the mighty socio-economic demands of urban business.[26] Chaucer's writing admits voices from that world, expressing its professional values and priorities, its cares and duties. His wording sometimes makes provocative

[25] Corsa, *Chaucer*; Blamires, *Ethics*, pp. 20–45; Wallace, *Chaucerian Polity: Absolutist Lineages and Associational Forms in England and Italy* (Stanford, 1997), pp. 83–103.

[26] John Wyclif, *Select English Works*, ed. Thomas Arnold, 3 vols (Oxford, 1869–72), vol. III, e.g. p. 390; William Langland, *Piers Plowman: A Parallel-Text Edition of the A, B, C and Z Versions*, ed. A. V. C. Schmidt, 2 vols (London and New York, 1995), vol. I, p. 125, lines 234–7.

contrasts with medieval Christian assumptions about asceticism, mutability and social bonds. Examples include the *Shipman's Tale*'s Merchant's comments on frugality and the care needed to maintain a good 'name' (essential for successful dealing on credit) and the tale's opening lines' perversion of the ideal of 'fellowship' that was central to conventional models of society (VII 1–20). These usher us into a world where social events and fashionable clothes are not valued by usual criteria, as good or bad: neither as worldly vanity nor fellowship. Here they are prudentially valued for their efficacy in a business community, especially one based on credit and 'name': the duty of fellowship perverted into the duty of business entertaining. The Reeve's portrait, like this tale, presents verbal analogies between spiritual asceticism and the self-control and dedication required for amassing wealth: the Reeve's friar-like dedication to profit and the Merchant's grave and anxious attitude to Fortune, mutability and the duties of 'chapmanhede'(VII 224–38). To lose the medieval equivalent of his credit ratings renders any merchant, he explains, useless: merely playing a pilgrimage (234). Scattergood argues that the tale's sympathy with the values of 'chapmanhede' follows a topos of celebrating 'winning' as socially necessary exemplified in *Winner and Waster*.[27] Blamires explores its challenge to the medieval 'ethics of sufficiency'.[28] An analogously worldly challenge to transcendental perspectives is the *Man of Law's Prologue*'s denigration of poverty as the worst of evils (II 99–133).

We hear the values of urban 'chapmanhede' also in Chaucer's quizzical use of 'worthy' to convey the respect of bourgeois society for the financially successful. Whereas his Knight is 'worthy' (I 43) in the older, aristocratic, sense of having chivalric prowess, late-fourteenth-century 'worthy' was also acquiring colloquial connotations of bourgeois criteria for respect: financially 'substantial' and 'respectable' citizens. Thus the Wife has been a 'worthy womman' – well-to-do and well respected – all her life (459): the adjective here hovers between that mercantile sense and a purely moral sense, just as her initial description 'good wif' (445) hovers between meaning 'virtuous wife' (subject to irony) and 'goodwife', the proprietor of a household or an establishment. The Friar cultivates 'worthy' women, respectably off citizens, whereas contact with lepers would be inappropriate for such a 'worthy', respectable, man (217, 243). Chaucer's use of 'worthy' in this sense may involve moral irony yet its repetition acknowledges the increased importance of socio-economic circles, with their own types of respect and endeavour, that had not usually got into serious medieval literature. It resembles his tendency to describe pilgrims as 'parfit praktisours' of their occupations, however worldly: there are disconcertingly perfections in the worlds of gaining *meed* as well as in godliness. Analogously the Physician's portrait includes features that medieval satirists had often attacked, but neutrally: as professional skills.[29]

The middle class, an ill-defined group yet growing, and growing in importance, is a social band stretching from rich peasants (peasant entrepreneurs like Symkyn) up to the Franklin on its upper boundary. We can hear the voice of the

27 'The Originality of the "Shipman's Tale"', *The Chaucer Review* 11 (1976–7), 210–31.

28 *Ethics*, pp. 107–29.

29 Jill Mann, *Chaucer and Medieval Estates Satire: The Literature of Social Classes and the* General Prologue *to the* Canterbury Tales (Cambridge, 1973), p. 91.

upwardly mobile, assessing what constitutes conduct unbecoming for the social state in which they now find themselves, when Symkin maintains that his position requires a bride who is virgin and well brought up, 'to saven his estaat of yeomanrye'. And, although Chaucer can include the cliché that churls' tales will lack morality (I 3167–84), he also depicts a man of the well-to-do tradesman class, Carpenter John, as someone who accompanies almost every comment he makes with a religious or sententious statement. He is energetically active to help Nicholas, tender over Alison, and the observations he makes in responding to Nicholas's strange malady (I 1325–491) are accompanied by moralizing references ranging variously over worldly mutability, the faults of sleeping all day, forbidden knowledge, the orthodox piety of his garbled prayers, the importance of keeping faith in Christ's Passion and avoiding *accidia* and lack of Christian hope. The remedy for the latter sin – trust in God – is presented as a virtue typical of his class, and with a sudden dignity: 'What! Thinke on God, as we doon, men that swynke' (3491). Chaucer's sensitivity to the moral vista of such a man (so unsophisticated he doesn't even know Cato's *Distychs*, a distinctly middle-brow life-guide) would be touching – if it were not also that John is patronizing, full of self-righteous class-contempt for the *clerk*, and that Nicholas is about to sweep solicitous John ruthlessly and hilariously off the board. Chaucer shows John's morality / moralizing as shaped by the parameters of his job and class: the priorities they embody are energy, hard work, not thinking over much, not speculating beyond what is correct, a trusting piety, and a readiness to hope. In a way too, the portrait of the vices of the riotous apprentice in the *Cook's Tale* depicts – negatively, by their absence – the virtues needed for a city tradesman's establishment. Unlike the *Pardoner's Tale* rioters' vices, Perkyn's faults exist not in a socio-economic vacuum but in contrastive proximity to the diligent tradesman, the master, who knows he must extirpate such habits from his household and the commercial microcosm it represents.

Sin and Virtue: Multiple Moral Perspectives

Chaucer's portraits of evil convey convictions about the nature of good. And sins against others – cruelty, exploitation and lack of charity – are often shown alongside spiritual sin. The profit motif produces both spiritual and earthly robbery when the Pardoner, for selfish gain, sells false indulgences, regardless of whether the buyers' souls 'goon a-blakeberyed' (VI 406). As the *Pardoner's Prologue and Tale* illustrate, speech and gesture are integral to Chaucer's ethical portraiture. Class is an element in this: courteous speech is also moral speech. The contemptuous manner in which boorish men, confident in their youthful strength or class status, address others in the *Pardoner's* and *Wife of Bath's Tales* (VI 717–59; III 1098–1104) dramatizes the nature of the evil that underlies their more serious assaults – murder and rape – and does so more graphically than Chaucer's descriptions of those atrocities, which use brevity and neutral language (III 888; VI 881, 888). *Gentils* who do not take advantage of superior rank in speech, like the Knight (I 79–81) and the *Book of the Duchess*'s Knight, are praised.

The *General Prologue*, as Jill Mann showed, draws on 'estates satire', which portrays the characteristics, especially the faults, of social types. The Monk's hunting, the Wife's headgear and the Friar's easy-going confession are traditional targets. Yet Chaucer relies only partly on estates traditions. Mann sees him creating an impression of individuality unknown in the genre, doing so less from adding non-traditional details than by manipulating the *reader*'s reactions, so that these resemble those of our real-life reactions to individuals: he evokes uncertain, mixed moral signals, rather than the absolute moral abstractions common in estates satire, and creates an illusion of the pilgrims' own viewpoints and their self-presentation. For example, the Sergeant of Law's portrait is filled with his professional skills, not traditional anti-lawyer satire; the extent of any moral condemnation is unclear and Chaucer constructs the lawyer's portrait 'in terms of his own façades'.[30]

Elsewhere Chaucer builds on and deepens established satirical tropes. Chaucer's *Summoner's*, *Friar's* and *Pardoner's Tales* brilliantly enact criticism of ecclesiastical abuses familiar to his readers from anticlerical satire. The friar's long speech in the *Summoner's Tale* dramatizes abuses regularly targeted in satires against mendicant friars: accusations of their rapacity, attempts to usurp the parish priest's role as confessor, and exploitation of the lucrative practice of enrolling laypeople in confraternities. The last practice triggers the well-to-do churl Thomas's revenge: he rates the friar's speech and pleas for donation worth only a fart. The friar's phrasing richly characterizes him as a religious hypocrite yet the tale includes within this vicious character's speech some genuinely valuable moral teaching against ire and drunkenness, particularly the dangers they represent for men of power (III 2010–88), a structure famously present in the *Pardoner's Prologue* and *Tale.* In dramatizing morality emanating from corrupt clergy, these particular tales can be seen as symbolizing the hope that a Church acknowledged to be imperfect can still disseminate God's message, but they also demonstrate how readily Chaucer jettisons the fiction of the pilgrim narrator's voice to create effects beyond novelistic realism. The abuses of the contemporary world appear very close to the terrifying boundaries of the next world, death and judgement in these three pilgrims' tales and prologues: the Summoner's story of friars in hell, the *Friar's Tale* consigning of a corrupt summoner to hell (III 1634–64), and the rioters' encounter with Death.

Biblical echoes and the medieval lexicons of astrology, physiognomy and antifeminist satire also suggest moral dimensions to words and scenes, though rarely without demanding a questioning attention from the reader. Thus January and May's sinful attitudes are not explicitly condemned but implied by parallels with Adam and Eve, but does that parallel imply that in this tale a virtuous man falls, through female guile, or is January fallen from the start of the tale? Lucrece's actions in the *Legend* (1879–82), though those of a pagan, are disconcertingly brought within the parameters of Christian moral approbation by an echo of Matthew 15: 28. Chaucer's allusion to the Franklin's 'sangwyn' humour seems morally neutral (I 333) but whether his desire to live 'in delit' like Epicurus should be read disapprovingly depends whether readers invoke strictly Christian moral criteria.

The presence in Chaucer's writing of multiple and overlapping ethical systems underlies some major critical debates. Most obviously critics divide over the

[30] Ibid., pp. 89, 90.

conflict between systems in *Troilus*, foregrounded by Chaucer's interweaving of a narrative informed by courtly, amorous ideals with passages evoking Boethian or Christian ideals. Some passages which provocatively place Troilus' love on a level with religious experiences contain echoes of writings – the Bible, Boethius or Dante – which intensify the disparity between sacred and sensual realms of experience. Examples include Boethius' metrum about divine love (*Consolation* II 8), the source of Troilus' song in III 1744–71, and the echoes of Dante in some of the cadences of Book III's invocations to pagan gods of love (III 39–42, 1261–7, 1807).[31] Robertson and Donald W. Rowe are among the most determined exponents of ethically unitary readings.[32] Ideological disparities between Chaucer's sources for *Troilus* are matched by its multiple endings: Windeatt argues that these form a process which takes readers out from the narrative's 'anticlimactic end' towards the 'rest and peace found in God', a resolution which is, however, 'achieved only after the end of the story for the reader, and only after death for the pagan hero'.[33]

Chaucer's final statement on Criseyde abjures moral judgement (*Troilus* V 1772–85). In both *Troilus* and the *Legend* a passive narrator, a mere translator or servant, pleading lack of responsibility, culpability and agency for what he depicts, leaves the reader with diverse criteria about how texts present morality and with questions about textual intention and interpretation, and how we judge these, as much as about female behaviour and how it is judged.

The Legend of Good Women

Women are the group for whom medieval culture most markedly prescribed specific virtues, arising from the attribution to them of particular vices: deception, infidelity, disobedience, and inclination to sinfulness, especially lust.[34] The stereotypes medieval feminists had to fight differed from those post-Victorian feminists faced. Defenders of women from Jerome on praised examples of female fidelity, modesty, chastity and deference to fathers and husbands.[35] Jerome's examples, emphasizing female virginity and chastity, often demonstrated through self-sacrifice and even a patriarchal form of female martyrdom, appear in a treatise, *Against Jovinian*, which is specifically arguing against the proposition that married people merit as much respect in the Church as the celibate, the clergy. In contrast, another source for the *Legend*, Ovid's *Heroides*, paints the psychology of passion, sharpened by sensationalism, agony, guilt and death: its focus is typically on its subjects' emotions, more than their moral valour. Chaucer's legends part company with the ethical attitudes of *Heroides* both in treating heroines they share (notably, for example, Dido) with more dignity and respect and also in presenting passion itself as an experience which can have, in certain noble personalities, moral qualities.

31 Barry Windeatt, *Troilus and Criseyde*, Oxford Guides to Chaucer (Oxford, 1992), pp. 125–37.

32 Robertson, 'Chaucerian Tragedy', *English Literary History* 19 (1952), 1–37; Donald W. Rowe, *'O Love, O Charite': Contraries Harmonized in Chaucer's Troilus* (Carbondale, 1976).

33 Windeatt, *Troilus*, p. 314.

34 See on this gendering of deception A. J. Minnis, *Fallible Authors: Chaucer's Pardoner and Wife of Bath* (Philadelphia, 2007), pp. 259–62.

35 *Adversus Jovinianum*, Patrologia Latina 23, ed. J. P. Migne (Paris 1883); also Alcuin Blamires, *The Case for Women in Medieval Culture* (Oxford, 1997).

The *Legend* departs also from contemporary conventions by dislodging traditional ideals of female virtue as inhering in sexual purity, as well as parodying Christian martyrdom narratives. These concepts are dislodged elsewhere in his oeuvre too: after the *Franklin's Tale* has listed female martyrs to conventional notions of sexual honour, Chaucer's tale dramatically sidelines this in favour of other models of honour based on *trouthe*. Moreover, in comic mode the Miller misapplies 'legende' for a tale of flagrant contempt for chastity (I 3141).

Yet the *Legend* rewrites in all seriousness the idea of a 'legende', a legend of exemplary women and Chaucer also rewrites both martyrdom traditions: the Christian and the patriarchal. Most of its legends honour heroines who are passionate and sexually experienced; arguably Chaucer's writing represents the intense, absolute, power of their emotional attachment to a sexual partner as the root of their exemplary moral power as good women. Intensity of passion seems to represent an existentialist part of the goodness the poem praises. That quality of absoluteness is central also to his heroines' virtues: they show utter sincerity and selfless giving. The self-emptying totality of those virtues matches their emotional intensity, and both involve complete sincerity: lack of calculation. Chaucer makes the quality of desire in his heroines of a piece with the high moral level of their other motivations, strengths and actions. Without claiming Chaucer as a D. H. Lawrence, a prophet of the holiness of the right kind of sexual emotion, the *Legend* conveys a differentiation between high and low, noble and ignoble, levels of desire: these passionate, sincere and generous women exemplify an ethically lofty love. That quality is pointed up by the shallow, calculating, mode of desire in a succession of exploitative, lustful males: Jason, Theseus, Aeneas, Tereus and Tarquin. Chaucer's satirical play on the language of masculine chivalry and *gentilesse* in describing these princes makes the sexual and financial exploitation of noblewomen seem appear to be the dirty little secret at the heart of aristocratic masculine identity and dynastic practices.

The *Legend* prologue includes – and from a queen – a passage of explicit advice for princes (F 345–411). The *Legend* is an unconventional mirror of princely qualities: its queens and royal heiresses, unlike its princes, display the qualities of ideal medieval rulers: courage, largesse, mercy and loyalty. Unconventionally too, and again overturning stereotypes of gendered virtues, Chaucer asserts in 'Thisbe' the two sexes' equal capacity for courage and fidelity.

Alceste represents (F 544–5) 'fyn lovyng' and 'wyfhod': twinned secular, non-celibate, virtues. Chaucer's ladies are mostly wives (or the medieval equivalent: Thisbe and Pyramus plight their troth). Unlike his sources, he makes Cleopatra's devoted 'wyfhod' central to her goodness and her death. The ethics of *Legend*'s handling of religious martyrdom and hagiography, and ideals about wives, have been found by readers difficult to judge. Is its alleged defence of women by praising sexually passionate women a sham, ironical and condemnatory? It parodies hagiography but is it blasphemous? Medieval use of religion as a language for a wide variety of subjects can disconcert modern readers (see Gillian Rudd's discussion, pp. 198–9, 207). It may help understanding to know that, in parish life and laywomen's experience, virgin martyrs were perceived as more roundly womanly, less exclusively virginal, than we might suppose: those most revered in England – Margaret, Catherine, Barbara – were patrons and helpers to women generally: aids in childbirth, their images shown on roodscreens near to the places where women in parish churches attended Mass.[36] At the same time, other, non-religious, female role models and exempla were gaining respect, with more purely secular qualities. The fourteenth century, which saw advanced poets like Machaut and Chaucer using classical material less constrained by moralizing traditions than earlier writers, also saw the Nine Female Worthies appearing as a theme in visual art. Like Richard II's development of the Ladies of the Garter, this furnishes figures to represent a respectful image of aristocratic laywomen. Rather than comparing Chaucer's passionate heroines from the classical world simply (and disapprovingly) with Christian virgin martyrs it is more apposite to compare them to classical male heroes like Hector, Jason or Alexander, who (though not perfect and pure saints) acted in medieval culture as avatars for contemporary aristocratic laymen. That would make particular sense if some of the heroines are compliments to particular contemporary royal ladies: Cleopatra for Constance of Castile and Alceste for Anne of Bohemia, perhaps.[37]

Lyrics

Chaucer's moral and philosophical ballades draw on multiple sources and diverse moral and religious systems, including the Bible, Boethius, Seneca, Ovid and the *Roman de la Rose*, together with oblique references to contemporary political concerns. They have a dazzling, shifting mix of tones and discourses: urbane, comic, earnest, reverent, didactic, teasing and diplomatic. Alfred David observes that, particularly following Deschamps, the ballade was a form where many worlds – moral, humorous, classical and Christian, and political and topical – interacted.[38]

'The Former Age' is based on descriptions of the Golden Age in Book Two of Boethius' *Consolation*, metrum 5, Ovid, and the *Roman de la Rose*, each source having an individual slant on the myth's import.[39] Chaucer's poem centres on one aspect of the concept of Nature, innocence, as well as implicitly another: social order, with mutual fellowship and absence of strife. Its praise of primitive simplicity creates a secular parallel to the admiration for poverty in medieval Christian morality.[40] Contentment is a virtue Chaucer often praises, and Burnley explores associated ideals, including asceticism, self-government and 'suffisaunce': not 'grucchinge' against worldly estate or fate.[41] These lend themselves to spiritual and political perspectives and, within the latter, both conservative and subversive political propaganda.

The classical and Christian myths of ancient perfection, an innocent past, provided a safely authoritative context for criticism of the present. Virtue is

[36] Eamon Duffy, *The Stripping of the Altars: Traditional Religion in England 1400–1580* (New Haven and London, 1992), pp. 171–7.

[37] Helen Phillips, 'Chaucer's Love Visions', *A Companion to Medieval Poetry*, ed. Corinne J. Saunders (Oxford, 2010), pp. 401–21.

[38] *Geoffrey Chaucer: The Minor Poems*, ed. George B. Pace and Alfred David, Variorum Chaucer 5 (Norman, OK, 1982), pp. 4–7.

[39] See John Scattergood, 'The Short Poems', *Oxford Guides to Chaucer: The Shorter Poems*, ed. A. J. Minnis, V. J. Scattergood and J. J. Smith (Oxford, 2000), pp. 455–512.

[40] Ibid., pp. 493–4.

[41] J. D. Burnley, *Chaucer's Language and the Philosophers' Tradition* (Cambridge, 1979), pp. 70–8

constructed upon absence of desire for luxury, power and artifice. Indeed, the ideal, if taken literally, is a world without civilization (agriculture, cookery, buildings, mining, and dyeing) as well as without war, covetousness and deceit. The sophistications of civilization, however, are metonymy for wider ethical concepts: dyeing, for example, stands for deception; house-building for robbery; mining for avarice. These fantastical binaries to modern corruptions allow more pointedly topical complaints to be included. Thus 'Nembrot' (58) represents tyranny, a political complaint against Richard II growing during the 1390s; 'taylage' (53) is another term of grievance in the 1390s.[42]

Chaucer's lyrics tend to move through multiple registers, literary modes, and levels of meaning. In 'Fortune', ostensibly a debate, both voices teach that ill fortune can teach the way to wisdom. The refrain used during lines 25–48, that discord can be brought into harmony by a ruling power's benignity, fits with other hints, especially in the envoy, that one of this lyric's modes may be a begging poem, complimenting a princely patron and expressing hope for continued support. Yet the supreme friend and ruler may also be Fortune. Chaucer's wording conveys a constantly oscillating image of power, as both instability and stable 'majestee' (65), while the speaker's stance vacillates between flight and hope of succour. Such inconsistencies create a mirror both of politics and a Boethian recognition that beyond Fortune's fickleness work the wise and stable purposes of God. Equally disconcerting and elusive, the language of the 'Complaint to Pity', outwardly a courtly allegory of unrequited love, runs through an extraordinarily vivid figurative panorama of conspiracies and the lexicon of treason, possibly evocative of Ricardian political contexts, whether of the Appellants' ascendancy in the late 1380s or the years before Richard's 1399 deposition. The multiple registers of 'Pity' also freight the ostensibly light allegory of pity's 'death' with a solemn marshalling of the moral terms used for *gentil* virtue: 'Bounte parfyt . . . Beaute, Lust, and Jolyte, / Assured Maner, Youthe, and Honeste, / Wisdom, Estaat, Drede, and Governaunce' (38–41), and more. The Death of Pity paints an aristocratic female ideal as much as the *Deeth of Blaunche the Duchesse*. Yet neither the fears nor the solemnity running through its wording possess a clear referent or tone.

The 'delivrance' (setting free) promised in 'Truth' may be spiritual, ethical or political. Stanza one gives counsel about conduct in worldly society: self-control and the avoidance of ambition. These are presented within a wholly secular condemnation of the dangers for the over-ambitious in the 'prees', meaning the fighting throng or rather, here, the rat-race at court. Scattergood links the counsel to Senecan, Stoic, advice about self-control and detachment from material affairs, and also to medieval curial satire: warnings for courtiers to shun the vices attendant on court life and high office.[43] Yet the introduction of the refrain in line 7, 'And trouthe shal delyver . . .', echoes 'the truth shall make you free' in John 8: 32, and though the word *truth* has in this poem its usual medieval sense, 'loyalty' – the correct stance of courtier to prince and the central principle of harmonious

[42] See Helen Phillips, 'Register, Politics, and the *Legend of Good Women*', *The Chaucer Review* 37 (2002), 101–28; Scattergood, 'The Short Poems', pp. 486–92.

[43] Ibid. pp. 493–4.

society – it also begins to connote God.[44] The third and fourth stanzas progressively reject the human, secular world, first with an image of distrusting Fortune, then a reformulating of the advice to flee the political 'prees' to stand now for rejecting this world. The perspective becomes that of a higher and lower vision: abandoning physical animal life for that of the spirit, using the biblical image of God's people travelling through 'wilderness' to a true home with God (Hebrews 11:8–10), and the Boethian image of wisdom as upward flight. The unequivocally spiritual word 'gost' moves the final lines firmly into the transcendental register. The Envoy, found only in one manuscript, personalizes the poem, with punning allusion to Philip de la Vache, who lost favour, as a king's man, during the Appellants' ascendancy. But it also unequivocally Christianizes it. The retreat is now from being 'thral' to this world, and the ambition is for heavenly 'meed' (wages): the source of princely reward will now be the divine monarch.[45]

'Gentilesse' also mixes religious and social perspectives. Its opening phrase, 'the firste stok', susceptible of multiple interpretations, becomes by the final lines a description of God himself, granting true nobility – now implicitly salvation–to those who please him, regardless of rank. Line one's 'first stok, fader of gentilesse', however, means high-born ancestor, the argument presented in the *Wife of Bath's Tale* that people now called *gentil* are descended from virtuous ancestors but do not merit the title, unless they act virtuously (III 1117–24).[46] The virtues listed in stanza two are not specifically Christian. They provide a list of virtues befitting a nobleman: 'ful of rightwisnesse [justice], / Trew of his word, sobre, pitous, and free, / Clene of his gost, and loved besinesse' (8–10). Largesse and loyalty to one's word are cardinal chivalric virtues, while the pair 'rightwisnesse' [justice] and 'pitous' corresponds to justice and mercy, twin princely duties which monarchs in their coronation oaths swore to exercise. Sobriety, purity and lack of idleness could be read as directly advice specifically for a young ruler or one criticized for luxury, like Richard II: Scattergood suggests a veiled address to Richard II.[47]

As in the *Wife of Bath's Tale* (III 1109–76), *gentilesse* is handled in moral and Christian terms but political viewpoints are also obviously present. The context might be that of the deposition of Richard II.

Whether 'Lak of Stedfastnesse' addresses contemporary politics or not, it, like 'Truth', makes loyalty its uniting concept. And, like 'The Former Age' and 'Gentilesse', it invokes the myth of Golden Age morality. The heading 'Lenvoy to King Richard' suggests to readers of modern printed texts that it indisputably addresses Richard II but only one manuscript carries it (Cambridge Trinity College R.3.20), and the envoy's opening words 'O prince' also echo a formula used at *puys*, poetry competitions, where envoys often address the so-called 'prince', the arbiter of the event. Yet, in favour of reading the lyric as an address to a ruler, Chaucer's ending does apply 'lak of steadfastness' specifically to the duties of a ruler. Cleverly he turns the subject's supreme virtue, loyalty, into a virtue for princes. The prince must take action, including punishment, to recall his people to loyalty, but must also himself cultivate virtues of loyalty, justice and refraining from extortion.

44 See Pace and David, *Minor Poems*, pp. 49–52, 61.
45 On, additionally, a humorous tone in the Envoy, see ibid., pp. 50–2.
46 See Scattergood, 'Short Poems'.
47 Scattergood, 'Short Poems', p. 486.

This lyric illustrates Chaucer's use of proverbial-style moral aphorisms. In contrast to the Elizabethans' admiration for Chaucer as a source of sententious epigrams and moral counsel, these elements in Chaucer's writings can pass modern readers by.[48] Examples of homely or proverbial styles of counsel include the proverbial crock spurning the wall in 'Truth' (12), and the 'dame's' advice at the end of the *Manciple's Tale.* In 'Lak of Stedfastnesse' stanza three employs the popular 'Complaint against the Times' kind of aphorism, in lines like 'Trouthe is put doun, resoun is holden fable' (15). Such verses, of which many examples survive, list social vices in formulas of this type:

> witte is turned into trechery,
> and love into lechery
> the holy day into Glotonye,
> and gentrie into vilanye.[49]

'Complaint against the Times' verse is a style possessing the advantage of indicating discontent with today while avoiding dangerously topical specificity and having an air of venerable moral lamentation.

Morality brings no calm or complacency to Chaucer's work. It is associated with some of his most provocative technical devices and with deep questions: questions about the intentions and interpretations of texts as well as about human conduct. Diversity is a recurrent theme when Chaucer writes about literature and morality, from the 'divers' responses to the *Miller's Tale* to the 'manye . . . weyes espirituels that leden folk to oure Lord Jhesu Crist', in the final Canterbury tale (X 78). Reluctance to assert unitary 'sentence' and 'conclusioun' appears to underlie the frequency of unfinished works and the inconclusive ends of those which are finished. *Troilus* has multiple conclusions; the *Book of the Duchess* ends with a return to its beginnings. *Anelida* seems to go round in circles. To the questions the *Parliament* raises about love, its ending provides no firm answer (even from Nature the best we get is an observation that loving emotions should be paramount when choosing a mate but royalty is likely to provide the be best candidate, 624–37). And for its narrator the end is a vista of endless books, endless reading and endless seeking. The image of travel recurs in Chaucer, with moral certainties located up and beyond this world, which seems a wilderness not only in offering its inhabitants no home (*Truth* 17), but also in being a far from orderly or comfortable realm of seeking, desiring, and questioning.

[48] See Clare R. Kinney, 'Thomas Speght's Renaissance Chaucer and the Solaas of Sentence in *Troilus and Criseyde*', *Refiguring Chaucer in the Renaissance*, ed. Theresa M. Krier (Gainesville, 1998), pp. 66–84.

[49] *Speculum Christiani*, ed. G. Holmstedt, EETS os 182 (London, 1933), p. xlxxxiv.

Teaching Chaucer Today

13

'To demen by interrogaciouns': Accessing the Christian Context of the *Canterbury Tales* with Enquiry-Based Learning

ROGER DALRYMPLE

THERE WOULD APPEAR to be a need for fresh pedagogic initiatives to assist students in accessing Christian context while continuing to enjoy freedom of interpretation and individual response. Can ecclesiastical and sacramental dimensions only be restored to Chaucer's work by the delivery of extensive didactic inputs in traditional lecture form? If so, at what point should these be delivered? To present extensive context to students *in advance* of their reading the primary texts risks compounding a sense of the alterity of medieval literature and supplies a further barrier to immediate engagement with Chaucer (alongside the linguistic challenges of reading Middle English).[1] Equally, to present religious context *retrospectively* once students have read the primary texts or even concomitantly with their study of the texts can imply that the process of uncovering Christian allusion is a rather mechanistic process, hardly an organic part of the initial reading experience. What would seem to be required is a supplementary teaching method whereby undergraduate study of Chaucer may include active engagement with Christian context from the outset.

'To demen by interrogaciouns'

Such a teaching method is available in a pedagogic model that proceeds from a principle of enquiry and discovery. Practised originally in medical disciplines in the 1970s, 'problem-based learning' (PBL) or 'enquiry-based learning' (EBL) advocates an approach in which students are given an initial impetus to investigate a new field of knowledge by approaching it from an investigative or exploratory aspect. Like Nicholas in Chaucer's *Miller's Tale* with his astrological investigations, students engaged in an enquiry-based activity proceed by asking questions,

1 The challenge of the perceived otherness or alterity of medieval literature is famously elaborated by Hans Robert Jauss, 'The Alterity and Modernity of Medieval Literature', *New Literary History* 10 (1979), 181–228.

to 'demen by interrogaciouns' (I 3194). As defined in one of the most influential anthologies on the teaching method,

> Problem-based learning is a way of constructing and teaching courses using problems as the stimulus and focus for student activity. . . . Problem-based courses start with problems rather than with exposition of disciplinary knowledge. They move students towards the acquisition of knowledge through a staged sequence of problems presented in context, together with associated learning materials and support from teachers.[2]

The present essay explores the value of adapting the EBL format to enable students to access Chaucer's religious contexts. My case-study, the *Miller's Tale*, is a central text in Chaucer syllabuses and a fabliau with a surprisingly high quotient of Christian allusion. As early as line 17 of the *Miller's Prologue* the drunken Miller is interrupting the Host 'in Pilates voys' and swearing by the Passion 'By armes, and by blood and bones' (3124–5). The tale itself of course, is mischievously advertised as 'a legende and a lyf / Bothe of a carpenter and of his wyf' (3141–2) and in the ensuing fabliau – the comic denouement of which turns upon a shared knowledge of the biblical story of the Flood – allusions are included to the hymn *Angelus ad Virginem*, the performance of 'Cristes owne werkes' (3308) at the parish church, the ecclesiastical duties of parish clerk Absolon, mystery plays, Ss Thomas, Frideswide and Benedict and the singing of lauds by friars.

All these allusions and the wider Christian hinterland of the poem can be illuminated by an enquiry-based approach where students are asked to explore two key literary questions. First, what is the relationship between religion and superstition in the tale, turning as it does upon the beguiling of a 'lewed man' by an undergraduate? Second, what is the relationship between sacred and profane in the poem, fond as it is of urging blasphemous juxtapositions of sexuality and spirituality upon us? These questions are designed to draw upon students' existing (modern) conceptions of piety, superstition and blasphemy so that these may form entry-points into the text, and hopefully take them beyond assuming such conceptions are entirely universal in all respects.

Superstition or Religion?

What is the relationship between devout piety and credulous superstition in the *Miller's Tale*? Of course, according to fabliau convention, we are not to scrutinize any character too far beyond a functional role in a plot centred upon themes of competition and sexual assertion. However, Chaucer nuances the portrait of John sufficiently that we are justified in exploring how far the character is to be seen as cruelly duped by Nicholas or as culpably gullible and wilfully credulous, courting disaster and wreaking his own undoing even as he avers:

> Men sholde nat knowe of Goddes pryvetee.
> Ye, blessed be alwey a lewed man
> That noght but oonly his bileve kan! (I 3455–7)

[2] *The Challenge of Problem-Based Learning*, ed. David Boud and Grahame Feletti (London, 1991), p. 14.

Critical views of John's character have varied. Robertson observes pertinently that when John accepts that a new Flood is imminent he overlooks 'as a "lewed man" that "oonly his bileve kan" the promise of Gen. 9.15' – that promise being that there will be no repeat of the deluge.[3] Ellis finds sufficient textual evidence for judging that Chaucer depicts a 'self-deluded fool';[4] Patterson detects an ominous quality in the silencing of the artisan's voice by his humiliation and cuckolding,[5] while Pearsall does not see John as 'a special target of ridicule. In fact, he is quite affectionately portrayed'.[6] An enquiry-based seminar might start with comparison of key passages of the text with contemporaneous Middle English material. For example, for John's 'nyght-spel', students might draw upon such revealing contextual materials as the following fifteenth-century charm against thieves:

> I Coniour hem in the name of the ffader, and sone, and holy gost;
> in hem ys vertu al-ther-most!
> In the bygynnyng & in the ending,
> And in the vertu of Al thing
> ys, & was, & euer schal be-
> In the vertu of the holy trinite –
> By the vertu of euery masse,
> that euer was seyde, more & lasse –
> In the vertu or erbe, gras, ston, & tre –
> And in the vertu that euer may be:
> yf here come eny fon
> me to robbe, other me to sclon;they stond as style ass eny ston,
> they haue no powere away to gon,
> By the vertu of the holy trinite,
> Tylle they haue lyve of me.
> lord iesu, Graunte me pys,
> as ȝe ben in heuen blys.[7]

Like John's 'white *pater noster*' this prays for divine protection from wrongdoers. Such material attests that, however credulous John may appear, there is a documentary context for his fervent piety. Another example is this charm 'ffor the nyȝthe-mare':

> Take a flynt stone þat hath an hole thorow of hys owene growing, & hange it ouer þe stabill dore, or ell ouer, horse, and ell writhe þis charme:
>
> In nomine Patris &c.
> Seynt Iorge, our lady knyȝth.
> he walked day, he walked nyȝth,
> toll pat he fownde pat fowle wyȝth;
> & whan þat he here fownde,
> he here bete & he here bownde,
> till trewly per here trowthe sche plyȝth
> þat sche scholde not come be nyȝthe,

[3] D. W. Robertson Jr, *A Preface to Chaucer: Studies in Medieval Perspectives* (Princeton, 1962), p. 385.
[4] Roger Ellis, *Patterns of Religious Narrative in the Canterbury Tales* (Beckenham, 1981), p. 285.
[5] '"No man his reson herde": Peasant Consciousness, Chaucer's Miller, and the Structure of the *Canterbury Tales*', *South Atlantic Quarterly* 86 (1987), 457–95.
[6] Derek Pearsall, *The Canterbury Tales* (London and New York, 1985), p. 172.
[7] *Secular Lyrics of the XIVth and XVth Centuries*, ed. Rossell Hope Robbins (Oxford, 1952), p. 58.

> With-Inne vij rode of londe space
> þer as Seynt Ieorge i-namyd was.[8]

Eamon Duffy presents such charms within a context, in a way that may give dismissive modern readers pause for thought, and bring Chaucer's text into relationship with more esoteric areas of the corpus of Middle English literature.[9] But these are written survivals of what, by its nature, was to be spoken: the property of the uneducated as well as those who wrote them down. And Chaucer's text renders John foolish, not just merely 'lewed', by the ironies in what he says, obvious to the reader but not to himself: he is the one who cannot see – who 'woot litel what hym shal bityde' (3450). And Chaucer soon makes explicit his mental blindness: 'Men may dyen of ymaginacioun' (3611). Students also gain from help with seeing not just the existence of such charms in Chaucer's period but from some sense of how to 'place' them in the period: how activities like such garbled prayers and charms may, within the culture, be associated with educationally backward groups or have a specific contemporary political resonance: Alan Fletcher shows how at this period conservative clerics were actually encouraging traditional religious practices and discouraging a questioning attitude.[10]

Blasphemy or Bawdry?

A second question students might explore in an enquiry-based seminar on the *Miller's Tale* is how are we to respond to the repeated and startling juxtaposition of sexual and sacred elements in a text, where the 'revel' and 'melodye' of lovemaking mingle with the strains of devotional song, where Nicholas courts Alison in an apparent parody of the Annunciation, and where parish clerk Absolon sings snatches of love songs at windows in the hope of a midnight tryst?[11] Are these to be viewed as blasphemy or cheerful bawdry? Are such juxtapositions characteristic or atypical of the age? Old-fashioned 'dramatic' criticism might attribute this conflation of secular and sacred discourses to the character of the drunken Miller. The text, after all, ends with this final mischievous and unconventional rhymed blessing:

> And Nicholas is scalded in the towte.
> This tale is doon, and God save al the rowte! (3853–4)

Within the tale itself there are some similarly startling juxtapositions. Nicholas makes his brash and explicit approach to Alison hard upon his singing of the devotional *Angelus ad Virginem* (a hymn celebrating the Incarnation); shortly after swearing by St Thomas of Kent to keep an adulterous tryst with Nicholas, Alison is making for church 'Cristes owene werkes for to werke' (3308); the clerk who

8 Ibid, p. 61

9 Eamon Duffy, *The Stripping of the Altars: Traditional Religion in England 1400–1580* (New Haven and London, 1992), 266–87.

10 'The Faith of a Simple Man: Carpenter John's Creed in the *Miller's Tale*', *Medium Ævum* 61 (1991), 96–105.

11 As Helen Cooper observes, 'motifs of the Flood and the "legende" of a carpenter and his wife are secularized to a point of near-blasphemy', *The Canterbury Tales*, Oxford Guides to Chaucer (Oxford, 1989), p. 101.

officiates at that church is meanwhile sketched as vainglorious and much distracted from spiritual concerns:

This Absolon, that jolif was and gay,
Gooth with a sencer on the haliday,
Sensynge the wyves of the parisshe faste;
And many a lovely look on hem he caste,
And namely on this carpenteris wyf.
To looke on hire hym thoughte a myrie lyf,
She was so propre and sweete and likerous.
I dar wel seyn, if she hadde been a mous,
And he a cat, he wolde hire hente anon.
This parissh clerk, this joly absolon,
Hath in his herte swich a love-longynge
That of no wyf took he noon offrynge;
For curteisie, he seyde, he wolde noon. (3339–51)

The juxtaposition of Nicholas and Alison's consummated lust with 'the belle of laudes' and singing of 'freres in the chauncel' (3653–6) has seemed to exegetical critics highly significant while others, such as Pearsall, counsel against taking earnest for game: 'The church and its activities are present in the poem as part of its naturalistic setting, part of the texture of town-life, and not, except in [a] jocular way, as a reminder to us of what the characters ought to be busy about.'[12] Students might draw upon the fifteenth-century lyric preserved in manuscript Sloane 2593, voiced by a girl enamoured of holy water clerk Jankin. In a set of pronounced juxtapositions, the courtship of the speaker takes place within the context of corporate worship and liturgy; the Yuletude procession, the offering at the Mass, the reading and the ringing of the sanctus bell at the consecration of the host form the reckoning points for the progress of the couple's relationship:

As I went on ȝol day in owr prosessyon,
Knew I Ioly Iankyn be his mery ton.
[kyrieleyson.]

Iankyn be-gan þe offys on þe ȝol day,
& ȝyt me þynkyt ot dos me good, so merie gan he say
kyrieleyson.

Iankyn red þe pystyl ful fayr & ful wel,
& ȝyt me þinkyt it dos me good, as euere haue I sel.

Iankyn at þe sanctus crakit a merie note,
& ȝyt me þinkyt it dos me good – I payed for his cote.
[kyrieleyson.]

Iankyn crakit notes an hunderid on a knot,
& ȝyt he hakkyt hem smaller þan wortes to þe pot.
[kyrieleyson.]

Jankyn begins a game of footsie as the pax bread is solemnly circulated around the church:

[12] Pearsall, *Canterbury Tales*, p. 175.

Iankyn at þe angnus beryt þe pax brede,
he twynkelid, but sayd nowt, & on myn fot he trede.

Yet the light-hearted tone gives way to a mournful coda:

Benedicamus domino, cryst fro schame me schyld.
Deo gracias þerto – alas, I go with chylde![13]

This short lyric both affords students a useful glimpse into medieval liturgy and church ritual and reveals that the currency of fabliau elements is widely spread in late-medieval England: Chaucer's tale's juxtaposition of secular and sacred is not without analogies. When students only read Chaucer it is all too easy for them to jump to the natural conclusion that such a juxtaposition on his part can only be original to him and betoken the deepest condemnation of what is going on, on religious grounds. Instead, the lyric illustrates, such juxtapositions, shocking even to moderns without strong religious beliefs, are more common in medieval humour and culture.

This theme of sacred and profane in the *Miller's Tale* can also be illuminated with reference to the English mystery cycles. The Miller's 'Pilates voys' (3124), and Absolon's involvement in a high-profile role – 'He pleyeth Herodes upon a scaffold hye' (3384) – and the evocation of the cycles' treatment of Noah's Flood with its negative portrayal of Noah's wife.[14] Many extant pageants introduce a fabliau sensibility and apparent irreverence into their treatment of the most sombre and serious biblical episodes. Particularly illustrative for the *Miller's Tale* is the N-Town *Trial of Joseph and Mary*.[15] Here Joseph and Mary put in an anachronistic appearance in a medieval court as they are summoned to appear in the company of an assortment of caricatured names for malefactors apparently drawn from an English city – 'Johan Jurdon', 'Geffrey Gyle', 'Malkyn mylkedoke', 'Thom tynkere' and others. After initial banter by the Summoner, the reverend characters of Joseph and Mary and the miracle of Christ's Incarnation are subjected to a fabliau-like reading, whereby a group of detractors cast Mary as the young faithless wife, the aged Joseph as the old jealous but impotent husband, and the incarnate Christ as the offspring of a local rake.

The detractors' depiction of Joseph as *senex amans*, the lustful old husband of fabliau tradition, is closely akin to the presentation of John the Carpenter:

ijus detractor
ȝa þat old schrewe joseph my trowth I plight
was so Anameryd upon þat mayd
þat of hyre bewte whan he had sight
He sesyd nat tyll had here a-sayd. (49–52)

Completing the fabliau picture they are painting, the detractors can only suspect that an intrigue with a young gallant lies behind Mary's pregnancy:

[13] Robbins, *Secular Lyrics*, pp. 21–2.
[14] Cooper, *The Canterbury Tales*, p. 97.
[15] *Ludus Coventriae or The Plaie called Corpus Christi*, ed. K. S. Block, EETS ES 120 (London, 1922), pp. 123–35.

1us detractor
A nay nay wel wers she hath hym payd
Sum fresch ȝonge galaunt she loveth wel more
Þat his leggys to here hath leyd
and þat doth greve þe old man sore

ijus detractor
be my trewth al may wel be
ffor fresch and fayr she is to syght
And such a mursel as semyth me
Wolde cause a ȝonge man to haue delight.
. . .
that olde cokolde was evyl be-gylyd
to þat fresche wench whan he was wedde
now muste he faderyn a-nothyr mannys chylde
and with his swynke he xal be fedde.

1us detractor
A ȝonge man may do more chere in bedde
to a ȝonge wench þan may an olde
þat is þe cawse such lawe is ledde
þat many a man is a kokewolde. (53–125–6)

Material like this can do more than reveal that juxtapositions of the sacred and profane are characteristic of the Gothic sensibility. It also offers the opportunity for students to explore further: looking at the context and range of the mystery cycles, their rationale and close relationship to ecclesiastical and civic drama and procession in the Middle Ages, and their origin in the Corpus Christi ritual at the heart of the liturgy. The mystery cycles are valuable primers of biblical narrative and of medieval Christian culture.

In seeking to restore the Christian context of Chaucer's work for modern readers, enquiry-based learning is a pedagogy with a distinct contribution to make. The author's experience of running enquiry-based sessions themed on these issues of superstition/religion and blasphemy/bawdry has shown that a good deal of context can indeed be explored and fruitfully applied to Chaucer's text, bringing a range of positive outcomes.[16] The present study in no way argues for replacing lectures and seminars but rather advocates the enquiry-based model as a supplementary pedagogy, extra materials, that can aid students in accessing the Christian context of the *Canterbury Tales*. Of course the number of contact hours in a course is always tightly limited, but introduction of some enquiry-based discussion or seminars enables students to engage proactively with the context of Chaucer's work and to study contextual materials first-hand. In the process, canonical and non-canonical texts can be brought into fruitful conversation with one another and it becomes increasingly possible to impart an image of Chaucer's religious contexts as diverse, rich and detailed, with the result that class discussion of context becomes increasingly nuanced and varied, eschewing unitary generalizations

[16] I am grateful to the English cohort of 2003–4 at St Hugh's College, Oxford, the Chaucer cohort of the Exeter College Oxford Summer Programme in English Literature (2004), the AS English 2004/5 cohort and Martin Nichols and Penny Maynard of The College of Richard Collyer, Horsham (2004–5), for their generous collaboration and feedback on EBL-led sessions.

about ‘the Church’ in the Middle Ages and substituting more particular and precise observations as to how varied dimensions of fourteenth-century Christianity inform Chaucer’s work. The introduction of enquiry-based sessions into undergraduate study of Chaucer seems to enhance discussion of the primary texts themselves. The investigative and exploratory aspect of such sessions tends to broaden rather than restrict the range of critical opinions expressed, as Hutchings and O’ Rourke remark:

> A literary text seldom, if ever, has a single issue or problem as its concern, even when a critic or even the author claims that it does. There will always be a diversity of potential response generated among diverse readers.[17]

Such a description of the effect of enquiry-based approaches seems particularly apposite for the *Canterbury Tales*, where the pilgrim audience is of course depicted at the close of the *Miller’s Tale* as ranging equally widely in interpretation: ‘diverse folk diversely they seyde’ (3857). It would seem that in meeting the challenge of recovering Chaucer’s Christian context for modern readers, enquiry-based learning has a valuable role to play, illuminating both text and context and enabling us ‘to demen by interrogaciouns’.

[17] Bill Hutchings and Karen O’ Rourke, ‘Problem-Based Learning: Evidencing and Evaluating the Student Experience’, at http://www.english.heacademy.ac.uk/explore/projects/archive/problearn/problem1.php, p. 73.

14

'Gladly wolde [they] lerne [?]': US Students and the Chaucer Class

D. THOMAS HANKS, JR

ALL TEACHERS OF CHAUCER, surely in the United Kingdom as in the United States, know the delights of teaching *The Canterbury Tales*. The delights may begin the moment students chuckle at the bawdy pun in the doubly directed 'So priketh' line in the first lines of the *General Prologue* –

And smale fowles / maken melodye
That slepen al the nyght / with open ye
So priketh hem nature / in hir corages
Thanne longen folk / to goon on pilgrimages[1]

Those delights may continue up to the intriguing ambiguity of the *Retraction*'s 'I revoke in my retracciouns . . . the tales of Caunterbury, thilke that sownen into synne' (X 328, 1084–5). Throughout the term, Chaucer slowly grows to giant stature in our students' eyes – at least when things go well. And we are allowed both to watch and to assist in the process.

To be sure, not all US courses, probably not even the majority, focus solely on the *Canterbury Tales*; if a department has only the one Chaucer course, many, perhaps most, instructors will choose to present Chaucer's breadth with perhaps a few of the shorter poems, a dream vision, sometimes the entirety of *Troilus and Criseyde*, and a representative sampling of *The Tales*. For a sampling of course outlines from US colleges and universities, visit the web syllabuses of Professors Edwin Duncan (Towson University),[2] Alan Baragona (Virginia Military Institute),[3] James M. Dean (University of Delaware),[4] Jennifer Bryan (Oberlin College),[5] David Wilson-Okamura (Macalester College),[6] Tamara O'Callaghan (Northern Kentucky University),[7] R. Alan Shoaf (University of Florida),[8] Steven F. Kruger (City University of New York),[9] or many others easily accessible on the

1 *Riverside Chaucer*, I 239–12; editorial punctuation deleted, Hengwrt manuscript punctuation included.
2 http://pages.towson.edu/duncan/chauhom2.html
3 http://academics.vmi.edu/english/baragonasyllabi.htm#EN%20413
4 http://www.english.udel.edu/dean/322/engl322.html
5 http://www.oberlin.edu/english/syllabi/fall01/jb201f01.html
6 http://geoffreychaucer.org/dswo/courses/chaucer/syllabus.htm
7 http://www.nku.edu/~ocallaghant/courses/401/eng401home.htm
8 http://www.clas.ufl.edu/users/ras/syll.html
9 http://web.gc.cuny.edu/English/fac_skruger70500.html

World Wide Web.[10] Several of those professors have chosen to focus on a variety of Chaucer's poems; this essay, however, focuses on my own course, where we read only the *Parliament of Fowls* and, chiefly, the *Canterbury Tales*. I discuss here two problems which seem to me paramount in the teaching of Chaucer in the United States: our students' failure to read in advance, and their failure to understand Chaucer's approach(es) to Christianity. The more crucial problem is the first; I shall deal with it last.

Engaging the Text and the Biblical Background

About Christianity: US students generally, even in the so-called 'Bible Belt', have little specific knowledge of the Bible (though many exceptions to that rule appear in the Christian institution where I teach). As W. Meredith Thompson has pointed out,[11] and as Lawrence Besserman has amplified,[12] Chaucer had an encyclopaedic knowledge of the Vulgate. Because our students do not have that knowledge, they do not recognize, for example, that Chaucer's tag in his *Retraction*, 'Al that is writen is writen for oure doctrine' (X 1083) comes from Paul's second letter to Timothy[13] and continues in a surprising way:

> 16 omnis scriptura divinitus inspirata et utilis ad docendum ad arguendum ad corrigendum ad erudiendum in iustitia 17 ut perfectus sit homo Dei ad omne opus bonum instructus
>
> (16 All scripture is inspired by God and profitable for teaching, for reproof, for correction, and for training in righteousness, 17 that the man of God may be complete, equipped for every good work. [RSV])[14]

Does Chaucer suggest that his work – or, perhaps, just the *Parson's Tale* – is inspired by God? Or is he, both here and in the *Nun's Priest's Tale*, just teasing? Our students do not reflect on this and other such possibilities; they do not recognize the biblical context. Helen Cooper has pointed out this lack:

> The loss of familiarity with Christian culture and allusion needs to be addressed as a matter of urgency. This is a cause on which the survival of any kind of deep appreciation and understanding of England's literary and

10 The web sites noted above were all current – i.e., their web-addresses produced the syllabus for each professor's class – as of 9 April 2009.

11 'Chaucer's Translation of the Bible', *English and Medieval Studies Presented to J. R. R. Tolkien on the Occasion of his Seventieth Birthday*, ed. Norman Davis and C. L. Wrenn (London, 1962), 183–99.

12 Lawrence Besserman, *Chaucer and the Bible: A Critical Review of Research, Indexes, and Bibliography* (New York, 1988); *Chaucer's Biblical Poetics* (Norman, OK, 1998).

13 The *Riverside Chaucer* note attributes the quotation here and in the *Nun's Priest's Tale* (VII 3441–2, p. 261) to Romans 15: 4: 'quaecumque enim scripta sunt ad nostram doctrinam scripta sunt ut per patientiam et consolationem scripturarum spem habeamus' ('for whatever was written was written for our doctrine so that through patience and the consolation of the writings we might have hope'). Given Chaucer's writing 'all that is written' rather than 'whatever was written', his passage seems to refer to 2 Timothy 3: 16, which passes unnoted by the *Riverside Chaucer* editors. Perhaps Chaucer had both Pauline passages in mind, since each seems echoed in his two references. It was the reference to 'doctrine', no doubt, that persuaded the editors that the passage reflects only Romans.

14 2 Timothy 3: 16–17 from http://www.biblegateway.org/cgi-bin/bible?passage=2TIM+3&language=latin&version=VULGATE

artistic heritage depends: strong words but no exaggeration.[15]

The only real remedy for this lack of 'familiarity with Christian . . . allusion' is for our students to gain a familiarity with the Bible similar to Chaucer's. That is not likely to happen soon if ever. What we can provide them with, however, is some knowledge of the cultural context of Chaucer's day (Christianity and Culture's CD-ROM, *Images of Salvation*,[16] is very helpful here), and, for allusions like this example from 2 Timothy/Romans, provide exercises in or out of class which will stimulate them to think out the implications of the passages as Chaucer uses them. For this specific passage, for example, one can present to one's students before class, or in class, a series of directions and questions like the following:

> Chaucer cites in this passage 2 Timothy 3: 16 (and possibly Romans 15: 4 as well), in both of which passages the early Christian writer Paul addresses fellow Christians, directing them to continue to read the Scriptures. Review both passages (easily locatable by Google), then consider these questions:
>
> 1. In citing these passages, what context does Chaucer give to his *Retraction*, and to his *Tales* overall – a context we saw earlier in the closing lines to the *Nun's Priest's Tale*? [The students usually reply, 'A Christian context'; some add, 'He's suggesting that his work is something like the Bible – useful not only as fiction, but for "instruction" as well.' One or two have even asked, timidly, 'Could he be suggesting that his work, too, is somehow God-inspired?']
>
> 2. Earlier, in the *Nun's Priest's Tale*, we thought that Chaucer was mocking sobriety when his narrator made the same statement, then assured us that his tale was not a mere 'folye . . . of a fox, or of a cok and hen' (VII 3438–9), but that instead he was dealing with 'moralite' (VII 3440). How do you read the same 'al that is writen' passage in the *Retraction*? Is Chaucer again mocking? Is he serious this time? Or is there another alternative?
>
> 3. Do you see Chaucer as being sacrilegious when he seemingly puts his text on the same plane as Scripture – 'inspired by God'? Or is he being massively egotistical? Or . . . what?

These questions lead the students to engage the text, and to engage the biblical background of the text. That does not remedy their lack of biblical background overall, of course, but it does suggest to them that one's reading of Chaucer's *Canterbury Tales* is enriched by biblical knowledge. One can add similar questions to one's presentation of biblical echoes throughout Chaucer – for another example, one might ask one's students to contrast the Gospel account of Jesus' Last Supper with the 'last supper' of the three 'riotoures' of the *Pardoner's Tale* (bread and wine, in each case), then ask them to find other parodic echoes of the Gospels in that tale. Though they do not have much background in the Bible or even in Christian doctrine (depending on what college or university one is discussing), students are aware of the importance of Christianity in Chaucer's time, and are willing to grant it their attention in the twenty-first century.

[15] http://www.york.ac.uk/projects/christianityandculture/index.html

[16] See http://www.york.ac.uk/projects/christianityandculture/index.html for this CD-ROM and *The Bible in Western Culture: A Student's Guide*, ed. Dee Dyas and Esther Hughes (London, 2005), a book which goes far toward remedying our students' lack of biblical background.

Preparation

Of course, asking questions like those above while in class, perhaps as a ten-minute variation in one's normal presentation, only works if students have read the text before class. In the United States, students most often have not read the text before class. If they are accustomed to lecture presentations – and most of them are, since this is still the primary mode of 'delivering instruction' in US colleges and universities – they will know that they will not be called upon to do more than passively take note of the professor's comments as he/she lectures. Moreover, one's reading for the day is not likely to affect 'the grade' – and, in the United States, 'the grade' is the end toward which we have taught students to work, the Grail of their quest. What our students are most likely to do, given the way they have been conditioned, is to prepare their days with a wary eye toward graded activities. That means that if other classes have graded activities that day – a test, a paper due, a quiz – then upon those activities the students will focus. Their daily Chaucer reading they will save for the time when they revise for the course's examinations. Many of us thus rely upon the 'pop quiz' to force our students to read; the success of the 'pop quiz' is minor, since even if a student does read, he/she is more likely to read for quiz details than to engage with the text.[17]

My colleague Anne-Marie Bowery (philosophy) introduced me several years ago to an assignment which has almost entirely remedied the situation described above. In almost any given class-period now, 85% or more of my students will have read the daily assignment and engaged with it to at least some degree beyond 'quiz details'. I have found this assignment particularly useful in prompting students actually to engage with Chaucer's Middle English text at least twice: once for the daily reading and once to revise for examinations and/or papers.

The assignment involves a daily electronic journal entry which each student sends in by email or other electronic means. The following is the formal assignment given out on the first day:

> JOURNAL ENTRIES. For each day's class where we have reading assigned, please do your reading beforehand and send to me via e-mail ONE insight or discussion question (with your answer) which seems to you to reflect the central concern, or one of the central concerns, of the reading for that class. Please begin with the reading for Wednesday, 3 September. I will sometimes use your insights and discussion questions in class; moreover, they will earn for you a total of 100 pts. As you see from the number of points (10% of your course grade), I take these insights/questions very seriously.
>
> NOTE: you must send these entries to me by 6 a.m. on the morning before our class: e.g., by 6 a.m. on the Sunday prior to our Monday class. I will not read entries marked later than 6 a.m., and will not count them toward your point total. I'm sorry to be so stringent, but the system doesn't work if I don't get the entries the morning before class. You may of course elect to send them in during the preceding day or evening.
>
> My chief evaluative criteria:

[17] A 'pop quiz' in the United States is an unannounced short test of minimal grade weight, typically containing objective questions only, often in multiple-choice, fill-in-the-blank, or even true/false format.

> 1. that you say something intelligent about the reading or readings;
>
> 2. that you support or develop your insight with enough details FROM the reading that even a professor can tell that you have read the material perceptively. Most excellent entries quote two-five lines central to the student's insight.

Students, having completed this assignment, come to class having engaged with all or part of the text to be discussed. Moreover, they have something to say; they can easily enter into the class conversation. I include below two representative 'e-journal' entries, the first referring to readings from the *Parliament of Fowls* and from the *Tales*:

> While anticipating finding like characteristics between the narrator of the *Parliament of Fowls* and the narrator in the *Canterbury Tales*, I unexpectedly discovered similarities between the narrator of *PF* and the clerk introduced in the prologue of *CT.* Just as the narrator of *PF* spends a majority of time reading, the clerk values books above all else, including his wealth or appearance. Although his clothes are 'thredbare' (290), nonetheless 'hym was levere have at his beddes heed / Twenty books, clad in blak or reed' (293–4). Also like the withdrawn, bookish narrator of *PF*, the clerk focuses mostly on his studies and 'Noght a word spak he moore than was neede' (304). What money the clerk does receive from his friends, he spends on books. While Chaucer does not portray learning or reading itself as negative, he seems to indicate that both these characters' obsessive focuses on these pursuits deprive them of other experiences or acquisitions in life. However, in making a pilgrimage rather than just reading about it, this student does seem more willing to act than the narrator of *PF*, but it will be interesting to discover if he will be able to leave the pages of his books long enough to learn from his experiences. (Lindsay Donham)
>
> INSTRUCTOR'S RESPONSE: Strongly perceptive, Lindsay. You do well to note the parallel between the narrator of *PF* and the Clerk – and you support your contention well.

The second relates to the *Nun's Priest's Tale*

> The *Nun's Priest's Tale* seems to be a compilation of the themes that have come before it. It addresses the role of women, predestination, and woe after joy. The tale even explicitly states two new themes of its own. The tale's take on the role of women can be seen in the discussion between Chauntecleer and his foremost concubine, Pertelote. The two debate the importance of dreams, and after Chauntecleer gives a much longer list of auctores than does Pertelote, he agrees with her simply because, when he looks upon her beauty, 'I am so ful of joye and of solas, / That I diffye bothe sweven and dreem' (3170–1). The narrator then spends several lines saying that the council of women is bad and was the cause of man's fall from grace. The concept of predestination is broached rather clumsily. The narrator considers the dream a warning from God. He then simply states the two sides of the argument: complete predestination versus free choice. The woe after joy theme is similarly obviously stated, 'For evere the latter ende of joye is wo' (3205), and later 'Lo, how Fortune turneth sodeynly' (3403). Each statement comes right before a turn of fortune: before Chauntecleer is captured by Daun Russell, and before Chauntecleer frees himself from the fox. These

various themes, as abruptly thrust into the text as they are, make the tale disjointed. The Nun's Priest seems to try to include everything and his tale suffers as a result. (Noah Peterson).

INSTRUCTOR'S RESPONSE: Perhaps the tale suffers, as you suggest; that's a valid reading. Another might be to suggest that the tale refers to and pulls together several other tales, and parodies them by doing so. The parody of the *Monk's Tale* is clear: Chauntecleer's 'fall' is made similar to all the falls of *MkT*, but he is a chicken. Good reading, Noah – we'll doubtless have some lively conversation about this tale tomorrow.

Neither of the student journal entries is necessarily 'correct', nor did I necessarily agree with them; I disagree with Noah's comment about incoherence in the *Nun's Priest's Tale*, for example. But each entry earned full marks for the journal assignment. As the reader sees above, each student has engaged with the text perceptively; that is the chief desideratum for this assignment. Each has also supported her/his comments with generous references to the text; in each case, the student entered into the class conversation with little prompting as the hour began. They had completed a graded assignment; they had read and thought about the assigned part of Chaucer's text; and they were wholly prepared to discuss the text in class.[18]

To conclude: students' grasp of Chaucer's work is hampered by their lack of biblical and doctrinal background, and by their customary mode of not reading daily assignments. This essay does not provide instant solutions for either problem; in it, I do suggest ameliorative approaches to the lack of Christian background, and an approach by which I have found that the great majority of my students have been stimulated to do their daily reading, think perceptively about it, and write, then later converse, interestingly about their insights. I asked a student in my most recent class – Noah Peterson, one of whose entries appears above – what he remembered most fondly from the class. He respondes: 'What I remember as especially good was the contribution from the various students on the ways they saw the pilgrims and the tales; I really liked the way different students had different views of the same text – and each one added something to my own view of the text.'

Noah's judgment parallels mine: I think that when students focus on Chaucer's text, rather than on the lecturer about Chaucer, the class is more likely to be a worthwhile learning experience for a greater number of students.

[18] A note about the instructor's part in the process: I respond to each entry, and find that I can read, respond, and mark the ejournal entries for a class of fifteen students in less than an hour – usually about 45 minutes, unless the entries are long and my own responses also lengthy. I have decided that the 45–60 minutes is time well spent in class preparation; my other preparation usually takes another hour. Two hours total preparation time for a class hour seems reasonable to me.

15

Teaching Teachers: Chaucer, Ethics and Romance

DAVID RAYBIN

FOR TWENTY YEARS, I have been directing a small annual conference for school teachers.[1] Each year in October, forty to eighty teachers from across my state of Illinois spend a day talking about a canonical book. Some of the teachers arrive the night before for an evening lecture, film, gallery show, or concert related to the world of Chaucer, Dickinson, Dante, Austen, or whoever our chosen author may be. In the morning we listen to a guest speaker discuss the author or book and then divide up into small groups for workshop sessions in which we discuss the topic from more directed perspectives. We repeat the procedure after lunch with a second speaker and additional workshops. These meetings are exciting: we make a point of inviting distinguished scholars who have a genuine interest in working with teachers, and the workshops that follow the lectures invariably provoke the kind of stimulating discussion one expects from highly motivated, self-selecting teachers. The participants, many of whom return year after year, say they appreciate the conference because of its emphasis on reading and on talking about books and ideas, with pedagogy a secondary consideration.

The principal limitation in these meetings is that the format of five or six hour-long blocks directed to a range of interests precludes concentrating very long on any one issue. With the support of my state Humanities Council, I have also been able to direct a longer conference that is more focused, more intense, and, happily, more leisurely: weekend seminars in which twelve to fifteen teachers and librarians gather in a lodge at a state park to eat, drink, and spend ten seminar hours and some free time pondering and arguing about my preferred topic: 'Chaucer Today: Romance and Ethics'.[2] The point of the seminar is to enjoy Chaucer, of course, but also to think about how his poetry and ideas matter. Romance and ethics are at the heart of the seminar because Chaucer frames an extraordinarily large part of his discussion of ethical behavior in terms of spouses, lovers, wooers, and rapists.[3] It is in bedrooms and gardens and woods, in private conversation and – surprisingly often – before an audience, that Chaucer's characters make the ethical decisions

1 The annual meeting is called the Eastern Illinois University Literature Conference. It began in 1988 with a conference on the *Canterbury Tales*, and we returned to the *Tales* in our twentieth anniversary conference in 2008.

2 These seminars took place in March 2004 and 2005. Cuts to the budget of the Illinois Humanities Council have since led the seminar program to be placed on hiatus.

3 The omnipresent correlation of ethics and gender in the *Canterbury Tales* has been treated most recently by Alcuin Blamires, *Chaucer, Ethics, and Gender* (Oxford, 2006).

that define them and, if we see character as a spiritual quality, determine their fates. In this essay I present the method I have employed for introducing Chaucerian ethics and spirituality in these seminars. It is a method that is particularly effective in teaching teachers and future teachers because by allowing us to focus on Chaucer's tales – in regard to both plot and language – it stimulates ways of thinking that get to the heart of Chaucer's poetic. We do not spend much time talking about education or process, but the excitement which we generate adapts readily to a classroom setting.

On the Association between Ethics and Religion

Given the subject of this volume, it is notable that the words *religion* and *Christianity* are not in the seminar title. This was a considered decision. Twenty-first-century assumptions about religion and Christianity are in many ways different from fourteenth-century notions,[4] and it is easy for teachers and their students to get caught up in or, worse, bored by discussion of the distinctions between modern and medieval attitudes. If Chaucer's ideas are to be relevant to a modern audience, it is salutary to consider subjects like his treatment of ethical behavior in modern terms, and therefore, in this case, to start from the premise that ethics is not a predominantly spiritual concern. One should not imagine, however, that Christianity and religion do not enter into our conversation. Of course they do, often. It would be disingenuous, and fundamentally misleading, to treat Chaucerian ethics without acknowledging the poet's faith and recognizing the centrality of Christian assumptions and issues to his thought. The key, I have found, is to focus initially on the ethical problems, and then to introduce Chaucer's spirituality in terms that enable us to recognize not only the differences in outlook, but also certain constants that bridge time, space, and cultural difference. Part of my job as seminar director is to explain the relevance of Chaucer's religious background in a way that enhances our understanding of the ethical questions he raises.[5]

On the Place of Critical Theory in a Seminar Directed to School Teachers

The scholarship and teaching of the past fifty years have made it evident that one cannot interpret without theorizing. I do not bring up theory at the start because it is peripheral to the seminar goal. I do address theoretical issues as they arise, either because a participant introduces a theoretical issue or approach directly, or because a participant brings up a question that a particular theoretical approach can help to resolve or that different theoretical approaches illuminate in different ways, or because I feel that a theory-inflected perspective can stimulate a productive response to a passage or issue that our discussion might otherwise ignore. Participants are

4 A good example of the conflation of modern and medieval views is the tendency of modern readers to treat Chaucer's pre-Reformation Christianity from a Protestant perspective; see the enlightening discussion by Linda Georgianna, 'The Protestant Chaucer', *Chaucer's Religious Tales*, ed. C. David Benson and Elizabeth Robertson (Woodbridge), pp. 55–69.

5 Were the seminar a bit longer, I would include the rape, bedroom, and trial scenes in the *Man of Law's Tale* and bring to centre stage the question of how a Christian ethic figures in Chaucer's conception of romance.

of course encouraged to pursue the diverse ways of thinking that theory elicits. It would be condescending to assume that teachers (and university students) are not able to understand or apply theoretical tools that might aid developing their ideas.

Organization and Content

The single most important consideration in teaching teachers is to respect their abilities and intellect. Teachers take classes, attend conferences, and join academic seminars for a supremely practical reason: they are interested in learning. A leader's task is to direct the group's energy and intelligence in a way that satisfies the teachers' desire by introducing ideas about literature and ways of thinking about a text that participants generally would not encounter on their own. A coherently structured seminar allows participants freedom to push their ideas about the readings further and to experiment more freely with interpretative strategies, and this in turn gives them a substantial voice in determining what goes on in each session. *Coherent* and *structured* do not, however, mean *linear*. When reading Chaucer one often finds that themes reappear from tale to tale, and that these multiple looks at common issues combine to establish an ethos that may not be apparent in any one context. I encourage participants to look out for and make sense of intertextual connections. Occasionally I suggest such connectivity by signaling that a question of minor import in one tale will come into greater play in a tale we look at later, but mostly I ask the teachers to play the lead role.

This said, I construct the seminar so as to introduce ethical issues in a generally progressive sequence. We begin with the old woman's bedroom lecture in the *Wife of Bath's Tale* (III 1086–1218) because in its short space Chaucer raises questions about ethical behavior in love and marriage that crystalize the seminar's theme. The old woman does not speak in terms of questions – she insists that what she says is grounded in moral absolutes – but it is each reader's task, as it is the young husband's, to interrogate her assertions. On the surface these declarations reflect a strong Christian tradition (*God* is referenced eight times, *Crist* and *Jhesus* once each), but their ethical force stands irrespective of the particular religious belief. Are a woman's age, physical appearance, and wealth merely superficial qualities, or do they betoken something fundamental about the marital relationship? The placing of a forceful argument against superficiality in the mouth of the aged wife seems to support the assertion that her knowledge makes her a desirable spouse, but as two generations of feminist critics have insisted, the wife's transformation into a young and elegant beauty undercuts the argument. And why are we talking about a woman here, when the tale's theme is supposed to be what women want, and not about the young rapist knight she has chosen to marry? One naturally wishes to debate correct – that is, satisfying – solutions, and we will do this when we return to the *Wife of Bath's Tale* in a later session, but at this early stage I try to steer the seminar away from answers and towards the questions Chaucer raises, questions that are central to each of Chaucer's tales of love and romance.

Following this introduction, we move to expand the grounds for discussion of ethical values by contrasting a scene of intense pathos in the *Knight's Tale* with one of gross burlesque in the *Miller's Tale*. Arcite's nasty death and doleful deathbed instructions (I 2743–97) bring into play the most fundamental questions of mortality, friendship, power, and love (does how one dies transform how one has lived? Can a satisfactory resolution to the triangle of love, friendship, and power be imposed by a benevolent external authority? Is redemption possible in a non-Christian world?), and in so doing demand that we determine the right and wrong and prioritize our different values. Nicholas's alternately rough and gracious wooing of Alisoun in the *Miller's Tale* (I 3271–306) complicates such prioritization, as Chaucer encourages readers to rethink their responses to the ethical dilemmas in a pagan romance in light of a Christian fabliau's satiric critique. Which is more outrageous or, alternatively, more chivalrous: to grab the crotch of a woman who welcomes gentler attention, and then respond in accord with her desire; or to battle a friend for a woman who wants no part of either lover, and then pass her on to that friend in a gesture of conciliation? And what of the two tales' endings: is the glorious death of a young man intrinsically more distressing than the injuring, cuckolding, and public mocking of an old man? A reader's typical response is to follow the lead of the two tales' narrators and more authoritative characters and therefore mourn Arcite and laugh at John, but the more closely we look at the characters' motivations, the less absolute the answers are.

Our next subject is Chaucer's parallel examination of what women want (the pivotal issue in the *Wife of Bath's Prologue and Tale*) and what men want (the corresponding issue in the *Clerk's Tale*). Our test passage for the *Wife of Bath's Tale* includes the young knight's formal declaration that 'Wommen desiren to have sovereynetee / As we over hir housbond as hir love, / And for to been in maistrie hym above' (III 1028–40) and the unexpected response of the old woman and the members of Arthur's court. For the *Clerk's Tale* we turn to Walter's proposal to Griselda, most especially his insistence that she be 'redy with good herte to al my lust' (IV 351–2) and her oath in response: 'nevere willyngly, / In werk ne thoght, I nyl yow disobeye' (IV 362–3). These passages become a springboard for understanding the testing that ensues in both tales (by the old wife of her reluctant husband, and by Walter of his willing wife). Are we to recognize in these contrasting story lines gender-defined differences in how men and women understand right and wrong behavior, or are we to see more absolute ethical standards that the gendered arena of marriage brings to the fore? In what spirit should we address the tales' closing reversals in which the Wife of Bath prays that Jesus send 'Housbondes meeke, yonge, and fressh abedde' and 'shorte [the] lyves' of husbands who 'noght wol be governed by hir wyves' (III 1259, 1261–2), and the Clerk equates Griselda's obedience to Walter with a Christian's proper submission to God: 'For sith a woman was so pacient / Unto a mortal man, wel moore us oghte / Receyven al in gree that God us sent' (IV 1149–51)?

As participants get increasingly comfortable with Middle English, it becomes more appropriate to deal with the subtleties of Chaucer's word choices. In our next session, we acknowledge the heightened comfort level by turning to the problematic of discordant words and deeds. May's assertion of her virtue in January's garden in the *Merchant's Tale* (IV 2132–218) furnishes our primary example, with secondary examples the discussion of crude and polite signifiers in the *Manciple's Tale* (IX 203–34) and the encomium for direct speech and action in the *General Prologue* portrait of the Parson (I 496–528). Chaucer, we remember, used a garden as a signifier of Emily's innocence in the *Knight's Tale*. Are signifiers so easily transferable? We remember also the rebellious unhappiness of mismatched young wives in the *Miller's Tale* and *Wife of Bath's Prologue*. Are deceptive words more troubling than deceptive deeds? It is with these contrasts in mind that we engage the tricky and overtly impious ethics of a wife whose loose-skinned husband is the most unbearable of all. Is pagan May truly sacrilegious? One god, the male Pluto, condemns her lecherous deceit, but the female Proserpine endorses at some length the young wife's thumbing of her nose in the face of patriarchy and proclaims May a model for all women: 'With face boold they shulle hemself excuse, / And bere hem doun that wolden hem accuse' (IV 2269–70). In her defiance, Proserpine recalls the famous allusion to the painting of lions in the *Wife of Bath's Prologue*, declaring passionately that 'I sette right noght, of al the vileynye / That ye of wommen write, a boterflye!' (IV 2303–4). How important are words – one's own or those of authorities – if they may be said aside so lightly?

This question provides the transition to our final subject: love and integrity as they are reflected first in Aurelius's wooing of Dorigen, and then in Dorigen's and Arveragus's responses in the *Franklin's Tale* (V 925–1011, 1311–51, 1457–1555). Here, in another of Chaucer's non-Christian tales, all the ethical questions we have been discussing come into play. Graciousness is said to matter, but it may conceal villainy. Meanings seem clear, but the words that express them prove to be slippery. The marriage of Dorigen and Arveragus is apparently marked by 'blisse' and 'solas', by 'joye', 'ese', and 'prosperitee' (V 802, 804). Nonetheless, trapped by desire, the three main characters discover that shame and honor have meanings they had not recognized, that solitude can be unbearable, and that death is a real choice. Is it possible, Dorigen asks, in what is perhaps the most fundamental ethical – and spiritual – question of all, that 'a parfit wys God and a stable' could have 'wroght this werk unresonable' (V 871–2)?[6]

Method

A seminar's method can be as important to its success as is its subject. The heart of the seminars I've offered to teachers, and, I would argue, of any class directed to training future teachers of Chaucer, is close reading of the text.[7] Close reading enables even teachers with little previous experience of Middle English to appreciate Chaucer's stories and his language, at the same time as it allows us to establish a basis for discussing ethics both in the terms Chaucer presents and our own. With this in mind, I offer the following model for conducting a seminar for teachers or course for future teachers.

• I ask participants to prepare for the course by reading in translation the tales that will be discussed. Those who have time are encouraged to read the entire *Canterbury Tales*. In situations where it is not possible to read in advance, participants are given time to read synopses on the first day, and are encouraged to read the tales before the second day.

6 For a feminist-inflected view of the characters' dilemmas, see David Raybin, '"Wommen, of Kynde, Desiren Libertee": Rereading Dorigen, Rereading Marriage', *The Chaucer Review* 27 (1992), 65–86.

7 Close reading is, at long last, returning into vogue. In Chaucer studies, this was evidenced in the well-attended sessions on 'The Value of Close Reading' at the Fifteenth Biennial Congress of the New Chaucer Society, New York, 27–31 July 2006.

• The text of the *Canterbury Tales* we use in the seminar proper is in Middle English. Early in the first session, I hand out a sheet explaining the basics of Middle English pronunciation and then read aloud the first passage we will consider. I read this by myself so that participants can be introduced to the flow and sound of Chaucer's verse. I then have the group join in reading the passage again, first with the participants reciting in unison, then going around the table and having each person read a few lines. It's important to have everyone read in this opening session, however reluctant some may appear. I make minor corrections (a vowel here and there – readers like to have some feedback, and the input helps them hear their own and others' sounds), but I emphasize that capturing the flow of the verse is more important than getting the sounds correct. In future sessions I continue the practice of having each member of the group involved in reading aloud, and I encourage those who wish to read more to do so.

• For each session, I choose a passage or passages that relate to the particular theme for discussion. After the reading in Middle English, I begin our discussion of the session's theme by inviting participants to present ideas and questions. I make a point of allowing participants to discuss issues and respond to one another without interference. I sometimes steer the conversation back to issues at hand when it has strayed too far or too long, but I do not expect participants to come up with a pre-ordained set of responses. I correct participants' misconceptions about Chaucer and medieval culture when it seems helpful, but with a light hand.

• I make it an absolute policy to avoid correcting participants' personal beliefs and their feelings about ethical issues, but I do not shy away from challenging participants to justify their assertions. The key here is to be fair-handed in questioning views from various perspectives, regardless of my own beliefs. I believe passionately in tolerance, and I am fervently opposed to sexism, racism, classism, and religious prejudices both particular and general. It seems to me, though, that to seek to impose my views and values is to adopt the very practices that I abhor, and to undercut the ethical values that the seminar asks participants to examine. It's also counter-productive: teachers, like students, instinctively resist indoctrination, while left to their own thoughts they tend toward tolerance.

• When it seems appropriate, I incorporate background material, useful critical strategies and the ideas they suggest, and secondary material. I also encourage participants to bring in materials that they would like the seminar to consider.

• When the seminar has progressed sufficiently for participants to feel comfortable reading aloud, I invite the group to perform a full tale (sometimes after-hours, sometimes in class), with self-selected participants taking on the different speaking roles. I have not had a problem getting enough volunteers: teachers and prospective teachers like to be involved (as do all but a few students). I usually take on the role of narrator. That helps to keep things flowing smoothly, and sometimes allows the surprising discovery that the narrator's role is not always the largest.

Closing Comments

I have taught Chaucer innumerable times – in university seminars and lectures; to graduate students, advanced English majors, and general education students;

in single-author classes, surveys, and introductory literature classes; and in workshops and seminars for school teachers. These experiences have been consistently satisfying – we are reading the *Canterbury Tales*, after all – but I have found that there is no other teaching quite like teaching teachers. With teachers, there is no need to perform, no need to explain the obvious, no need to wake the class up. The discussion may lack the theoretical sophistication of an advanced graduate class, but there is a welcome maturity to the teachers' discourse that is unavailable to younger, more sheltered students. When adult participants bring their lived experience to bear on Chaucer's narratives, they discover poems that those who read in order to develop an idea or validate a theory tend to overlook. Adult teachers do not just discern pathos or bitterness; they interrogate the circumstances that produce such feelings. They do not just notice an emotive or introspective line; they appreciate its sentiment. They do not just point out unexpected or contradictory ideas; they respond to those ideas with insight and debate their ethical basis with passion. This is what happens, at least, on the good days. And when the subject is Chaucer, almost every day, and almost every hour, is good.

16

Reflections on Teaching Chaucer and Religion: The *Nun's Priest's Tale* and the *Man of Law's Tale*

GILLIAN RUDD

ANY DISCUSSION of teaching is necessarily closely related to the constraints and freedoms offered by the system and community in which one teaches, so it is probably useful to begin this reflection on teaching with a brief description of my current position. I do not wish to suggest that my position is in any way unusual, quite the opposite; I offer what follows in the belief that many will see much they recognize here and in the hope that some may find it useful.[1] My university, the University of Liverpool, is a large civic university in the north-west of England. We offer three-year BA honours programmes, a variety of MA programmes and have roughly forty doctoral students on the books at any one time, researching a wide range of subjects from medieval to contemporary literature, from historical or linguistic language work to the theory and practice of teaching English as a foreign language. While our BA is available for full-time study only, many of our postgraduates study on a part-time basis. We have a noticeable constituency of local students, 'local' meaning those whose permanent home address lies within Merseyside or Cheshire (an area which, pleasingly for lovers of *Sir Gawain and the Green Knight*, includes the Wirral). These students could commute from home to the main campus on a daily basis with journey times of around an hour, although many of the younger ones prefer to live in student houses with their peers rather than at home with their parents.

Students taking modules in English may be following single honours degree programmes, or joint (a 50/50 split of English and another subject) or combined (three subjects in the first year, two thereafter). We operate a modular system and do not distinguish between these three types of student in this modular provision, which means that any given seminar group is likely to contain students from all three types of degree programme. Therefore, although we have one medieval text on our first year syllabus (*Sir Orfeo*), and offer medieval modules in both second and third years, it is not possible to assume that everyone in a class has taken the same previous modules, a fact which brings both opportunities and challenges to teaching modules on Middle English literature which are delivered over twelve weeks and

1 I would like to thank the many teachers at all levels with whom I have discussed teaching matters over the years. I am conscious of drawing on all those conversations as well as my own habits and practices in what follows.

examined either by a series of coursework pieces, or by traditional examination in conjunction with one assessed coursework exercise. We do not have a dedicated Chaucer module; rather his work appears on the modules offered at levels 2 and 3 alongside other texts from the twelfth to the fifteenth century, although it is not unusual for undergraduates who elect to do a dissertation to write on Chaucer.

Finally, like many of my colleagues at my own and other British universities, I also regularly run seminars or lectures for secondary-school (high-school) pupils studying Chaucer for their A-levels (public examinations taken in the final year of schooling, typically at age 17–18).[2] At the request of the teachers and pupils, these sessions often combine some general knowledge about Chaucer with a period of focused analysis and discussion of whichever one of the *Canterbury Tales* they happen to be studying that year. In the last ten years the tales I have discussed with A-level students have been those of the Pardoner, Miller, Merchant, Nun's Priest and, of course the Wife of Bath. Somewhat to my surprise, it is no longer habitual to include even a cursory reading of the *General Prologue* alongside deeper study of the particular tale to be examined.

For this discussion I will focus on two tales: the *Nun's Priest's Tale*, the one I have most recently explored with secondary-school pupils as well as undergraduates, and the *Man of Law's Tale*, which I have taught at both undergraduate and postgraduate MA level. In each case, given the kinds of teaching we do, I have roughly three hours to give to each tale and that time needs to include some general information about Chaucer and his time or at least his literary endeavours as well as time focusing on the details of the tale. That makes it sound much bleaker than it actually is, because of course one is never teaching in a vacuum; the students already know many things and come with a wide variety of assumptions, expectations, ideas and random bits of knowledge about Chaucer, the medieval world, religion (then and now) and humanity, all of which feeds into their (and thus also my) reactions to and understandings of the texts in hand. Indeed finding ways of forging links between these tales and what the students already know is inevitably the most exhilarating and frequently most unexpected part of the whole process.

The Nun's Priest's Tale

The two tales I have chosen offer useful grounds of comparison, not least because their very titles offer such different initial approaches to the question of how religion operates within these texts. We might presume that the double emphasis offered by a title which tells us we are about to hear a story that is told not just by a priest, but a nun's priest at that, acts as a fanfare introducing an overtly religious tale. There is obvious support for this view in the Nun's Priest's closing exhortation:

> Taketh the moralite, goode men.
> For Seint Paul seith that al that writen is,

2 Four informed and informative essays, by Alan Baragona, Donna Dermond, Rosalind Field and Mary Ryant, on teaching at school and university levels, teaching practices, overviews and statistics, in the United States and the United Kingdome may be found on the companion website for *Chaucer: An Oxford Guide* ed. Steve Ellis: http://www.oup.com/uk/booksites/content/0199259127/resources/.

> To oure doctrine it is ywrite, ywis;
> Taketh the fruyt, and lat the chaf be stille. (VII 3440–4)

These lines feed into a common expectation that I have encountered, particularly when exploring this Tale with school students, that it must have been (and so ought still to be) received primarily as a Christian moral fable. Yet to accept this is the only response available overlooks the previous line, which acknowledges the possibility of an entirely secular appreciation of the story, one which 'holde[s] this tale a folye, / As of a fox, or of a cok and hen' (3438–9). There are several points to make here. One is to recall the Nun's Priest's opening willingness to be entertaining: 'But I be myrie, ywis I wol be blamed' (2817). This leads into debates about how far the line is a pointed comment on most people's inability to attend to serious literature (a remark that often elicits rueful recognition from university and school students alike) and how much a skilled speaker's acknowledgement that if one is asked to entertain one is rightly criticized if instead one bores, as the Monk has clearly done in his preceding marathon of summaries of tragedies. On the other hand, this line of argument can be countered by noting that, while the Nun's Priest knows he will be blamed if he is not entertaining, he does not explicitly endorse the views of those who do the hypothetical blaming. It is possible to makes this into a covert criticism of his audience's lack of religious insight as well as lack of literary appreciation, and thus to link back to those closing lines and wonder about the implications of the phrase 'goode men'.

Another option here is to highlight the way entertainment and serious intent can co-exist in a text. When dealing with students who are studying this Tale in isolation, this argument has to be made with reference to the debates within the Tale alone, perhaps by looking at the range of views on dreams that Pertelote and Chauntecleer offer. The irony of the cock who asserts the prophetic value of dreams and then fails to heed the warning in his own is not lost. Where students are studying a range of tales it is of course possible to draw comparisons between the use of entertainment in this Tale with its avowed moral intent and that of the Pardoner's, with its effectiveness as an income-stream. Regardless of how much of the *Tales* as a whole the group is looking at, I have often found it effective to provide a short section of the opening of the *Parson's Tale* as the most marked contrast available. Without necessarily going into the detail of why this is not strictly a sermon, nor indeed a homily, the simple fact of having such a thing included in the collection called the *Canterbury Tales* with its framework of storytelling competition is enough to elicit some challenging discussions about what counts as entertaining and the role of what is deemed appropriate both as a 'story' and as subject matter for a moral or improving tale.

Focusing in this way on individual lines and their connotations is often what is most welcome when addressing secondary-school groups and their teachers. The general Christian context has usually been dealt with more than adequately, but demonstrations like this of how an unspecific awareness of religious assumptions and debates is reflected at the level of Chaucer's language can help to demonstrate how living within a religious framework does not actually mean living a life of pious devotion. This in turn makes it possible to harness the current noticeable inclination on the part of students at both school and undergraduate level to latch on to any overt Christian element and assume that they are required to judge the text against a rigorous Christian code. Showing that moral allusion is possible without being inevitably accompanied by castigation of sin allows readers to gain huge satisfaction from spotting clues to such potentially moral and religious elements in the *Nun's Priest's Tale*. Before long someone will point out that Chauntecleer is proud of his voice, and from there it is a quick move to 'pride coming before a fall' and the evils of vanity, but these are no longer held up for high-minded opprobrium – they have become elements to enjoy within a lively and witty tale.

Equally swift, particularly amongst school pupils, is the urge to identify the devil in the story. It is as if any Christian moral tale *must* have a devil figure in it.[3] Luckily, this one does – the cunning fox is introduced in all his devilish cunning, and so one easily moves into explorations of the animal fable that for many is the main part of this Tale. Students who have also read Jonson's *Volpone* are often pleased to recognize the underlying fable and its moral, religious message and these students will also soon comment that, as in *Volpone*, the fox is not allowed to triumph. This then throws up some interesting questions about Chauntecleer's escape: does not he use the same ruse of flattery that the fox employed? And if so, and if the fox is the devil, then is that allowed? Once one has got to this point, the Tale has been freed from being held within a necessarily single message and the ambiguities at work within the moral standing of this central fable can be revealed and explored in depth.

One other device that works particularly well, for both school and university students alike, is introducing the descriptions of the hen, cock and fox found in the bestiaries and their accompanying illustrations. The Aberdeen bestiary, so conveniently found online, and Richard Barber's edition of manuscript Bodley 764, with its modernized text and beautifully reproduced illustrations, are both invaluable sources of material.[4] The fox lying in the dust with the crows gathering around him shows a further side of his trickery but the satisfaction we as readers gain from correctly interpreting the image creates the same kind of connection between reader and animal as is found in the *Nun's Priest's Tale* – we rather like the fox and laugh at his ploy, even as we know he is the villain of the piece. The cock is resplendent in gold, red, blue and green: the very picture of vanity, which indeed the text tells us he represents, but the prick of conscience that comes with his association with reminding Peter of his denial of Christ often surprises. But it is the hen that is most useful, and the picture of her found in a French manuscript of Bartholomaeus Anglicus' encyclopaedic *De Proprietatibus Rerum* is particularly apposite.[5] Here the hen nestles with wings slightly raised as some chicks

[3] Interestingly, there is no concomitant urge to find a Christ figure. I did once have a particularly interesting and stretching discussion about how far Chauntecleer could be regarded as the Christ figure, but that has happened only once, thus far.

[4] *Bestiary: Being an English Version of the Bodleian Library, Oxford M.S. Bodley 764*, ed. and trans. Richard Barber (Woodbridge, 1992); the Aberdeen Bestiary: http://www.abdn.ac.uk/bestiary

[5] Barthélemy l'Anglais, *Le livre des propriétés des choses*: Anjou, Maine, 15th century, Bibliothèque nationale de France, MS Fr 136, fol. 21v; see http://www.luminarium.org/medlit/nptimage.htm. Other useful websites include the Chaucer Metapage, http://www.unc.edu/depts/chaucer, Intute Arts and Humanities Page, http://www.intute.ac.uk/artsandhumanities, the Labyrinth, http://labyrinth.georgetown.edu/.

shelter beneath and others hop towards her, presumably summoned by a motherly cluck. The interpretation of hen as Mother Church finally opens up the whole of the *Nun's Priest's Tale*, as it soon becomes apparent that while Pertelote does not easily match this characterization of a hen (she is closer to the nagging wife who hen-pecks her husband), the widow at the start of the Tale does. It may be traditional to ask what she represents, to encourage readers to note the various types of structure in which she lives (cottage with a compound in which the hen-house and its enclosure are situated) and the fact that she also keeps sheep, with all the religious resonances they may offer, but it is also useful. A final twist can then be added by referring to the *Physiologus* in which the fox is not just the devil, but also men who mislead by speaking fair but thinking foul ('For wo so seieth other god / & thenketh iuel on his mod': 'whoever says good to another person and thinks evil in his mind'), and in particular Herod, who said he would believe in Christ, but sought ways to betray him.[6] For some groups this brings the animal allegory as a whole back to the human level and offers the notion of the average man (represented by Chauntecleer) being led astray by wayward companions, rather than deliberately caught by a figure of the devil. For others this leads into discussion of how we can read the widow's cottage and small-holding, now possibly either a convent or the Church in general, as being under threat from the errant heretic who makes sly invasion and threatens to carry off the inhabitants.

Moving between attention to the detail of everyday life offered by such descriptions and the way such details can also be read allegorically frees us from trying to find a fixed 'answer' to the Tale and makes students aware that the rhetorical tricks used to make an entertaining story can be the same as those used to create a religiously informed tale. As will by now be obvious, my aim, particularly when addressing school pupils, is to move beyond the simple, and often unstated, assumption that because the Church was a powerful institution in fourteenth-century England and the default position for most of the populace was to be Christian, that the Middle Ages were necessarily pious and that every text that indicated any degree of religious engagement must be read as being religiously earnest throughout. Even in a text as explicitly engaged with Christian codes of conduct as *Sir Gawain and the Green Knight* there are phrases that are more common exclamations than expressions of religious fervour. One such is the 'Bigog' uttered by the Green Knight in line 390. Having just the week before overheard the word 'omged' (pronounced 'o-em-geed' and derived from the abbreviation of 'oh my God' commonly used when sending sms text messages) I was delighted to be able to suggest to my second years that the poet's 'bigog' was a similar creation of an expressive and emphatic exclamation that had little to do with the appeal to the Deity that seemingly lies at its root. Such serendipitous discoveries are godsends to us medieval tutors.

6 *The Middle English 'Physiologus'*, ed. Hanneke Wirtjes, EETS os 299 (Oxford, 1991), p. 12. I have modernized the letter forms in this quotation. The significance of the fox is explained in slightly obscure terms, partly in order to fit into the rhyme pattern, but his interpretation clearly leads to a more general association of fox and heretic via hypocrisy. For a lively discussion see Jeffrey Jerome Cohen, 'Inventing with Animals in the Middle Ages', *Engaging with Nature: Essays on the Natural World in Medieval and Early Modern Europe*, ed. Barbara A. Hanawalt and Lisa J. Kiser (Notre Dame, 2008), pp. 39–62.

In the space allocated to schools lectures and seminars, or indeed to undergraduate lectures and classes of whatever kind, it is not possible to cover every element of this Tale, nor is it desirable. Rather than arrive at consensus over a single reading of the text, I am happy if I send the group away aware of a multiplicity of responses to religion, ideas of right and wrong and the range of possible representation of the Church and its members, including some notion of the variety of positions open to its clergy. If students have encountered the *Miller's* and *Reeve's Tales* it is possible to raise the question of how far the Nun's Priest may be using his Tale as a form of revenge for his social position, or simple narrative repost to the other Pilgrims, but for school pupils who may not be reading any other Chaucer, such questions are too likely to result in a rather meaningless discussion. It is possible to touch a little on the gender politics at work in the relation between a Nun and her Priest, with the different levels of religious and social hierarchy that might indicate, but without the time to explore the social and religious context in some detail, I find such areas are best left as questions demanding further investigation.

It may be relevant that discussions with secondary-school teachers at a variety of kinds of school about how they tackle the religious elements in Chaucer revealed that when it comes to religious context, they tend to assume ignorance and work up from there. As one teacher at a large state school commented: 'We are very much a secular school. We find the best way is to assume nothing and things can only get better, or we are pleasantly surprised.' The same teacher also pointed out that the difficulties encountered concerning the religious context in Chaucer are the same they encounter in teaching any literary text with a religious context, regardless of period; this is a comment many of us teaching in the tertiary sector will recognize. Often religious elements are not dealt with in detail. In particular, questions of the standing of and attitude towards non-Christian religions, specifically Judaism and Islam, are left aside, partly because the teachers feel ill-equipped to discuss such matters (a feeling I often share) but mainly because the tales they are called upon to teach are not ones that include overt references to these faiths. The classical gods do come up, most obviously if the *Knight's Tale* happens to be on the syllabus, but there at least, with classical religions safely in the area of being material for literary tradition, not practised belief, they do not have to tangle with the complexities that surround the question of how Chaucer and his Christian contemporaries might have regarded practitioners of other creeds, or with the combination of respect and suspicion, and its associated racism, accorded to the learning and learned of the East.

As mentioned above, and like many other teachers, I find pictures a valuable tool and am frequently struck by how visually literate students are. In part this comes from the prevalence of television and films in our society, but often this brings with it the concomitant problem of an automatic and unexamined assumption that pictures, whether moving or not, are realist. The trend for fantasy fiction helps enormously here. From books to computer games, there is a popular corpus of material that not only happily works with the belief that mythical beasts and talking animals exist, but also with the need to read symbolically at the *same time* as reading mimetically. Once students realize that it is legitimate to make connections between the way they respond to current popular literature and the way they read Chaucer, they are several steps on the road to freeing Chaucer's tales from a perceived medieval religious strait-jacket and noticing instead how the *Nun's Priest's Tale* in particular moves between intellectual debate about the role of dreams, common gender politics, popular literature (in the form of the fable), social anxiety about the rise of new religious groups, and religious teaching. Although church-going is by no means the norm in Britain, it is helpful if there is someone in the group who will admit to having attended regularly at some point in their lives. Perhaps this is where Liverpool's Catholic inheritance comes to my aid, but it is very unusual to encounter a group in which no-one recollects sitting through sermons based on anecdotes and fables. This allows for a further connection to be made between the medieval use of fables as sources of 'ensaumples' for sermons addressed to the majority of people, as opposed to the more abstruse discussions of text that formed the basis of the university sermon, or the penitential handbook as represented by the *Parson's Tale* and frankly unbelievable as a reading matter of choice to the typical modern student. So between fantasy and pulpit, we find grounds for comparison between how we experience and interpret stories today and how Chaucer's contemporaries might have done in the fourteenth century.

The Man of Law's Tale

Visuals and contemporary comparisons open the way to insightful discussions of the *Man of Law's Tale* too. My preferred comparison is with Olivia Hetreed's adaptation in 2003 for the BBC series that recast the nine of the Tales in modern guise. The *Man of Law's Tale* was perhaps one of the furthest removed, but for me it is an impressive recasting of the story which makes Custance into Constance, an illegal immigrant and refugee from Nigeria, who is found washed up in Chatham docks by Mark, who takes her to his home, where she forms a close friendship with his wife, Leila, whose own immigration to England happened many years ago and perfectly legally. As in the Chaucer tale, Constance is devout, and her piety disconcerts many of those who befriend her. This adaptation inevitably conflates episodes from different sections of the original Tale and necessarily alters the overall structure to keep this version of the Tale within the required hour's space of viewing. However, much has been done to include elements of the Tale as a whole. The Northumbrian knight who kills the kindly Hermengild in order to frame Custance for her murder is referenced in the scenes of flashback to the religious and bloody conflicts in Nigeria that made Connie (daughter of a mixed Muslim/Christian marriage) flee her country. Hermengild becomes Leila, whose own faith is revitalized by Constance's presence, to the detriment of her own marriage. The murderous Sowdanesse mother-in-law and Donegild are conflated and rewritten as an equally devious and plotting British, presumably Anglican, mother-in-law-to-be who ensures Constance's deportation back to Africa in the hope of preventing her marriage. Yet within such changes specific details are retained. Although obviously genuinely traumatized, it is not always clear that Constance's partial and gradual recollection of the appalling events that necessitated her flight is due to memory lapse alone. There are hints that such forgetting may be defensive or even strategic plays for support, hints which pick up lines 526–7 of Chaucer's Tale which read 'She seyde she was so mazed in the see / That she forgat hir mynde, by hir trouth'. There is even a voyage in a rudderless and unprotected boat; indeed it is with this that the television version begins. As in Chaucer's version Constance's strong belief in God and evangelical Christianity mark her out as very different from those who take her in, and her direct and often literal faith disconcerts her companions and eventually sows suspicion in their minds.

One of the most striking changes in the casting of the Tale is to make Constance Nigerian, thus making immediately obvious the fact that she is a stranger in a strange land for much of the action of the story. This is also true of Chaucer's Custance, who begins in Rome, finds herself first sent to Syria as a wife, then washed up in Northumbria and finally returned to Rome again, but this simple change effectively highlights how closely connected the questions of race and religion are in Chaucer's text. It is an element easily overlooked by students finding it tricky enough to keep track of the plot-line as they read the Tale for the first time, but is one that is particularly resonant in our own troubled times. It is also a topic that can be difficult to explore with students in a group which may meet only once a week and who may not know each other well at all. Embarrassment competes with ignorance in a desire not to offend: but all of that is easily exacerbated if there is, as so often, an exchange student in the group.

However, my sense from my own experience and from talking to colleagues at my own and other institutions, is that such embarrassment is often more keenly felt by the tutor than the student group. It is dangerous to generalize, as the mixture of personalities within any one group necessarily makes certain kinds of discussion more or less easy or appropriate, and indeed more or less fruitful, but I frequently recall the experience of discussing the *Man of Law's Tale* with one particular postgraduate group taking our MA in Women and the Word: Gender, Literature and Spirituality. Most unusually, that year's group was made up of three American students (hailing from New York, California and Kentucky), one Omani, a Tunisian, one person from Hong Kong and four British students, one of whom was a mature student. In this one small group were gathered representatives of the two main faiths operating in Chaucer's tale as well as those of the several degrees of secularization that dominates all levels of the British educational system. The range of awareness of religion and degree of religious engagement in the group members' various backgrounds was striking. Not that individual religious affiliations were always declared; to this day I am sure one student had a Jewish background, but she never referred to it, and why should she? Likewise the second Muslim never drew directly on his faith in discussions. The simple fact that only some referred to their faith, or lack thereof, made me realize that my apprehension was ill-founded. Each student, as each reader, takes their own line on how far individually practised faith and literary study must interact. Couching the discussion in terms of what the text offers and how it represents the attitudes and figures within it, rather than seeking to determine from it what Chaucer must have believed himself, makes exploration of this Tale and others like it both less anxious and more illuminating. It is worth noting, for example, that insights often came from those with entirely secular outlooks who were struck by some of the assumptions behind the narrative or the characterization. Indeed it was one such student who pointed out how many of Custance's circle die as a result of being converted by her, thus exposing not only the subtext of martyrdom, but helping to explain one way in which she is such a disconcerting figure. It was also useful that in previous weeks, and in casual conversation with the individual students of this MA group, what emerged most strongly was how lacking in religious awareness (and morals) England appears to those coming from societies where religious faith is expected to form part of the day-to-day habit of life, one way or another. This sense of a lack of religious sensibility was felt as much by the very secular student from Kentucky as by the practising Muslim from the Sultanate of Oman. It is a particularly ironic impression for a city with two cathedrals, within five minutes walk of each other and the university campus these students attended, but it is not an inappropriate one for readers of the *Man of Law's Tale*. On reflection I wonder if the description of Northumberland as a place from which 'Alle Cristen fold been fled' (541) carried an echo of their own reaction, although they were tactful enough not to say so outright.

More striking, though, was the way that the figure of Custance as an ideal woman, powerful in her ability to affect others, yet unendingly accepting of her bad treatment, was instantly comprehensible to the whole group, but for very different reasons. To those with religious backgrounds, whether Christian or Muslim, practising or not, she was instantly recognizable as the type of the true and devout woman. For those with entirely secular backgrounds, she was also familiar, as representative of women's lot down the ages, passed from man to man and often the victim of hatred from her mother-in-law. For each, the extreme passivity of Custance was familiar, although for the secular it was hard to admire and for those from British Catholic backgrounds it was a role model they consciously sought to overthrow. Studying Chaucer's text made us all consider exactly how and why such devout figures are disconcerting as they command a mixture of admiration and suspicion. Interestingly, and perhaps due to the specific focus of that MA, the question of religion was more immediately apparent and easier to discuss than that of race with this group. The reasons for Custance's position as someone who elicits suspicion through steadfast faith lead to some searching discussion about how far the Tale rings changes on its theme and its role model, and how far it simply uses the repetitive pattern to provide some sense of completeness at the end. Custance's position as recurring religious exile seemed to over-ride any issue of race and although the question why those who convert others elicit such profound hatred was touched on, it proved to be a step further than that particular group was willing to go. In this case, then, the notion of being made an exile first because one was a woman, and thus easily moved between men, and second because one is an example of religious faith, and thus liable to be tested as well as rescued, was where in the end Chaucer's *Man of Law's Tale* rested.

With undergraduate groups, typically lacking the diversity of background and experience of that remarkable MA group, the religious aspect of the Tale tends to be taken for granted, rather than dominating discussion. Custance is easily read as an iconic figure, representing true faith, and the assumption that this Tale is thus mainly about religion and the superiority of Christianity is frequently accepted without demur. Indeed the question of religion is normally set aside in favour of reading it in terms of its representation of women. Here, too, it is easy to overlook Custance's position as foreigner for much of her tale, but again this is where the

BBC adaptation helps things along. Making the issue explicit by discussing the possible reasons for changing the nationalities of the characters for the television version draws attention away from discussions focused too exclusively on matters of sexual politics, to include debates about the effect of mixed-race as well as mixed-religion marriages. Thus sometimes beginning with questions of race before moving onto those of religion can offer a more open-ended way in to the text. Discussion may well touch on complex questions concerning how the West views Africa and the East, and on the couple of occasions this has surfaced in my seminars, it has proved to be a very useful way in to Chaucer's text. Thus far, though, it has been rare to move on to deal explicitly with the different faiths represented in the Tale, and I suspect this has been as much due to my sense of the students' potential embarrassment or unwillingness to tackle such a tricky area, as their own real awareness of what is going on. It is easy to allow difficult topics to be glossed over as being firmly in the past, particularly when undergraduates are still finding dealing with Chaucer's text itself challenging enough.

Frequently I have found it more effective to move to the question of allegory rather than tackle religion and race head on at once: how far is Custance a figure of constancy and to what is she constant? Or how much does the categorization of the Tale as allegory make it easier to accept the various points of extreme behaviour? Inevitably underlying such discussion is the ever-present issue of how much we read literary characters as real people, but with the BBC version to hand as a comparison, it is also possible to examine our latter-day casting of the Middle Ages, arguably paralleled by our view of Africa as a third world country. It can also open the way into explorations of perceptions of the medieval in general, which allows for certain 'givens' to be challenged. The Middle Ages were neither uniformly bawdy and violent, nor uniformly pious and elegant, but we rather like the idea that they were. Knights in shining armour co-exist with phrases like 'getting medieval on your ass' to quote Tarantino's *Pulp Fiction*, and we should never underestimate the persistent effect of Monty Python and the Holy Grail. At the time of writing, it remains to be seen what effect the television serials *Robin Hood* and *Merlin*, aimed at teenage audiences, will have on those coming through the educational system to study Chaucer at university. However I would hazard a guess that they will contribute to making the concept of a heroine who is self-effacing and utterly and uncomplainingly obedient increasingly alien. Custance, like Griselda and Virginia, is so far removed from the feisty, independent portrayals of particularly Maid Marion and Morgan le Fey that have come to predominate our received version of the Middle Ages that it often takes some deliberate consideration to discover how such figures can be admirable. Such film and television versions will also, I suspect, increase the secularization of the image of the Middle Ages and that in turn could contribute to the frequently encountered assumption that all of Chaucer's portrayals of people professing religion, particularly members of the clergy, are satirical if not downright sarcastic.

The figure of Custance is a check to such presumptions. It is impossible to read the *Man of Law's Tale* without noting the genuine faith Chaucer portrays, even if one is not quite sure what to do with it. Stanzas such as those at lines 470–83, in which the narrator addresses his audience directly with the question 'Who myghte hir body save?' (471) and answers with the assertion 'No wight but God' (476) can create an air of puzzlement in our typically secular student cohorts, but Custance's own personal devotion is not in question. It may be this focus on her, coupled with the power of the story, that means that readers who are often alienated by the overt Christianity of other texts find that they can read this Tale on the level of story alone. I suspect it helps that this is the Tale of a Man of Law, rather than one told by a character whose title indicates religious conviction. It is in fact noteworthy that, with the exception of the Parson, the religious pilgrims do not tell overtly and unambiguously religious tales. Chaucer himself thus goes some way to combat the guardedness that often accompanies reading religious texts, particularly by those of no particular conviction themselves. The questions of law and justice that this Tale raises can indeed be revealed to be those of divine law, justice and reward, but on an immediate level this appears to be a tale told about a young girl with faith in her religion, more than being a religious tale *per se*. Readers are astounded at a human level at the sowdaness's actions and only later pause to consider how far her actions are motivated by her own religious conviction. Focusing on her motivation can lead into discussions of the attitude towards Muslims within this Tale, but here again Chaucer himself proves the tutor's greatest ally by following her actions with the equally outrageous actions of the unnamed Northumbrian knight and Donegild, both of whom are pagan. At this juncture it often comes as a surprise to point out that this story is rooted not in England, but Italy, and that England is put on a par with Syria. Our tendency to overlook this fact may seem to be reflected in Hatreed's adaptation, as much of the action is set in England. However, the film ends with the Alla figure finding Constance and their son in Nigeria, in the care of a priest. After all her affliction, Constance, like her Chaucerian counterpart, is thus back in her home country and it is left open whether or not the three will finally return to England. What this says about the England of both Chaucer's day and ours is a question I tend to leave hanging at the end of a seminar.

Many students have done some post-colonial and feminist literary theory, either at school or on other modules of their degree programme, and this is often very useful when studying the *Man of Law's Tale*. Representations of the East, the idea of Africa as the dark Other and of women as objects to be passed around, and written over, redefined by the context in which they find themselves, help illuminate a tale in which all these aspects combine. Added to that, however, is the concept of the woman as a figure of religious conviction. Not militant, indeed not very pro-active, despite her gift for conversion, but certainly strong in faith; it is this definition of constancy that often emerges from seminar debates over the character of Custance. The urge to project onto such female figures a kind of sentimental piety can be swiftly illustrated by showing Burne-Jones's illustration of this tale for the Kelmscott Chaucer. In it Custance is standing, hands clasped and up to one shoulder, in a clinker built boat, afloat on a choppy sea with sea-gulls swooping overhead. She looks across the swell with her head turned away from the viewer. She is less obviously the epitome of piety than a frightened young woman, helplessly at the mercy of the sea and brewing storm. Discussing why Burne-Jones chose that particular moment to illustrate and matching his picture to the relevant text can lead into discussions of representation, what women are expected to stand for and how they are perceived. In Custance's case it can also add a level of complexity to the question of her own culpability: how far does she bring her misfortunes on herself by not adapting her behaviour to suit her new surroundings? It is here that the comparisons with immigrants, particularly those from conflict areas, so deftly raised by the BBC version can be most thought-provoking. Conversations of that kind can finally offer a view of Chaucer as a man aware of the diversity of religious and social exchange, interaction and their possible consequences, and also aware of the richness such topics offered to a creative mind.

So much for Chaucer; when it comes to the students, I have frequently been pleasantly surprised by insightful comments from people not used to thinking within a religious framework at all. Rather than being put off, many come to regard religion as just one of the many aspects of a text that is odd to them and so invites some thought. Instead of approaching Chaucer's texts from the vantage point of latter-day Christianity, such students feel free to examine the moral codes offered, explored or challenged by the texts they read and discover from them which elements are endorsed, which criticized. Alongside these insights come those from students who do practise religion, and who thus vouch for the continued currency of many of the attitudes towards sin, obedience and utter trust in God that Chaucer represents in his *Tales*. Usefully, though, these students can often be the ones who also question how far Chaucer can really mean what his texts seem to say in purely religious terms. Let me not, though, be naive and paint too sunny a picture. One aspect that both sets of students have in common is a lack of awareness of the many changes in Christianity during the six hundred years between Chaucer and ourselves. Tenets of faith and terms of expression are often assumed to be fixed and it takes a little effort to point out that even in the space between their generation and the one above there have been substantial changes. Most striking, however, are the gaps in knowledge of the basic Christian story. In a brief survey of second- and third-year students taking medieval literature modules one year it was revealed that out of a group of five biblical stories chosen for their presumed common currency (Adam and Eve in the Garden of Eden, the Ten Commandments, Noah's Flood, the Annunciation, Herod) it was the Annunciation that was least recognized, with many admitting they had never heard of it and only a few feeling they could say what it was with confidence. Thankfully, we as teachers can trust a good deal to the texts we deal with to solve the problems of gaps in knowledge. By encouraging reading the texts themselves first and then working out from them what they are expected to know, the students often find that in fact much of what they need for initial understanding is provided by the tale itself. Further research may well be required in order to really engage with the debates or attitudes that inform the texts. In the case of the *Man of Law's Tale*, we are explicitly invited to compare Custance to Jonah, and thus read a very different story about a figure cast adrift at the mercy of God and whose destiny was also to travel to foreign lands and convert them. The Nun's Priest explicitly invites us to consider his story as one of a fox, or a cock and a hen, and if we do, following that thread through the Bestiaries, we will find ourselves again returned to religious instruction. Such research is easier and more interesting to do when it is overtly linked to the text or topic under discussion.

So finally Chaucer's own interest in the knowledge of his time and how people from many walks of life used and reacted to it saves the day. The fact that he is also typically guarded about his own views, preferring to offer many alternatives, often with his famously ironic stance, seems to free students to give their own responses, rather than feeling they must first divine and then concur with whatever message Chaucer is sending. What emerges is a Chaucer who was conscious of living within one religious framework and aware of those living in others, someone adept at satire, but also with time for genuine religious conviction (although how far he shared that himself remains, in my view, impossible to say). Above all, a man fascinated by the effects of narrative, the power of telling stories and the variety of topics, moral, social and religious that can be treated within the space of a single tale.

Index

CPSIA information can be obtained at www.ICGtesting.com
223943LV00002B/2/P

9 781843 842293